306

SIMMEL ON CULTURE

Theory, Culture & Society

Theory, Culture & Society caters for the resurgence of interest in culture within contemporary social science and the humanities. Building on the heritage of classical social theory, the book series examines ways in which this tradition has been reshaped by a new generation of theorists. It will also publish theoretically informed analyses of everyday life, popular culture, and new intellectual movements.

EDITOR: Mike Featherstone, *Nottingham Trent University*

SERIES EDITORIAL BOARD
Roy Boyne, *University of Durham*
Mike Hepworth, *University of Aberdeen*
Scott Lash, *Lancaster University*
Roland Robertson, *University of Pittsburgh*
Bryan S. Turner, *Deakin University*

THE TCS CENTRE
The Theory, Culture & Society book series, the journals *Theory, Culture & Society* and *Body & Society*, and related conference, seminar and postgraduate programmes operate from the TCS Centre at Nottingham Trent University. For further details of the TCS Centre's activities please contact:

Centre Administrator
The TCS Centre, Room 175
Faculty of Humanities
Nottingham Trent University
Clifton Lane, Nottingham, NG11 8NS, UK
e-mail: tcs@ntu.ac.uk

Recent volumes include:

The Body and Society
Explorations in Social Theory
Second edition
Bryan S. Turner

The Social Construction of Nature
Klaus Eder

Deleuze and Guattari
An Introduction to the Politics of Desire
Philip Goodchild

Pierre Bourdieu and Cultural Theory
Critical Investigations
Bridget Fowler

Re-Forming the Body
Religion, Community and Modernity
Philip A. Mellor and Chris Shilling

The Shopping Experience
edited by Pasi Falk and Colin Campbell

Undoing Aesthetics
Wolfgang Welsch

SIMMEL ON CULTURE

Selected Writings

edited by
David Frisby and Mike Featherstone

SAGE Publications
London · Thousand Oaks · New Delhi

Introduction © David Frisby 1997
Editorial arrangement © David Frisby and Mike Featherstone 1997
'Introduction' to *Philosophical Culture* © Mark Ritter and David Frisby 1997
'The Concept of Culture' © Tom Bottomore and David Frisby 1990
'On the Essence of Culture' © D.E. Jenkinson 1976
'Female Culture' © G. Oakes 1984
'The Concept and Tragedy of Culture' © Mark Ritter and David Frisby 1997
'The Conflict of Modern Culture' © D.E. Jenkinson 1976
'The Crisis of Culture' © D.E. Jenkinson 1976
'The Future of Our Culture' © Mark Ritter and David Frisby 1997
'The Change of Cultural Forms' © Mark Ritter and David Frisby 1997
'Sociology of the Senses' © Mark Ritter and David Frisby 1997
'The Sociology of Sociability' © *American Journal of Sociology* 1949/50
'Sociology of the Meal' © Mark Ritter and David Frisby 1997
'The Sociology of Space' © Mark Ritter and David Frisby 1997
'Bridge and Door' © Sage Ltd 1994
'The Metropolis and Mental Life' © Kurt H. Wolff 1950
'The Philosophy of Fashion' © Mark Ritter and David Frisby 1997
'Adornment' © Kurt H. Wolff 1950
'The Problem of Style' © Sage Ltd 1991
'The Alpine Journey' © Sage Ltd 1991
'The Adventure' © Kurt H. Wolff 1958
'On the Psychology of Money' © Mark Ritter and David Frisby 1997
'Money in Modern Culture' © Sage Ltd 1991
'The Berlin Trade Exhibition' © Sage Ltd 1991
Infelices Possidentes! (Unhappy Dwellers) © Mark Ritter and David Frisby 1997
'Some Remarks on Prostitution in the Present and in the Future' © Mark Ritter and David Frisby 1997
'The Women's Congress and Social Democracy' © Mark Ritter and David Frisby 1997
'On the Sociology of Religion' © Mark Ritter and David Frisby 1997
'A Few Words on Spiritualism' © Mark Ritter and David Frisby 1997

First published 1997

Published in association with *Theory, Culture & Society*, Nottingham Trent University

SAGE Publications Ltd
6 Bonhill Street
London EC2A 4PU

SAGE Publications Inc
2455 Teller Road
Thousand Oaks, California 91320

SAGE Publications India Pvt Ltd
32, M-Block Market
Greater Kailash – I
New Delhi 110 048

British Library Cataloguing in Publication data

A catalogue record for this book is available from the British Library

ISBN 0 8039 8651 3
ISBN 0 8039 8652 1 (pbk)

Library of Congress catalog card number 97-069473

Typeset by Type Study, Scarborough, North Yorkshire.
Printed in Great Britain by The Cromwell Press Ltd, Broughton Gifford, Melksham, Wiltshire

CONTENTS

ACKNOWLEDGEMENTS

The editors and publisher would like to thank the following for permission to include translations of Simmel's work in the present volume: Routledge for permission to reproduce 'The Concept of Culture' from *The Philosophy of Money* (2nd edn) Routledge 1990; Nelson for permission to reproduce 'On the Essence of Culture', 'The Conflict of Modern Culture' and 'The Crisis of Culture' from Peter Lawrence (ed.), *Georg Simmel Sociologist and European*, Nelson 1976; the *Americal Journal of Sociology* for permission to reproduce 'The Sociology of Sociability; volume 55, 1949/50; The Free Press for permission to reproduce 'The Metropolis and Mental Life' and 'Adornment' from Kurt H. Wolff (ed.) *The Sociology of Georg Simmel*, 1950; Yale University Press for permission to reproduce part of 'Female Culture' from *Georg Simmel: On Women, Sexuality and Love*, 1984; the Ohio State University Press for permission to reproduce 'The Adventure' from Kurt H. Wolff (ed.) *Georg Simmel 1858–1918*, 1958. Full bibliographical information on these and all other selections in this volume are printed at the end of the Simmel texts.

The editors wish to thank Mark Ritter for his translations of some of the selections contained in this volume.

Thanks are also due to Maureen McQuillan and Ann Settle for typing the final versions of much of the material contained here.

D.F.
M.F.

INTRODUCTION TO THE TEXTS

Simmel has often been described as a philosopher of culture. One could just as well call him a philosopher of the soul, of individualism, or of society. All of these labels, however, are imprecise and one-sided and do not even begin to encompass the scope of his work.

Siegfried Kracauer (1995)

A sociology of culture such as has been undertaken by Max Weber, Troeltsch, Sombart and others – however much they might all also wish to distance themselves from him methodologically – has surely only been made possible on the foundation created by him.

Georg Lukács (1991)

Simmel as a critic of culture is in a peculiar way both near to, and far away from us.

Jürgen Habermas (1996)

Now, how does the philosopher view the culture of our time? Very differently, to be sure, from how it is viewed by those professors of philosophy who are so well contented with their new state.

Friedrich Nietzsche (1983)

The texts assembled in this volume are drawn from Georg Simmel's writings over more than two decades on cultural themes. That these texts span such a large time scale indicates that reflection upon culture and aspects of cultural life are a continuous concern in Simmel's extensive works and is not confined merely to his later and perhaps best known writings on the conflict and tragedy of culture.[1] This is one of the reasons why some of Simmel's essays from the 1890s (and even an essay from 1889) are included in the present collection as well as earlier versions of later works.

From the outset, it should be emphasized that the writings assembled here do not appear in Simmel's work under the headings provided for the sections in this collection. Just as Kracauer and others have frequently pointed out how difficult it is to subsume Simmel's work under a single concept,[2] so too the location of the articles and extracts in this collection should not be given a reified position by the reader. A close reading of many of these essays would reveal that thematically they could be located under other categories that are relevant to and for us. This flexibility of location of essays – and even sections of them – is in keeping with Simmel's own practice of placing sections of essays and thematic issues in a variety of different contexts within his own work. It is a practice which, in part, creates the impression of developing a conscious perspectivism – a viewing of themes from a variety of standpoints.

This mutability that is present in the content of Simmel's writings in the essay form and even in other forms is also relevant, as we shall see, to his discussion of the concepts of form and culture themselves. The essay, as Adorno pointed out, 'refuses the definition of its concepts . . . The essay . . . takes up the anti-systematic impulse into its own procedure and introduces concepts unmodified, "immanently", just as it receives them. They are only made more precise through their relationship to one another'.[3] Simmel's mastery of the essay form, which gradually takes on distinctive features from the mid-1890s onwards, should lead the reader to see essays and themes in relation to one another. For Simmel, it is not merely social circles that intersect with one another but his texts too.

This should not be surprising in a philosopher, sociologist and cultural theorist one of whose key concepts, in these and other spheres, is that of reciprocal effect or interaction (*Wechselwirkung*). Viewed substantively, the interaction between form and content, between subjective and objective culture, and the results of these interactions in the *crystallization* of contents as culture and the *cultivation* of supra-individual culture all constitute some of the foundations for a fuller understanding of Simmel's *cultural* analysis and *analysis* of culture.

Indeed, the very fact that Simmel has been designated as a philosopher, sociologist, social psychologist, and cultural theorist and critic should sound a cautionary note for those who wish to subsume Simmel's work under any one of these titles. It is true that, with regard to establishing the foundations for some of these disciplines such as sociology or philosophy, Simmel sought to demarcate their distinctive features.[4] And, in the sphere of theorizing about culture, it should not be forgotten that the epithet 'culture' (*Kultur*) was applied in Simmel's lifetime to a whole range of disciplines and theoretical practices: to the philosophy of culture (*Kulturphilosophie*),[5] to the historical study of culture (*Kulturgeschichte*),[6] to the development of a sociology of culture (*Kultursoziologie*),[7] to the development of a psychology of culture (*Kulturpsychologie*),[8] to a critique of (contemporary) culture (*Kulturkritik*)[9] and, by Simmel himself, to a distinctive philosophical culture (*philosophische Kultur*),[10] as well as more general references to the culture of peoples (*Völkskultur*), social classes and strata, and so on. In some of Simmel's early work we can also see evidence of his confrontation with attempts to establish a moral cultural sphere: an ethical culture (*ethische Kultur*).[11] Germany itself, after unification, was also the site of a religious struggle over culture (*Kulturkampf*). It should not be forgotten here that Simmel also drew attention to the gendered nature of culture, indeed to its hitherto male-dominated nature, and examined the possibilities for the alternative development of a female culture (*Weibliche Kultur*).[12]

Virtually every one of these dimensions of culture within the academic sphere was the site of often contested attempts to establish academic disciplines around sciences of culture, be they historical, philosophical, sociological, anthropological, psychological, and so on. By the late nineteenth century, the newer of these disciplines were struggling to demarcate themselves from more general, all-encompassing foundations for human sciences (*Geisteswissenschaften* – the Germany translation of J.S. Mill's 'moral sciences' but epitomized by the philosophical works of Wilhelm Dilthey, a colleague of Simmel's), or cultural sciences (*Kulturwissenschaften* – epitomized in the foundational demarcations of human studies from the natural sciences in the works of Wilhelm Windelband and especially Heinrich Rickert, with both of whom Simmel was asociated).[13] Within the domain of the social sciences (*Sozialwissenschaften*), Simmel's early career at Berlin University was supported by the historical economist Gustav Schmoller and Simmel's early attempt (1890) to establish sociology as an independent discipline rested ostensibly on the foundations of social science (though in fact focused upon sociology).[14] In Simmel's case, the interest in cultural phenomena can be traced to his study of ethnology (and his earlier writings abound with references to anthropological instances of cultures drawn from the literature of the Darwinian tradition and that of Simmel's teacher Adolf Bastian), but more significantly to the work of Moritz Lazarus who, together with Heymann Steinthal, was the founder of an important tradition of *Völkerpsychologie* (conceived as a broad social psychology of human life).[15] When Simmel published one of his crucial foundational essays on sociology in 1894 ('The problem of sociology'),[16] he acknowledged to Lazarus the central role of his *Völkerpsychologie* which 'forcibly directed me to the problem of the supra-individual'.[17] Lazarus's *Völkerpsychologie* aimed both to study the development and evolution of human culture and to analyse contemporary cultural phenomena in terms of language and meaning, social psychological foundations and social formation. Although the notion of the 'supra-individual' often appears in Simmel's writings on culture as explorations of the objective spirit or mind (*objectiver Geist*) – and thus draws upon Lazarus's *Völkerpsychologie* and, earlier, Hegel – his investigation of cultural phenomena is certainly not confined to this level of generality. Rather, Simmel draws upon another feature of Lazarus's work, namely, a concern for the emergence of independent cultural phenomena arising out of everyday interaction in the social world. The constellations and configurations of individuals interacting with one another generate supra-individual phenomena that are condensed, distilled or crystallized into distinctive forms. It is a feature of Simmel's writings on culture that he continually has recourse to the exploration and analysis of cultural forms in their emergence in everyday mundane interactions between individuals, however fleeting they might be. Thus, this study of cultural forms can focus upon the condensation or crystallization (*Verdichtung*) of interactions in cultural forms at the point of their emergence – as Simmel often states it, *in statu nascendi*. Of course, Simmel also has an interest in the persistence of cultural forms over time and space, as well as their massification in objective forms that confront individuals as estranged entities.

What should be apparent from even the present selection of his writings on culture is, therefore, both the consistency of Simmel's concern with the development of cultural analysis itself and the ability to direct his explorations to such a wide variety of cultural phenomena. Indeed, many of his contributions to the sociology of forms of social interaction and the

everyday world of confrontation and interaction with cultural forms should
be an indication of Simmel's contribution to the systematic study of cultural
forms. The systematic nature of such a study should not be seen as a mere
classification of cultural forms but rather as a critical confrontation with the
dynamic and often antagonistic and contradictory development of cultural
forms that are to be located within his major contribution to the study of
modernity. Simmel engaged critically with his society and its cultural
phenomena, producing an analysis that focused not upon abstract themes
but, according to his contemporaries, upon 'all that which to us and to him
appeared problematical as human beings of the turn of the century. In so
doing, he became the greatest philosopher of culture of our times'.[18]

Part I: Defining culture

There exist a number of significant strands or dimensions to Simmel's
various attempts to define culture. His introductory remarks to his hugely
popular *Philosophische Kultur* (which draw upon the already drafted introduction to the French selection of his writings *Mélange de la philosophie rel-
ativist* of 1912)[19] should indicate that Simmel was firmly commited to
developing a distinctive philosophical culture within the parameters of
which it would be possible to analyse the everyday world of relationships
and objects. The notion of developing and influencing German philosophical culture was later highlighted in his concern at leaving Berlin for a chair
of philosophy at Strasbourg University in 1914. In January 1914 he declared
that 'the influence I have upon our philosophical culture, which I can exercise in Berlin, will not be achieved so easily elsewhere',[20] a concern which
led him to suggest to Rickert in the same month that a student interchange
between Strasbourg, Freiburg and Heidelberg might create 'a south-west
German corner of philosophical culture' so that eventually one could
'enlarge the concept of "philosophical culture"'.[21]

Then, as now, though for different reasons, culture and its investigation
and analysis was a contested domain – one that is perhaps masked by
Simmel's statement on his undoubted contribution to a 'philosophical'
culture, to a distinctive mode of philosophizing. For the concept of culture
itself was the subject of several attempts by Simmel to clarify this phenomenon. In his early writings, it is possible to discern the foundation for the
concept of culture in the distinction between contents and forms. In however temporary a manner, the contents of experience take on a structure
(*Gestalt*) or form through human interaction that condenses or coalesces
into something other than mere content – what Weingartner has termed
'proto-culture'.[22] In his early work Simmel uses the rich concept of *Verdichtung* which means condensation, coalescence and crystallization. Cultural
artefacts created out of the contents of human experience can achieve their
own objective existence in distinctive forms that may be temporary but
which may also persist over time in, say, cultural traditions. The aesthetic

mode of crystallization (*Verdichtung*), for instance, is already intimated in the concept itself which can also be translated literally as 'rendering into poetry (*Dichtung*)', that is, the process of giving an aesthetic form to particular contents. But other spheres of human existence, such as the cognitive or moral spheres, may also be crystallized into independent forms that may persist over time. Interaction within these spheres can create autonomous and objective cultural forms or crystallizations.

In the extracts from Simmel's writings presented here from around 1900 onwards, the focus of attention shifts towards the process of the creation or *cultivation* of culture. Culture is, as it were, formed intentional subjectivity that emerges out of human life and its interactions and is created by human beings as objectified contents or entities in language, religion, normative orders, legal systems, traditions, artistic artefacts, and so on. This process of the objectification of the subject that is simultaneously 'the desubjectification of the individual'[23] implies, as Guy Oakes has formulated it, following Simmel's terms, that culture is

> the process in which life first reproduces itself as 'more life' and then transcends itself by generating forms that qualify as 'more-than-life'. Simmel represents culture as a two-dimensional process. On the one hand, the energies and interests of life are defined and moulded by the forms of 'objective culture', the world of cultural forms and their artefacts that have become independent of individual human existence . . . On the other hand, these cultural forms and their artefacts are incorporated into the 'subjective culture' of the individual, the state of the personality which is the ultimate result of the process of cultivation . . . Subjective culture is the personal culture of the individual, or the life of the individual as a cultural being.[24]

Simmel regards the process of cultivation as emerging out of 'the use of purposively formed *objects*' in such a way that human beings create forms of culture that 'take the process of perfection into real and ideal spheres beyond the individual'.[25]

However, the coordination or reciprocal interaction between life and form and between subjective and objective culture is itself seldom 'perfected'. Indeed, as the selections from his writings indicate, the relationship is viewed as conflictual, crisis-ridden and tragic, and, for Simmel, crucial to understanding 'the disharmony of modern life'. The development of forms of objective culture may be accompanied by high levels of differentiation (accelerated by the division of labour), functionalization and abstraction (notably with the development of the mature money economy), and distinctive forms of domination (as in the gendered nature of objective culture).

Some of the problems associated with a gendered objective culture are addressed in Simmel's essay on 'Female culture', published in 1902. For Simmel, there exists no neutral ungendered culture since 'with the exception of a very few areas, our objective culture is thoroughly male',[26] so much so that there is a human/man identification manifested in the fact that 'many languages even use the same word for both concepts',[27] and in the fact that 'deficient performances in the most diverse areas are degraded as "feminine", whereas outstanding performances of women are celebrated as "thoroughly manly"'.[28] Within this objective culture, 'the naive conflation of male values with values as such . . . is based on historical power relations'. Indeed, 'the fact that the real contents of our culture exhibit a male character . . . is grounded in a multifaceted interweaving of historical and psychological motives'.[29] Within this context, Simmel explores the possibilities for the development of a distinctive female culture emerging out of the 'objectivation of the female nature' and developing counter to the objective, differentiated male culture which is more conducive to the realization of male abilities. (Simmel's problematical evaluation of the possibilities for the development of a distinctive female culture later elicited a response by Marianne Weber in 1913, taking issue with many of its assumptions.)[30] Despite the limitations of Simmel's conceptualization of the gendered nature of objective culture,[31] his discussion is an indication of an intention to develop a critique of dimensions of contemporary culture and a recognition of contemporary cultural conflicts.

Among the dimensions of Simmel's cultural analysis that are not fully developed in the present collection is the confrontation with cultural movements themselves. Kurt Gassen's lecture notes on the course "Ethics and Problems of Modern Culture' (1913) (Gassen, 1949)[32] reveal Simmel's interest – already evident at least two decades earlier in his critique of absolute ethical systems and ethical movements – in the conflict between culture and ethics (the latter as an 'alternative culture' and exemplified in Leo Tolstoy), and culture and morality (here 'Charles Baudelaire and Oscar Wilde are flagrant examples'). Again, much of the discussion of the relationship between culture and morality is located within the framework of the 'cultural schisms (*Zwiespältigkeiten*)' of subjective and objective spirit in which 'culture itself appears to stand as a permanent extension of this schism, of the quantitative and qualitative conflict between subjective and objective spirit'.[33]

Part II: Culture and crisis

Even Simmel's various attempts at clarifying essential features of culture and its conceptualization reveal that his aim was not to lay the foundations for a synthetic science of culture (*Kulturwissenschaft*), which was certainly an intention of several of his neo-Kantian contemporaries. Rather, his writings on culture and his explorations of cultural forms display an intention to confront the transformation of cultural formations brought about by metropolitan and capitalist – for Simmel often primarily the advanced capitalist money economy – modernity. Such interventions into the culture of modernity can be traced back at least as far as to his writings of the 1890s ('Money in modern culture' from 1896 (cf. Part VII) would be an example of this) and are not merely confined to those essays presented here from the first two decades of the twentieth century. However, what all these essays have in common is a genuine confrontation with the transformation ('change'), future, crisis, conflict and tragedy of culture. In other words, for Simmel, there is a sense of urgency present in his cultural analysis and diagnosis that highlights the tensions between a break with the past to which we cannot return, a present that is in a state of crisis and a future that offers uncertain possibilities.

'The concept and tragedy of culture' (cf. Part II) appeared in the journal *Logos* in 1911. It was one of the intentions of this journal, then in its second year of publication (and of which Simmel was an associate editor), to create a forum for the development of a new philosophical culture and new philosophical directions (including those provided by younger philosophers such as Ernst Cassirer and Edmund Husserl). The essay develops out of earlier reflections upon the problematical relationship between subjective and objective culture. 'On the essence of culture' (1908; cf. Part I) concludes with the apparent paradox that although 'subjective culture is the overriding final goal ... there can be no subjective culture without an objective culture, because a subjective development or state constitutes culture only by virtue of its inclusion of such objects. Objective culture, on the other hand, can, relatively speaking, become substantially (though not completely) independent of subjective culture'.[34] The often radical implications of this disjunction between subjective and objective culture are explored in the essays contained in Part II.

The fact that what is of cultural value must be objectified already points to a potential distance between subject and object in cultural objectifications. In his essays on the development and crisis in modern culture, this separation of subjective and objective culture is radicalized as a widening gap between the two, with objective culture extending itself and accelerating its growth at a faster rate than subjective culture to the point of rendering problematic the possibilities for the development of subjective creativity, the personality and individuality. At the same time, culture as the synthesis of the subjective and the objective is threatened where objectifications attain an autonomous development, creating a discrepancy between the objective and cultural meaning of the same object. The exploration of 'the fateful autonomy' of cultural production following 'an immanent developmental logic' constitutes Simmel's extension of Marx's theory of commodity fetishism into the cultural realm.[35]

'The conflict of modern culture' (cf. Part II) – Simmel's lecture published in 1918 as a highly successful pamphlet – commences with this autonomous development of cultural forms with 'their own logic and laws', which gives culture 'a history' and is 'the subject of history'. At the same time, Simmel deepens the conflict between subjective and objective culture into one between life and form, in which life creates forms that increasingly lose their meaning for the human subject. The result in modern culture is the search for expressions of life that seek to avoid this loss by bestowing meaning upon the immediacy of life itself. Simmel gives a number of instances of the reaction to perceived static forms such as Expressionism, the reaction against closed systems in philosophy, the development of a new morality of personal relations and a movement towards religious 'life', away from its institutional forms.[36]

In these and other essays on contemporary, objective modern culture there is a concern with technology and the proliferation of technical solutions to the increase in, and greater differentiation of, means and ends. In 'The crisis of culture' – another wartime piece first published in 1916 – the consequence is that 'the ends of life become subordinate to its means', which themselves become ends. Elsewhere, this proliferation of means is viewed as a developmental tendency in modern cultures, in modernity itself, creating a situation in which 'technology, . . . the sum total of the means of civilized existence, becomes the essential object of struggle and evaluation . . . [creating] a criss-crossing jungle of enterprises and institutions in which the final and definitely valuable goals are missing altogether'.[37] The crisis of culture is variously described as a 'pathology of culture', a 'tragedy and chronic crisis of all culture', 'a chaos of disjointed individual elements devoid of any style', and 'the disintegration and perversion of cultural life' in this wartime essay, with its questionable temporary synthesis in war activity itself.

'The future of our culture' is Simmel's response to a request by the editors of the *Frankfurter Zeitung* in 1909 to twenty leading figures – 'fighters for culture' – to address 'the future of our culture' and 'a conscious politics of culture'.[38] Again the focus is upon 'the widening gulf between the culture of things and personal culture [. . .] of individuals who feel this objective culture to be something alien, which does violence to them and with which they cannot keep pace'.[39] Whilst recognizing that a political cultural policy could not eliminate this widening gap, the education of the individual could contribute to enabling individuals to make use of aspects of objective culture.

'Change in cultural forms' is yet another wartime article published in 1916, one which commences with the cultural extension and qualification of Marx's historical materialism that is apparent already in Simmel's aim in *The Philosophy of Money* (1990) to build a new storey beneath historical materialism and his extension of the theory of commodity fetishism to the cultural sphere. Here Simmel extends the theory of the relationship between the forces of production that create and eventually transcend modes of forms of production into a theory of cultural forms. The attempts to break the bonds of existing cultural forms, even to reject form as such (as in Futurism, or in religion as 'formless mysticism'), are part of wider attempts to assess the way in which we think about our life, our culture and its forms.

Part III: Culture of interaction

Probably unique among his sociological contemporaries, Simmel explored time and time again the world of everyday social interactions and their cultural manifestations. This investigation of the mundane everyday interactions and our experience of them places this aspect of his work in relatively close proximity to the symbolic interactionist and phenomenological traditions, even though adherents of both traditions can hardly be said to have drawn as fully as they might upon his work in this area.

Indeed, in the first essay presented in this Part, on the sociology of the senses, Simmel asserts that the seemingly insignificant mundane everyday interactions are constitutive for sociation, society and culture. The opening argument of this essay 'The sociology of the senses' (1907), which was incorporated into the opening chapter of his major work on sociology (*Soziologie*, 1908), forms one of the later attempts to justify his particular approach to the study of social phenomena (in the 1890s many of his sociological essays open with a justification for his sociological analysis). The methodological significance of the initial argument in the essay on the senses lies in the fact that, not only does Simmel claim that sociology should study the 'microscopic-molecular' processes within human interaction and hence justifiably study micro-sociology as well as the study of major social structures and formations, but he also asserts that such an investigation will produce a 'deeper and more accurate' understanding of society – and, we might add here, equally of cultural formations.

Substantively, the exploration of the role of the senses in social interaction and cultural differentiation devotes most attention to sight and hearing but covers only briefly – as Simmel admits – the sense of smell. The tactile sense receives no treatment at all. In many respects, such an order of depth of treatment corresponds to the history of explorations of the senses, with the greatest attention having been devoted to the sense of sight.[40] Yet despite this limitation, Simmel's early investigation of the senses draws attention to the neglected role of bodies and their senses in social interaction. Cultural variations in modes of seeing others, hearing others and smelling others have begun to receive more attention in recent decades. And, as with many of Simmel's other essays, the theme of sensory distance and proximity – to take but one example – is clearly relevant for themes in other works, especially the study of space.

The role of the senses is significant too for Simmel's exploration of sociability. 'The sociology of sociability' (1910) is the opening address by Simmel to the first meeting of the German Sociological Association held in Frankfurt in 1910. The concept of sociability (*Geselligkeit*) is obviously closely related to that of society (*Gesellschaft*). Indeed, for Simmel, sociability is 'the play form' of society, 'the pure form, the free-playing interacting interdependence of individuals'. Sociability is a form of social interaction that is freed of content or substance since it possesses 'no ulterior end, no content, and no result outside itself . . . [and] is oriented completely around personalities'.[41] Freed from the real consequences of social life and its contents, sociability is a 'social game', 'a pure interaction' in which 'people actually "play" society'.[42]

This play element emerges because sociability is, as it were, a pure *form* of interaction (Simmel's other instance is exchange which, in his *Philosophy of Money* [1990], he declares to be 'a sociological phenomenon *sui generis*', an '*actus purus*').[43] Sociability posseses 'no ulterior end, no content, and no result outside itself'. It is therefore 'a pure interaction', 'an ideal sociological world' of equal participants. As a social game, it may take many forms from the most universal that is to be found in 'that most extensive instrument of all human common life, conversation'; indeed conversation and talking is seen as an end in itself. As a gendered game, it may be found in the erotic play form of flirtation (the subject of a separate essay by Simmel)[44] in which flirtation or coquetry 'plays out the forms of eroticism'. As a formalized and rigidly rule-governed game, the configurations of sociability can become ossified in a set of formal and formally binding rules of etiquette and deport-ment which always run the risk of being a caricature of themselves (as in the French *ancien régime*) such that, at the moment in which the social forms became ends in themselves, sociability disintegrates.

One of the sites for sociability within which the forms of its social game – conversation, flirtation and etiquette, among others – are displayed is the meal. Since Simmel's brief exploration of interaction at mealtimes, 'Soci-ology of the meal', was published in 1910 it may well have been conceived by him as part of his broader study of sociability.[45] The development of eating habits from the context of a natural act of necessary nourishment to the elaboration of rules for communal eating – indeed for an aesthetics of the meal – is a topic which accords with Simmel's interest in the develop-ment of forms from specific contents of interaction: the crystallization of interactions into distinctive forms of rule-following. As in many of his other cultural analyses, Simmel indicates the extent to which the civilizing process, in this cases the rules for communal eating and their domination by aesthetic principles, remain connected with the basic physiological need for nourishment.[46] The higher level, which often seeks to affirm its inde-pendence, is still intimately connected with the lower level, as it were. The aesthetic dimension and its elaboration hides the more basic, organic dimension. Elsewhere, in his essay on style, Simmel maintains that it is the dining room which initially felt the impact of the drive towards 'stylization' in the later decades of the nineteenth century – creating 'relaxation' and 'a broader comfort shared with others'.[47]

Part IV: Spatial and urban culture

It is a feature of Simmel's extensive investigations of the forms of social interaction and the foundations of sociation or of the processes by which we become members of society that they have a spatio-temporal location. One of Simmel's more ambitious tasks was the study of the formal preconditions for the possibility and existence of forms of social interaction. Along with time, quantity and mass, all of which receive varied treatment by Simmel during various stages of his career, it is the study of space which constitutes one of the most extensive chapters of his major sociological work *Soziologie* in 1908, especially if the supplements to that chapter – 'Sociology of the senses', 'The sociology of the boundary' and 'The stranger' – are included. The study of social space as a crucial dimension of social interaction and also of cultural formations constitutes one of those projects in which it can be said that Simmel, in many respects, was a pioneer.[48] And, as with many of his analyses of the foundations of interaction and cultural formation, the subject matter of social space and spatial relations was explored from a variety of perspectives. Here we need merely indicate the very different approaches to the study of the sociology of space, the quasi-phenomenological exploration of the bridge and the door (undoubtedly significant for Heidegger's later investigations) and the highly influential essay on the modern metropolis.

Although the essay translated and included here, 'The sociology of space', was reworked with a further essay on space 'On the spatial projection of social forms'[49] to constitute a major chapter of Simmel's *Soziologie* in 1908, both earlier essays were first published in 1903 – the same year in which his most famous essay 'The metropolis and mental life' appeared. This suggests that although the essay on the metropolis has usually been read in conjunction with Simmel's *Philosophy of Money*, it could equally be read in the context of his more systematic explorations of social space and the social psychological impact of socio-spatial relations.

Simmel's exploration of space goes beyond Kant's notion of space as the abstract possibility of being together (*Beisamkeit*) in the direction of human interactions as modes of filling in space. Sociation fills in space. But, as Lechner (1991) has pointed out, Simmel's argument concerning the 'spatial embeddedness of social configurations should not be confused with the actual causes of social processes. And yet, while he shows how space is in some ways socially formed, he does not treat space as simply a social construct. It retains a reality of its own. Simmel's overall position, then, lies somewhere between spatial determinism and social constructionism' (Lechner, 1991: 196). The specific explorations of aspects of space such as exclusivity, boundaries of space, fixity of social forms in space, spatial proximity and distance, and mobility in space all contain significant contributions to the formal presuppositions for social interaction and cultural formation, their historical transformation, and the modern configurations of social space in modernity. There is evidence of the spatial implications of the development of an objective culture, a culture of abstraction based upon functionalization and forms of social interaction detached from space that are delineated from a different direction in his *Philosophy of Money*. In this context, it is fruitful to read this exploration of social space in conjunction with Simmel's reflections upon the metropolis, since for him the city is 'not a spatial entity with sociological consequences, but a sociological entity that is formed spatially'.[50]

The themes of distance and proximity, separation and connection, the boundary and openness are all central to Simmel's exploration of space. These and other themes receive a different treatment in his essay 'Bridge and door' (1909). The subtlety of his examination of the differences between the bridge and the door – with its rich interplay of dimensions of connection and separation, outside and inside, unity and separation – already testifies to the development of a phenomenology of our experience of connection and separation that also reveals elements of another of Simmel's projects after the completion of his *Philosophy of Money* in 1900: a philosophy of art and aesthetics. The richness of Simmel's play with the juxtaposition of that which connects and that which separates and opens up the world to us was not lost on later phenomenological explorations of space and place. Martin Heidegger's essay, 'Building, dwelling, thinking', for instance, seems to draw upon Simmel's discussion of the bridge in the context of his examination of 'what is a built thing?'[51]

Simmel's reflections on the metropolis (more accurately translated as metropoles),[52] published as an essay in 1903, were in fact presented in a lecture given during the winter of 1902–3 in Dresden as part of a series on the city and associated with an exhibition on the modern metropolis.[53] It is one of Simmel's most famous essays, described by Louis Wirth in 1925 as 'the most important single article on the city from the sociological stand-point',[54] and praised more recently by Manfredo Tafuri on the grounds that 'Simmel's considerations on the great metropolis contained *in nuce* the problems that were to be at the centre of concern of the historical avant-garde movements' in the first half of the twentieth century (Tafuri, 1976: 88). Indeed, with some exaggeration, Massimo Cacciari has claimed that 'The problem of the Metropolis, as a problem of the relation between modern existence and its forms, is the point from which all of Georg Simmel's philosophy develops'.[55]

More modestly, we can see Simmel's reflections upon the modern metropolis as an investigation of the one of the crucial sites of modernity – the point of its intensification – along with the mature money economy. Significantly, in the context of social theory, it is the metropolis, rather than the industrial enterprise or production or rational organization, that is a key site of modernity. The analysis of the metropolis as the focal point of the circulation of commodities and individuals also concentrates upon the sphere of circulation, exchange and consumption, as did the exploration of modern society in Simmel's *Philosophy of Money* upon which the former rests. What does not comes to the fore – though would not be excluded from Simmel's analysis elsewhere of social circles or networks and their intersection or lack of contact – is the highly stratified nature of experience of the metropolis according to social class, status, gender and ethnicity. Similarly, the power structure of the metropolis – except at the significant individual level of personal freedom – is largely absent, perhaps, like the other dimensions of stratification, because other lectures in the Dresden series were presumed to cover these topics. On the other hand, the focus upon the personal consequences of engagement within the spheres of circulation, exchange and consumption (and fashion is perceived as rooted in a metropolitan setting) gives Simmel's analysis affinities with some postmodern discussions of the city. However, as the opening paragraphs of the essay make clear, the metropolis is the site of the domination of objective culture and indeed of 'the culture of things'. The problematization of the maintenance and development of personal identity as a crucial dimension of the experience of metropolitan modernity remained at the forefront of Simmel's concerns.

Part V: Fashion, adornment and style

On more than one occasion, Simmel indicates that the metropolis was the site, above all others, upon which one of the crucial manifestations of modernity could flourish: namely, fashion. Later commentators such as Benjamin were to view fashion as the epitome of modernity, as 'the tireless helpmaiden of modernity'.[56] Certainly, fashion was a theme to which Simmel returned on several occasions. If we include in this context his explorations of adornment (a concept, the translation of which would legitimately include ornament) and style, then there is revealed in his work a preoccupation with key conceptualizations and debates that stand at the centre of concern by his contemporaries in the late nineteenth and early twentieth centuries in a variety of spheres, many of which are associated with dimensions of 'modern' life and society and the ambiguity of modernity.

The first of the selections in this context is the complete translation of Simmel's short book or brochure, *The Philosophy of Fashion* (1905). Yet this was not the first of his reflections upon the theme of fashion since he had already published a 'Psychology of fashion' (Simmel, 1895b), a brief discussion of fashion in *The Philosophy of Money* and an English version of his 1904 article titled 'Fashion' in the American *International Quarterly* journal (among whose editorial advisors on sociology were Simmel, Gabriel Tarde, Franklin Giddings and J.S. Mackenzie). The extended essay translated here subsequently appeared in Simmel's essay collection *Philosophische Kultur* (1911, 1919) – one of the most successful of his publications.

Within the extensive literature on fashion from the late eighteenth century onwards and relevant to Simmel's reflections are: Kant's interest in fashion as the 'game of imitation', the interaction between the new and the useless, indeed a fascination for 'purposiveness without purpose' (Kant 1964); Friedrich Vischer's influential discussion of fashion *Fashion and Cynicism* (1879); Nietzsche's association of modernity with fashion[57] and the extension of this negative association of the merely fashionable and the stylized with the modern into areas extending beyond clothing to architecture and other spheres.[58] Among Simmel's contemporaries, the exploration of conspicuous differentiation through consumption of fashion was highlighted by Thorstein Veblen in his *Theory of the Leisure Class* (1899)[59], while the imitative dimension of fashion was generalized into a crucial feature of human interaction in Gabriel Tarde's *Law of Imitation* (which Simmel reviewed).[60] Werner Sombart in *Economy and Fashion* (1902) drew upon existing reflections upon the large scale enterprise of consumption and concluded that 'the driving force throughout in the creation of modern fashion is the capitalist enterprise' (1902). Substantively, it is worth noting that one of the themes at the 1896 Women's Congress in Berlin, upon which Simmel reported in another context (see below), was women's fashion and the reform of dress (in turn drawing upon efforts made by the Rational Dress Association and other bodies since the early 1880s).[61]

Simmel's exploration of the philosophy of fashion is initially unfolded through the dialectical interplay of individual imitation and differentiation; the desire, on the one hand, to be like others and, on the other, the desire for difference from others. Fashion as the continuous announcement of newness always disturbs and destroys that which is already in existence. The absolute newness of fashion is simultaneously associated with its demise, its death. Although Simmel indicates that fashion is continuously produced and reproduced to accelerate the turnover time of new commodities, he also reveals that the economic production of things 'simultaneously produces the aesthetic realm as its veil'.[62] This aesthetic dimension of the life of the commodity is also relevant for the individual within the accelerated circulation of metropolitan modernity. The search for recognition, for difference, for identity within the ceaseless interaction of metropolitan existence is facilitated and encouraged by an adherence to the fashionable – and its extreme forms of becoming a slave to fashion and the dandy (who draws attention to himself but does not reveal an inner self).

Simmel's brief exploration of adornment, which appears as an 'Exkursus' in his major work *Soziologie* (1908), is itself clothed in ambiguity. The German concept under discussion – '*Schmuck*' – may be variously translated as adornment, as jewelry and as ornament. On the one hand, Simmel's discussion may be seen in the context of bodily adornment and, on the other, more generally as a contribution to the contemporary discussion of ornamentation, ongoing in the nineteenth century but accentuated by the debate at the turn of the century over art nouveau and its putative emphasis upon ornament and stylization, and therefore upon the surface of buildings and their 'cladding'.[63] Perhaps even more generally, and thematized briefly in Simmel's essay, is the debate upon art itself – the distinction between the work of art as a self-enclosed entity and the applied arts as for ourselves and our needs. Further, as is so often the case with Simmel's essays read out of context, it is surely relevant to note its position within the work; the exkursus on adornment is located within a chapter of his *Soziologie* entitled 'The secret'.[64] Both adornment and ornamentation in the contexts outlined above may be seen as means of preserving the inside, and masking it both from and by the outside – perhaps even deliberately through ostentatious outward forms of display.

Not unrelated to some of these themes is Simmel's essay 'The problem of style', again on a theme which is dealt with in other contexts – not least in the *Philosophy of Money* in its final synthetic chapter on 'the style of life', and specifically with reference to the 'proliferation' of styles and the 'stylessness' of the times. However, the fact that the essay appeared in 1908 in one of the leading German journals on the applied arts (*Dekorative Kunst*) should draw our attention to a more specific set of debates with respect to the applied arts. The debates on building and furnishing within particular styles and the proliferation of styles may be traced back to the first half of the nineteenth century. In the second half of the century, the excessive eclecticism of styles associated with historicism was responded to at the turn of the century by attempts to develop a 'modern style' in what was variously described as the 'modern movement', 'art nouveau', and '*Jugendstil*'. The stylization of ornamentation itself provoked debate on the shallowness of the modernist movement's purported connections with 'mere' style, with what was merely 'fashionable',[65] and in 1908 – with Adolf Loos's lecture 'Ornament and crime'[66] – upon ornament itself. Further, Simmel's colleague in Berlin, Werner Sombart was writing on the state of the applied arts too (including an essay published in 1907).[67]

Part VI: Leisure culture

If fashion was one of the crucial manifestations of modernity for Simmel and a phenomenon which flourished within the metropolitan context, then the pursuit of the fashionable by the slaves to fashion, whose orientation he sought to explore, itself constituted a significant dimension of a much wider phenomenon, whose parameters Simmel investigated: namely, leisure.[68] The selections here consist of two very different approaches to the theme of leisure, the one an early piece on tourism and the other a much more substantial phenomenology of the experience of the adventure as a constellation extracted from the mundane everyday world. However diverse their respective treatments may be, they both contribute to our understanding of contemporary leisure culture. Again, it should be noted that they do not constitute Simmel's only forays into the culture of leisure, some of which are contained in a later part of this text from a quite different and more political perspective. Here, as elsewhere, we can see the virtue of Kracauer's delineation (see Kracauer, 1995) of one of the basic features of Simmel's analyses: namely, that of the 'fundamental interrelatedness of phenomena', their lack of isolation and mistaken attempts to treat them in isolation from one another. With regard to the present theme, the essays on sociability, fashion, the trade exhibition, and leisure establishments are all instances of contributions to the study of leisure.

In his essay on the metropolis, Simmel refers to the wealth of possibilities and distractions available within the capitalist metropolitan milieu. The metropolis is the site in which 'stimulations, interests, fillings in of time and consciousness are offered' in profusion. Such fillings in of time and consciousness would include the search for the fashionable, the whole variety of leisure activities, urban spectacles such as exhibitions (whether of commodities or artistic and cultural works) and the many attempts to escape from the tumult of the metropolitan 'secret restlessness', to a 'mania for travelling', to a desire to escape from 'the trite everyday world'. In this context, one possible escape is ostensibly provided by an escape to nature, to the mountains – in this case, to the Alps. 'The alpine journey' (1895) in part explores an instance of the impact of metropolitan culture upon nature and the accompanying transformation of the landscape and those who are in it.

Simmel's reflections upon the alpine journey examine the consequences of extending travel (by railway) to hitherto inaccessible areas in the Swiss and Italian Alps, and increasingly into the mountains themselves. The contrast with the individual exploration of nature and its mass tourist form is used by Simmel to highlight the development of a new phenomenon: 'the large-scale enterprise of the enjoyment of nature', a 'standardized' and, in the light of another of Simmel's essays (on the picture frame),[69] an already 'framed' consumption of nature itself as a 'prepared' landscape. In this context, such experience is not an 'escape' from modernity but another manifestation of its aesthetic. The search for excitement and stimulation associated with the metropolis is extended through alpine sports to individual challenges to the forces of nature, challenges that may themselves be extensions of the modern thirst for new stimulations.

The escape from the mundane everyday world is only one of the major themes of one of Simmel's richest essays 'The adventure' (1911), which first appeared in the Berlin newspaper *Der Tag* under the title 'The philosophy of adventure' in 1910. Thematically, the essay may also be related in some respects to the earlier discussion of spatial distance (in this case, its distance from our everyday experience), sexual relations (the erotic adventure) and time consciousness (Simmel's exploration here of the 'unconditional presentness' of the adventure). And although not intended as such, the exploration of representation of the adventure is directly relevant to modes of advertising holiday and leisure activities in recent decades.

For Simmel, however, the adventure is constituted by a distinctive 'form of experiencing' life as a 'closed entity' that is totally dissociated from an everyday mundane world which is hostile to this experience of the adventure. This dissociation from the everyday world is formed by an explicit 'dropping-out of the continuity of life', as 'that which has been torn away' from the everyday continuity and transformed itself into 'an island in life' that is 'something alien, untouchable, out of the ordinary'. In contrast to work activity, which consciously coalesces around human purposive interaction with the world and its contents, the adventure is experienced as an abandonment to the momentary, even to 'a fragmentary incident'.

The mode of experiencing the adventure is characterized by an acceleration, a heightening of time consciousness as absolute or 'unconditional presentness, the quickening of the process of life to a point that possesses neither past nor future'. When it is subsequently recalled in our memory, it seems unconnected to the continuity of life experience and acquires 'the nuance of dreaming', so much so that 'the more "adventurous" an adventure is . . . the more dream-like it will be for our memory'. In these and other respects, Simmel's exploration of the adventure is an instance of a practical phenomenology that may have appealed to those, such as Edmund Husserl, intent on analysing 'internal time consciousness' (Husserl, 1964).

However, there is another direction in which Simmel's own analysis of the adventure takes him. The adventure is viewed as exemplary of the experience of modernity itself. For Simmel, 'the adventurer is ... the most powerful example of the unhistorical person of the contemporary essence. On the one hand, he is determined by no past ... on the other, the future does not exist for him'.[70] The experience of immediate presentness promises an eternal presentness, and the moment lasting for an eternity. This 'contemporary essence' of modernity, with its acceleration and heightening of time consciousness of the present and, simultaneously, its transcendence of mundane time as a dream experience, and its promise of eternal presentness – all of which deserve comparison with Bergson's contemporary discussion of time consciousness and subsequent explorations by Husserl and Benjamin – must be set against metropolitan modernity's proliferation of 'the fillings-in of time and consciousness'. Indeed, Simmel recognizes that the experience of the adventure must be set in the context in which, in the mundane everyday world, 'so much of life is hostile to adventure'. It is precisely upon this disjunction between the adventure and the mundane world that decades of advertising the time and space of leisure and tourism has drawn to convince consumers of the extraordinary nature of this commodity – as an 'island', an 'exclave', 'torn away' from the everyday world.

Part VII: Money and commodity culture

The preceding explorations of significant facets of metropolitan modernity would be incomplete without reference to one of the most significant correlations between the features of metropolitan existence and the mature money economy. At the conclusion of his essay on the metropolis, Simmel indicates that the central features of metropolitan existence to which he has alluded and which he has explored have been dealt with more extensively in his earlier (1900) study *The Philosophy of Money* (see Simmel, 1990).

In turn, the origins of this most systematic investigation of the features and consequences of the development of the mature money economy may be tracked back at least to Simmel's paper of 1889, 'On the psychology of money', presented to Gustav Schmoller's seminar in that year. The notion of a 'psychology' of money as a project was maintained by Simmel until 1897 when he refers to 'a future "Philosophy of Money"'.[71] The early psychology of money commences with the relationship between means and ends and the implications for the lengthening of this teleological chain through the intervention of the 'indifferent' means of money. Where the circulation process is interrupted at various stages, the psychological traits of greed, avarice, extravagance, etc. are generated. The 'indifference' of the absolute means, which cannot possess psychologically an absolute value, creates the blasé attitude among the wealthier strata. Money's lack of quality comes to adhere to those who deal with it, in turn highlighting the impersonality of money. This very indifference and impersonality of money is, in turn, capable of creating an affinity with the concept of God as the reconciliation of all diversity – God in the form of belief, money in the form of the concrete abstraction. These are all themes given much fuller treatment in Simmel's *Philosophy of Money* in 1900.

Chronologically, the next major indicator of the project on money is Simmel's 'Money in modern culture' (1896). This was originally a lecture given to the Society of Austrian Economists in Vienna which may well have been attended by some of the Society's figures such as Carl Menger (who subsequently reviewed Simmel's *Philosophy of Money*),[72] Friedrich von Wieser and Eugen von Böhm-Bawerk – all of them opponents of the Historical School of Economics with which Simmel, through his connection to Schmoller, would have been associated. 'Money in modern culture' is the first overview of some of the central themes of his *Philosophy of Money*. One such theme is the seemingly contradictory development of the individual personality accompanied by an increasing inner and external freedom of movement and, on the other hand, the enormous expansion of the objective contents of life liberated from any individual nuance. The money economy has both contributed substantially to the development of the most individual aspects of the personality and to an increasing social levelling. In turn, this contradiction between qualitative and quantitative evaluation has been resolved in favour of quantification in the money economy, in the development of a blasé attitude to the value of things and, with the increasing focus upon means and technique over ends, to a growing 'Americanism of the times'. Money as a universal equivalent of all values is capable of bringing the most diverse things into relationship with one another, indeed with a dynamic flux of things that are assessed on the basis of exactitude and calculability. The totally dynamic impetus of the money economy, throwing everything into the circulation process, shatters stable and constant relations and creates a transitory constellation of relations – one that may be elevated into a worldview of modern life: everything in flux with no secure resting points. And although this may intimate the 'darker sides' of the money economy, these same processes in the money economy are also responsible for 'the finest and highest elements of our culture'.

Whereas the philosophical writings on culture explore the theoretical implications of the widening gap between subjective and objective culture – many of whose dimensions are already present in his *Philosophy of Money* – the final chapter of his major study of money contains a more substantive treatment of the increasing gap between the culture of things (*Sachkultur*) and personal culture (*Persönlichkeitskultur*). There, Simmel explicitly attributes the increasing separation of the two to the division of labour and consumption. On the one hand, this account of the consequences of the division of labour has remarkable affinities with Marx's earlier, but then not yet discovered, discussion of alienation in his *Paris Manuscripts*; on the

other, Simmel's examination of the negative impact of the 'capitalist' division of labour within the production process is located in the context of an
exploration of objective culture rather than a critique of capitalist society.
As Schmoller indicated, with respect to Simmel's *Philosophy of Money* but
relevant in this context too, 'his theme is the retroactive effect of the most
important institution of the modern economy – money – upon all sides of
life, of culture'.[73] Further, given Simmel's focus upon money, he is able to
extend his analysis to consumption as well as production – and indeed to
the sphere of consumption in general – in order to take in, briefly, modern
consumption, fashion and style.

Indeed, the focus of Simmel's exploration of socio-economic life – with
some exceptions where production is discussed – is largely upon the spheres
of circulation, exchange and consumption. In particular, as in the essay on
fashion, he was interested in modes of representation and masking things
within the context of metropolitan modernity. A significant mode of representing the wealth of commodity production from the nineteenth century
onwards was through world exhibitions. Due in part to the resentment of
the other states within the German Empire, the exhibition of 1896 in Berlin
became merely the Berlin Trade Exhibition. Simmel responded to this exhibition – which was taken to symbolize Berlin's elevation from a mere city
(*Grossstadt*) into a world metropolis (*Weltstadt*) – in his short essay 'The
Berlin Trade Exhibition' (1896). The confined space within which a plethora
of objects are displayed creates a disorientation, a mass effect upon perception, indeed 'a true hypnosis'. And whereas it is impossible to comprehend all 'the objects produced in a single city', the exhibition of
commodities strives to achieve this. The exhibition reveals 'how much the
form of modern culture has permitted a concentration in one place . . . [and]
through its own production a city can represent itself as a copy and a sample
of the manufacturing forces of world culture'. This concentrated unity of
commodities is, however, only a temporary phenomenon, an impression
that is confirmed by the transitory nature of its architecture. Together with
the modes of display – 'the struggle to render the graceless graceful for consumers' – the effect is to accentuate the shop-window quality of things. As
with the study of fashion, Simmel's concern is not merely with the circulation of commodities – here temporarily frozen in space – but with the aesthetic significance of the commodity form, its 'aesthetic super-additum'.

Part VIII: Politics of culture

Simmel's investigations of the permeation of the mature money economy
into modern culture may sometimes leave the impression that they are
merely concerned with its influence upon forms of interaction and cultural
forms. This would remain merely a partial perspective. There exists within
the total body of Simmel's works extensive evidence of his political concerns
and his awareness of the political dimensions of culture. How far this was

equally evident to his contemporaries must remain more open to question, given that Simmel's political commentaries often appeared anonymously or were published under a pseudonym.

Aside from his wartime writings, some of which were intended to have a political impact, the majority of known contributions to discussion upon political issues and, in the most general sense, to the politics of culture are located in the decade of the 1890s.[74] Those selected for inclusion here form part of Simmel's extensive explorations of gendered dimensions of culture and are to be understood in the context of his recognition of objective culture as being historically a predominantly male culture. This selection should be read in conjunction with the collection of essays *On Women, Sexuality and Love* (see Oakes [ed.], 1984).

With respect to the political writings of Simmel, it is most often the case that although political processes and institutions are discussed in many of his major works, his own political commentary on contemporary society usually is confined to newspaper and journal articles outside the academic arena.[75] Thus, reviewing Simmel's *Philosophy of Money*, Alfred Vierkandt could claim that many readers will

> miss a forceful word of judgment on some of the darker sides of our culture. In fact, the book distances itself from such a critique. It does indeed distinguish between the lighter and darker sides of our culture, but not really between good and evil in the sense of what is worth striving for and what not. It holds fast unperturbed ... to the pantheistic standpoint'.[76]

Yet it is also during the 1890s that we find Simmel's articles in support of free trades unions, socialized medicine, against political censorship of the theatre,[77] and, presented here, on aspects of prostitution and the development of the women's movement in Germany.

The first essay presented in this context is '*Infelices possidentes*', published in *Die Zukunft* in 1893 under the pseudonym Paul Liesegang. It is the only one of Simmel's several contributions in this important critical journal, edited by Maximilian Harden, which he felt necessary to publish under a pseudonym. Its authorship has affinities with the article published in the preceding October by Paul Liesegang in the socialist newspaper, *Vorwärts*, on the topic of spiritualism. Thematically, it has closer affinities with the anonymous article on prostitution published in the socialist journal, *Die Neue Zeit*, in 1892. Simmel's critique of the superficial entertainments for the bourgeois male runs counter to the notion of Simmel's cultural critique as élitist, for it is invariably directed at the bourgeoisie. The entertainment's superficial excitement and stimulation is a transportation of the stimulations of the metropolis into the sphere of comfort, amusement and withdrawal from the tension of everyday experience of modernity in the metropolis. This retreat into an unchallenging leisure sphere is not without its political dimension, as when – in the same year – Simmel decries the government restrictions upon Berlin performances of Gerhart Hauptmann's 'The Weaver' while encouraging the establishments which he describes in 'Unhappy dwellers'.[78]

As Simmel indicates in 'Unhappy dwellers', the focus is upon 'the excitement of sexual feelings' which is seen more as distraction from the bourgeoisie's more 'serious' concerns. However, his anonymous piece for *Die Neue Zeit* in the previous year, entitled 'Some remarks on prostitution in the present and the future', although directed again at bourgeois hypocrisy, has a more substantial import. The provocative nature of Simmel's position in the context of socialist discussion is revealed by the actions of the editors of *Die Neue Zeit* (Mehring and Kautsky), who distanced themselves from Simmel's article and indicated that they would publish an article replying to Simmel's piece from a presumably more ideologically sympathetic standpoint.[79] Dimensions of the relationship between prostitution, family, social class and the money economy recur in Simmel's writings in the 1890s: in his essay on 'The sociology of the family' (1895c)[80] and in early versions of sections of his *Philosophy of Money* (1900), in which the reciprocal affinity between prostitution and the money economy becomes an exemplar for his exploration of the relationship between the money economy and personal values.

The article on 'The Women's Congress and social democracy', also published in Harden's journal *Die Zukunft* in 1896, is indicative of Simmel's changing political position in favour of social reform and against aspects of the socialist women's movement exemplified by Clara Zetkin and Lily Barun.[81] Simmel himself attended the 1896 Women's Congress, to which the socialist wing of the women's movement was invited. Although the general invitation was rejected, two of its leaders – Zetkin and Braun – did attend what they viewed as the 'ladies movement' (*Damenbewegung*) and denounced the efforts of the latter to transform fundamentally the position of working class women within the existing social structure in favour of a revolutionary transformation. Simmel explores the alternative positions and presuppositions of the two tendencies within the women's movement: the socialist, working class movement associated with the Social Democratic Party and ideologically, at least, committed to a political revolution and socialization of the means of production on the one hand, and the middle class reformist movement in favour of piecemeal amelioration. Thus, the same socioeconomic formation creates not merely significantly differentiated responses on particular issues but, Simmel argues, the class differentiated society generates opposing perspectives on women's position within that society. The so-called bourgeois movement favours increased participation within the economic order whereas the working class movement seeks release from an inferior position within the capitalist individual labour process. The 'atrophy' of personal development in the one case, and the 'misery' of personal circumstances in the other, are two outcomes of the same socioeconomic formation.

Part IX: Beliefs and culture

Simmel's interest in the consolidation or coalescence of belief systems was extended to its broadest dimensions in his studies of religion. Like his contemporaries Emile Durkheim, Max Weber and Ernst Troeltsch, but with much less impact upon subsequent debates, Simmel wrote extensively on religion and, more occasionally, upon belief systems. What is presented here are two very different contributions to this area: an early (1898) essay on religion and an even earlier (1892) article on spiritualism.

Simmel's essay 'On the sociology of religion' constitutes his first significant published contribution to the study of religion, thus predating and differing substantially from his later book on religion published in 1906, and itself substantially revised and enlarged in its 1912 edition, but on both occasions being entitled simply *Die Religion* (See Simmel, 1906). The monograph appeared in a series edited by his student, Martin Buber. There followed a number of other contributions to the philosophy and sociology of religion, either in article form or as discussions within other contexts.

The inclusion of Simmel's 1898 essay in the present collection should be viewed as further evidence that his concern with cultural forms is not confined to his later writings that explicitly contain the concept 'culture' in their title. Further, the essay stands as an example of Simmel's interest in developing a sociology of religion. In the following year, in the summer semester of 1899, Simmel was offering a course on the philosophy of religion, as he informed Heinrich Rickert in July 1899: 'Have I already written to tell you that I am lecturing in this semester on the philosophy of religion? It is giving me greater satisfaction than all the other courses, and although it is probably one of the most difficult courses that is offered in German universities, there are nonetheless those who are interested in it'.[82] Three years later, in 1902, Simmel published (in English only) an essay entitled 'Tendencies in German life and thought since 1870', which contained a significant section on religious culture in contemporary Germany.[83] There, after examining the political strength of both Catholicism and Protestantism with their tendencies towards centralization and – along with the state – their demands for conformity, Simmel detects an increase in 'the need for religion . . . now that the two great intellectual currents, the scientific and the social, have lost much of their intoxicating power' (Frisby, 1994: 22). This 'transcendental impulse' to go beyond the everyday world will not be satisfied with the aesthetic realm but will turn 'to the deepest and profoundest things in life, which are thoroughly religious in character, even though they refuse to have anything to do with the Church, on the one hand, and just as little, on the other, with much extolled conversion of religion into morality' (Ibid.: 23). The latter is perhaps an oblique reference to the development of an ethical culture sponsored by several associations at the turn of the century.

In his 1898 essay, Simmel views the everyday world as the source of the development of higher cultural manifestations, including religion. This emphasis upon the everyday world and the delineation of its features again makes his analysis close to the phenomenological tradition. His explorations of faith, unity, origin and emotion in relation to religion all reveal connections with other dimensions of social life, whether these are the interaction of faith and religion with political domination, the crystallization of the lowest and the highest to constitute a unity, or the search for historical origin as located in the present.

Simmel's brief exploration of spiritualism – the impact of which upon intellectual and other circles should not be underestimated before, throughout and after the period in which Simmel was writing – was published in the leading Social Democratic newspaper *Vorwärts*. Aside from his scepticism in relation to spiritualism, there are a number of aspects of his analysis worthy of consideration. In the context of belief systems, Simmel commences with a contrast between a belief in science and its truths as a mode of making sense of the world and spiritualism which also seeks to make sense of the world. The latter is subsequently interpreted, at least with respect to bourgeois intellectuals' interest in the phenomenon, as in part a yearning for a simpler past – a nostalgia for a less complex world. This juxtaposition between the scientific and spiritualist cultures of belief was itself unified in many contemporaries. A significant example is Conan Doyle, who created in Sherlock Holmes a representation of the scientific – or at least the logical – detective, while also being a convinced spiritualist.[84]

From another perspective, we may see Simmel's brief exploration of spiritualism as an investigation of what he was later to describe as 'the culture of things as the culture of human beings'. In this context, the nineteenth century abounds in creations of phantasmagoria and simulacra – often with an accompanying elaborate technology – and an attendant fascination for, and fear of, the autonomous world of things.[85]

Concluding remarks

If we seek, somewhat artificially, to abstract some of Simmel's writings on culture and his contributions to the analysis of culture – and it must be emphasized that his contribution to a philosophical culture should be placed alongside his foundation for sociology, his extensive and relatively neglected philosophical studies, and his contributions to social psychology and to aesthetics – then we do so in order to bring to the foreground the significance of this cultural analysis. It would be difficult to summarize briefly the impact of Simmel's explorations of culture upon his contemporaries and students. The sociology of culture was continued during and after Simmel's lifetime by those who had attended his lectures, had been his erstwhile colleagues or had been, in a closer sense, his students. The contributions of Max Scheler, Karl Mannheim and many others to this mode of cultural analysis remain indebted to Simmel's impetus. The philosophy of culture that is to be found in the work of such diverse figures as Ernst Cassirer, Arnold Gehlen, Heinrich Rickert and Martin Heidegger contains echoes and confrontations with Simmel's work. Indeed, the important journal *Logos*, intended as an 'international journal for the philosophy of culture' and with which Simmel was closely associated from its inception, was edited by Richard Kroner – a student of Simmel. The critique of culture, and especially of contemporary modern culture, was developed far beyond Simmel's original contributions by his students such as Georg Lukács, Ernst Bloch and Siegfried Kracauer as well as by those within the Critical Theory tradition who took up aspects of Simmel's cultural analysis, such as Walter Benjamin. If the perspective on the debates on culture and crisis are widened, then Simmel's impact upon such movements as German Expressionism (not least in the work of his erstwhile student, Kurt Hiller) is worthy of further investigation. And in contemporary discussion, Habermas's somewhat limited evaluation of Simmel's diagnosis of modernity and philosophy of culture as that of 'a child of the fin de siècle' with its reliance upon 'the neo-Kantian notion of culture' should provoke a confrontation with Critical Theory's persistently ambiguous relationship to his work (Habermas, 1996). For it is Adorno, cited by Habermas, who declares that Simmel, 'for all his psychological idealism, [was] the first to accomplish the return of philosophy to concrete subjects, a shift that remained canonical for everyone dissatisfied with the chattering of epistemology or intellectual history' (Ibid.: 406).

The mode of exploration of concrete cultural phenomena is illuminated by some of his students. Some, such as Karl Mannheim, commented upon his preoccupation with the everyday and seemingly insignificant elements of social and cultural life. Others, such as Kracauer, drew attention to Simmel's explorations of conceptual, interpretive and insignificant entities, often bringing things that seem far apart into connection with one another, creating 'in us a sense of unified connectedness of the manifold' of the world and its fragments. He often explores 'the relations between objects that are entirely foreign to each other on the surface and that stem from radically different material worlds. He especially enjoys leaping from one or another layer of being into the experiential realm of the intimate personality' (Kracauer, 1995: 250). This gives Simmel's cultural analysis a resonance not merely for concrete objects but also for our relationship to them and their impact upon our psychological and emotional states as well as our social being.

Rather than deducing individual facts from abstract general concepts, Simmel's

> conceptual articulations cling to an immediately experienced (but admittedly not universally accessible) lived reality . . . Simmel never engages in acts of thought that are not supported by a perceptual experience of some sort and that cannot accordingly be realized through such an experience . . . He has no interest in grasping a phenomenon in terms of its obvious meaning, but instead wants to allow the entire plenitude of the world to pour into it. (Ibid.: 257)

The multiplicity of perspectives, grounded as it is in experience, allows Simmel to create a comparative exploration of cultural phenomena through historical and ethnographic comparison, and through a comparison of the diversity of forms within which cultural phenomena reveal both their affinities and differences.

Thus, although Simmel's contributions to the study of culture may appear, at first sight, removed from those of much of contemporary cultural theory and its applications, it is possible to detect certain affinities. Kracauer's reference to Simmel's attempts to explore experiential and emotional dimensions of cultural phenomena still has relevance to the wealth of explorations of the everyday world and problems of accessing experience of it. The critical dimension of contemporary cultural analysis, and its often uncertain affinities with an elastic use of the term 'critical theory', is also not absent from Simmel's critique of aspects of the dominant culture of his society. This is revealed, at times, by means of a relativization of the accepted, seemingly unproblematical dominant cultural phenomena which is achieved through reference to ethnographic and comparative data. Present, accepted cultural forms are never timeless and can be revealed to be part of a series of other historical or not yet realized possibilities. Further, although Simmel's cultural analysis seldom covers what we term 'popular culture' – which was to become central to the explorations of modernity by his students such as Kracauer and Bloch – it is the case that Simmel does provide, on occasion, a direct political critique of the dominant cultural order and its contradictory presuppositions. Equally significant in this respect are his frequent attempts to reveal that 'high' culture is embedded in 'low' culture. It is not surprising, therefore, that Simmel's work has been drawn upon increasingly in the exploration of cultural phenomena from a range of different disciplinary and critical perspectives.

Indeed, if the present limited selection of Simmel's writings is effective, then it will have encouraged the reader both to cross the boundaries of particular cultural constellations into other spheres and to search beyond the selection provided here to other instances of Simmel's cultural and social analysis. In other words, the present volume should be seen as complementing existing selections from Simmel's work that are readily available and accessible, upon general social themes, upon sociology and upon gender. It is for the reader to judge to what extent the contributions to the understanding of cultural phenomena assembled in the present volume are relevant to those intellectual fields of the present day that have expanded in recent decades into cultural studies, the sociology of culture and critical (cultural) theory in all their diversity, as well as the philosophy of culture.

David Frisby
Glasgow, 1997

Notes

1. It is true that the more systematic and extensive treatments of the problem of culture do emerge in Simmel's work from around 1900, but the exploration of culture is not confined to this period. The recent outstanding study by Klaus C. Köhnke on Simmel and his early works should substantially shift our orientation to his writings on culture, sociology and philosophy. See Köhnke (1996).

2. See Kracauer (1995: 225–57).

3. Theodor W. Adorno (1958: 26–7).

4. On Simmel's various attempts to establish sociology as an independent discipline, see Section 5 of Frisby (ed.) (1994, vol. 1: 309–73; vol. 2: 3–173). On the Berlin context, see Köhnke (1990: 99–108).

5. For a general overview of conflicting disciplines studying culture in Germany, see Smith (1991). For a recent collection on the philosophy of culture, see Konersmann (1996).

6. As a contemporary representative of this tradition, see the works of Karl Lamprecht, such as *Die Kulturhistorische Methode* (1900). His work is discussed in Smith (1991).

7. Simmel's student Georg Lukács claimed that the sociology of culture as it developed in the early decades of the twentieth century was only possible on the basis of the foundational work of Ferdinand Tönnies and Simmel. The work of Max Weber, Ernst Troeltsch, Werner Sombart, Max Scheler, Alfred Weber and Karl Mannheim may be viewed in this context.

8. This tendency may be exemplified in some of the work of one of Simmel's contemporaries, Alfred Vierkandt. See, for example, Vierkandt (1896).

9. On some of the issues involved in this extensive tradition, see Adorno (1967), and the opening essay on 'Cultural criticism and society'

10. This is the title of one of Simmel's most popular works, *Philosophische Kultur* (1911). On this work, see Jürgen Habermas (1996: 403–14).

11. Ethical societies and movements for ethical renewal were already common in the late nineteenth century.

12. See 'Weibliche Kultur', in Simmel (1911). This essay appears in English as 'Female culture' in Oakes (1984: 65–101). The complete translation of 'Female culture' is contained in this volume. It also includes a useful introduction by Oakes.

13. See Köhnke (1990, 1996).

14. See 'Einleitung. Zur Erkenntnistheorie der Sozialwissenschaft', in Simmel (1890: 1–20).

15. For an introduction to this context, see 'Georg Simmel and social psychology', in Frisby (1992: 20–41). A detailed discussion is to be found in Köhnke (1996).

16. Georg Simmel (1894: 271–7). In English this was published as 'The problem of sociology' (Simmel. 1895: 52–63); reprinted in Frisby (1994: vol. 1, pp. 28–35).

17. Letter to Lazarus, 5.11.1894, cited in Frisby (1992: 20). For more detail, see Köhnke (1996).

18. Fritz Hoeber (1918: 475–7, esp. 475).

19. See Rammstedt (1996). For the original French collection, see Simmel (1912).

20. Letter to Adolf von Harnack, 3.1.1914, in Gassen and Landmann (1958: 82).

21. Letter to Heinrich Rickert, 28.1.1914, in Gassen and Landmann (1958: 111–12).

22. For discussions on Simmel's concept of culture, see Weingartner (1960); Guy Oakes's 'Introduction' to Simmel (1980); Lawrence A. Scaff (1990: 283–96); Birgitta Nedelmann (1991: 164–94); Donald L. Levine's 'Introduction' to Simmel (1991: xv ff.).

23. Cited in Oakes (1984: 3).

24. Oakes (1984: 6–7).

25. G. Simmel, 'On the essence of culture' this volume (p. 40).

26. Oakes (1984: 67).

27. Ibid.

28. Ibid.: 72.

29. Ibid.: 69.

30. Marianne Weber (1919: 95–133). For a discussion of this essay, see Suzanne Vromen (1987: 563–79).; reprinted in Frisby (1994: vol. 2, 393–410). A more detailed discussion is found in Lieteke van Vucht Tijssen (1991: 203–18); reprinted in Frisby (1994: vol. 2, 19–31).

31. For a more general discussion of Simmel on women, see Kandal (1988: ch. 4); Felski (1991: ch. 2). For a collection of Simmel's essays on women, see Dahme and Köhnke (1985).

32. Kurt Gassen (1949: 310–44).

33. Ibid.: 340.

34. See this volume, p. 45.

35. These and other issues are dealt with in detail by Oakes in his introduction to Simmel (1980). A more provocative account is provided by Cacciari (1993).

36. On Simmel's and other German social theorists' relationship to Expressionism, see Frisby (1993: 88–111).

37. See G. Simmel (1986: 4).

38. Simmel's piece is one of a series published during April 1909 in the *Frankfurter Zeitung*. The questions here are from the editors of this series. Other contributors included Henry van de Velde, Friedrich Naumann, Peter Behrens and Karl Lamprecht. A selection is available in English as 'The future of our culture' in Francesco Dal Co. (1990: 292–312).

39. This volume, p. 101.

40. There has been a resurgence of interest in social and historical studies of the senses in recent years. See, for instance, Jay (1993); Corbin (1986); Classen et al. (1994); Goldstein (1996). See also the journal, *Body and Society* (Sage).

41. See this volume, p. 122.

42. See this volume, p. 125.

43. G. Simmel (1990: 100).

44. Simmel (1909); expanded as 'Koketterie', in Simmel (1911: 11–28); and published in English as 'Flirtation' in Oakes (1984: 133–52).

45. It was published in the same year as Simmel gave his lecture on sociability.

46. On meals, see also Mennell (1985).

47. See this volume, p. 215.

48. Even recent discussions of social space make little reference to Simmel's work. See Urry (1987: 213–38); Lefebvre (1991). An exception is Werlen (1993).

49. Simmel (1903: 287–302).

50. See this volume, p. 143.

51. See Martin Heidegger (1978: 323–59).

52. Since the title of Simmel's lecture was 'Die Grossstädte und das Geistesleben'.

53. On some of the context within which this lecture took place, see Smith (1991: 209–18).

54. See Park and Burgess (1967: 219).

55. Cacciari (1993: 3). The volume contains a detailed critical account and contextualization of Simmel on the metropolis.

56. On Walter Benjamin's theory of modernity, see Buck-Morss (1989); Frisby (1986); McCole (1993); Gilloch (1996).

57. Nietzsche associates fashion with other dimensions of modernity – *Mode* (Fashion), *Meinung* (opinion) and *Moment* (the momentary). See Frisby (1986: 31).

58. For a recent collection of essays on the significance of fashion in architecture, see Fausch et al. (eds) (1994).

59. See Veblen (1953).

60. Tarde (1890). See also Simmel's review of Tarde's volume in Simmel (1891: 141–2).

61. See, for example, Brigitte Stamm (1978).

62. See Lenk (1986: 415–37).

63. See the discussion in Fausch et al. (1994), as well as Loos (1982).

64. See Simmel (1950: 330–76).

65. See Fausch et al. (1994).

66. Loos (1985). On Loos in this context, see Colomina (1994).

67. Sombart (1907: 513–36).

68. For an overview of Simmel's contributions to the sociology of leisure, see Frisby (1992: 118–34).

69. Simmel (1902a); published in English as 'The picture frame: an aesthetic study', Simmel (1994: 11–17).

70. This volume, p. 223.

71. See my 'Afterword: the constitution of the text', in Simmel (1990: 513–34, especially 517). See also the critical German edition, *Philosophie des Geldes*, Frisby and Köhnke (eds) (1989).

72. See Menger (1901: 160–1).

73. Cited in Frisby (1992: 94).

74. On Simmel's wartime writings, see Watier (1991: 219–34). On Simmel's political writings, see also Frisby (1991), especially Chapter 5.

75. On the context of some of Simmel's early contributions, see Köhnke (1996).

76. Vierkandt (1901: 637–48, esp. 641); also cited in Simmel (1990: xviii).

77. For a brief discussion, see Frisby (1991), Chapter 5.

78. Simmel (1892–3: 283–4).

79. Blashko (1892: 10–18; 164–72).

80. Simmel (1895c); reprinted in Dahme and Köhnke (1985).

81. On the history of the women's movement in Germany in this period, see Evans (1976). On the wider context and significance of Simmel's essay, see Köhnke (1996: 462–6); Oakes (1984), 'Introduction'; Vromen (1987: 563–79).

82. Letter to Heinrich Rickert, 27.10.1899, in Gassen and Landmann (1958: 98).

83. Simmel (1902b: 93–111, 166–84); reprinted in Frisby (1994: 5–27).

84. See, for example, Jones (1989).

85. See Crary (1992); Asendorf (1994).

SHORT BIBLIOGRAPHY

Adorno, Theodor W. (1958) 'Der Essay als Form', in *Noten zur Literatur*, vol. 1. Frankfurt: Suhrkamp.

Adorno, Theodor W. (1967) 'Cultural criticism and society', in *Prisms*. London: Neville Spearman.

Asendorf, Christoph (1994) *Batteries of Life*. Berkeley, CA: University of California Press.

Blashko, A. (1892) 'Die moderne Prostitution', *Die Neue Zeit*, 10.

Buck-Morss, Susan (1989) *The Dialectics of Seeing*. Cambridge, MA: MIT Press.

Cacciari, Massimo (1993) *Architecture and Nihilism: On the Philosophy of Modern Architecture*. New Haven/London: Yale University Press.

Classen, Constance; Howe, David; Synnott, Anthony (1994) *Aroma. The Cultural History of Smell*. London/New York: Routledge.

Colomina, Beatriz (1994) *Privacy and Publicity. Modern Architecture as Mass Media*. Cambridge, MA: MIT Press.

Corbin, Alain (1986) *The Foul and the Fragrant*. Cambridge, MA: Harvard University Press.

Crary, Jonathan (1992) *Techniques of the Observer. On Vision and Modernity in the Nineteenth Century*. Cambridge, MA: MIT Press.

Dahme, Heinz-Jürgen and Köhnke, Klaus C. (eds) (1985) *Georg Simmel. Schriften zur Philosophie und Soziologie der Geschlechter*. Frankfurt, Suhrkamp.

Evans, Richard J. (1976) *The Feminist Movement in Germany 1894–1935*. London/Beverley Hills, CA: Sage.

Fausch, Deborah, et al. (eds) (1994) *Architecture: In Fashion*. Princeton, NJ: Princeton University Press.

Felski, Rita (1991) *The Gender of Modernity*, Cambridge, MA: Harvard University Press.

Francesco Dal Co. (1990) *Figures of Architecture and Thought*. New York: Rizzoli.

Frisby, D. (1986) *Fragments of Modernity*. Oxford: Polity Press/Cambridge, MA: MIT Press.

Frisby, D. (1991) *Sociological Impressionism* (second edn). London/New York: Routledge.

Frisby, D. (1992) *Simmel and Since*. London/New York: Routledge.

Frisby, D. (1993) 'Social theory, the metropolis and expressionism', in Timothy O. Benson (ed.), *Expressionist Utopias*. Los Angeles, CA: LA County Museum of Art/Seattle, WA: University of Washington Press.

Frisby, D. (ed.) (1994) *Georg Simmel. Critical Assessments*. (3 vols) London/New York: Routledge.

Frisby, D.P. and Köhnke, K.C. (eds) (1989) *Philosophie des Geldes*. Frankfurt: Suhrkamp.

Gassen, Kurt (1949) 'Georg Simmel's Vorlesung "Ethik und Probleme der modernen Kultur" 1913', *Philosophische Studien*, 1.

Gassen, K. and Landmann, M. (eds) (1958) *Buch des Dankes an Georg Simmel*. Berlin: Duncker & Humblot.

Gilloch, Graeme (1996) *Myth and Metropolis. Walter Benjamin and the City*. Cambridge: Polity Press.

Goldstein, Kurt (1996) *The Organism*. Cambridge, MA: MIT Press.

Habermas, Jürgen (1996) 'Georg Simmel on philosophy and culture: postscript to a collection of essays', Mathew Deflem (trans.), *Critical Inquiry*, 22(3): 403–14.

Heidegger, Martin (1978) 'Building, dwelling, thinking', in David Farrell Krell (ed.), *Basic Writings*. London: Routledge.

Hoeber, Fritz, (1918) 'Georg Simmel: Der Kulturphilosoph unserer Zeit', *Neue Jahrbücher für das Klassische Alterum*, 21: 475–7.

Husserl, Edmund (1964) *The Phenomenology of Internal Time Consciousness.* Bloomington, IN: Indiana State University Press.

Jay, Martin (1993) *Downcast Eyes.* Berkeley, CA: University of California Press.

Jones, Kelvin I. (1989) *Conan Doyle and the Spirits.* Wellingborough: Aquarian Press.

Kant, Immanuel (1964) *Anthropologie in pragmatische Absicht,* (Werke xii), Frankfurt: Suhrkamp.

Kandal, Terry R. (1988) *The Women Question in Classical Sociological Theory.* Miami: Florida International University Press.

Köhnke, Klaus C. (1990) 'Four concepts of social science', in Michael Kaern et al. (ed.), *Georg Simmel and Contemporary Sociology.* Dordrecht: Kluwer.

Köhnke, Klaus C. (1996) *Der junge Simmel – in Theoriebeziehungen und sozialen Bewegungen.* Frankfurt: Suhrkamp.

Konersmann, Ralf (ed.) (1996) *Kulturphilosophie.* Leipzig: Reclam.

Kracauer, Siegfried (1995) 'Georg Simmel', in Thomas Y. Levin (trans., ed.), *The Mass Ornament. Weimar Essays.* Cambridge, MA: Harvard University Press.

Lamprecht, Karl (1900) *Die Kulturhistorische Methode.* Berlin: Weidmann.

Lechner, Frank J. (1991) 'Simmel on social space', *Theory, Culture & Society,* 8(3): 192–202.

Lefebvre, Henri (1991) *The Production of Space.* Oxford: Blackwell.

Lenk, Elizabeth (1986) 'Wie Georg Simmel die Mode überlistet hat', in S. Bovenschen (ed.), *Die Listen der Mode.* Frankfurt: Suhrkamp.

Levine, Donald N. (1991) 'Introduction', in G. Simmel, *On Individuality and Social Forms.* Chicago: Chicago University Press.

Loos, Adolf (1982) *Spoken into the Void.* Cambridge, MA: MIT Press.

Loos, Adolf (1985) 'Ornament and crime', in *The Architecture of Adolf Loos.* London: Arts Council of Great Britain.

Lukács, Georg (1991) 'Georg Simmel', *Theory, Culture & Society,* 8(3): 145–50.

McCole, John (1993) *Walter Benjamin and the Antinomies of Tradition.* Ithaca: Cornell University Press.

Menger, Carl (1901) 'Simmel, Georg. Philosophie des Geldes', *Literarische Centralblatt,* 52(4).

Mennell, Stephen (1985) *All Manners of Food.* Oxford: Blackwell.

Nedelmann, Birgitta (1991) 'Individualization, exaggeration and paralysation: Simmel's three problems of culture', *Theory, Culture & Society,* 8(3): 169–94.

Nietzsche, Friedrich, *Untimely Meditations* (trans. R.J. Hollingdale). Cambridge: Cambridge University Press.

Oakes, Guy (ed.) (1984) *Georg Simmel: On Women, Sexuality and Love.* New Haven: Yale University Press.

Park, R.E. and Burgess, E.W. (1967) *The City.* Chicago, IL: Chicago University Press.

Rammstedt, Otthein (1996) 'Editorische Bericht', in G. Simmel, *Philosophische Kultur.* Frankfurt: Suhrkamp.

Scaff, Lawrence A. (1990) 'Georg Simmel's theory of culture', in M. Kaern (ed.), *Georg Simmel and Contemporary Sociology.* Dordrecht: Kluwer.

Simmel, Georg (1890) *Über sociale Differenzierung.* Leipzig: Duncker & Humblot.

Simmel. G. (1891) 'Besprechung von: Tarde, Gabriel, Les lois de l'imitation', *Zeitschrift für Psychologie und Physiologie der Sinnesorgane,* 2.

Simmel, G. (1892–3) 'Gerhart Hauptmann's "Weber"', *Sozialpolitisches Zentralblatt,* 2.

Simmel, Georg (1894) 'Das Problem der Soziologie', *Schmollers Jahrbuch für Gesetzgebung, Verwaltung und Volkswirtschaft,* 18: 271–7.

Simmel, Georg (1895a) 'The problem of sociology', *Annals of the American Academy of Political and Social Science,* 6: 52–63.

Simmel, G. (1895b) 'Zur Psychologie der Mode: Soziologische Studie', *Die Zeit* (Vienna), 5 and 12 October.

Simmel, G. (1895c) 'Zur Soziologie der Familie', *Vossische Zeitung,* 30 June, 7 July.

Simmel, Georg (1902a) 'Der Bildrahmen', *Der Tag* (Berlin), 541.

Simmel, G. (1902b) 'Tendencies in German life and thought since 1870', *The International Monthly,* 5.

Simmel, G. (1903) 'Über räumliche Projektionen sozialer Formen', *Zeitschrift für Sozialwissenschaft*, 6.

Simmel, G. (1904) 'Fashion', *International Quarterly*, 10.

Simmel, G. (1906) *Die Religion*. Frankfurt: Rütten & Loening.

Simmel, G. (1908) *Soziologie*. Leipzig: Duncker & Humblot.

Simmel, G. (1909) 'Die Zukunft unserer Kultur', *Frankfurter Zeitung*, 14 April 1909.

Simmel, G. (1909) 'Psychologie der Koketterie', *Der Tag* (Berlin). 11 and 12 May.

Simmel, G. (1911) *Philosophische Kultur*. Leipzig: W. Klinkhardt.

Simmel, G. (1912) *Mélange de philosophie relativiste*. Paris: Alcan.

Simmel, G. (1916) 'Die Krisis der Kultur', *Frankfurter Zeitung*, 13 February 1916.

Simmel, G. (1916) 'Wandel der Kulturformen', *Berliner Tageblatt*. 27 August 1916.

Simmel, G. (1950) 'The secret', in Kurt H. Wolff (ed.), *The Sociology of Georg Simmel*. Glencoe: Free Press.

Simmel, Georg (1980) *Essays on Interpretation in Social Science*. Manchester: Manchester University Press.

Simmel, Georg (1986) *Schopenhauer and Nietzsche* (trans. H. Loiskandl). Amherst, MA: University of Massachusetts Press.

Simmel, G. (1990) *The Philosophy of Money* (second enlarged edn). London/New York: Routledge.

Simmel, Georg (1994) 'The picture frame: an aesthetic study', *Theory, Culture & Society*, 11.

Smith, Woodruff D. (1991) *Politics and the Sciences of Culture in Germany, 1840–1920*. New York/Oxford: Oxford University Press.

Sombart, Werner (1902) *Wirtschaft und Mode*. Wiesbaden: J.F. Bergmann.

Sombart, Werner (1907) 'Probleme des Kunstgewerbes in der Gegenwart', *Die Neue Rundschau*, 18(1).

Stamm, Brigitte (1978) 'Anf dem Wege zum Reformkleid', in Eckhard Siepmann (ed.), *Kunst und Alltag um 1900*. Giessen: Anabas.

Tafuri, Manfredo (1976) *Architecture and Utopia. Design and Capitalist Development*. Cambridge, MA: MIT Press.

Tarde, Gabriel (1890) *Les lois de l'imitation*. Paris: Alcan.

Urry, John (1987) 'Nature and society: the organization of space', in R.J. Anderson; J.A. Hughes; W.W. Sharrock (eds), *Classic Disputes in Sociology*. London: Unwin Hyman.

Veblen, Thorstein (1953) *The Theory of the Leisure Class*. New York/Toronto: New American Library.

Vierkandt, A. (1896) *Naturvölker und Kulturvölker. Ein Beitrag zur Sozialpsychologie*. Leipzig: Duncker & Humblot.

Vierkandt, Alfred (1901) 'Einige neuere Werke zur Kultur-und Gesellschaftslehre', *Zeitschrift für Sozialwissenschaft*, 4.

Vischer, Friedrich T. (1879) 'Mode und Cynismus', in *Kritische Gänge*, New Series. Stuttgart.

Vromen, Suzanne (1987) 'Georg Simmel and the cultural dilemma of women', *History of European Ideas*, 8: 563–79.

Vucht Tijssen, Lieteke van (1991) 'Women and objective culture', *Theory, Culture & Society*, 8(3): 203–18.

Watier, Patrick (1991) 'The war writings of Georg Simmel', *Theory, Culture & Society*, 8(3).

Weber, Marianne (1919) *Frauenfragen und Frauengedanken. Gesammelte Aufsätze*. Tubingen: Mohr.

Weingartner, Rudolf H. (1960) *Experience and Culture. The Philosophy of Georg Simmel*. Middletown, CT: Wesleyan University Press.

Werlen, Benno (1993) *Society, Action and Space*. London/New York: Routledge.

PART I

DEFINING CULTURE

'INTRODUCTION'[1] TO
PHILOSOPHICAL CULTURE

When essays such as the following are presented in collected form, essays which, as far as their material content is concerned, possess no unity, then the internal justification for this can lie only in an overall intention which transcends all the diversity of content. Here such an intention commences from the concept of philosophy: the fact that what is essential to it is not or is not merely the content which is known, constructed or believed in each particular instance, but rather a specific intellectual attitude to the world and life, a functional form and manner of perceiving things and dealing with them internally. In so far as philosophical assertions diverge so much that they cannot be united and not one of them possesses uncontested validity, but since nonetheless one senses something in common among them, the value of which survives any criticism of the individual element and carries the philosophical process further and further onwards, then that which they have in common cannot lie in any particular content but only in this process itself. This may of course be obvious as a reason for leaving the name philosophy unscathed, despite all the contrariness of its doctrines. Yet it is not equally obvious that what is essential and significant in philosophy should rest upon this functional and, as it were, formal movement of the philosophizing mind – at least as compared to the dogmatically expressed contents and results, without which, of course, the philosophical process cannot inherently and independently proceed.

Such a separation between function and content, between the living process and its conceptual result, signifies a quite general tendency of the modern spirit. If epistemology, often declared to be the sole remaining object of philosophy, separates the pure process of knowing from its objects and analyses it; if Kantian ethics transfers the essence of all morality into the form of pure or good will, whose value exists self-sufficiently and free from all determination by purposive contents; if, for Nietzsche and Bergson, life as such is the genuine reality and signifies the ultimate value, not determined by any substantive contents, as it were, but instead creating and ordering them in its own right – then in all these instances, this separation between process and content and the independent accentuation of the former has already taken place.

Thus one can now conceive of the metaphysical impulse, process or state of mind that flows from it as a character or a value which is unaffected by all the contradictions and untenability of its content or results. And freed in principle from the rigid connection to the latter, it gains a flexibility and opportunity to expand, a lack of prejudice *vis-à-vis* any possible contents, which would have been unthinkable when people still sought to determine the essence of philosophy or metaphysics from their *objective* problems. If one conceives of the functional aspect, the attitude, the deep tendency and rhythm of the cognitive process to be the factors which make it philosophical, then its objects are unlimited from the outset and in that commonality of manner or form of thinking they acquire a unity for the most heterogeneous investigations, the kind of unity which the studies presented here claim for themselves.

Historical experience indicates that any fixing of the metaphysical tendency to a systematic content has left enormous cosmic and social areas outside philosophical interpretation and absorption. This occurs not only as a consequence of the always merely relative efficacy of any absolute principle, but above all because of its rigidity and lack of plasticity, which rule out the inclusion of the inconspicuous segments of existence into a metaphysical depth. Not even the most fleeting and isolated superficial phenomena of life should be able to escape this movement; but it appears that there is no single fundamental metaphysical concept from which a guideline leads from each phenomenon of that type. Although the philosophical process is really supposed to proceed from the universal breadth of existence, it seems instead compelled to run in innumerable directions. Some phenomena, some moods and some connections of thought point philosophical reflection in a direction that would be a form of pantheism if pursued to the absolute, whereas others, on the contrary, point toward individualism. Sometimes this reflection seems bound to end in an idealistic conclusion and sometimes in a realistic one, here in a rational one and there in a voluntaristic one. Obviously, then, there exists a most intimate connection between the full plenitude of actual existence, which demands to be led to the philosophical depths, and the full plenitude of possible metaphysical absolutes. The flexible articulation between the two, the possible connection to get from every point of one to any point of the other is offered by that mobility of the mind, not tied to any absolute, which is inherently metaphysical. Nothing prevents it from taking the path indicated, and many others by turn, and it is now more faithful and adaptable to the symptoms of things in such devotion to the metaphysical function than the jealousy of a material exclusivity would permit. The demand of the metaphysical impulse is not redeemed only at the end of these paths; indeed, the entire concept of path and destination, which brings with it the illusion of a necessarily uniform endpoint, is inappropriate here and is only a misuse of spatial analogies. Only if the qualities of any motion had a name, as it were, could they confront the absolute principles as an ideal final goal. A contradiction exists between them only in dogmatic crystallization, but not within the mobility of philosophical life itself, whose individual path can be a uniform and personally characterized one, no matter how many turns and twists it passes through.

This point of view is as distinct as possible from eclecticism and the wisdom of compromise. For both, after all, are no less anchored in the fixed results of thought than is any one-sided exclusive philosophy; the only difference is that they fill the same form, not with a single principled thought but with a mosaic of pieces of such thought, or gradually reduce their differences to the point of compatibility. Here we are concerned, however, with the quite fundamental turn, as it were, from metaphysics as dogma to metaphysics as life or function; not with the kind of contents of philosophy but with the type of its form, not with the differences between dogmas but with the unity of cognitive movement, which all these differences have in common until they harden into dogmas and thereby cut off the return to the intersection of all philosophical paths, and thus to the wealth of all possibilities of movement and inclusion.

Now there is no doubt that this shift of emphasis from the *terminus ad quem* to the *terminus a quo* in philosophical efforts would probably not be admitted by a single one of the brilliant creators within the history of philosophy. Intellectual individuality is so strong among them that it can be projected only into a worldview that is completely and unilaterally determined according to its content, and that the radicalism of the formal philosophical attitude to life indissolubly and intolerantly fuses together with this content. Thus the religiosity of all really religious human beings always implies an eternally equal being and inner behaviour, but in the individual – and particularly in a religiously creative one – it becomes such an organic unity, with a definite content of belief which stamps this particular individuality, that for this person only this particular dogma can be a religion. If, therefore, the individual nature of the productive philosopher always condenses into an absolute conception of the world which excludes others – which, by the way, could happen in parallel with the recognition in principle of that shift of emphasis in metaphysics – then such a conception appears to me to be the condition for a 'philosophical culture' in a broader and modern sense. This culture does not in fact consist in the knowledge of metaphysical systems or the confession of faith in individual theories, but rather in a consistent intellectual attitude toward all existence, in an intellectual motion towards the stratum in which, in the broadest variety of profundities and connected to the broadest variety of actualities, all possible currents of philosophy run. Similarly, a religious culture does not consist in the recognition of a dogma, but rather in the interpretation and structuring of life with continuous regard to the eternal fate of the soul; and an artistic culture does not consist of the sum of individual works of art, but rather in sensing and forming the contents of existence in general according to the norms of artistic values.

Even if philosophy also remains in its inner orientation in the discontinuity of dogmatic partisanship, then there are still two uniformities on either side of the latter; the functional one, of which I first spoke, and this teleological one, for which philosophy is an exponent, an element or a form of culture in general. Both uniformities, as it were, are connected below ground; philosophical culture in any case must act flexibly and must be able to see and go back from any single theory of the functional common ground of all theories. The results of the effort may be fragmentary, but the effort itself is not.

The treatment and condensation of the problems of this volume commenced from the interest in this philosophical attitude in general. Demonstrating how precisely its individuality and heterogeneity supports this fundamental concept of philosophical culture, or is supported by it, is no longer a matter of the programme but of the work itself. According to the particular perspective adopted, philosophical culture rests upon the presupposition or furnishes evidence for the following: it is a prejudice that delving into things from the surface of life, excavating the respective succeeding strata of ideas under each of its phenomena, or what one could call *giving it meaning*, must necessarily lead to a *single* ultimate point or must hover unsupported in the air if it does not take its direction from such a point.

In a fable, a peasant on his deathbed tells his children that there is treasure buried in his field. Thereupon they dig deeply all over the field, without finding the treasure. The next year, however, the field prepared in this way yields a triple harvest. This symbolizes the line of metaphysics indicated here. We will not find the treasure, but the world we have dug through in search of it will bring a triple harvest to the spirit, even if in reality there was no treasure at all but only the fact that this excavation is the necessary and inner determination of our minds.

THE CONCEPT OF CULTURE

If we define culture as the refinement, as the intellectualized forms of life, the accomplishment of mental and practical labour, then we place these values in a context in which they do not automatically belong by virtue of their own objective significance. They become manifestations of culture to us inasmuch as we interpret them as intensified displays of natural vitality and potential, intensified beyond the level of development, fullness and differentiation that would be achieved by their mere nature. A natural energy or allusion, which is necessary only in order that it may be surpassed by actual development, forms the presupposition for the concept of culture.

From the standpoint of culture, the values of life are civilized *nature*; they do not have here the isolated significance that is measured from above, as it were, by the ideals of happiness, intelligence and beauty. Rather, they appear as developments of a basis that we call nature and whose power and intellectual content they surpass in so far as they become culture. Therefore, if a cultivated garden fruit and a statue are both equally cultural products, then language indicates this relationship in a subtle manner by calling the fruit tree 'cultivated', whereas the bare marble block is not 'cultivated' to produce a statue. For in the first case one assumes a natural driving force and disposition of the tree to bear these fruits which, through intelligent influence, grow beyond their natural limits; whereas we do not presuppose a corresponding tendency as regards the statue. The culture embodied in the statue constitutes an enhancement and refinement of certain human energies whose original manifestations we term 'natural'.

At first glance, it seems reasonable to describe impersonal objects as cultured only as a figure of speech. For to develop through will and intelligence what is naturally given beyond the limits of its merely natural capacities is reserved for ourselves or such objects whose growth is connected with our impulses and, in their turn, stimulate our feelings. The material products of culture – furniture and cultivated plants, works of art and machinery, tools and books – in which natural material is developed into forms which could never have been realized by their own energies, are products of our own desires and emotions, the result of ideas that utilize the available possibilities of objects. It is exactly the same with regard to the culture that shapes people's relationships to one another and to themselves: language, morals, religion and law. To the extent that these values are interpreted as cultural, we distinguish them from such levels of growth of their innate energies that they may accomplish, as it were, by themselves, and that are only the raw material for the process of civilization, like wood and metal, plants and electricity. By cultivating objects, that is by increasing their value beyond the performance of their natural constitution, we cultivate ourselves: it is the same value-increasing process developing out of us and returning back to us that moves external nature or our own nature. The fine arts reflect this concept of culture most clearly because they display the greatest tension between these opposites. For the shaping of the object seems completely to escape being adapted to the process of our subjectivity. The work of art interprets the meaning of the phenomenon itself, whether it is embedded in the shaping of space or in the relations of colours or in the spirituality that exists, as it were, both in and beneath the visible. Yet everything depends on discovering the meaning and secret of things in order to represent them in a form that is purer and clearer than their natural development – not, however, in the sense of chemical or physical technology, which explores the law-like nature of objects in order to incorporate them into human purposes that are intrinsic to them. Rather, the artistic process is completed as soon as it has succeeded in presenting the object in its unique significance. This, in fact, also fulfils the purely artistic ideal, since the perfection of the work of art is an objective value in itself, completely independent of its success in our subjective experience. The slogan '*l'art pour l'art*' characterizes perfectly the self-sufficiency of the purely artistic tendency. But from the standpoint of a cultural ideal the situation is different. Here it is essential that the independent values of aesthetic, scientific, ethical, eudaemonistic and even religious achievements are transcended in order to integrate them all as elements in the development of human nature beyond its natural state. More accurately, they are the milestones which this development has to pass. At each moment cultural development is located somewhere along this road; it never can proceed purely formally and independently of some content even though it is not identical with this content. Cultural contents consist of those forms, each of which is subordinate to an autonomous ideal, though here they are viewed from the standpoint of the development of our energies or our being beyond the degree considered to be purely natural. In refining objects, man creates them in his own image. The cultural process, as the supra-natural growth of the energies of things, is the manifestation or embodiment of the identical growth of *our* energies. The borderline at which the development of specific life-content passes from its natural form into its cultural form is indistinct and is subject to controversy. But this is merely one of the most universal difficulties of thought. The categories under which specific phenomena are subsumed in order to incorporate them into knowledge, its norms and relationships, are marked off from each other and often gain their meaning only from this contrast. These concepts form sequences with discontinuous levels. Yet the particulars that are supposed to be covered by these concepts usually cannot be located with the same degree of certainty. Rather, their quantitative characteristics often determine whether they belong to the one or the other concept so that, because of the continuity of everything quantitative and the ever-possible *intermediate position* between two entities, each of which corresponds to a specific category, the specific phenomenon may well be placed sometimes with one, sometimes with the other. Thus there seems to be an indeterminacy between them, even a mixture of concepts which, according to their actual meaning, exclude one another. The fundamental certainty of the demarcation between nature and culture, that the one starts where the other leaves off, is just as little affected by the uncertainty as to where to locate individual phenomena as are the concepts of day and night which do not merge into one another because dawn and dusk may sometimes be attributed to the one, sometimes to the other.

I will now contrast this discussion of the general concept of culture with a specific relationship within contemporary culture. If one compares our culture with that of a hundred years ago, then one may surely say – subject to many individual exceptions – that the things that determine and surround our lives, such as tools, means of transport, the products of science, technology and art, are extremely refined. Yet individual culture, at least in the higher strata, has not progressed at all to the same extent; indeed, it has even frequently declined. This does not need to be shown in detail. I only wish, therefore, to emphasize some aspects of it. Linguistic possibilities for expression, in German as well as in French, have become much more refined and subtle in the last hundred years. Not only do we now have Goethe's language, but in addition we have a large number of refinements, subtleties and individual modes of expression. Yet, if one looks at the speech and writing of individuals, they are on the whole increasingly less correct, less dignified and more trivial. In terms of content, the scope of objects of conversation has been widened during that time through advances in theory and practice, yet, nonetheless, it seems that conversation, both social as well as intimate and in the exchange of letters, is now more superficial, less interesting and less serious than at the end of the eighteenth century. The fact that machinery has become so much more sophisticated than the worker is part of this same process. How many workers are there today, even within large-scale industry, who are able to understand the machine with which they work, that is the mental effort invested in it? The same applies to military culture. The work of the individual soldier has essentially remained the same for a long time, and in some respects has even been reduced through modern methods of warfare. In contrast, not only the material instruments but, above all, the completely impersonal organization of the army have become extremely sophisticated and a real triumph of objective culture. In the purely intellectual sphere, even the best informed and most thoughtful persons work with a growing number of ideas, concepts and statements, the exact meaning and content of which they are not fully aware. The tremendous expansion of objective, available material of knowledge allows or even enforces the use of expressions that pass from hand to hand like sealed containers without the condensed content of thought actually enclosed within them being unfolded for the individual user. Just as our everyday life is surrounded more and more by objects of which we cannot conceive how much intellectual effort is expended in their production, so our mental and social communication is filled with symbolic terms, in which a comprehensive intellectuality is accumulated, but of which the individual mind need make only minimal use. The preponderance of objective over subjective culture that developed during the nineteenth century is reflected partly in the fact that the eighteenth century pedagogic ideal was focused upon the formation of man, that is upon a personal internal value, which was replaced during the nineteenth century, however, by the concept of 'education' in the sense of a body of objective knowledge and behavioural patterns. This discrepancy seems to widen steadily. Every day and from all sides, the wealth of objective culture increases, but the individual mind can enrich the forms and contents of its own development only by distancing itself still further from that culture and developing its own at a much slower pace.

How can we explain this phenomenon? If all the culture of things is, as we saw, nothing but a culture of people, so that we develop ourselves only by developing things, then what does that development, elaboration and intellectualization of objects mean, which seems to evolve out of these objects' own powers and norms without correspondingly developing the individual mind? This implies an accentuation of the enigmatic relationship which prevails between the social life and its products on the one hand and the fragmentary life-contents of individuals on the other. The labour of countless generations is embedded in language and custom, political constitutions and religious doctrines, literature and technology as objectified spirit from which everyone can take as much of it as they wish to or are able to, but no single individual is able to exhaust it all. Between the amount of this treasure and what is taken from it, there exist the most diverse and fortuitous relationships. The insignificance or irrationality of the individual's share leaves the substance and dignity of mankind's ownership unaffected, just as any physical entity is independent of its being individually perceived. Just as the content and significance of a book remains indifferent to a large or small, understanding or unresponsive, group of readers, so any cultural product confronts its cultural audience, ready to be absorbed by anyone but in fact taken up only sporadically. This concentrated mental labour of a cultural community is related to the degree to which it comes alive in individuals just as the abundance of possibilities is related to the limitations of reality. In order to understand the mode of existence of such objective intellectual manifestations, we have to place them within the specific framework of our categories for interpreting the world. The discrepant relationship between objective and subjective culture, which forms our specific problem, will then find its proper place within these categories.

ON THE ESSENCE OF CULTURE

All series of events arising from human activity can be regarded as nature, that is to say, as a causally determined development in which each stage must be explicable in terms of the configuration and dynamic forces of the preceding situation. Nor need any distinction be made between nature and history, thus understood. What we call history takes its place, when considered purely as a sequence of events, within the natural pattern of events in the material world, which can be causally apprehended. But as soon as any of the elements of these series are grouped under the concept of culture, the concept of nature thereby takes on a more restricted specific meaning. The 'natural' development of the series then only leads to a certain point, at which it is replaced by cultural development.

The wild pear tree produces hard, sour fruit. That is as far as it can develop under the conditions of wild growth. At this point, human will and intelligence have intervened and, by a variety of means, have managed to make the tree produce the edible pear; that is to say, the tree has been 'cultivated'. In just the same way we think of the human race first developing, by virtue of psycho-physical constitution, heredity and adaptation, to certain forms and modes of existence. Only then can teleological processes take over and develop these existing energies to a pitch that was quite impossible, in the nature of things, within the limits of their foregoing development. The point at which this change to a new evolutionary energy occurs marks the boundary between nature and culture.

Since, however, culture can also be causally derived from its 'natural' origins, we see, first, that nature and culture are only two different ways of looking at one and the same thing, and secondly, that 'nature', for its part, is being used in two different senses. It means both the all-embracing nexus of causally and temporally connected phenomena, and also a phase of development, namely that phase in which only inherent energies are developed. This phase ends as soon as an intelligent will with *means* at its disposal takes up these energies and, with them, creates states which could not be attained by those energies unaided. If this seems to mean that the concept of culture is identical with that of purposive human activity in general, the concept needs to be qualified in order to pin down its special meaning. If one schoolboy trips another up so as to make him fall and make his friends laugh, this is without doubt an eminently teleological action, in which will and intelligence make use of natural circumstances. But it will not be regarded as an element of culture. The use of that concept depends, rather, on a number of conditions – operating unconsciously, if one wishes to put it thus – which can be determined only by a process of analysis which is not immediately obvious.

Cultivation presupposes the prior existence of an entity in an uncultivated, i.e. natural state. It also presupposes that the ensuing change of this entity is somehow latent in its *natural structure or energies*, even if it cannot be achieved by the entity itself but only through the process of culture. That is to say, cultivation develops its object to that perfection which is predetermined as a potential of its essential underlying tendency.

Hence we regard the pear tree as cultivated because the work of the gardener only develops the potential dormant in the organic constitution of its natural form, thus effecting the most complete evolution of its own nature. If, on the other hand, a tree trunk is made into a ship's mast, this, too, is undoubtedly the work of culture, but not a 'cultivation' of the tree trunk, because the form given it by the shipbuilder is not inherent in its nature. It is, on the contrary, a purely external addition imposed by a system of purposes alien to its own character.

Thus all cultivation, as the word is generally understood, is not only the development of some entity beyond the form attainable by natural processes alone. It is development in accordance with an original inner essence, the perfection of an entity in terms of its own significance, its most profound impulse. But this perfection is unattainable at the stage which we call natural, which consists in the purely causal development of initial inherent energies. It comes into being, rather, by the combination of those energies and the new teleological intervention, an intervention in the potential direction of the entity itself, which may thus be called the culture of that entity.

Strictly speaking, this means that only man himself is the real object of culture. For he is the only being known to us with an inherent a priori demand for perfection. His 'potential' is not simply the fact of latent energies, not the considerations and speculations aroused in the mind of an onlooker (as is the 'potential' garden pear seen in the wild pear tree), but rather it already has, so to speak, its own language. Whatever can be attained by the development of the soul is already present in its state at any time, as a feeling of urgency, as some invisible inner pattern. Even if its content is actualized only in a vague, fragmentary way, it is, for all that, a positive feeling of direction. Full development, as destiny and as capacity, is inseparably bound up with the existence of the human soul. It alone possesses the potential for development towards goals that are exclusively inherent in the teleology of its own being. However, it too cannot attain these goals purely through that growth from within which we call natural growth, but beyond a certain point it requires a 'technique', a procedure directed by the will.

Thus when we speak of the 'cultivation' of lower organisms, plants and animals (usage does not permit the term to be applied to inorganic entities), this is clearly only a transference based on the loose analogy between man and other organisms. For even if the state to which culture develops such entities is a potential of their organization and is in due course reached with the aid of their own energies, it is never inherent in the same way in the intrinsic meaning of their existence, it is never predetermined in their natural state as a kind of activity, in the way that the perfection attainable by the human soul is inherent therein.

This consideration, however, necessitates a further qualification of our concept. Even if culture is a perfection of man, it is by no means the case that any perfection of man constitutes culture. There are, on the contrary, developments which the soul achieves purely from within, or in the form of a relationship to transcendental powers, or in a direct ethical, erotic or emotional relationship with other people, and which cannot be included in the concept of culture. Religious exaltation, ethical dedication, strict preservation of the personality for its own unique task and mode of existence – all these are values which the soul achieves instinctively by its own nature or by self-improvement. They may entirely accord with our concept of culture: the maximum development of a person's potential from its natural stage, following the authentic intrinsic direction of the particular personality while necessitating the intervention of the highest spiritual powers to guide his energies. But for all that, it is not a matter of culture as we conceive it.

For culture implies also that such human development involves *something external to man*. Certainly, cultivatedness is a spiritual state, but of such a kind as is attained by the use of purposively formed *objects*.

This external, objective aspect is not to be understood only in a spatial sense. For example, forms of etiquette; refinement of taste revealed in critical judgement; the acquisition of tact, making the individual an agreeable member of society – all these are forms of culture which take the process of perfection into real and ideal spheres beyond the individual. Perfection here does not remain a purely immanent process, but takes the form of a unique adaptation and teleological interweaving of subject and object. If the development of the subjective soul does not involve any objective artefact as a means and stage of its progress back to itself, then even if values of the highest order are created, within the soul or in the outside world, it is not by way of culture in our specific sense. This also explains why certain highly introverted individuals, to whom it is abhorrent that the soul should seek self-perfection indirectly via anything external to itself, can feel hatred for culture.

This necessary duality in the concept of culture can be seen equally with regard to its objective element. We are accustomed automatically to label as cultural values the great series of artistic and moral, scientific and economic achievements. Perhaps they all are; but they are certainly not so by virtue of their purely objective, as it were autochthonous significance. The cultural significance of any particular achievement is by no means equivalent to its significance within its own series as determined by its specific nature and purpose. For example, a work of art is subject to quite different criteria and norms when considered within the sphere of art history or aesthetics, than when its cultural value is involved.

Each of these great series can be regarded on the one hand as an end in itself, so that each individual member of them constitutes a value which is proven directly by being enjoyed and giving satisfaction. On the other hand, they can all also be included in the cultural series, i.e. considered in respect of their significance for the overall development of individuals and society at large. Standing on their own ground, all these values resist inclusion in the cultural series. A work of art aspires only to perfection as measured by purely artistic criteria. In scientific research, all that matters are correct results; for the economic product, only the most efficacious manufacture and profitable utilization are of importance. All these spheres of the inner and outer world are developed teleologically beyond their 'natural' limitations; they thus, of course, become capable of functioning as cultural values. But, as autonomous objective spheres, they are *not* such values *per se*, but are subject to criteria and norms derived only from their objective content, not from the requirements of the unified centre of human personality. Their contribution to the development of human personality, i.e. their cultural value, is a different matter. Their status in this regard is by no means the same as in relation to the requirements of those specific interests pertaining only to one objective aspect of our lives. However excellently they may serve our specific ends, their value for our lives as a whole, for the wellspring of our being in its struggle for development, may be very slight. Conversely, they may be imperfect and insignificant in the objective, technical perspective of their specific province, but may, for all that, offer precisely what our life needs for the harmony of its parts, for its mysterious unity over and above all specific needs and energies.

We only ever perceive 'unity' as the interaction and dynamic interweaving, coherence and balancing of multiplicity; and so it is with that point of unity within us, whose inner significance and energy reach perfection in the cultural process by way of enhanced and perfected objects. To be more explicit: the various aspects of our lives exist in close interaction, each supporting and supported by the others, harmoniously balancing and exchanging their vitality. That is why we are not cultured simply by virtue of particular knowledge or abilities. That is why specialist expertise, of no matter what objective degree, is not of itself culture, which is only created when such one-sided attainments are integrated into the soul in its entirety, when they help to resolve discords between its elements by raising them all to a higher level, in short, when they help to perfect the whole as a unity. The criterion for assessing whatever we contribute or are able to appreciate within the categories of their specific objective series, must not be confused with the other criterion for evaluating these same things in the category of culture, i.e. the development of our inner *totality*.

This distinction illuminates the paradox that it is precisely the supreme achievements in various fields, especially those of a personal kind such as art, religion or speculative philosophy, whose *cultural* value is relatively secondary. The most impressive works and ideas impose their own intrinsic content and criteria on us so powerfully that their cultural significance is overshadowed. They refuse, as it were, to collaborate with other elements in the evolution of our whole being. They are too supreme within their own sphere for the subordinate role entailed in treating them as cultural factors, as means to the creation of a spiritual unity.

This will clearly apply with most force to those products of culture from which a personal life speaks most directly to the recipient. The more distinct a product is from the subjective spirituality of its creator, the more it belongs to an objective order with its own validity, then the more specific is its *cultural* significance, the more suitable it is to play a general part in the spiritual development of a large number of people.

The same is true of the 'style' of a work of art. We tend scarcely to consider the style of a really great work of art in which a sovereign spirit has found its unique mode of expression. For style is a *general* manner of expression common to many works, a form which can be abstracted from any particular content. But in the supreme work of art, the general foundation and the particular details of form are one unified revelation, in which any elements it may share with other works are wholly irrelevant. Such a work compels us to appreciate it in its uniqueness, not as an example of some general stylistic principle.

Likewise, anything very great or very personal may, in fact, have a very considerable cultural effect, but this category cannot provide the most significant locus to give the greatest prominence to its value. It can only do this with achievements which are essentially of a more general, impersonal kind, which are objectified at a greater distance from the subject, and can therefore more 'selflessly', as it were, provide stages in spiritual development.

Because culture, in a unique way, sets the contents of life at a point of intersection of subject and object, we may legitimately interpret the concept in two ways. The name of objective culture can be given to things, extended, enhanced and perfected as described above so as to lead the soul to its own perfection, or to constitute a part of the road to higher life of the individual or the community. By subjective culture, on the other hand, I understand the degree of personal development thus attained. Thus objective and subjective culture are coordinated concepts only if the former is understood in a figurative sense, namely if one ascribes to things an independent impulse towards perfection, a consciousness that they ought to develop beyond their natural limits. The human energy which brings this about is then imagined to be only the means used by things, as it were, to this end. To describe things, the material contents of life, as 'cultivated' is to invert the order of the real process of cultivation which takes place within man. It is to create a symbolic parallel to this process by treating the development of things as if it were *per se* a teleological process, and then dividing it into a natural and a cultivated stage; the latter, as a self-sufficient and definitive state proceeding in its ascent, or a part thereof, by means of the intervention of human activity.

But when understood more precisely, the two senses in which the concept of culture is used are not at all analogous. On the contrary, subjective culture is the overriding final goal, and its measure is the measure of how far the spiritual process of life has any part in those objective entities and their perfection. Clearly there can be no subjective culture without an objective culture, because a subjective development or state constitutes culture only by virtue of its inclusion of such objects. Objective culture, on the other hand, can, relatively speaking, become substantially (though not completely) independent of subjective culture, by the creation of 'cultivated' objects – i.e. 'cultivating' objects, as they should properly be understood, whose value as such is subjectively utilized only to an incomplete degree. Especially in highly developed epochs based on division of labour, the achievements of culture acquire the extent and coherence of a realm with its own kind of independent existence. Objects become more perfect, more intellectual, they follow more and more obediently their own inner logic of material expediency. But real culture, that is, subjective culture, does not progress equally; indeed, it *cannot* in view of the vast expansion of the objective realm of things, divided up as it is between innumerable contributors. To put it at its lowest, historical development tends increasingly to widen the gap between concrete creative cultural achievements and the level of individual culture. The disharmony of modern life, in particular the intensification of technology in every sphere combined with deep dissatisfaction with it, arises largely from the fact that things become more and more cultivated but people are capable only to a lesser degree of deriving from the improvement of objects an improvement of their subjective lives.

FEMALE CULTURE

Culture can be regarded as the perfection of individuals achieved as a result of the objectified spirit at work in the history of the species. Subjective being appears as cultured in its unity and totality by virtue of the fact that it is consummated in the acquisition of objective values: the values of morality and knowledge, art and religion, social formations and the expressive forms of the inner life. Thus culture is a distinctive synthesis of the subjective and the objective spirit. Its ultimate purpose, of course, can lie only in the enrichment of individuals. However, the contents of the objective spirit must first be juxtaposed to this process of perfection as autonomous and detached, both from those who create the contents and from those who appropriate them. Only by this means can they then be incorporated into the process as its instruments or stages. As a result, these contents – all that is expressed and formed, what exists ideally and what has real force, the complex of which constitutes the cultural capital of an era – may be designated as its 'objective culture'. From the determination of this objective culture, we can distinguish the following as the problem of 'subjective culture': To what degree, both extensively and intensively, do individuals have a share in the contents of objective culture?

From the perspective of both reality and value, these two concepts are quite independent of each other. The great mass of personalities that comes into question may be excluded from a highly developed objective culture. On the other hand, this same mass can participate in a relatively primitive culture in such a way that subjective culture attains a relatively extraordinary level. Value judgements vary in a corresponding fashion. Those who have purely individualist convictions, and especially those who have purely social convictions, will link the entire significance of culture to the question of how many persons participate in it and to what extent. How much cultivation and happiness, beauty and morality, does the life realized in the individual draw from it? On the other hand, consider those who have a commitment not only to the utility of things but also to the things themselves, not merely to the turbulent stream of action, pleasure, and suffering but also to the timeless meaning of the forms on which the spirit has left its stamp. They will be interested only in the development of objective culture. They will appeal to the consideration that the objective value of a work of art, a piece of knowledge, a religious idea, or even a law or an ethical norm is quite irrelevant to the question of how frequently or infrequently the fortuitous course of the reality of life has incorporated all this into itself.

The two value questions posed by the modern women's movement also divide at the point that these two tendencies branch off. The genesis of this movement seemed to confine it completely to the course of subjective culture. In so far as women proposed to move into the forms of life and achievements of men, for them the question concerned their personal participation in cultural goods that already existed and to which they had merely been denied access, regardless of whether these goods might provide them with a new source of happiness, new obligations, or a new form of personality. In this case, the struggle is invariably only on behalf of individual persons, regardless of how many millions of people may have a stake in it in both the present and the future. It is not a struggle for something that in itself transcends everything individual and personal. How often a value is realized is at issue here, not the creation of objectively new values. Perhaps all the eudaemonistic, ethical, and social emphases of the women's movement are grounded in this tendency. However, the other tendency, which is much more abstract and produced by a need that is much less pressing, does not disappear: the question of whether qualitatively new entities and an expansion of the objective content of culture arise from this movement, the question not only of a multiplication of reproduction of what already exists but rather of creation as well.

Suppose that the women's movement, in accordance with the view of its advocates, immeasurably extends the domain of subjective culture. Or suppose, as its opponents prophesy, that it threatens to debase the value of subjective culture. The gains the women's movement produces for the contents of objective culture would be independent of both cases. The prospects for the latter development will be considered here. More precisely, we shall consider the *basis* for these prospects: the fundamental relations of the female nature to objective culture.

In this context, it is important at the outset to affirm the fact that human culture, even as regards its purely objective contents, is not asexual. As a result of its objectivity, there is no sense in which culture exists in a domain that lies beyond men and women. It is rather the case that, with the exception of a very few areas, our objective culture is thoroughly male. It is men who have created art and industry, science and commerce, the state and religion. The belief that there is a purely 'human' culture for which the difference between man and woman is irrelevant has its origin in the same premise from which it follows that such a culture does not exist – the naive identification of the 'human' with 'man'. Many languages even use the same word for both concepts.

At this point, I shall not consider the issue of whether this masculine character of the objective elements of our culture is a result of the inner nature of the sexes or is a consequence of male dominance, a matter that really has no relation to the question of culture. In any case, this naive identification is responsible for the fact that deficient performances in the most diverse areas are degraded as 'feminine' while outstanding performances of women are celebrated as 'thoroughly manly'. It is why not only the scope but also the nature of our cultural activity turn on specifically male energies and emotions and a distinctively male intellectuality.

This is important for culture as a whole, and especially for those strata that can be called semi-productive. These are the strata in which nothing absolutely new is brought forth from the spiritual springs of creativity. However, they are also not characterized by mechanical reproduction according to models that are exactly prescribed. On the contrary, these strata constitute a certain middle ground. Thus far, cultural history has not adequately investigated this distinctive quality, which is of infinite importance for the more subtle aspects of the structure of society. In many areas of technology and commerce, science and warfare, literary activity and art, innumerable achievements of what could be called secondary originality are called for: achievements which take place within given forms and on the basis of given presuppositions, but which also demonstrate initiative, distinctiveness, and creative power. The claims of the specifically male energies are especially evident in these cases. That is because the forms and presuppositions in question have their origin in the male spirit. They transmit its character to these achievements, which may be described as epigonal.

I shall single out only one example of this masculine nature of cultural contents that seems to be completely neutral. Frequently the 'legal antipathy' of women is stressed: their opposition to legal norms and judgements. However, there is no sense in which this necessarily implies an animus against the law itself; instead, it is only against *male* law, which is the only law we have, and for this reason seems to us to be the law as such. In the same way, our historically defined morality, individualized by considerations of both time and place, seems to us to fulfil the conditions of the concept of morality in general. The female 'sense of justice', which differs from the male in many respects, would create a different law as well. The entire logical problematic of this sense should not conceal the fact that, ultimately, legislation as well as the administration of justice rest on a basis that can be characterized only in this way. Suppose that there were an objectively determinable ultimate purpose of all law. In that case, of course, it would be possible to construe every single legal definition on its basis and in a way that is, in principle, purely rational. However, this ultimate purpose itself could be posited only by a metalogical act that would constitute nothing more than another form of this 'sense of justice' and its crystallization in a stable and distinctive logical entity. But since this has not happened, the sense of justice remains in a more or less fluid state, in which it effectively and decisively enters into every single definition and decision, just as some quantum of the undifferentiated protoplasm still remains in almost every cell of even the fully developed animal organism. Thus every immanently defined and pervasive sense of justice would produce its own law. A body of law that developed in this fashion on the basis of the specifically female sense of justice could be denied acknowledgement as an objectively valid body of 'law' only because the objective is a priori identified with the male.

However, the fact that the real contents of our culture exhibit a male character, rather than their apparently neutral character, is grounded in a multifaceted interweaving of historical and psychological motives. Culture, which in the final analysis is a state of subjects or persons, does not trace its path merely through objectivations of the spirit. On the contrary, with the progress of each of its great periods, this sphere of real objects becomes increasingly extensive. The sojourn of individuals – with their interests, development, and productivity – becomes increasingly protracted in this transitional region. Ultimately, objective culture takes on the appearance of culture as such. Its consummation in subjects no longer seems to be the aim and purpose of culture but rather the purely private concern of these subjects, and otherwise is of no real relevance. The accelerated rate of development applies more to things than to persons. The 'separation of the worker from the instruments of production' appears as only a quite specific economic instance of a general tendency to shift the praxiological and axiological emphasis of culture away from human beings and onto the perfection and self-sufficient development of objects.

The objectification of our culture, which requires no proof, stands in a most intimate mutual relationship with its other most salient characteristic: its specialization. Suppose that the person, instead of constituting a whole, increasingly becomes nothing more than a dependent and inherently insignificant aspect of such a whole. In that case, it becomes increasingly difficult for him either to bring to bear the unified totality of his personality on his work or to recognize this totality in his work. There is an invariable connection between the inherent uniformity of the performance and that of the performer. It is exhibited most significantly in a work of art, the distinctive and self-sufficient unity of which requires a homogeneous creator and unconditionally resists all fabrication on the basis of differentiated and specialized performances. If these specialized performances are present, the subject as such is detached from them. The product of labour is coordinated with an impersonal structure whose objective requirements it is obliged to meet. This product is juxtaposed to each of those who contributed to it, as a totality which he does not comprehend and which does not reflect his self. If the objective element of our culture did not occupy such a decisive prerogative over its personal element, then the modern division of labour simply would not be feasible. And conversely, if this division of labour did not exist, then the contents of our culture could not have that objectivistic character.

However, as the entire history of work demonstrates, it is obvious that the division of labour is incomparably more congruent with the male nature than with the female. Even today, when it is precisely the division of labour that has removed from the household a large number of differentiated tasks that were formerly carried out within its unity, the activity of the housewife is more diversified and less specialized than any male occupation. It seems as if the man has more opportunity to allow his energy to flow in a unilinear direction without threatening his personality. This is precisely because he experiences this differentiated activity from a purely objective standpoint, and as detached from his own subjective life, a standpoint clearly distinguished from what could be called the private existence of his subjective life.

Moreover – and this is quite curious and difficult to express conceptually – this holds true even if he is committed to this objective and specialized task with a total intensity.

However – and this is the second point – the more refined sensitivity and the pronounced vulnerability of women may also rest on this disposition rather than upon the more fragile or delicate structure of their individual psychic elements. There is a sense in which the lack of differentiation and the self-contained uniformity of woman's psychic nature make it impossible for any attack upon her to remain localized. Every assault continues from the point of attack until it covers the entire personality, in which case it quite readily affects all possible points that are easily vulnerable or injured. It is repeatedly said of women that they are more easily offended than men under the same circumstances. However, this simply means that they frequently perceive a singular attack aimed at some specific point as touching their entire person. This is because they have a more integral nature, in which the part has not differentiated itself from the whole and taken on an autonomous life.

This fundamental structure of the female nature – which achieves historical expression only in its estrangement from culture as specialized and objective – can be epitomized in a psychological trait: fidelity. Fidelity signifies that the totality and integrity of the psyche are indissolubly connected with one single element of its contents. There is probably universal agreement concerning the observed fact that women, compared with men, have a more constant nature. This begins with the woman's dependence upon old articles of possession – her own as well as those belonging to persons dear to her – and also upon 'recollections', tangible as well as those of the most intimate sort. The undivided unity of her nature holds together whatever has taken place. As regards values and feelings that were once associated with each thing and related to the same centre, the unity of her nature links these values and feelings to the thing in question in such a way that they are very difficult to separate.

The male is less pious. This is due to his differentiated quality, as a result of which he sees things more in terms of their autonomous objectivity. Consider the capacity to decompose oneself into a plurality of distinctly different essential tendencies, to detach the periphery from the centre, and to make interests and activities independent of their integral interconnection. All this creates a disposition in favour of infidelity. In this case, the development can seize upon first one and then another interest, bring the person into changing forms, and make each present moment completely free to choose on its own terms and in a purely objective fashion. However, this presents the development with a profusion of different modes of action, each of which has the same unprejudiced status – a possibility that fidelity excludes.

From the perspective of the logic of psychology, differentiation and objectivity are the antitheses of fidelity. Fidelity unconditionally fuses the totality of the personality with a single interest, feeling, and experience.

Simply because such an interest, feeling and experience existed, fidelity remains fused with them. For this reason, it represents an obstacle to that retreat of the ego from its individual embodiments. There is something faithless in the separation of the person from the object. In this respect, it is opposed to the more constant nature of women. It estranges women – inwardly, of course – from a productive culture that is objectified on the basis of its specialization, and specialized on the basis of its objectivity.

Thus, in so far as women are lacking in objective cultural accomplishments, this need not signify a dynamic deficiency in relation to a general human requirement. On the contrary, it may signify only the incongruity between a mode of being in which all the contents of life exist solely through the energy of an indivisible subjective centre with which they are directly fused, and authentication in a world of objects as structured by the differentiated nature of the male.

It is true that men are more objective than women. However, suppose that the male is regarded quite self-evidently as the more consummate being, and that a life in which there is no differentiation of the individual from the totality is regarded as deficient and 'undeveloped'. This is possible only by means of a vicious circle. From the outset, the relative value of the male and the female is decided on the basis of a male rather than a neutral value idea. It follows that only a thoroughly radical dualism can help us here. The naive conflation of male values with values as such can give way only if the female existence as such is acknowledged as having a basis fundamentally different from the male and a stream of life flowing in a fundamentally different direction: two existential totalities, each structured according to a completely autonomous rule.

This naive conflation is based on historical power relationships that are logically expressed in the fateful dual meaning of the concept of the 'objective'. On the one hand, the objective seems to be a purely neutral idea, equidistant above the one-sidedness of both the male and the female. On the other hand, the objective is also the specific form of achievement that corresponds to the distinctively male mode of being. The former is a conception of transhistorical and transpsychological abstraction. The latter is a historical configuration that has its origins in the differential quality of masculinity. As a result, the criteria that are derived from the latter conception employ the same word and assume the same thoroughly ideal status characteristic of the former conception. Thus the being whose nature excludes the possibility of authentication by means of the specifically male conception of objectivity seems to be devalued from the standpoint of the transhistorical and inherently human conception of objectivity (which in our culture is either not realized at all or is realized only very sporadically).

This male capacity for not allowing his personal existence to be torn apart by a specialized performance that entails no inherent psychic unity is due to the fact that he places this performance in the remote distance of objectivity. It seems that this is exactly what the female nature lacks, not in the sense of a gap, but rather in that what is expressed here as a deficiency stems completely from the positive qualities of this nature. For if there is any sense in which the distinctive psychic quality of woman's nature can be expressed symbolically, it is this: Its periphery is more closely connected with its centre and its aspects are more completely integrated into the whole than holds true for the male nature. Here the authentication of the single individual does not lie in a distinctive development and a differentiation from the self with its emotive and affective centres; a process shifts the performance into the domain of the objective, with the result that its lifeless specialization becomes compatible with a complete and animated personal existence (which, of course, does not deny that there are male phenomena in which the latter suffers at the expense of the former).

At this point, I shall consider only two aspects of this homogeneity of the female nature. They are specific and quite remote from one another. Perhaps we designate them with concepts that are as negative as diffuseness and lack of objectivity only because, in the main, language and concept formation conform to the male nature.

As regards the introduction of female prison attendants, experienced penitentiary experts have stressed that only quite well-educated women should be accepted. As a rule, the male prisoner is quite docile in obeying his guard, even if the guard is far beneath him in education and culture. However, female prisoners have almost always created difficulties for a female guard inferior to them in education and culture. In other words, the man differentiates his total personality from the individual relationships in which he finds himself. He experiences this relationship in a purely objective fashion, detached from all factors that are external to it. The woman, on the other hand, cannot permit this momentary relationship to transpire in an impersonal fashion. On the contrary, she experiences it as inseparable from her integral total being. For this reason, she draws the consequences and makes the comparisons which the relationship between her complete personality and that of her female guard implies.

The opposition at stake here spans the relationship between the completely general nature of women and the completely general form of our culture. Thus, within this culture, the female performance will be all the more inhibited the more this most universal and formal element confronts her as a *demand*. This holds true most certainly in the case of original creativity. If contents which are already formed are taken up and their combinations are further worked out, this rather easily results in an accommodation to the total character of the area of culture in question. However, if a spontaneous creation emerges from the most distinctive qualities of the subject, this requires an absolutely active and total formation, beginning with the most elemental features of the contents at stake. In the extreme case, this activity finds no aspect of the general form in the material itself. On the contrary, the distance from the material to the general form must be surmounted step by step and without any residue by the creative psyche. This results in the sequence in which female activities are successful within an objective culture defined in male terms.

Within the arts, the woman's domain lies in those which are reproductive: from the art of dramatic acting (to be discussed below from another aspect) and musical performance, to that most distinctive type of embroidery in which the mark of incomparable skill and industry consists precisely in its reproduction of a 'given' pattern. In the sciences, her abilities as a collector and a 'carrier' are noteworthy; and this capacity to work with what she is given progressively advances to her considerable accomplishments as a teacher – for, all its functional independence notwithstanding, teaching still consists in transmitting what is given. In short, within the limits of hitherto existing culture, woman is more successful to the extent that the material of her work has already incorporated the spirit of this culture – that is, the male spirit – into itself. She fails to the extent that an act of original production is demanded: in other words, an act which requires that she commit her original energies, which are a priori quite differently disposed, solely to the forms that are required by the objective – and thus, the male – culture.

It could be said, however, that there is a twofold sense in which this culture is male. It is male not only because it transpires in an objective form determined by the division of labour but also because the realizations of this form prescribe single accomplishments and synthesize the elements of these accomplishments into specific professions in a way that conforms to the distinctive rhythm and intention of the male capacity. Thus, independent of the fundamental difficulty concerning forms noted above, there would still be an inadequacy, and even a disavowal, of the creation of new intensities and qualities of culture if women undertook to become natural scientists or engineers, physicians or artists, in the same sense that men are.

Of course this will happen often enough, and the quantum of subjective culture will still be amply increased. However, if objective culture is to exist, and if women are to accommodate themselves to its form, then new nuances and a new extension of its limits are to be expected from women only if they accomplish something that *men cannot do*. This is the core of the entire problem, the pivotal point of the relationship between the women's movement and objective culture. In certain areas, a decomposition of the activity that is now regarded as an objective unity (even though, in reality, this synthesis of partial functions conformed to the male mode of work) will create distinctively female spheres of activity. English workers have carried this principle out in a limited area of material life. There are many cases in which women have used their inferior and cheaper standard of living in order to undercut men. As a result, the standard wage declines, so that in general the trade unions are most bitterly opposed to the use of female labour in industry. Some trade unions – the cotton weavers and the stocking weavers, for example – have found a way out of this problem by introducing a standard list of wages for all factory work, even for the most trivial constituent functions. Everyone receives the same pay for these functions, regardless of whether they are performed by men or women.

This was intended as a way of eliminating competition between men and women. However, it has developed, as if independently, a division of labour in which women in a sense have monopolized the functions for which their physical powers and skills are adequate, leaving to men those functions that conform to *their* abilities. The best expert on conditions among English industrial workers offers the following judgement: 'As regards manual labour, the women form a special class of workers who have abilities and needs that differ from those of the men. In order to maintain both sexes in the same state of health and performance capability, a *differentiation of tasks* is frequently necessary'. Here, therefore, there is a sense in which the immense problem of female cultural activity is already solved in a naive fashion. The new line is drawn through the complex of tasks, connecting those points for which distinctively female abilities have a predisposition and defining them as special occupations. Even in this context, it holds true that women do something that men are unable to do. Although they were previously done by men, the tasks that conform to the powers of women are certainly better performed by distinctively female labour.[2]

Notes to Part I

1. Georg Simmel (1911) *Philosophische Kultur: Gesammelte Essais* [Philosophical Culture: Collected Essays]. Potsdam: Gustav Kiepenheuer Verlag.

2. This is an extract from Simmel's much longer essay on 'Female Culture' (cf. Oakes [ed.] 1984).

PART II

CULTURE AND CRISIS

THE CONCEPT AND TRAGEDY OF CULTURE

The fact is that, unlike animals, humanity does not integrate itself unquestioningly into the natural facticity of the world but tears loose from it, confronts it, demanding, struggling, violating and being violated by it – and it is with this first great dualism that the endless process between the subject and the object arises. It finds its second stage within the spirit itself. The spirit produces countless constructs which continue to exist in a peculiar autonomy, independent of the soul that created them as well as of any of the others that accept or reject them. This is the way the human subject confronts art as well as law, religion as well as technology, science as well as custom. The human subject is not only attracted and then repelled by their content, now fused together with it as with a part of itself and then again estranged from and untouched by it; it is also the form of solidity, of immobility, of lasting existence, with which the spirit, having become an object in that way, opposes the flowing liveliness, the inner self-responsibility and the changing tensions of the subjective psyche. As mind it is intimately connected with the spirit, but also experiences for that very reason countless tragedies in this antagonism of forms: between subjective life, that is restless but infinite in time, and its contents which, once created, are immovable but timelessly valid.

In the midst of this dualism resides the idea of culture. It is based on an inner fact which can be expressed completely only allegorically and somewhat vaguely as the path of the soul to itself. For no idea is ever only what it is at this moment, but always something more: a higher and more perfected form of itself within itself, not concrete but still somehow present. We are not referring here to a nameable ideal, fixed at some point in the intellectual world, but rather to the release of tensions residing within it, to the development of its individual embryonic form obeying an inner formal impulse. Just as life – and most of all its elevation in consciousness – contains its past inside itself in an unmediated form as some part of the inorganic, and just as this past element lives on according to its original content and not only as the mechanical cause of later transformations in consciousness, so life also includes its future in a manner to which non-living matter has no analogy. The later form is present at every moment of existence for an organism that can grow and reproduce, with a prefiguration and an inward necessity that cannot be compared, for instance, with the presence of the expanded form in a compressed spring.

Whereas every inanimate thing only possesses simply the moment of the present, that which is alive extends in an incomparable way over the past and the future. All the psychological motions such as those of volition, duty, vocation and hope are the intellectual continuations of the fundamental determination of life: to contain its future in its present, in a special form existing only in the life process. And this pertains not only to individual developments and perfections; rather, the personality as a whole and as a unity contains within itself an image drawn as if with invisible lines, and whose realization, as it were, would only be its full reality rather than its potentiality. No matter how much the psychological forces may have matured and proven themselves in individual and parochial tasks and interests, as it were, still – somehow behind or above this – there lies the demand that in all those things the psychological totality as such should fulfil a promise made with itself, and all the individual formations thus appear only as a multitude of ways in which the soul comes to itself. This is, if you will, a metaphysical prerequisite of our practical and emotional nature, no matter how far removed from concrete behaviour this symbolic expression may consider itself: namely, that the unity of the psyche is not simply a formal bond that forever encloses the elaborations of its individual forces in the same way, but rather that a development as a totality is carried by these individual forces and this development of the totality is inwardly preceded by the goal of a cultivation of itself, for which all those individual abilities and perfections are considered means to an end.

Here we see the first determination of the following concept of culture which, for the time being, simply follows our linguistic instincts. We are not cultivated simply because we have formed this or that individual item of knowledge or ability within ourselves, but only if all those things serve the development of that psychological centrality which is connected to culture but does not coincide with it. Our conscious and specifiable efforts are aimed at particular interests and potentialities, and this is why the development of every person, viewed according to that which can be named in them, is a bundle of lines of growth that extend in quite different directions and with quite different lengths. However, it is not all these, with their individual perfections, which make a person cultivated, but only their significance for or their development of the individual's indefinable personal unity. Or, to put it another way, culture is the path from the closed unity through the developed diversity to the developed unity. Yet under all circumstances, this can only refer to a development toward a phenomenon which is laid out in the embryonic forces of the personality, sketched, as it were, as an ideal plan into the personality itself.

Here too, linguistic usage provides safe guidance. We term cultivated a piece of fruit from the orchard which has been developed by the gardener's efforts from a woody and inedible wild fruit, or, one could say, this wild tree has been cultivated into an orchard tree. If, however, a ship's mast is produced from the same tree – and therefore a no less purposeful effort has been applied to it – then we do not say that the trunk has been cultivated into a mast. This linguistic nuance obviously indicates that the fruit, despite the fact that it could not have come about without human effort, still ultimately springs from the tree's own motive forces and only fulfils the possibilities which are sketched out in its tendencies, whereas the mast form is added to the trunk from an instrumental system quite alien to it and without any preformation in the tendencies of its own nature.

In precisely the same sense, all possible knowledge, virtuosities and refinements of a person cannot lead us to credit that person with genuine cultivation if they simply act like additions, as it were, that come from a sphere of values external to, and always remaining external to, their personality. In such a case, a person has aspects of cultivation, but they are not yet cultivated; for the latter occurs only if the elements absorbed from the supra-personal sphere appear to be developing within the psyche, as if through a predetermined harmony, that which already exists in it as its inmost drive and as an inner prefiguration of its subjective perfection.

And here, finally, there emerges the conditionality of culture through which it represents a solution to the subject–object equation. We deny that the concept of culture applies to those cases where perfection is not felt to be the personal development of the psychological centre. Similarly, the concept does not hold where it appears only as such a personal development that requires no objective means and stages external to itself. Many types of movement really lead the psyche, as that ideal demands, to itself – that is to the realization of its full and most personal being, superior to it, but initially existing only as a possibility. Yet if, or in so far as, the soul achieves this purely from within – in religious exaltations, moral self-sacrifice, dominant intellectuality or harmony of the totality of life – then it still cannot dispense with the specific attribute of cultivation. It is not merely that it may thereby lack that totality or relatively external element which linguistic usage dismisses as mere civilization. That would really not matter. But cultivation in its purest and deepest sense does not exist where the psyche travels that path from itself to itself, from the possibility of our truest self to its reality, exclusively under its own subjective powers – even though, when viewed from the supreme standpoint, it may be precisely these kinds of refinement which are the most valuable; all of which would only prove that culture is not the only determinant of value for the soul.

The specific meaning of culture is thus fulfilled only where a person adds something external to that development, where the path of the soul leads through values and scales that are not themselves subjectively psychological. Those objectively intellectual constructs of which I spoke initially – art and morality, science and practical objects, religion and the law, technology and social norms – are stations through which the human subject must pass in order to acquire the specific personal value known as its culture. Individuals must include *these* constructs and constraints within themselves, but they must really include them within the individual *self*, and not simply allow them to continue to exist as objective values. The paradox of culture is that the subjective life, which we feel in its continual flowing and which pushes of its own volition towards its inner perfection, cannot, viewed from the idea of culture, achieve that perfection on its own, but only by way of those self-sufficient crystallized structures which have now become quite alien to its form. Culture comes into being – and this is what is absolutely essential for understanding it – by the coincidence of two elements, neither of which contains culture in itself: the subjective soul and the objective intellectual product.

This is where the metaphysical significance of this historical construct is rooted. A number of the decisive activities of human nature build bridges between subject and object that are not capable of completion or, once completed, immediately torn down: these include knowing and, most of all, work, and in some senses also art and religion. The spirit confronts a being towards which both the constraint and the spontaneity of its nature drive it; but it remains eternally spellbound with movement within itself, in a circle that only touches on being, and at any moment when it would like to turn off from the tangent of its orbit and penetrate into being, the immanence of its law pulls it back again into its self-enclosed rotation. In the formation of the concepts 'subject' and 'object' as correlates, each of which finds meaning only in the other, there is already the longing and anticipation of a transcendence of this rigid and ultimate dualism. Those movements referred to above now transport it into special atmospheres, in which the radical estrangement of its antitheses is diminished and allows certain fusions. Yet because the latter can only occur under the modifications produced, as it were, by the atmospheric conditions of a special nature, they cannot overcome the deepest basis of that arrangement between the two elements, and thus they remain finite attempts to solve this infinite problem. Yet our relationship to those objects with which we become cultivated by incorporating them into ourselves is a different one, since they are themselves spirit, which has taken objective form in those ethical and intellectual, social and aesthetic or religious and technical forms. This dualism, with which the subject – reliant upon its own limits – faces the object, that exists for itself, experiences an incomparable formation when both elements are spirit.

Thus, the subjective spirit must abandon its subjectivity but not its intellectuality in order to experience that relationship to the object through which it becomes cultivated. This is the only way in which the dualistic form of existence, immediately posited with the existence of the subject, organizes itself into an inwardly uniform referentiality. An objectification of the subject and a subjectification of the object occurs here, which constitutes the specific nature of the cultural process, and in which, beyond the latter's individual contents, its metaphysical form is displayed. A deeper understanding of it thus requires a further analysis of this objectification of the spirit.

These pages started out from the deep estrangement or enmity which exists between the life and creative process of the psyche, on the one hand, and its contents and products on the other. The vibrating, boundlessly developing, restless life of the creative soul of any type is confronted by its fixed and intellectually unshakeable product, with the uncanny retroactive effect of tying down and even hypostatizing that liveliness; it is often as if the creative movement of the soul were dying from its own product. Herein lies a fundamental form of our suffering from our own past, our own dogma and our own fantasies. This discrepancy, which exists, as it were, between the aggregate condition of inner life and that of its elements, is thereby to some extent rationalized and made less perceptible by the fact that, through their theoretical or practical creativity, human beings confront and view those products or contents of the soul as a cosmos of the objectified spirit which, in a certain sense, is independent. The external or immaterial world in which the life of the soul takes form is felt to be a value of a special type. No matter how much life enters a cul-de-sac as it flows into them, or flows onwards, leaving these cast-up objects in its place, this is still the specifically human type of wealth: namely, that the products of objective life belong at the same time to a persisting, objective order of values, be they logical or moral, religious or artistic, technical or legal. By revealing themselves to be the exponents of such values, or the members of such a series, they are not merely removed from rigid isolation by the mutual interweaving and systematization with which they separated themselves from the rhythm of the life process; but rather this process itself has thereby taken on a significance which could not be gained from the unstoppability of its mere course.

The objectifications of the spirit receive a value emphasis which originates, to be sure, in the subjective consciousness but it is one by which that consciousness refers to something beyond itself. The value here need by no means always be something positive, in the sense of good; rather, the mere formal fact that the subject has set down something objective, which his or her life has embodied from within itself, is felt to be something important, because only the independence of the object thus formed by the spirit can resolve the fundamental tension in consciousness between process and content. For just as spatially natural ideas calm the uneasiness of persisting as something with a completely fixed form by legitimating this stability with their relationship to an objectively external world, so the objectivity of the intellectual world performs a corresponding service.

We consider the whole liveliness of our thought to be connected to the immovability of logical norms, the entire spontaneity of our hearts is connected to moral ones, and the entire course of our consciousness is filled up with knowledge, traditions and impressions of a milieu somehow shaped by the spirit. The solidity and the almost chemical insolubility of all this confronted with the restless dynamism of the subjective psychological process, displays a problematic dualism in which it is indeed produced as a conception, as a subjectively psychological content. But because it belongs to an ideal world above the individual consciousness, this contrast is given a foundation and a justification. Certainly, the crucial thing for the cultural meaning of the object – which is what we are ultimately concerned with here – is that will and intelligence, individuality and emotion, the forces and the mood of individual souls (and also of their collectivity) are gathered within it. Only because this has occurred have those psychological meanings reached the endpoint of their destiny.

In the happiness of the creative person in his or her work, no matter how great or small it might be, and alongside the release of inner tensions, the proof of subjective strength and the satisfaction at having fulfilled a demand, there also exists a kind of objective satisfaction, as it were, at the fact that this work is now in existence – that the cosmos of somehow valuable objects has been enriched by this particular piece. Indeed, there is perhaps no more sublime personal enjoyment of our own work than when we feel its impersonality and its separation from everything subjective in us. And just as the objectifications of the spirit are valuable in that way, beyond the subjective life processes which have entered into them as causes, they are also beyond the others which depend on them as results.

No matter how much and how overwhelmingly we scrutinize the organizations of society and the technical shaping of the facts of nature, the work of art, customs and morality with regard to their radiation into life and the development of psyches, there is often and perhaps always a recognition woven into this that these constructs exist in the first place, that the world also includes this creation of the spirit. It is a directive in our valuation processes which stops short at the inherent existence of the spiritually objective, without enquiring beyond the definitive nature of these things into their psychological consequences. Alongside all the subjective enjoyment with which, for instance, the work of art enters us, as it were, we consider it a special value that it exists at all, that the spirit has created this vessel for itself. Just as at least one line within the artistic volition issues into the inherent existence of the work of art, and weaves a purely objective valuation into the self-enjoyment of exultant creativity, so a line also runs in the same direction within the attitude of the recipient. This is clearly in contrast to the values which clothe what is purely objectively given, what is *by nature* objective. For it is precisely such combinations as the sea and the flowers or the Alps and the starry sky which possess what one may call their value only in terms of their reflexes within the human soul. For as soon as we set aside mystical and fantastic anthropomorphizing of nature, it is just a continuous interdependent totality, whose indifferent regularity does not grant any part of itself an accent based on its objective existence, indeed, not even an existence that is objectively delineated off from other parts. Only our human categories cut individual pieces out of it, to which we attach aesthetic, inspiring, or symbolically significant reactions. The idea that natural beauty is 'blissful in itself' rightly exists only as a poetic fiction; for the consciousness that strives for objectivity there is no bliss connected to it other than that which it arouses in us.

Thus, whereas the product of purely objective powers can only be subjectively valuable, so conversely the product of subjective powers is objectively valuable to us. The material and immaterial constructs – in which human will and ability, or knowing and feeling, are invested – constitute that objectively existing entity which we consider to be significant and an enrichment of existence, even if we abstract completely from its being seen, used or enjoyed. If value and significance, meaning and importance, may be produced exclusively in the human psyche, so this constantly proves true with respect to all of existing nature, but it does not hinder the objective value of these constructs in which the creating and shaping forces and values *have* already been invested. A sunrise unseen by any human eye in no way makes the world more valuable or sublime, because its objective facticity has no place at all for these categories. Yet once a painter has invested his mood, his sense of form and colour and his expressive abilities into a picture of this sunrise, then we consider this work (leaving aside for now in which metaphysical category) to be an enrichment, an elevation of the value of existence in general. The world appears to us more worthy of its existence, as it were, and closer to its meaning when the source of all values, the human soul, has poured itself into such a fact which now also belongs to the objective world – independent in this peculiar meaning of whether a later soul will once again release the value conjured into it and dissolve it into the flood of its subjective feeling. The natural sunrise and the painting both exist here as realities, but the former finds its value only in living on in psychological subjects, whereas in the case of the latter, which has already absorbed such life into itself and shaped it into an object, our evaluating sense stops short, as it would with a definite object not in need of any subjectification.

If one draws these factors out into a polemical polarity, then on the one side there stands the exclusive estimation of subjectively animated life, from which not only all meaning, value and significance is produced, but also only within which all of them reside. On the other hand, however, the radical accentuation of objectivized value is no less understandable. Of course, this is not tied to the original production of works of art and religions, technologies and forms of knowledge; but whatever a person also does should provide a contribution to the ideal, historical and materialized cosmos of the spirit in order to be considered valuable. This does not belong to the subjective immediacy of our being and action, but rather to its objectively regulated and objectively ordered content, so that ultimately only these regulations and orderings contain the substance of value and transmit it to fleeting personal events. Even the autonomy of the moral will in Kant's work is said not to involve any values of that will in its psychological factuality, but instead ties it to the realization of a form existing in objective ideality. Even attitudes and the personality have their significance, in both the good and bad senses, in the fact that they belong to a supra-personal realm.

In so far as these valuations of the subjective and the objective spirit confront each other, culture directs its unity through both of them: for it implies that kind of individual perfection which can take place only by receiving or using a supra-personal construct, located in some sense outside the subject. The specific value of cultivation is not accessible to the subject unless it reaches him or her by way of objectively spiritual realities. The latter, for their part, are only *cultural* values in that they direct through themselves that path of the soul from itself to itself, from what one could call its state of natural state to its cultural state.

Thus one can also express the structure of the concept of culture in the following way. There is no cultural value that would merely be a cultural value; rather, in order to acquire this significance, each must also be a value on an objective scale. Wherever there is a value in this sense and where some interest or capability of our nature is advanced by it, even then it is a cultural value only if this partial development simultaneously raises our total self one step closer to its unity of perfection. Only in this way do two corresponding negative phenomena of intellectual history become comprehensible. The first is the fact that people with the deepest interest in culture often exhibit a remarkable indifference to, and even a rejection of, the individual elements of culture – in so far as they are incapable of discovering the supra-special-ized benefit of the latter for the advancement of the whole personality. And there is probably no human product which *must* of necessity show such benefit, nor probably any product that *could* not show it. On the other hand, however, phenomena appear which seem to be *merely* cultural values *alone*, certain formalisms and refinements of life of the type that belong in par-ticular to over-mature and exhausted epochs. For where life has become hollow and senseless in and of itself, there all possible and desirable develop-ment toward its fulfilment is only a schematic one, and no longer capable of drawing nourishment and encouragement from the factual content of things and ideas – just as the sick body can no longer assimilate the substances from its nourishment which provide growth and strength to the healthy body. Here individual development can draw no more than socially correct conduct from social norms, only unproductive enjoyment from the arts, and only the negative elements of effortlessness and smoothness of daily life from technical progress. There thus arises here a kind of formal-subjective culture, lacking that inner *interweaving* with the objective element through which the concept of a concrete culture first fulfils itself.

On the one hand, then, there is such a passionately centralized emphasis upon culture that the actual content of its objective factors is too much and too distracting, since that content *as such* is not and cannot be absorbed within its cultural function. On the other hand, there is such a weakness and emptiness of culture that it is incapable of incorporating the objective factors into itself in accordance with their objective content. Both phenom-ena, though appearing at first glance to be counter-instances against the tie between personal culture and impersonal conditions, upon closer inspection actually confirm this tie.

That the ultimate and decisive factors of life are thus united in culture is revealed precisely in the fact that the development of every one of them can take place with an independence that can not only dispense with motivation by the cultural ideal, but also one that virtually rejects it. For a glance in one direction or another feels distracted from the unity of its intention if it is supposed to be determined by a synthesis between the two. Particularly the intellects that create lasting values, that is to say, the objective element of culture, would probably deny borrowing the motif and the value of their achievement directly from the idea of culture. Instead, the following inner situation exists here. In the case of the founder of a religion and the artist, the statesman and the inventor, the scholar and the legislator, there is a double process at work: the discharging of their essential forces, the elevation of their natures to the height at which they set free the elements of cultural life – and the passion for the object, in the autonomous perfection of which the subject becomes indifferent to itself and is obliterated. In the genius, both of these currents are one: the development of the subjective spirit for its own sake, for the sake of its urgent powers, is indistinguishably united for the genius with the completely self-negating devotion to the objective task.

As has been seen, culture is always a synthesis. But synthesis is not the only and not the most immediate form of unity, since it always presupposes the separation of the elements as its starting point or as its correlate. Only a period so marked by analysis as the modern age could see in synthesis the most profound aspect, the one and all of the formal relationship between spirit and world – whereas there is in fact an original and pre-differentiated unity of the two. Since it is this latter which brings forth the analytic elements from its midst, just as the organic embryo branches out into the multiplicity of separate limbs, so this unity stands beyond analysis and synthesis – regardless of whether these two develop out of it reciprocally, the one at each state presuming the other, or the synthesis subsequently brings the analytically separated elements into a unity, which, however, is something quite different from the unity preceding all separation. Creative genius possesses that original unity of the subjective and the objective, which must first separate itself in order to be reconstituted as it were, in a totally different, synthetic form, in the cultivation process of individuals. This is why the interest of culture in both – the pure self-development of the subjective spirit and pure absorption in the object – does not lie on one level, but occasionally attaches itself, secondarily and in reflection, to the object, as an abstract general entity, beyond the inwardly unmediated value impulses of the soul. Culture remains out of the picture as long as the soul takes a path only through its own sphere, as it were, and perfects itself in the pure self-development of its own nature – no matter how the latter may be objectively determined.

If we look at the other dimension of culture – namely, that leading to an ideal separate existence, independent now of all psychological dynamics and as matured products of the spirit, in its self-sufficient isolation – then we see that its most fundamental significance and value by no means coincides with its cultural value, that indeed, for its part, it leaves its cultural meaning

completely open. The work of art is supposed to be perfect according to the
norms of art, which enquire into nothing other than themselves and would
give or deny the work its value, even if, so to speak, there were nothing other
than this work in the world. Similarly, the result of research as such is supposed to be true and absolutely nothing more; religion contains its meaning
within itself in the salvation it brings to the soul; the economic product wants
to be perfect as something economic and in that sense recognizes no other
standard of value for itself. All these series proceed within the enclosed
nature of purely internal regulation, and whether and with what values they
can be employed in the development of subjective souls is irrelevant to their
significance, which is measured according to purely objective standards that
are valid only for them.

This state of affairs explains the fact that we often find an apparently
remarkable indifference, even an aversion to culture, both among people
oriented only towards the subject and those oriented only towards the
object. Whoever cares only about the salvation of the soul or the ideal of
personal strength or individual inner development, in which no external
factor may intervene, then such a person's evaluations will lack precisely the
one integrating factor of culture. Conversely, the other type of person will
also be missing this factor, namely the one who cares only about the pure
objective perfection of our works, so that they fulfil this idea of *theirs* and
not that of those somehow connected to it. The extreme of the first type is
the ascetic saint, and that of the other is the specialist completely and
fanatically wrapped up in his or her specialism.

At first sight, there does appear something astonishing when the exponents of such indubitably 'cultural values' as religiosity, the formation of
the personality or technologies of all sorts despise or oppose the concept of
culture. This is immediately explained, however, by the insight that culture
in fact always implies only the *synthesis* of a subjective development and an
objective spiritual value, and that the advocacy of any one of these elements, in so far as it is exclusive, must reject the interweaving of both to the
extent of its exclusivity.

Such dependency of the value of culture upon the cooperation of a second
factor that stands beyond the objective-inherent value scale of the object
enables us to understand that the latter often attains a quite different level
on the scale of cultural values than it does on that of mere objective meanings. Many kinds of works, which remain beneath the level of what has
already been achieved in artistic, technical or intellectual respects, nevertheless have the capability of fitting most efficaciously into the developmental path of a great many people, as unfolders of their latent powers, as
a bridge to their next higher level. It is not only the most enormous or aesthetically perfect impression of nature which provides us with a very deep
rapture and the feeling that very vague and unresolved elements within us
have suddenly become clear and harmonious; rather, we often owe this to
a very plain landscape or the play of shadows on a summer afternoon. In
the same way, the significance of a work of the spirit, no matter how high

or low it may stand on its own scale, cannot be discerned from what the work can do for us for the path of culture. For in this case, everything depends upon the fact that this special meaning of the work has the additional benefit, as it were, of serving the central or general development of personalities, and there are many reasons why this benefit can be inversely proportional to the inherent or internal value of the work. There are human creations of the ultimate attainable perfection to which we have no access precisely because of this unbroken well-roundedness, or which have no access to us for that same reason. Such a work remains in solitary perfection, as it were, in its place, from which it cannot be transplanted to our street. We can visit it, perhaps, but cannot take it with us in order to elevate ourselves upon it in the perfection of our selves.

For the modern spirit of life, antiquity frequently possesses this self-sufficiently perfect enclosed nature, which resists absorption into the pulsations and restlessness of the tempo of our development. And today this may be what moves some to seek precisely for our culture a different fundamental factor. It is the same with certain ethical ideals. The constructs of the objective spirit characterized in this way are destined, perhaps more than others, to carry development from the mere possibility to the highest reality of our totality and to determine its direction. Yet some ethical imperatives contain an ideal of such rigid perfection that no energies which we could absorb into our development can be produced from them. For all their height on the scale of ethical ideals, the latter, as cultural elements, may quite easily lie beneath others, which are more able on their own at that lower position on this scale to assimilate themselves to the rhythm of our development and to incorporate themselves strongly into it.

Another motive for such a disproportion between the objective value and the cultural value of an object lies in the unilateral nature of the support that we receive from the former. Many of the contents of the objective spirit make us wiser or better, happier or cleverer, but do not actually develop *us* in that way but, as it were, only an objective side or quality which pertains to us. We are concerned here, of course, with variable and infinitely delicate differences, not externally tangible at all, and connected to the mysterious relationship between our unified wholeness and our individual energies and perfections. Of course, we can characterize the complete, enclosed reality which we call our subject only by means of the sum of such details, although it cannot be put together from them, and the only category available – that of the whole and the parts – by no means exhausts this unique relationship.

All of this singularity, however, has an objective character when viewed in isolation. In its isolation, it could be part of many different subjects, and it only acquires the character of our subjectivity on its inner side with which it permits that very unity of our nature to develop. With our subjectivity, however, it in a sense builds a bridge to the values of objectivities; it lies on our periphery, with which we are wedded to the objective, both external and intellectual, world. The aforementioned discrepancy occurs when this outward-directed and externally nourished function is cut off from its inward-directed meaning which issues into our centre. We become learned, more efficient, richer in enjoyment, perhaps even more 'cultured', but our cultivation cannot keep in step, because in that way we pass from a lower state of possession and ability to a higher one, but not from ourselves as something lower to ourselves as something higher.

I have only emphasized this possibility of a discrepancy between the objective meaning and the cultural meaning of one and the same object in order to be able to illustrate more emphatically the fundamental divided-ness of the elements whose interweaving is the sole prerequisite of culture. This interweaving is a purely unique one in that the culturally significant development of personal existence is a condition existing solely in the subject, but one which can be achieved in no other way than through the absorption and utilization of objective elements. For that reason, cultivation is, on one hand, a task lying in the realm of the infinite – since the utiliza-tion of objective factors for the perfection of individual being can never be considered finished. On the other hand, the nuances of linguistic usage follow this state of affairs very exactly by generally using culture in con-nection with an objective element – religious culture, artistic culture and the like – only for characterizing the general spirit and not for the condition of individuals. In this sense, the term means that there are especially many or particularly impressive intellectual elements of a certain type in a particu-lar period, through which the cultivation of individuals takes place.

In the strict sense, individuals can only be more or less cultivated, but not cultivated as specialists in this or that way. An objectively separated culture of the individual can only mean either that the cultural and, as such, over-specialized perfection of the individual has occurred mainly by means of this unilateral element, or that a considerable ability or knowledge with respect to subject matter has been developed, alongside that person's individual cul-tivation. The artistic culture of an individual – for instance, if it is to be something more than artistic perfection, which can also occur in an other-wise 'uncultivated' person – can only mean that in this case it is precisely *these* objective perfections which have brought about the perfection of the personal being as a whole. Now, however, there emerges a split within this structure of culture, one that is in fact already located in its foundations, and which turns the subject–object synthesis – the metaphysical meaning of its concept – into a paradox, indeed, into a tragedy. The dualism of subject and object that is presupposed by their synthesis is after all, not merely, so to speak, a substantial one which affects the being of both. Rather, the inner logic, according to which each of the two develops, by no means coincides self-evidently with that of the other.

Once certain primary motifs of law, art or morality have been created – perhaps following our most personal and innermost spontaneity – then the issue of what individual forms these will grow into is no longer in our hands. Instead, we produce or receive these forms as we follow the connecting theme of an individual necessity which is completely objective and no more concerned with the demands of our individuality, regardless of how central these might be, than are physical forces and their laws. It is certainly true in general that language composes and thinks for us, that is to say, it takes in the fragmentary or bounded impulses of our nature and leads them to a perfection which they would never have been able to attain otherwise, even purely for ourselves. Yet this parallelism of objective and subjective developments nevertheless possesses no fundamental necessity. Occasionally, we even feel language to be an alien natural force, which distorts and curtails not only our utterances, but also our innermost intentions.

And even religion, which certainly developed out of the soul's search for itself, the wing brought forth by the soul's own forces to raise it to their own height, once emerged, has certain laws of formation which elaborate its inner necessity but not always that of our own. What is often condemned as religion's anti-cultural spirit is not just its occasional hostility to intellectual, aesthetic and moral values, but also this deeper aspect: the fact that it takes its own path determined by its inherent logic. It does pull life onto this path, but no matter what transcendent values the soul may find along this path, often enough it does not lead it to the perfection of its totality, which is where its own possibilities direct it, and which, absorbing the significance of objective structures into itself, is precisely what is called culture.

In so far as the logic of impersonal structures and circumstances is laden with dynamism, a harsh friction results between them and the inner impulses of the personality, and this friction undergoes a unique concentration in the form of culture itself. Ever since human beings began referring to themselves as 'I', having become an object above and against themselves, and ever since the contents of our soul have belonged to its centre by virtue of such a form, the ideal has grown out of this form that these things, which are connected in such a way to the centre, are also a self-enclosed unity, and therefore a self-sufficient totality.

Yet the contents with which the self is supposed to conduct this organization into a personal, unified world do not belong to it alone; they are *given* to it from some spatial, temporal and ideal entities external to it. They are simultaneously the contents of some other worlds – social and metaphysical, conceptual and ethical – and in the latter they possess forms and connections among themselves which are not apt to coincide with those of the self. The external worlds seize hold of the self with these contents, in order to draw it into themselves, and because they form the contents according to their *own demands*, they do not permit them to become centred around the self.

This may find its broadest and deepest manifestation in the religious conflicts between the self-sufficiency or freedom of the human being and his or her integration into the divine order. But like the social conflict between the person as well-rounded individual and as the mere member of the social organism, this is only *one* case of that purely formal dualism in which the fact that our life contents belong to other groups than our own inevitably involves us. It is not just that human beings are countless times caught in the intersection of two spheres of objective powers and values, each of which would like to pull them along with it. They also consider themselves the centre which orders all the elements of its life about itself, harmoniously and according to the logic of their personalities – and at the same time they feel a solidarity with each of these peripheral elements, each of which, after all, also belongs to another sphere and is claimed by another law of motion. Hence, it is the case that our nature constitutes, as it were, the intersection of itself and an alien sphere of demands. Now the fact of culture pushes the parties of this collision extremely tightly together by virtue of tying the development of the one to its incorporation of the other (that is, by permitting them to become cultivated only in that way). That is to say, it presupposes a parallelism or a mutual adaptation of both. The metaphysical dualism of subject and object, which this structure had overcome in principle, revives as a discordance of the individual empirical contents of objective and subjective developments.

The chasm yawns perhaps even wider when its sides are not occupied by opposite elements, but when instead the meaning of the objective factor escapes the subject due to its formal determinations: independence and impersonality. The formula of culture, after all, has been that subjective and psychological energies attain an objective form which is subsequently independent of the creative life processes and that this form is once again drawn into subjective life processes in a way that will bring its exponent to a well-rounded perfection of his or her central being.

Now, however, this flow from subjects through objects to subjects, in which a metaphysical relationship between subject and object takes on historical reality, can lose its continuity. The object may move away from its mediating activity in a more fundamental fashion than has been indicated so far, and may thereby cut off the bridges over which its cultivating path led. It is seized, in the first instance, by such an isolation and alienation *vis-à-vis* creative subjects through the division of labour. The objects that are produced by the cooperation of many persons form a scale, according to the extent to which their unity derives from the uniform intellectual intention of an individual or whether it was produced without such an origin, by itself, from the partial contributions of those engaged in cooperation. The latter pole would be occupied by a city that was not built according to any pre-existing plan, being instead built up only according to the chance needs and inclinations of individuals but which is nonetheless a construct that is meaningful as a whole, visibly enclosed and organically interconnected within itself. The other pole is perhaps exemplified by the product of a factory in which twenty workers have worked together, each with no knowledge of the other components and no interest in how they fit together – whereas the whole product, of course, is directed by a central personal will and intellect. One could also cite the performance of an orchestra, in which the oboist or the tympanist has no knowledge of the violin or cello part, but which is nonetheless brought into a perfect unity of effect by virtue of the conductor's baton. Between these phenomena, perhaps, might be the newspaper, for instance, whose external unity at least goes back to a leading personality in its appearance and significance, but which consists to a considerable extent of mutually coincidental contributions of the most diverse character, written by a great variety of mutually unacquainted persons.

In absolute terms, this type of phenomenon is characterized as the following: a cultural object grows out of the efforts of different persons, a work which, as a whole, as an existing and specifically effective unity, *has no single producer* – not one emerging out of a corresponding unity of a mental subject. The elements have composed themselves as if following a logic and form-giving intention inherent to themselves as objective realities, not one which their creators have invested in them. The objectivity of the intellectual content, which makes it independent of any absorption or non-absorption, here already falls on the side of its production. No matter what the individuals may or may not have intended, the finished object, realized in purely physical form with no spirit feeding its now effective significance, nevertheless possesses one and can pass it on in the cultural process – only differing in degree from a small child playing with alphabet blocks and arranging them fortuitously into a coherent meaning. This meaning exists in them in intellectual objectivity and concreteness, regardless of the extent of the ignorance from which it was produced.

Viewed more closely, however, this is only a very radical case of a quite general human spiritual fate, one which also encompasses these cases of the division of labour. The great majority of products of our intellectual creation contain a certain portion of significance which we did not ourselves create. I am not referring here to lack of originality, inherited values or dependency upon exemplars, because in all of these cases the entire content of the work could still be born of our consciousness, even though this consciousness would only be transmitting *tale quale* what it had received. Rather, the great majority of our creations which present themselves objectively contain something of significance that can be extracted by other human subjects, but which we ourselves did not place there. The saying that 'no weaver knows what he's weaving' is, of course, never absolutely true, but always relatively so. The finished product contains nuances, relations and values, purely according to its objective existence and quite independently of whether the creator knew that these would be the result of his or her creation. It is a fact, as mysterious as it is indisputable, that an intellectual meaning, objective and reproducible for every consciousness, can be tied to a material object, a meaning not put in it by any consciousness, but adhering instead to the pure and most inherent facticity of this form.

The analogous case *vis-à-vis* nature poses no problem: no artistic will bestowed southern mountains with the stylistic purity of their contours or the stormy sea with its striking symbolism. In the first instance, that which is purely natural, if it is equipped with such possible meanings, has or can have a share in all creations of the spirit, but this is also true for the spiritual content of its elements and for the connection that naturally results from them. The possibility of deriving a subjective spiritual content from them is invested in them as an objective formation that cannot be described any further and has now left its origin completely behind.

To take an extreme example, suppose a poet has composed a riddle with a certain solution in mind. If another word is found which is just as fitting, meaningful and surprising as the first, then it too is just as 'correct' and, although it was far removed from his creative process, it is contained in his creation as an ideal object just as much as is the first word, for which the riddle was written. As soon as our work exists, it not only has an objective existence and a life of its own that have detached themselves from us, but it also contains in this being for itself – as if by the grace of the objective spirit – strengths and weaknesses, components and meanings of which we are completely innocent and which often completely surprise us.

These possibilities and dimensions of the autonomy of the objective spirit are only supposed to clarify the fact that, even where produced from the consciousness of a subjective spirit, it possesses a validity that is detached from the latter and an independent opportunity for re-subjectification after the objectification has occurred. Of course, this opportunity need not be realized, since, as in the example above, the second solution to the riddle rightly exists in its objective spirituality, even before it was discovered and even if it were never to be discovered. This peculiar quality of cultural elements – which has until now applied to individual and, as it were, isolated elements – is the metaphysical foundation for the fateful autonomy with which the realm of cultural products grows and grows as if an inner logical necessity were sprouting one branch after the other, often almost unrelated to the will and personality of the producers, and as if unaffected by the question as to how many subjects absorb it and lead it to its cultural meaning, and how deeply and completely they do so.

The 'fetishistic character' which Marx attributed to economic objects in the epoch of commodity production is only a particularly modified instance of this general fate of the contents of our culture. These contents are subject to the paradox – and increasingly so as 'culture' develops – that they are indeed created by human subjects and are meant for human subjects, but follow an immanent developmental logic in the intermediate form of objectivity which they take on at either side of these instances and thereby become alienated from both their origin and their purpose. It is not physical necessities, for instance, that would come into question here, but really only cultural ones, which of course cannot surmount their physical determinations. But what drives on the products, as spiritual ones, seemingly one after the other, is the cultural and not the natural scientific logic of the objects.

Herein lies the fateful inner compulsion of all 'technology', as soon as its development has elevated it beyond the reach of immediate usage. Thus, for instance, the industrial manufacture of some products may suggest that of by-products, for which no need actually exists; yet the constraint of fully utilizing already existing installations pushes for this; the technical scale demands of its own accord to be completed by links, which the psychological scale – actually the definitive one – does not require, and that is how the supply of commodities comes into existence, commodities which for their own part are only artificial and which, when viewed from the standpoint of the culture of human subjects, call forth meaningless needs.

It is no different in some branches of scholarship and science. Philological technique has been developed, on the one hand, to an unexcelled refinement and perfection, whereas, on the other, the number of objects which it is of real interest for intellectual culture to treat in that way do not grow to the same extent, and thus philological effort often becomes a micrology, a pedanticism and a treatment of the unessential – an idle running of the method, as it were, a continuation of the objective norm, the independent path of which no longer coincides with that of culture as a perfection of life. In this way, what could be called superfluous knowledge is accumulating in many areas of scholarship and science – a sum of methodologically faultless knowledge, unassailable from the standpoint of an abstract concept of knowledge, but nonetheless alienated from the genuine purpose and meaning of all research. Here, it goes without saying, I am referring to the ideal and universal purpose of all research, not an external purpose.

The enormous supply of people willing to engage in intellectual production and often gifted for it, a supply favoured by economic factors, has led to an autonomous evaluation of *all* scholarly work whose value is indeed often only a convention, almost a conspiracy of the scholarly caste; all this has led to an uncannily fertile inbreeding of the scholarly mind, the offspring of which, both inwardly and in the sense of having a wider effect, is infertile. This is the basis of the fetishistic worship which for a long time has been conducted with regard to 'method' – as if an achievement were valuable simply because of the correctness of its method. This is a very clever means for the legitimation and appreciation of an unlimited number of works which are invalid for the meaning and context of the advancement of knowledge, no matter how generously the latter is framed. It is natural to object that this development has at times been advanced in the most overhasty manner by even the apparently most inconsequential studies. These are fortuitous opportunities of the type that occur in every sphere, but they do not deter us from granting or denying the truth and value of an activity on the basis of our currently existing – even though not omniscient – rationality. No one would consider it sensible to drill for petroleum or dig for coal at some random place in the world on the off chance, no matter how undeniable the possibility is that he or she might really find something in so doing. There simply is a certain threshold of probability for the usefulness of scholarly or scientific work, which may prove erroneously applied in one of a thousand cases but would not justify the effort for the next nine hundred and ninety-nine fruitless attempts.

Viewed from the position of cultural history, this is also merely a particular phenomenon of that hypertrophy of cultural contents in a soil in which forces and purposes, other than those which are culturally meaningful, drive and hold them, and in which they inevitably often produce unfruitful blossoms. The same ultimate formal theme is present when, in the development of art, technical ability becomes sufficiently large that it can emancipate itself from the general cultural purpose of art. Now obedient only to its own objective logic, technique develops refinement after refinement, yet ones that are only instances of *its* perfection, but not in fact the perfection of the cultural meaning of art.

All the excessive specialization, about which people complain in all areas of endeavour and yet, with demonic inexorableness, subjects the further development to its own law, is only a special formation of this general fate of cultural elements: namely, that objects have their own developmental logic – not a conceptual or a natural one, but only a logic of development as cultural human works – and in consequence of this, they deviate from the direction in which they could incorporate themselves into the personal development of human minds. Hence, this discrepancy is not identical to the one that is so often emphasized, namely the growth of means into the value of ultimate ends, which advanced cultures display at every turn. For this is something purely psychological, an accentuation based on psychological coincidences or necessities, and without any firm relationship to the objective connection of things. Here, however, we are concerned precisely with the latter, with the immanent logic of the cultural formations of things. The human being now becomes the mere bearer of the compulsion with which this logic rules developments and leads them onward, as in the *tangent*, to the path by which they would again return to the cultural development of living humanity.

This is the real tragedy of culture. We would probably characterize the following as a tragic fate – as opposed to a sad or, viewed from outside, a destructive one – the fact that the annihilating forces aimed against an entity stem from the deepest layers of this very entity; when it is destroyed, a fate is completed which is planned within itself and is the logical development, so to speak, of the very same structures with which the entity built up its own positive nature. The concept of all culture is that the spirit creates something independent and objective, through which the development of the subject from itself to itself makes its way. But, in so doing, this integrating and culturally determining element is predestined to an autonomous development, which still consumes the forces of human subjects, and still draws such subjects into its orbit, without elevating them to its own height: the development of the subjects now can no longer take the path followed by the objects; where the former follow it nonetheless, the development runs into a cul-de-sac or a vacuity of our innermost and most genuine life.

The development of culture externalizes the subject in an even more positive way through the already indicated formlessness and absence of boundaries which the objective spirit experiences from the numerical unrestrictedness of its producers. Everyone can contribute to the stock of objectivized cultural elements without any consideration of the other contributors. This stock may indeed possess certain nuances in individual cultural periods, and thus an internal qualitative limit, but no corresponding quantitative one. In fact, there is no reason not to expand indefinitely, not to line up book after book, work of art after work of art, discovery after discovery: the form of objectivity as such possesses an unlimited capacity for accomplishment.

However, this inorganic accumulative capacity, as it were, makes it profoundly incommensurable with the form of personal life. For the latter's absorptive capacity is not only limited by strength and longevity, but also by a certain unity and relative closure of its forms, and it therefore makes a selection with a determined scope from among the elements offered to it as means of individual development. Now it would seem that this incommensurability need not become a practical problem for the individual because it leaves aside what his or her personal development cannot assimilate. However, this is not so easily done. The infinitely growing stock of the objectified mind makes demands on the subject, arouses faint aspirations in it, strikes it with feelings of its own insufficiency and helplessness, entwines it into total constellations from which it cannot escape as a whole without mastering its individual elements.

There thus emerges the typical problematic condition of modern humanity: the feeling of being surrounded by an immense number of cultural elements, which are not meaningless, but not profoundly meaningful to the individual either; elements which have a certain crushing quality as a mass, because an individual cannot inwardly assimilate every individual thing, but cannot simply reject it either, since it belongs potentially, as it were, to the sphere of his or her cultural development. One could characterize this with the exact reversal of that saying, '*Nihil habentes, omni possidentes*', which characterized the blissful poverty of the early Franciscans in their absolute liberation from all things that would somehow still tend to divert the soul from its path through themselves and thereby make it an indirect route. Instead of that, human beings in very rich and overburdened cultures are '*omnia habientes, nihil possidentes*'.

These experiences may have already been expressed in a great variety of forms.[1] What is at issue here is their deep rootedness in the centre of the concept of culture. The entire wealth which this concept embodies lies in the fact that objective constructs, without losing their objectivity, are integrated into the perfection process of human subjects as their path or means. Whether, viewed from the subject's position, the highest type of perfection is achieved in this way can be left open, yet for the metaphysical intention, which seeks to bring the principle of the subject and that of the object together, this is one of the ultimate guarantees of not having to recognize itself as an illusion. In this way, the metaphysical question finds a historical answer. In cultural constructs, the spirit has gained an objectivity that makes it independent of all the fortuitousness of subjective production and at the same time serviceable to the central goal of subjective perfection. Whereas the metaphysical replies to this question actually tend to cut it off by somehow demonstrating the subject–object opposition to be invalid, culture in fact holds fast to the full confrontation of the two elements, to the supra-subjective logic of spirit-formed things among which the subject elevates itself to itself.

The mind's fundamental ability to detach itself from itself, to confront itself as if it were a third party – shaping, recognizing and valuing – and first to gain consciousness of itself in this form, has attained, as it were, the broadest radius in the factual existence of culture, and has brought the object most forcefully to the highest point of tension against the subject in order to lead it back to the latter. But precisely in this inherent logic of the object, from which the subject regains itself as something perfect in itself and in accordance with itself, the integration of the two sides breaks into two. Something that was pointed out previously in these pages – namely, that the creator tends to think only of the objective meaning of the work, not of its cultural value – slides into caricature with the imperceptible transitions of a purely objective developmental logic, into a specialization cut off from life, into the self-enjoyment of a technique that can no longer find its way back to the subject. This very objectivity makes possible the division of labour, which collects the energies of an entire complex of personalities in the individual product, without regard to whether a subject can develop the amount of spirit and life invested in it for his or her advancement, or whether merely an externally peripheral need is satisfied with it. Herein lies the profound basis for Ruskin's ideal of replacing all factory labour with the artistic work of individuals. The division of labour separates the product as such from each individual aspect of the contributors. The product exists in an independent objectivity, which indeed makes it suitable to fit into an order of things or to serve an objectively determined individual purpose, but in so doing it loses that inner pervasive psychological dimension which only the whole individual can give to the whole work and which supports its incorporation into the psychological centrality of other human subjects.

For this reason, the work of art is such an immeasurably important cultural value because it is inaccessible to any division of labour, that is to say, because here (at least in the sense which is now essential, and aside from meta-aesthetic interpretations) the product created most profoundly preserves the individuality of the creator. What might appear to be a hatred of culture in Ruskin's work is, in reality, a passion for culture: it aims at the reversal of the division of labour, which deprives the content of culture of its subject, providing it with a soulless objectivity, with which it detaches itself from the real cultural process. And then the tragic development was revealed which binds culture to the objectivity of its contents, but ultimately relegates these contents, precisely through their objectivity, to a logic of their own and removes them from assimilation by human subjects; this development is revealed in the arbitrary reproducibility of the contents of the objective spirit. Because culture has no concrete unity of form for its contents, but instead each creative person contrasts his or her product to those of the others as if they were in an unlimited space, so that mass-like quality of things arises, each of which can lay claim – with some justification – to a cultural value and can also awaken in us a desire to utilize it in that way.

The formlessness of the objectified spirit as a totality grants it a developmental tempo which must leave that of the subjective spirit behind by a rapidly growing margin. The subjective spirit, however, is simply unable to protect the closed nature of its form completely against contacts with all those 'things' and their temptations and distortions. Hence, the superior power of the object over the subject, generally realized by the course of the world, transcended in culture to yield a propitious equilibrium, once again becomes palpable within culture through the limitlessness of the objective spirit.

That which is criticized as the encumberment and overladening of our life with a thousand superfluous things from which in fact we are unable to free ourselves, as the continuous 'stimulation' of the cultured person, who is not stimulated by all this into his or her own creativity, as the mere knowledge or enjoying of a thousand different things which our development cannot assimilate into itself and which remain behind in it as ballast – all these often-formulated specific ailments of culture are nothing other than the phenomena of the emancipation of this objectified spirit. The fact that the latter exists simply implies that the contents of culture ultimately follow a logic independent of their *cultural* purpose and one leading further and further away from it, but without the path of the human subject being unburdened of all of these things which have become so qualitatively and quantitatively inappropriate.

Rather, since this path, as a cultural one, is determined by the fact that psychological contents become independent and objective, there emerges the tragic situation that, already in its first moments of existence, culture conceals within itself the form of its contents, those of its inner essence: the path of the soul from itself as incomplete to itself as the completed essence. The great undertaking of the spirit in thus transcending the object as such by creating itself as an object, in order to return to itself with the enrichment from this creation, succeeds on countless occasions. But it must pay for this self-perfection with the tragic opportunity – determined by the autonomy of the world it has created – of finding itself creating a logic and dynamic which – at an ever increasing rate and creating an ever widening gap – diverts the contents of culture from the goal of culture.

THE CONFLICT OF MODERN CULTURE

As soon as life progresses beyond the purely biological level to the level of mind, and mind in its turn progresses to the level of culture, an inner conflict appears. The entire evolution of culture consists in the growth, resolution and re-emergence of this conflict. For clearly we speak of culture when the creative dynamism of life produces certain artefacts which provide it with forms of expression and actualization, and which in their turn absorb the constant flow of life, giving it form and content, scope and order: for example civil laws and constitutions, works of art, religion, science, technology and innumerable others. But a peculiar quality of these products of the life process is that from the first moment of their existence they have fixed forms of their own, set apart from the febrile rhythm of life itself, its waxing and waning, its constant renewal, its continual divisions and reunifications. They are vessels both for the creative life, which however immediately departs from them, and for the life which subsequently enters them, but which after a while they can no longer encompass. They have their own logic and laws, their own significance and resilience arising from a certain degree of detachment and independence *vis-à-vis* the spiritual dynamism which gave them life. At the moment of their establishment they are, perhaps, well-matched to life, but as life continues its evolution, they tend to become inflexible and remote from life, indeed hostile to it.

This is ultimately the reason why culture has a *history*. Life, as it becomes mind, continuously creates such artefacts: self-sufficient and with an inherent claim to permanence, indeed to timelessness. They may be described as the *forms* which life adopts, the indispensible mode of its manifestation as spiritual life. But life itself flows on without pause. With each and every new form of existence which it creates for itself, its perpetual dynamism comes into conflict with the permanence or timeless validity of that form. Sooner or later the forces of life erode every cultural form which they have produced. By the time one form has fully developed, the next is already beginning to take shape beneath it, and is destined to supplant it after a brief or protracted struggle.

The transformation of cultural forms is the subject of history in the widest sense. As an empirical discipline, it is content to identify in each individual case the concrete basis and causes of these external manifestations of change. But the deeper underlying process is surely a perpetual struggle between life, with its fundamental restlessness, evolution and mobility, and its own creations, which become inflexible and lag behind its development. Since, however, life can take on external existence only in one form or another, this process can be clearly identified and described in terms of the displacement of one form by another. The never-ending change in the content of culture, and in the long run of whole cultural styles, is the sign, or rather the result, both of the infinite fertility of life and of the profound opposition between its eternal evolution and transformation and the objective validity and self-assertion of those manifestations and forms in which, or by means of which, it exists. It moves between the poles of death and rebirth, rebirth and death.

This nature of the process of cultural history was first observed in respect of economic developments. The economic forces of any age give rise to an appropriate form of production: slavery, the guilds, peasant statute labour, free wage-labour, and all the other forms of the organization of labour.

When they arose, they were all the adequate expression of the capacities and aspirations of the age. But always within their norms and restrictions there arose economic energies whose nature and proportions could not find adequate scope in these forms. They therefore broke free of them, either gradually or in violent upheavals, and the former mode of production was replaced by one more suited to the current energies. But a mode of production has, as a form, no inherent energy to oust a different mode. It is life itself (in this case in its economic aspect) with its impetus and dynamism, its transformation and differentiation, which provides the driving force behind the entire process, but which, being itself formless, can only manifest itself as a phenomenon by being given form. However, it is the essence of form to lay claim, the moment it is established, to a more than momentary validity not governed by the pulse of life. This can be seen even more clearly in intellectual than in economic spheres. That is why there is from the very outset a latent tension between these forms and life, which subsequently erupts in various areas of our lives and activity. This can, in the long run, accumulate as a pervasive cultural malaise in which all form comes to be felt as something forcibly imposed on life, which then tries to break out of any form, not just one specific form or other, and to absorb it into its own spontaneity, to put itself in the place of form, to allow its force and plenitude to gush forth in their primal untrammelled spontaneity, and in no other way, until all cognition, values and structures can only be seen as the direct revelation of life. We are at present experiencing this new phase of the age-old struggle, which is no longer the struggle of a new, life-imbued form against an old, lifeless one, but the struggle against form itself, against the very principle of form. The moralists, the eulogists of the good old days, the stylistic purists have the facts on their side when they complain of the ubiquitous and growing formlessness of modern life. But they tend to overlook the fact that what is happening is not merely something negative, the death of traditional forms, but that an altogether positive vital impulse is sloughing off these forms. But because the magnitude of this process does not as yet permit this impulse to focus on the creation of new forms, it makes, as it were, a virtue of necessity and feels obliged to struggle against form simply because it *is* form. This is perhaps only possible in an age which feels that all cultural forms are like exhausted soil, which has yielded all it can but which is still entirely covered with the products of its earlier fertility. In the eighteenth century, of course, something similar occurred, but first it happened over a much longer period of time, from the English Enlightenment of the seventeenth century to the French Revolution; and secondly, each upheaval was inspired by a very definite new ideal: the emancipation of the individual, the rational conduct of life, the reliable progress of humanity towards happiness and perfection. And from each upheaval there arose, giving men a sense of inner security, the image of new cultural forms which in a way were already prefigured. Hence they did not produce the cultural malaise as we know it, which we of the older generation have seen grow gradually to the point where it is no longer a question of a new cultural form struggling against an old, but of life, in every imaginable sphere, rebelling against the need to contain itself within any fixed form at all.

This situation, which is now clear for all to see, was anticipated in a way some decades ago when the concept of life began to assume a dominant role in philosophy. In order to relate this phenomenon correctly to the general history of ideas, it is necessary to digress a little. In any great cultural era with a definite character of its own, one particular idea can always be discerned which both underlies all intellectual movements and at the same time appears to be their ultimate goal. Whether the age itself is aware of this idea as an abstraction, or whether it is merely the ideal focal-point of such movements, whose import and significance for the age become apparent only to later observers, makes no difference. Every such central idea occurs, of course, in innumerable variants and disguises, and against innumerable opposing factors, but it remains withal the hidden governing principle of the intellectual era. In every such era it is to be found (and can hence be identified), where the highest life, the absolute, the metaphysical dimension of reality coincides with the supreme value, the absolute demand made of ourselves and of the world. A logical paradox is involved here, of course: what is absolute reality does not need anything to make it real; it cannot, clearly, be said that what most indubitably exists has yet to come into being. But at its highest peaks, philosophy is not inhibited by this conceptual difficulty; indeed, the point where this paradox appears, where the series of that which is and that which ought to be, otherwise alien to each other, meet, is, one may be sure, an authentic central aspect of that particular philosophy of life.

I will only indicate with the utmost brevity the ideas which seem to me to be central in this way to certain broad eras. In the era of Greek classicism, it was the idea of *being* – being which was unified, substantive and divine, but not of a pantheistic formlessness, yet which rather existed, and could be shaped, in meaningful concrete forms. The Christian Middle Ages replaced this idea with that of God, at once the source and goal of all reality, the unconditional lord of our lives, yet one who demanded free obedience and devotion from those lives. From the Renaissance onwards, this supremacy was gradually accorded to the idea of Nature: it appeared to be the absolute, the sole embodiment of existence and truth, but at the same time also the ideal, that had yet to be endowed with presence and authority – initially in artistic activity, for which, of course, the vital prerequisite is a priori the unity of the ultimate essence of reality and the highest value. Then the seventeenth century focused its philosophy on the idea of natural laws, which alone it regarded as fundamentally valid, and the century of Rousseau erected upon this foundation an ideal of 'nature' as the absolute value, aspiration and challenge. In addition, at the end of the era, the ego, the spiritual personality, emerges as a central idea: on the one hand, existence in its entirety appears as the creative idea of a conscious ego, while on the other hand personality becomes a goal. The assertion of the pure individual ego comes to be seen as the absolute moral imperative, indeed the universal metaphysical goal of life. The nineteenth century, with its motley variety of intellectual currents, did not produce any comparable all-embracing guiding concept. If we restrict ourselves to the human sphere, we might here speak of the idea of society, which in the nineteenth century is proclaimed for the first time to be the true reality of our lives, reducing the individual to a point of intersection of various social series, or even a hypothetical entity such as the atom. But, on the other hand, man is *required* to relate his entire life to society; complete social integration is regarded as an absolute obligation subsuming all other obligations, moral or otherwise. Only at the turn of the twentieth century did large groups of European intellectuals appear, as it were, to be reaching out for a new basic idea on which to construct a philosophy of life. The idea of *life* emerged at the centre where reality and values – metaphysical or psychological, moral or artistic – both originate and intersect.

As for which individual phenomena, among those which make up the general tendency of our most recent culture as described above, find in the multifaceted 'metaphysics of life' the soil to nourish their growth, the vindication of their proclivity, their conflicts and their tragedies – this will be investigated later. But it must be mentioned here how remarkably the emergent philosophical significance of the concept of life is anticipated and confirmed by the fact that the two great adversaries in the modern articulation of values, Schopenhauer and Nietzsche, have precisely this idea in common. Schopenhauer is the first modern philosopher to enquire at the most profound, crucial level, not into any specific contents of life, any conceptions or aspects of existence, but to ask exclusively: what is life, what is its pure significance *qua* life? The fact that he does not use the term, but speaks only of the will to life, or just of the will, must not be allowed to obscure this fundamental stance. Notwithstanding all his speculative exploration of areas beyond life, the 'will' provides his answer to the question of the meaning of life as such. This answer is that life cannot attain to any meaning and goal beyond itself, because it always follows its own will, albeit in innumerable shapes and forms. Precisely because its metaphysical reality condemns it to remain within its own bounds, any apparent goal can only bring disappointment and an endless series of further illusions to pursue. Nietzsche, on the other hand, started in exactly the same way from the idea that life is entirely self-determining and constitutes the sole substance of all its contents. But he found in life itself the purpose that gives it the meaning which it cannot find outside itself. For the essence of life is intensification, increase, growth of plentitude and power, strength and beauty from within itself – in relation not to any definable goal but purely to its own development. By its increase, life itself takes on potentially infinite value. However profoundly and vitally these two opposing responses to life, despair and jubilation, differ – beggaring any attempt to make a rational choice or compromise between them – they have in common the basic question which sets them apart from all earlier philosophers: what does life mean, what is its intrinsic value? For them, questions of knowledge and morality, of the self and reason, art and God, happiness and suffering, can only be asked after they have solved that prime mystery; and the answer to them depends on the solution given. Only the fundamental fact of life itself gives to all other things positive or negative value, meaning and proportion. The idea of life is the point of intersection of the two diametrically opposed ways of thinking, which between them have mapped out the crucial decisions to be taken in modern life.

I shall now attempt to illustrate in relation to some of the manifestations of our most recent culture, that is, that which had evolved up to 1914, how it has diverged from all former cultural evolution. In the past, old forms have always been destroyed by a desire for new forms. But today the ultimate impulse underlying developments in this sphere can be identified as opposition to the principle of form as such, even where consciousness is actually or apparently advancing towards new forms. The fact that for at least several decades we have no longer been living by any sort of shared idea, nor indeed, to a large extent, by any idea at all, is perhaps – to anticipate a later point – only another manifestation of the negative aspect (as regards its identifiable phenomena) of this intellectual current. The Middle Ages, by contrast, had the idea of the Christian Church; the Renaissance had the restoration of secular nature as a value which did not need to be legitimized by transcendental forces; the eighteenth-century Enlightenment lived by the idea of universal human happiness through the rule of reason, and the great age of German idealism suffused science with artistic imagination, and aspired to give art a foundation of cosmic breadth by means of scientific knowledge. But today, if one were to ask educated people what idea actually governs their lives, most of them would give a specialized answer relating to their occupation. One would not hear much of any cultural idea governing them as whole men and guiding all their specialized activities. If even within the individual cultural sphere the present peculiar stage of historical evolution is a stage where life aspires to manifest itself in pure immediacy; and, this being possible only in some form or other, if the inadequacy of any such form reveals that this is indeed the truly decisive impulse, then not only is there no raw material, as it were, for an all-embracing cultural idea, but also the spheres whose new forms it would encompass are far too diverse, indeed disparate, to permit any such ideal unification.

Turning now to specific phenomena, I propose first to discuss art. Of all the hotch-potch of aspirations covered by the general name of futurism, only the movement described as Expressionism seems to stand out with a certain identifiable degree of unity and clarity. If I am not mistaken the point of Expressionism is that the artist's inner impulse is perpetuated in the work, or, to be more precise, *as* the work, exactly as it is experienced. The intention is not to express or contain the impulse in a form imposed upon it by something external, either real or ideal. Thus the impulse is not concerned with the imitation of any entity or event, either in its objective natural form or, as was the ambition of the Impressionists, as registered by our momentary sense impressions. For, after all, even this impression is not the artist's purely personal creation, coming exclusively from within. It is, rather, something passive and secondary, and the work which reflects it is a kind of blend of artistic individuality and a given alien entity. And just as this non-subjective element is rejected, so likewise is the formal procedure, in the narrower sense, which is only available to the artist from some external source: tradition, technique, a model or an established principle. All these are obstructions to life, whose urge is to pour out spontaneously and creatively. If it were to accommodate itself to such forms it would survive in the work only in a distorted, ossified and spurious guise. I imagine the creative process, in its purest form, of an Expressionist painter (and similarly, though less simple to formulate, in all the other arts) as a process whereby the emotional impulse is spontaneously transferred into the hand holding the brush, just as a gesture expresses an inner feeling or a scream expresses pain. The movements of the hand obediently follow the inner impulse, so that what eventually takes shape on the canvas is the direct precipitate of inner life, unmodified by any external alien elements. The fact that even Expressionist paintings have names denoting objects, although they bear no 'resemblance' to them, is, of course, rather puzzling, and perhaps superfluous, but it is not as pointless as it is bound to appear in the light of traditional expectations regarding art. The artist's inner impulse, which simply gushes forth as an Expressionistic work, can, of course, originate in nameless or unidentifiable spiritual sources. But it can clearly also originate in the stimulus of an external object. It used to be thought that the artistically productive result of such stimulus must show a morphological similarity to the object that provided it (the entire Impressionist movement was based on this assumption).

But Expressionism rejects this assumption. It takes seriously the insight that a cause and its effect can have wholly dissimilar external manifestations, that the dynamic relationship between them is purely internal and need not produce any visual affinity. The sight of a violin or a human face, for example, may trigger off emotions in the painter which, transmuted by his artistic energies, eventually produce an artefact with a completely different appearance. One might say that the Expressionist artist replaces the 'model' by the 'occasion' which awakens an impulse in that life in him which is obedient only unto itself. In abstract terms (but describing a very real act of will), it is the struggle of life to be itself. Its ambition is to express itself purely as itself, and hence it refuses to be contained in any form which is thrust upon it by some other reality which is valid because it is real, or by a law which is valid because it is a law. Conceptually speaking, the artefact eventually produced in this way does, of course, have a form. But as far as the artistic intention is concerned, this is merely an unavoidable extraneous appendage, as it were. It does not, as in all other conceptions of art, have any significance in itself, requiring creative life merely as the basis of its actualization. That is why this art is also indifferent to beauty or ugliness. These are qualities associated with such forms, whereas the significance of life lies beyond beauty and ugliness, for its flux is governed not by any goal but merely by its own driving force. If the works thus created do not satisfy us, this merely confirms that a new form has not been discovered, and is thus not at issue. Once the product is completed, and the life process which engendered it has departed from it, we see that it lacks that meaning and value of its own which we expect from any objective created thing existing independently of its creator. Life, anxious only to express itself, has, as it were, jealously withheld such meaning from its own product.

Perhaps this is the basic explanation of the peculiar preference for the late works of the great masters observable in recent times. Here creative life has become so sovereignly itself, so rich in itself, that it sloughs off any form which is at all traditional or common to other works also. Its expression in the work of art is purely and simply its own inmost essence and destiny at that particular time. However coherent and meaningful the work may be in relation to this essence, it often appears, when measured against traditional forms, uneven, fragmentary and disjointed. This is not a senile waning of formal artistry; it reveals not the infirmity but the strength of old age. Having perfected his creative powers, the great artist is so purely himself that his work shows only the form spontaneously generated by the flow of his life: form has lost its autonomy *vis-à-vis* this life.

It would, in theory, be perfectly possible, of course, for a form with its own intrinsic perfection and significance to be the wholly appropriate expression for such spontaneous life, to fit it like a living skin. This is doubtless the case with the truly great classic works. But, disregarding these works, one can observe here a peculiar structural feature of the spiritual world which far transcends its consequences for art. It is true to say that, in art, whose forms are available in their perfection, something which exists beyond those forms is articulated. In all great artists and all great works of art there is something more profound, more expansive, of more mysterious origin than is offered as art considered purely as artistry, something which is, however, accommodated, presented and made visible by art. In the case of the classics, this something fuses entirely with art. But where it actually conflicts with, or indeed destroys, the forms of art, we feel it, we are conscious of it rather as something separate, something with a voice of its own. An example of this is the inner fate which Beethoven attempts to articulate in his last works. Here it is not a matter of a particular art form being shattered, but rather of the form of art itself being overwhelmed by something different, vaster, something from another dimension. The same applies to metaphysics. Its aim, after all, is knowledge of truth. But in it something which lies beyond knowledge struggles to be heard, something greater, or more profound, or merely different, which reveals itself unmistakably by doing violence to truth as such, making paradoxical, easily refutable claims. It is a typical intellectual paradox (which, of course, a superficial and complacent optimism tends to deny) that some metaphysical beliefs would not have the truth they do as symbols of life or the expression of a particular typical human stance towards life as a whole if they were true as 'knowledge'. Perhaps there is in religion also something that is not religion, something profounder lying beyond it which transcends all its concrete forms, however genuinely religious these are, and reveals itself as heresy and dissent. Some, perhaps all, human creations which spring entirely from the creative power of the soul, contain more than can be accommodated in their form. This property, which distinguishes them from anything produced in a purely mechanical fashion, can only be seen unmistakably when there is a tension between the work and its form.

This is the reason, in a general if not so extreme a way, for the interest currently enjoyed by the art of Van Gogh. For here, more than with any other painter, one surely feels that a passionate vitality far transcending the limits of painting, erupting from an altogether unique breadth and profundity, has merely found, in the gift for painting, a way of channelling its surging flux – by chance, so to speak, as if it could equally well have found fulfilment in religious, literary or musical activity. It seems to me that it is more than anything else this incandescent, palpable spontaneous vitality – which, it is true, only occasionally conflicts with its pictorial form to the extent of destroying the latter – which attracts large numbers of people to Van Gogh in line with the general intellectual tendency under discussion. The existence, on the other hand, in some young people of today of a desire for a wholly abstract art probably arises from the feeling that an insurmountable paradox is created when life acquires – no matter how blithely – a passion for direct, unveiled self-expression. It is precisely the tremendous dynamism of these young people which pushes this tendency to an absolute extreme. It is, incidentally, perfectly understandable that the movement we are describing is, above all, a movement of the young. Revolutionary historical change, external or internal, is generally brought about by the young, and this is particularly true of the current change with its special nature. Age, with flagging vitality, concentrates more and more on the objective *content* of life (which in the present context can equally appropriately be described as its form). But youth is primarily concerned with the *process* of life, it is anxious only to develop to the utmost its powers and its surplus vitality; it is relatively indifferent, and quite often unfaithful, to the particular objects involved. In a cultural climate which enthrones life itself, with its utterances that are well-nigh contemptuous of all form, the significance of youthful life as such is, as it were, objectified.

Finally, we encounter within our sphere of discourse a further fundamental confirmation both in the pursuit of art and also, to a large extent, in other areas. The *mania for originality* in so many young people of today is often, but by no means invariably, vanity and sensationalism, both private and public. In the better cases, the passionate desire to articulate an authentic personal sense of life plays an important part, and the conviction that it really is authentic appears to require the exclusion of anything pre-established or traditional – any permanent forms objectified independently of spontaneous creativity. For when personal life is channelled into such forms, it not only forfeits its uniqueness, it also runs the risk of squandering its vitality on something that is no longer alive. The intention in these cases is to preserve not so much the individuality of life as the life of individuality. Originality is only the *ratio cognoscendi*, so to speak, which guarantees that life is purely itself and that no external, objectified, rigid forms have been absorbed in its flux, or its flux in them. We may have here a more general underlying motive for modern individualism (a point which I can only suggest in passing here).

I shall now try to demonstrate the same basic impulse in one of the most recent movements in philosophy, one which departs most radically from the historically established modes of philosophy. I will refer to it as pragmatism, because the best-known offshoot of the theory, the American version, has acquired this name – a version, incidentally, which I consider to be the most narrow and superficial one. Independently of this or any other specific version that has become current hitherto, the following seems to me to be the crucial motivation in the context of our present interests. Of all the individual spheres of culture, none is as independent *vis-à-vis* life, none as autonomous, as remote from the stress and turbulence, the individual patterns and destinies of life, as knowledge. Not only are the statements that twice two is four, or that matter attracts matter in inverse proportion to the square of distance *true*, regardless of whether they are known to any living minds or not, or of what changes the human race may undergo during the period in which they are known. It is also true to say that knowledge which is directly interwoven with life owes its importance precisely to its complete independence of the fluctuating fortunes of life. Even so-called practical knowledge is, of course, simply theoretical knowledge that is put to practical use at some later stage, but which, *qua* knowledge, remains part of an order of things obedient to its own laws, an ideal realm of truth.

This independence of truth which has always been accepted in the past is denied by the pragmatists. Both inner and outer life are based at every step – so their argument runs – on particular imagined ideas. These ideas sustain and foster our lives if they are true, or they bring us to ruin if they are false. But our ideas are dependent on our mental make-up, they are by no means a mechanical reflection of the reality with which our practical life is interwoven. It would therefore be the most remarkable coincidence if ideas shaped exclusively by the logic of subjective thinking were to produce desirable and predictable results within that reality. On the contrary, it is more likely that of the innumerable ideas which determine our practical life some are regarded as true because they affect that life in a dynamic, positive way, while others which have the opposite effect are dismissed as false. There is therefore no independent, pre-existent truth which is merely later incorporated, as it were, into the stream of life in order to guide its course. On the contrary, the opposite is the case: among the vast mass of theoretical elements which are engendered by the stream of life and are subsequently fed back and affect its course, there are some whose effects match our vital desires (by chance, one might say, but without this chance we could not exist). These we call true, epistemologically correct. The truthfulness of our ideas is not a matter of objects *per se*, nor of any sovereign intellect in us.

Life itself, rather, creates, sometimes on the basis of crude expediency, sometimes of the most profound spiritual needs, the scale of values within our ideas, the one pole of which we call the complete truth, the other complete error. I can neither elaborate nor criticize this doctrine here. I am, indeed, not concerned with whether it is correct or not, merely with the fact that it has evolved at the present time, and that it denies the time-honoured claim of knowledge to be an autonomous realm governed by independent, ideal laws. It now becomes one element interwoven with and sustained by life, guided by the totality and unity of vital impulses and goals, and legitimized by the fundamental values of life. Life has thus reasserted its sovereignty over a sphere which hitherto appeared to be separate and independent of it. In more profound philosophical terms: the forms of knowledge whose internal consistency and self-sufficient meaning constitute a firm framework or an indestructive backcloth for our entire mental world, are dissolved by and in the ebb and flow of life. They are seen to be moulded by its evolving and changing energies and ambitions, not standing firm in their own rightness and timeless validity. Life as the central concept of philosophy finds its purest form where, far transcending the reformulation of the problem of epistemology, it becomes the prime metaphysical fact, the essence of all being, making every existing phenomenon a heart-beat, or a mode of representation, or a stage of development of absolute life. Life ascends as spirit, in the course of the overall evolution of the world towards spirit; it descends as matter. This theory answers the question of knowledge in terms of an 'intuition' which transcends all logic and all the operations of the intellect and directly apprehends the essential inner truth of things – which means that only life is capable of understanding life. That is why, in this way of thinking, all objective reality (the *object* of knowledge) had to be transformed into life, so that the epistemological process, conceived entirely as a function of life itself, could be sure of encountering an object essentially similar to itself, which it can thus wholly penetrate. Thus, whereas the original pragmatism dissolved our conception of the world into life only from the point of view of the subject, this has now been performed from the point of view of the object also. Nothing remains of form as a universal principle external to life, as a governing factor of existence with its own import and its own power. Any surviving remnant of form in this conception would exist only by the grace of life itself.

The repudiation of the principle of form culminates not only in pragmatism, but also in all those thinkers imbued with a modern sense of life who reject the coherent systems in which an earlier age, dominated by the classical notion of form, saw its entire philosophical salvation. Such systems attempt to unify all knowledge (at least with regard to its most general concepts) symmetrically, as it were, in a regular, harmonious edifice with dominant and subordinated elements, all based on one fundamental principle. In such a system, the architectural, aesthetic perfection, the achieved harmony and completeness of the edifice is regarded as proof (and this is the crucial point) of its objective correctness, the proof that existence has been truly grasped and comprehended in its entirety. This is the final culmination of the principle of form, for it makes intrinsic formal perfection and completeness the ultimate touchstone of truth.

It is against this that life is now on the defensive, for although it is forever creating forms, it is also forever bursting their bounds. These theories specify in two ways the philosophical significance which they claim for life. On the one hand, mechanism is rejected as a fundamental principle of the universe; it is, perhaps, a technique employed by life, perhaps a symptom of its decadence. On the other hand, the belief in ideas as metaphysically autonomous, as the supreme and absolute guiding principle or substance of all existence, is also rejected. Life refuses to be governed by anything subordinate to itself, but it also refuses to be governed at all, even by any ideal realm with a claim to superior authority. If, for all that, no higher life can escape the awareness of some guiding idea, be it a transcendental power, or some ethical or other value-based obligation, if this is so, it now seems to be possible, or to have any prospect of success, only by virtue of the fact that the ideas themselves come from life. It is the nature of life to produce within itself that which guides and redeems it, and that which opposes, conquers and is conquered by it. It sustains and enhances itself by way of its own products. The fact that these products confront it as independent judges is the very foundation of their existence, their *modus vivendi*. The opposition in which they thus find themselves to the life which is superior to them is the tragic conflict of life as mind. This conflict is now, of course, becoming more perceptible with the growing awareness that it is in fact created by life itself, and is therefore organically and ineluctably bound up with life.

In the most general cultural terms, this entire movement constitutes the repudiation of classicism as the absolute ideal of humanity and its evolution. For classicism is altogether dominated by form: harmonious, fulfilled, serene and self-contained, the confident norm of life and creativity. Here, too, it is certain that nothing positive, clear and satisfactory has, as yet, been found to put in place of the former ideal. This is why one can see that the battle against classicism is not, for the moment, concerned with creating a new cultural form at all. What is happening is simply that life, with its own self-assurance, is endeavouring to emancipate itself altogether from the formal restraint historically embodied in classicism.

A very brief look may be taken at the same basic trend underlying a specific phenomenon from the sphere of ethics. The term 'the new ethics' has been adopted for a critique of existing sexual relationships being propagated by a small number of people, but whose aspirations are widely shared. The critique is directed chiefly against two elements of the existing order of things: marriage and prostitution. The theme of the critique is, fundamentally, that erotic life is striving to assert its own authentic, inmost energy and natural proclivity against the forms in which our culture has in general imprisoned it, robbed it of its vitality and caused it to violate its own nature. Marriage is contracted in innumerable cases for other than actual erotic reasons, and thus, in innumerable cases, the vital erotic impulse either stagnates or perishes when its individuality comes up against inflexible traditions and legal cruelty. Prostitution, which has almost become a legalized institution, forces young people's love life to take on a debased form, a caricature which transgresses against its inmost nature. These are the forms against which authentic spontaneous life is in revolt. Under different cultural conditions, they would perhaps not be quite so inadequate, but at the present time they are being challenged by forces which spring from the deepest source of life. One can see here very much more clearly than in the other areas of our culture the almost complete lack hitherto of any positive new forms as a concomitant of the basic (and entirely positive) desire to destroy existing forms. No proposal put forward by these reformers is regarded at all generally as an adequate substitute for the forms which they condemn. The typical process of cultural change – struggle against an old form by a new form in a successful bid to replace it – has conspicuously failed to occur. The energy which should by rights occupy the new form is, for the time being, aimed directly, as it were naked, against those forms from which authentic erotic life has departed. Thus, in perpetrating the paradox which has by now been repeatedly stressed, it finds itself in a vacuum, for the moment erotic life enters any sort of cultural context, it simply must adopt a form of some kind. For all that, as in the areas discussed earlier, it is only the superficial observer who sees here merely licentiousness and anarchic lust. In this sphere, formlessness in itself does indeed appear in such a light; but at a deeper level (wherever this exists) matters are different. Authentic erotic life flows along wholly individual channels, and the above forms arouse hostility because they trap this life in institutionalized patterns and thus do violence to its special individuality. Here, as in many of the other cases, it is the struggle between life and form which, in a less abstract, metaphysical way, is being fought out as a struggle between individuality and standardization.

A tendency in current religious life must, it seems to me, be interpreted similarly. I refer here to the fact, which has been observable for the past ten or twenty years, that quite a number of intellectually progressive people find satisfaction for their religious needs in mysticism. It can be reasonably assumed, by and large, that they all grew up within the intellectual orbit of one of the existing churches. Their turn to mysticism very clearly reveals two motives. First, the forms which channel religious life by means of a series of specific, objective images no longer do justice to that life. Secondly, religious longings are not thereby killed, they merely seek other paths and goals. The decisive factor in the turn towards mysticism seems to be more than anything else its freedom from the clear contours and boundaries of religious forms. Here there is a divinity which transcends any personal (and hence, in people's minds, ultimately specific) form. Here there is an indefinite expansiveness of religious emotion, free from all dogmatic restrictions, given profundity in a formless infinity, and evolving solely from the yearning of the soul, transmuted into energy. Mysticism appears to be the last resort of religious individuals who cannot as yet dissociate themselves from all transcendental forms, but only (for the time being, as it were) from any fixed, specific form.

But the most profound impulse (no matter if it be self-contradictory and its goal eternally remote) is to my mind the impulse to replace the structures of faith by a religious life that is purely a functional quality of inner life: the spiritual state which once gave rise, and still does give rise, to such structures of faith. In the past, the evolution of religious culture has followed the course demonstrated throughout these pages: a particular form of religious life, initially wholly appropriate to the nature and energies of that life, gradually becomes externalized, constricted and inflexible. It is then ousted by a new form, which once again accommodates the spontaneous dynamism of the religious impulse in its current manifestation. What takes the place of the obsolete form is thus still a religious form, with various articles of faith. Today, however, the other-worldly objects of religious faith are being radically rejected, at least by very many people. But this does not mean that these people no longer have any religious needs. In the past, these basic needs revealed themselves in the creation of appropriate new dogmas. But today the whole situation of a believing subject confronted by something that is believed in is no longer felt to be a proper expression of the religious life. Taken to its ultimate conclusion, this whole spiritual evolution would make religion into a kind of direct mode of living, not a single melody, so to speak, within the symphony of life, but the key of the entire symphony. Life, in all its secular aspects, action and fate, thought and feeling, would be permeated in its entirety by that unique inner blend of humility and exaltation, tension and peace, vulnerability and consecration, which we can describe in no other way than as religious. Life thus lived would itself produce the sense of absolute value which, in the past, appeared to be derived from the specific forms of religious life, the particular articles of faith in which it had crystallized. A pre-echo of this, albeit transposed into the last surviving form of mysticism, can be heard in the writings of Angelus Silesius, where he rejects any restriction of religious values to specific forms and locates them in life itself as it is lived: 'The saint, when he drinks, pleases God as much as when he prays and sings'. It is not a question of so-called secular religion.

This, too, is still associated with a specific content, which is simply empirical rather than transcendental. It, too, channels religious life into certain forms of beauty and grandeur, sublimity and lyric emotion. It is, in essence, an obscure hybrid form, animated by the disguised surviving remnants of transcendental religiosity. What we are speaking of is religiosity as an all-embracing, spontaneous process of life. It is a state of being, not of having, a piety which is called faith when it has an object, but which now lies in the way life itself is lived. Needs are no longer satisfied by anything external. (The Expressionist painter likewise does not satisfy his artistic needs by faithful adherence to an external object.) What is sought is a continuity at that profound level where life has not yet split into needs and satisfactions and thus requires no object which would impose a specific form upon it. Life seeks religious expression of a direct kind, not using a language with a given vocabulary and fixed syntax. One might say (and it only appears to be a paradox) that the soul desires to preserve the quality of faith even though it no longer accepts any specific predetermined articles of faith.

This desire of religious souls is often perceptible in tentative beginnings, bizarre confusion, and critique that is wholly negative because its proponents do not understand their own sentiments. It faces, of course, the most intractable difficulty in the fact that spiritual life can, from the outset, only become articulate in *forms*. Its *freedom* likewise can only be actualized in forms, even though they also immediately restrict that freedom. Certainly piety or faith is a spiritual state entailed by the very existence of the soul; it would give life a particular colouring even if it never had any religious object – just as people of an erotic temperament would perforce retain and fulfil that temperament even if they never met anybody worthy of their love. Nevertheless, I doubt whether a fundamental religious need does not inevitably require an object. A purely functional quality, a formless dynamism which does no more than give a colour, a spiritual quality to the universal ebb and flow of life, appears to be the essence of much contemporary religious feeling. But I doubt whether this is not merely an interlude of an ideal nature which can never become reality, the symptom of a situation where existing religious forms are being repudiated by the inner religious life, which is, however, unable to replace them with new ones; and where, as elsewhere, the notion then arises that this life can entirely dispense with forms that have their own objective significance and legitimate claims, and be content to give free rein to its eruptive inner force. One of the most profound spiritual dilemmas of innumerable modern men is that although it is impossible to preserve the traditional church religions any longer, the religious impulse still exists. No amount of 'enlightenment' can destroy it, for it can only rob religion of its outer garment, not of its life. The intensification of religious life to the point of complete self-sufficiency, the transformation, as it were, of 'faith' from a transitive into an intransitive concept, is a tempting way out of the dilemma, but one which in the long run perhaps involves no small degree of self-contradiction.

Thus all these phenomena (and a number of others besides) reveal the conflict which arises from the inescapable essence of all cultural life in the widest sense of the word, whether creative or responsive to what has already been created. Such life must either produce forms, or proceed within given forms. What we *are* is, it is true, spontaneous life, with its equally spontaneous, unanalysable sense of being, vitality and purposiveness, but what we *have* is only its particular form at any one time, which, as I have stressed above, proves from the moment of its creation to be part of a quite different order of things. Endowed with the legitimacy and stature of its own provenance, it asserts and demands an existence beyond spontaneous life. This, however, goes against the essence of life itself, its surging dynamism, its temporal fortunes, the inexorable differentiation of all its elements. Life is ineluctably condemned to become reality only in the guise of its opposite, that is as *form*. This paradox becomes more acute, more apparently insoluble, to the degree that the inner being which we can only call life *tout court*[2] asserts its formless vitality, while at the same time inflexible, independent forms claim timeless legitimacy and invite us to accept them as the true meaning and value of our lives – that is the paradox is intensified, perhaps, to the degree to which culture progresses.

Thus life here aspires to the unattainable: to determine and manifest itself beyond all forms, in its naked immediacy. But knowledge, volition and creation, though wholly governed by life, can only replace one form by another; they can never replace form itself by the life that lies beyond form. All the onslaughts on the forms of our culture, passionate and iconoclastic or slow and cumulative, which either overtly or covertly oppose them with the power of life purely *qua* life because it is life, are revelations of the most profound internal paradox of the spirit wherever it evolves as culture, that is to say, takes on forms. Indeed it seems to me that of all the periods of history in which this chronic conflict has become acute and affected the entirety of life, no period has revealed as clearly as our own that this is its fundamental dilemma.

It is, however, pure philistinism to assume that all conflicts and problems are meant to be solved. Both have other functions in the history and make-up of life which they fulfil independently of any solution. Hence they are by no means pointless, even if the future resolves them not by solving them but merely by replacing their forms and contents with others. For, of course, all these problematic phenomena which we have discussed make us aware that the present state of affairs is far too paradoxical to be permanent. The dimensions of the problem clearly indicate some more fundamental change than the mere reshaping of an existing form into a new one. For, in such cases, the link between the past and the future hardly ever seems so completely shattered as at present, apparently leaving only intrinsically formless life to bridge the gap. But it is equally certain that the movement is towards the typical evolution of culture, the creation of new forms appropriate to present energies. This will only replace one problem, one conflict by another; though it may perhaps take longer to become conscious of it, open battle may be postponed for a longer period. But this is the true destiny of life, for life is struggle in the absolute sense that overrides the relative distinction between struggle and peace, while absolute peace, which perhaps also overrides this distinction, remains a divine mystery.

THE CRISIS OF CULTURE

Anyone who discusses culture must define this ambiguous concept in accordance with his particular purpose. I understand it to be that improvement of the soul which the latter attains not directly from within, as with the profundity that is the fruit of religion or with moral purity and primary creativity, but indirectly, by way of the intellectual achievements of the species, the products of its history: knowledge, lifestyles, art, the state, a man's profession and experience of life – these constitute the path of culture by which the subjective spirit returns to itself in a higher, improved state. Therefore all behaviour intended to increase our culture is bound up with the form of means and ends. This behaviour is, however, fragmented into countless separate activities. Life is made up of modes of action which, only to a very limited extent, have, or can be seen to have, any common direction. The resulting tendency towards fragmentariness and uncertainty of purpose is maximized by the fact that the various means which serve our ends, our 'technology' in the widest sense of the word, are constantly becoming both more extensive and more intensive. The resulting immensity of the series of ends and means gives rise to a phenomenon of incalculably far-reaching consequences: certain members of these series become, in our consciousness, ends in themselves. Innumerable things which, objectively speaking, are no more than a transitional stage, a means to our real ends, appear to us while we are striving for them, and often even after we have achieved them, as the fulfilment of an ultimate ambition. We need this relative emphasis within our aspirations because they are so extensive and complex that our energy and courage would flag if we had only our real ultimate goal (which is Heaven knows how remote) as an incentive. The vast intensive and extensive growth of our technology – which is much more than just material technology – entangles us in a web of means, and means towards means, more and more intermediate stages, causing us to lose sight of our real ultimate ends. This is the extreme inner danger which threatens all highly developed cultures, that is to say, all eras in which the whole of life is overlaid with a maximum of multi-stratified means. To treat some means as ends may make this situation psychologically tolerable, but it actually makes life increasingly futile.

A second internal contradiction of culture arises from the same source. Those objective artefacts which are the precipitate of a creative life and which are, in due course, absorbed by other people as a means of acquiring culture, immediately begin to develop independently in accordance with the particular *objective* factors involved in their creation. Industries and sciences, arts and organizations impose their content and pace of development on individuals, regardless of or even contrary to the demands that these individuals ought to make for the sake of their own improvement, that is the acquisition of culture. The more finely wrought and perfect in their own way are those things which both have their basis in culture and are themselves the basis of culture, the more they follow an immanent logic which is by no means always appropriate to the process of individual development and self-realization, which is the whole point of all the products of culture as such. We are confronted by countless objectifications of the mind: works of art, social forms, institutions, knowledge. They are like kingdoms administered according to their own laws, but they demand that we should make them the content and norm of our own individual lives, even though we do not really know what to do with them, indeed often feel them to be a burden and an impediment. But it is not only this qualitative dissociation that sets a barrier between the objective and the subjective aspects of higher cultures. It is also, in a crucial way, a matter of quantitative vastness. One book after another, one invention after another, one work of art after another all add up to an endless, formless mass confronting the individual with the demand that he absorb it all. But the individual, with his predetermined nature and limited capacity for absorption, can only meet this demand to a visibly diminishing degree. This creates the typical problematic situation of modern man: the feeling of being overwhelmed by this immense quantity of culture, which he can neither inwardly assimilate nor simply reject, since it all belongs potentially to his cultural sphere. Left to evolve in its own way, what one might call the culture of *things* has unlimited scope for development, and the result of this is that people's interests and hopes increasingly turn towards *this* culture, at the expense of the apparently much more restricted finite task of individual personal culture.

These, then, are the two most profound dangers for ripe and over-ripe cultures: first, that the ends of life become subordinate to its means, with the inevitable result that many things which are only means acquire the psychological status of ends; and secondly, that the objective products of culture develop independently in obedience to purely objective norms, and thus both become profoundly estranged from subjective culture and advance far too rapidly for the latter to keep pace with them.

As I see the matter, all the phenomena which have, for some time now, given us the sense of an impending cultural crisis can be attributed to these two basic factors and their ramifications. All the restlessness, the overt covetousness and craving for pleasure of our age are merely a consequence of, and a reaction to, this situation: that people seek personal values on a plane where they are simply not to be found. The fact that technological progress is unquestioningly equated with cultural progress; the fact that, in intellectual fields, methods are often considered sacred and more important than results; the fact that the desire for money far exceeds the desire for the things it can buy; all these facts prove that ends and goals are gradually being usurped by means and methods. If these are the symptoms of an ailing culture, does then the war mark the outbreak of the crisis, which can become the first step towards recovery?

I do not venture to assert without reservation that the first group of phenomena in this pathology of culture – the disparity between personal culture and the culture of things – offers any prospect of a cure. We probably have here an internal paradox inseparable from the very nature of culture. For culture, after all, means the cultivation of the individual by means of the cultivation of the world of things, and the latter is capable of unlimited refinement, acceleration and expansion, whereas the capacity of the individual is ineluctably one-sided and limited. Therefore I do not see any way in theory of preventing fragmentation and the state of simultaneous dissatisfaction and over-satiation. Even so, the war does seem to be helping to narrow the rift in two ways. For the soldier, the whole system of culture pales into insignificance, not only because he is, in fact, compelled to do without it, but because in wartime the meaning and demands of life are focused on activity of whose value one is conscious without the mediation of any external things. Strength and courage, skill and stamina, prove themselves in direct activity as the values of life, and the 'war machine' visibly has a quite different, infinitely more vital relationship than a factory machine to the men involved in its operation. This is the only sphere where personal life is not usurped by objective activity, however much the vast expansion of events and the negligible quality of the individual contribution provide the conditions for this usurpation, conditions which under normal circumstances would certainly have that effect. Of course, the war situation has no actual bearing on the general cultural tension between the subjectivity of life and its material content. Of course, this tension is in the nature of things insurmountable. But even so, people who have seen it surmounted on the battlefield may perhaps also perceive the significance of their other anonymous, partial contributions to society more clearly and in a more personal way. They may more resolutely seek the connection between the work they do for the means of life and the ultimate values of personal life. And whether they find it or not, the search itself is of immeasurable value. If there is a general hope that this war may create closer bonds between the individual and the community, and may somehow temper the dichotomy of the individual as an end in himself and as a member of the community, then the problem touched on here is one context in which this dichotomy operates. By seeing how the tiny scope of his individual activity can completely absorb all his energy and will-power, the soldier – and to a certain extent also the wartime civilian – will have been given a sense at least of the *form* such a reconciliation might take, a sense of some meaningful relationship between the part and the whole, the *thing* and the *person* – even if this is no more than a pause for breath before fresh strife and alienation.

This theme can be elaborated in a particular direction in the light of our present situation. It seems to me that a number of particular contemporary cultural phenomena demonstrate in the clearest possible fashion a process which can be observed throughout the entire history of culture. It is, on the one hand, the process of interaction between life, which is in a constant state of flux and expansion of its energies, and on the other hand its historical forms of expression on forms which remain, or at least attempt to remain, fixed and permanent. The growth of Naturalism in the arts towards the end of the last century was an indication that the dominant art forms inherited from the classical era were no longer capable of accommodating a life which was clamouring for expression. It was hoped that it would be possible to capture this life in direct images of reality which, as far as possible, were not filtered through any personal artistic conception. But naturalism failed to satisfy this crucial need, just as contemporary Expressionism, which replaced concrete images by the direct expression of psychological processes, surely also fails. Here the idea is that by externalizing inner dynamics in a work of art without regard to either the form appropriate to that work or to objectively valid norms, life could at last be given the form of expression genuinely appropriate to it without any falsification by external forms. But it seems to be in the nature of inner life that it can only ever be expressed in forms which have their own laws, purpose and stability arising from a degree of autonomy independent of the spiritual dynamics which created them. Creative life is constantly producing something that is not life, that somehow destroys life, that opposes life with its own valid claims. Life cannot express itself except in forms which have their own independent existence and significance. This paradox is the real, ubiquitous tragedy of culture. What individual genius, and eras of special creativity, achieve is to give to the creative life that wells up from the inner fountain-head a felicitous and harmonious form which, for a time at least, preserves that life without hardening into an independent existence hostile to it. But, in the great majority of cases, the paradox is unavoidable. Where the expression of life attempts to avoid it by presenting itself, as it were, formless and naked, what actually results is unintelligible, inarticulate, not an expression of anything at all, but merely a chaos of fragmentary vestiges of form as a substitute for a form which is unified, even if it is also inflexible, alien and at odds with its content.

Futurism has advanced to this extreme consequence of our situation in the arts: a passionate desire for the expression of life, for which traditional forms are inadequate, but for which no new forms have been devised, and which therefore seeks pure expression in a negation of form, or in forms that are almost provocatively abstruse - a violation of the very nature of creativity in order to escape its other inherent paradox. Nowhere, perhaps, do we see more forcefully than in some of the manifestations of futurism that once again the forms that life created as dwelling-places have become its prisons.

It is, perhaps, not possible to determine how matters stand in this respect with regard to religion, because the decisive factors are not visible phenomena but the inner life of the soul. As regards Christianity specifically, what has been stated in these pages as a fundamental intellectual result of the war holds good: that it has given both inner and outer reality to those rifts which, though structurally inherent in our society, were not actualized in peacetime. We all know the great polarization that has split the religious life in our times, affecting everyone except Christians of convenience and people with absolutely no religious sense at all: the split between Christianity and a religion with repudiates any historical content, whether it be undogmatic monotheism, or pantheism, or a purely inward spiritual condition not entailing any specific beliefs. The age, with its universal religious tolerance, exerted no pressures on men to choose. If I am not mistaken, it frequently allowed a situation to arise where, on the more conscious level of the mind, a man could believe he had adopted one of those positions, while deeper down the other belief (whether old or new) was, in fact, more powerful and influential. The spiritual forces of religion have been unmistakably vitalized and enhanced by the war to a degree which demands from each and every man a decision as to where he ultimately stands. The peaceful age of gradual transitions, of hybrid forms, of that pleasant twilit zone where one can indulge alternately even in mutually exclusive attitudes – this age, we may safely assume, is past and gone. It is to be hoped that the resoluteness with which, in these years, the German people is travelling along its appointed road will also penetrate to this inmost area of decision. But nowhere will it encounter such a hollow truce as in the religious sphere, where real Christians, in obedience to some intellectual quirk, adopt an undogmatic pantheistic stance, while decided unbelievers talk themselves into a kind of Christianity by 'symbolically' adapting basic Christian teachings. Any person of some maturity will presumably have long since made his decision – except that because of the peculiar cultural broadmindedness which our situation seemed to permit, or even demand, that decision was often intermingled with, or concealed by, its opposite. This is, however, no longer possible in a period of radical eruption of man's religious depths. No matter how far either attitude is visible to the outside world: within men's souls, what is ripe for supremacy will come into its own.

In our present context the essential fact is the existence of large social groups who, in pursuit of their religious needs, are turning away from Christianity. The fact that they are turning to all sorts of exotic, far-fetched and bizarre new doctrines appears to be of no importance whatsoever. Nowhere among them, except in isolated individual cases, can I discern any genuinely viable belief providing an adequate and precise expression of the religious life. On the other hand, the widespread rejection of any fixed form of religious life is in keeping with our general cultural situation. Thus supra-denominational mysticism has by far the strongest appeal to these groups. For the religious soul hopes to find here direct spontaneous fulfilment, whether in standing naked and alone, as it were, before its God, without the mediation of dogma in any shape or form, or in rejecting the very idea of God as a petrefaction and an obstacle, and in feeling that the true religion of the soul can only be its own inmost metaphysical life not moulded by any forms of faith whatever. Like the manifestations of futurism touched on above, this wholly formless mysticism marks the historical moment when inner life can no longer be accommodated in the forms it has occupied hitherto, and because it is unable to create other, adequate forms, concludes that it must exist without any form at all.

Within the development of philosophy, this crisis seems to me to be more far-reaching than is generally admitted. The basic concepts and methodology which have been elaborated since classical antiquity and applied to the raw material of life in order to shape it into philosophical images of the world, have, I believe, achieved this to the highest degree of which they are capable. The philosophical instinct of which they were the expression has, with their help, evolved into ways of thinking, impulses and needs to which they are no longer appropriate. If the signs do not deceive us, our entire system of philosophy is beginning to become an empty shell.

It seems to me that there is one category of phenomena where one can see this particularly clearly. All the great concepts in the history of philosophy have served the task of bringing absolute unity into the fragmented, chaotic plenitude of life. But, alongside each such concept, there also exists, or arises, another concept incompatible with the first. Thus these basic concepts appear as pairs of opposites, between which one is expected to make a choice. Any phenomenon which is incompatible with one concept must of necessity be compatible with the other: one must say Yea or Nay, there is no third way. To this category belong the antinomies of the finiteness and infinity of the universe; the mechanism and teleology of organisms; free will and determinism; phenomenon and noumenon; absolute and relative; truth and error; unity and multiplicity; progress and immutability of values in human evolution. It seems to me that a great number of these pairs of opposites no longer permit a clear decision to allocate any dubious case definitely to one concept or the other. This whole conceptual logic is felt to be so undesirably constricting, and at the same time its solutions are so rarely derived from any previously discovered third factor, but rather remain a challenge and a gap in our understanding, that this must surely indicate a profound philosophical crisis, one which brings all the specialized problems together in a general trend, albeit one which for the moment can only be negatively defined. The failure of the conceptual alternatives hitherto accepted as logically valid, and the demand for an as yet indefinable third possibility, make it more unmistakably clear than does anything else that our resources for mastering reality by giving it intellectual expression are no longer adequate to their task. They no longer accommodate what we wish to express, it transcends them, and seeks new forms, which as yet announce their arcane presence only as intuition or perplexity, desire or clumsy groping.

Perhaps the war, for all its destruction, confusion and danger, would not have had such a shattering effect had it not encountered cultural forms that were already so eroded and lacking in self-assurance. Here, also, what it has done is to make external reality give more scope and clarity to inner necessity. It has forced the individual to face the drastic decision as to whether he wishes to keep intellectual life on the old beaten track at any price, or whether he has the courage to seek new paths through the new terrain of life, whatever the risk, or whether perhaps he shall attempt what is even more perilous: to salvage the values of the former life from the collapse of their forms and carry them over into the new life. And here, at least, we can perhaps already discern the quest for a universal interpretation of life, even if as yet feeble and blurred: an illuminating basic concept, which I shall attempt to indicate in due course, which might make possible a continuity between the values of yesterday and those of tomorrow.

With more tangible significance, contemporary experience appears to play a part in the other cultural development, the elevation of means to ends in themselves. This modification of the teleological sequence has occurred, above all, in a sphere which provides the most far-reaching example in world history of the superimposition of means upon ends: the economic sphere. This example, it need scarcely be said, is *money*: a medium of exchange and balancing of values which, apart from this mediating function, is totally devoid of value and meaning, an absolute nullity. And it is precisely money which, for the majority of men in our culture, has become the supreme end. It is the possession of money which tends to be the ultimate goal, however rationally unfounded, of all the purposive activity of this majority. True, the expansion of the economy makes this dislocation of values understandable. For since it has ensured that any commodity can be obtained at any place and any time, the satisfaction of most human desires depends solely on possessing the required amount of money. In the mind of modern man, to be in need means not to be in need of material goods, but only of the money to buy them. The exclusion of Germany from the world market, which used to supply it with whatever quantities of goods were desired (making consumption purely a question of money) has brought about a most revolutionary change. Food, which used to be freely accessible provided one had money, has become scarce and its provision unreliable, and this has re-established its status as an absolute value. Money, on the other hand, which has at least forfeited its previous *unlimited* efficacy, can be seen to be in itself utterly powerless.

Even if this development is by no means complete, the bread ration-card at least symbolizes the uselessness of even the greatest wealth. In former times, the concepts of thrift and wastefulness, even when applied to particular material objects, only ever really referred to their monetary value. But now monetary value has become quite irrelevant. At last people are again being asked to economize with meat and butter, bread and wool, for the sake of these commodities themselves. This change may sound simple, but it totally reverses a sense of economic value which has been nurtured for centuries in the civilized world. A single gap has appeared in the most far-reaching example in the history of civilization of the concealment of what is really of value behind the means of obtaining it. There is, of course, no doubt that the gap will be closed again. The efficiency and omnipresence of the world economy will, in due course, make us forget that it is not money that is valuable, but things. Nobody will imagine that the grave consequences of this misconception will not reappear: the idea that everything has its price, the evaluation of things purely in terms of their monetary value, scepticism regarding any values that cannot be expressed in terms of money. The creeping crisis of culture arising from these attitudes will undoubtedly continue. But it is equally beyond doubt that the discovery that money is not what matters – is, indeed, of no use at all at the present time – will in a peculiar way jolt many people into reconsidering their attitudes. Such psychological moods and changes of mood cannot, of course, be documented. But however uncertain the consequences, and however superficial the occasion, for once a blow has been dealt to the absolute status of money value. For once it has been seen that money is no substitute for the value of economic commodities, and this mere fact in itself seems to me to be a profound psychological gain. A more sensitive, less blasé – I would even go so far as to say a more reverent – relationship to the commodities which we consume daily cannot but be felt by people who have been compelled for once to see their direct importance and the unimportance to which money is reduced the moment it ceases to function as a medium.

There is one further sense, and this time an absolute sense, in which the war reverses the relationship of ends and means. Self-preservation is customarily man's central concern. Work and love, thinking and volition, religious practices and our attempts to influence the course of our destiny: all these are aimed, by and large, at preserving the existence and development of the self, which are constantly threatened – by external danger and inner weakness, by our problematic relationships with the outside world, and by the insecurity of our material circumstances. Apart from those very rare people who really do devote their lives solely to an objective goal, the preservation of the self – which may include the selves of one's nearest and dearest – is *the* end, and all life the direct or indirect means to it. But, above this end, the war has, for millions of people, set the end of victory and the preservation of the nation, an end to which the individual life has all at once become a mere means, in respect of both its preservation and its sacrifice. The former appears even more important than the latter. The idea that a soldier goes into battle in order to sacrifice himself is emotionalism, and highly misleading. The fatherland is served not by dead soldiers, but by living ones. Where this service demands the sacrifice of life, this is, so to speak, an extreme case, which merely shows with maximum clarity that the self has lost its status as an ultimate end and, whether preserved or sacrificed, has declared itself a means to a higher end.

Of course, self-preservation will regain its old position at the head of the teleological series. But even so, one thing seems to me undeniable. The malaise of our culture, the elevation of everything that is relative and provisional into ultimate values, will not come about quite so easily in a generation which has seen for itself that it was possible even for self-preservation, usually the most autonomous of ultimate ends, to become a mere means to an end. From the very beginning of the war, there has been a prevalent feeling that, in an indefinite number of ways, it will bequeath to us a new scale of values; and in this one respect, at least, this will prove to be true. To attach ultimate significance to relatively secondary aspects of life is one of the psychological dangers of long periods of comfortable and undisturbed peace. They provide unrestricted scope for the greatest variety of activities; no violent upheavals compel men to make their choice between what is of primary and what is of secondary importance. But anyone who has once seen what is usually the most important thing in life – the self and its preservation – becomes a means to something higher, ought to be immune for a while to that squandering of end-status on what is relatively insignificant and peripheral.

These dangers which I have indicated converge, as if in a common symptom, in the fact that all the spheres of culture to which I have alluded have developed independently of and alien to one another – that is, until recent years, when, it is true, more unified overall tendencies have again become discernible. This is the reason for the much-discussed *lack of style* of our era. For style is always a general form which gives a common quality to a variety of individual artefacts of differing content. The more the spirit of the people (to use this problematic phrase for the sake of brevity) colours everything that is created during a particular period by virtue of its unity of character, the more style that period appears to us to have. That is why earlier centuries, which were not burdened with such an abundance of heterogeneous and infinitely seductive traditions and resources, had so much more style than the present, where in innumerable cases one individual activity is completely isolated from all others. True, in recent years, perhaps since Nietzsche, a certain change has begun here. The concept of *life* now seems to permeate a multitude of spheres and to have begun to give, as it were, a more unified rhythm to their heartbeat. I believe that the war will be very conducive to this process. For, apart from the common ultimate goal which contemporary cultural movements of all kinds have embraced, they are all suffused with a passionate vitality bursting forth as if from one common source of energy.

Countless forms which had begun to harden and become immune to creative dynamism have been drawn back into the stream of life. We suspected recently that all the diverse phenomena of culture were emanations or media, heartbeats or products of the process of life itself. Now all the aspects of our consciousness seem even more palpably to have been melted down and re-fused in the increased momentum of the stream of life. It seems certain that the soldier, at least when engaged in vigorous action, feels this action to be an enormous increase in the quantity of life, so to speak, and to be in more direct proximity to its surging dynamism than he is able to feel in his usual working activities. The supreme concentration of energy pervading the life of an entire nation does not allow that independent consolidation of its diverse elements which, in peacetime, sets up these elements of culture as separate, mutually alien entities, each obeying only its particular individual laws. There is a mysterious congruence in the fact that the immense events of our day came, in a way, at the right time to vindicate this incipient spiritual tendency to seek the unity of divergent phenomena in the depths of the life process itself. Of course, the experience of these events has no direct visible effect on the rifts and internal disparities in the moral, intellectual, religious and artistic spheres of our culture. And it is equally certain that, even if such an effect occurs, it will gradually fade away again in that tragic development which appears inevitable in highly developed objective cultures. But there is to my mind no doubt that, within these limits, the war does have this positive significance, on the *form* of our culture, notwithstanding its destruction of the substance of that culture. Not only have the common goal and the common danger given our people, as the sum total of its individuals, an unsuspected unity – regardless of how far it is permanent, how far only temporary. The unprecedented enhancement and excitement in the lives of each and every one of us has also promoted this fusion, this coming together in one single stream. And, likewise, it will for a while give a new dynamic impetus to the objective elements of culture, and thus new scope and encouragement to become reintegrated, to break out of that rigidity and insularity which had turned our culture into a chaos of disjointed individual elements devoid of any common style. As I have said, we shall not, in the long run, escape this tragedy and chronic crisis of all culture. But, for a certain period, its progress will be slowed down, its intensity tempered.

Faced with the ultimate paradoxes of cultural life, we cannot, however, hope for more than this. They are, indeed, developing as if towards a crisis, and thus towards strife and gloom to which we can see no end. That mere means are regarded as ultimate ends, completely distorting the rational order of both inner and practical life; that objective culture is developing to an extent and at a pace that leaves subjective culture, which alone gives significance to the perfection of objects, further and further behind; that the separate branches of culture are evolving in different directions towards mutual estrangement, that culture as a whole has already, in fact, suffered the fate of the Tower of Babel and its most profound value, which lies precisely in the integration of its parts, appears threatened with annihilation: all these things are paradoxes which are probably inseparable from the evolution of culture as such. Their ultimate logical consequence would be the continuation of this development to the point of destruction, if they were not repeatedly opposed by the positive and meaningful forces of culture, and if upheavals did not come from totally unsuspected quarters, which – often at a high price – temporarily bring cultural life, that is approaching total disintegration, to its senses.

The devastation of the war belongs, as far as we can see, to this category. It will, perhaps, once and for all remove some individual elements of contemporary culture, and create some new ones. But, as regards its effect on the fundamental inner form of all cultures, which at the summit of their development take the form of a permanent imminent crisis, it can inaugurate only a single scene or act of this endless drama. We can thus understand how this war, which seems to us to be the most momentous event since the French Revolution, with the most decisive implications for the future, can, in our prognosis, create these disparate consequences for our culture. On the one hand, it will remove certain things for ever and create certain entirely new things; but on the other hand, it will retard or reverse certain developments, which nonetheless seem inevitably certain to revert to their former course. The former relates to individual elements of culture, the latter to the innermost fate of its forms. Thus the merely relative and temporary quality of the latter effect does not in any way diminish the significance of the war for our culture. For this very quality integrates it into the fundamental rhythm – a tragic one, it is true – of culture, its constantly jeopardized balance, which can only be preserved by constant defensive action. Here, where it is a matter of the life of an entire form of culture, to expect any absolute, definitive solution (even within the limits of what is possible in a historical perspective) would do not more but less justice to that very life itself.

As I have said, the most basic comprehensive definition of the destiny of a highly developed culture is that it is a constant delayed crisis. I mean by this that its tendency is to cause life, in which it originates and which it is intended to serve, to disintegrate into futility and paradox. Again and again the fundamental dynamic unity of life defends itself against this tendency. Drawing on the very source of life itself, it reimposes unity on that objectivity which is alien to life and which estranges life from itself. And that is why we, in this era, stand at a high-water mark of history, because the disintegration and perversion of cultural life has reached an extreme, and life has risen in revolt against it in the shape of this war, with its unifying, simplifying and concentrated force. Even if this be only one wave in the infinite ocean of the life of mankind, no other wave has been raised to such a height and breadth by the friction of its forces. We stand deeply moved before the magnitude of this crisis, which it is utterly impossible for the individual to take the measure of. But, at the same time, the crisis is deeply familiar and intelligible to us. For in each of us it is, consciously or not, the crisis of our own soul.

THE FUTURE OF OUR CULTURE

As far as I can see, the reason for the apparent pessimism of the majority of philosophical minds regarding the present state of culture is the widening gulf between the culture of things and personal culture. As a result of the division of labour during the last few centuries, the technology at our service and the knowledge, arts, lifestyles and interests at our disposal have expanded to an unprecedented variety. But the individual's capacity to use this increased raw material as means of personal culture increases only very slowly and lags further and further behind. We can no longer absorb into our lives all those things, which multiply as if in obedience to an inexorable fate indifferent to us. They develop their own purely objective life, which we are almost entirely unable even to understand.

What the Ancient Greeks created in politics and science, strategy and scope for pleasure, had a sufficiently consistent style and simple structure to be grasped to some extent by any educated man. He could, without difficulty, make use of the sum total of objective culture to build up his own subjective culture. Thus they could both evolve in a harmony which, in the modern age, has been destroyed as they have become independent of each other. In our indescribably complex culture, individual ideas and achievements leave behind permanent forms in which the fruits of individual lives become independent of those lives. There are too many of them for the individual to absorb them all: their inevitable lack of a common style is enough to make this profoundly impossible. The subjectivism of modern personal life, its rootless, arbitrary character, is merely the expression of this fact: the vast, intricate, sophisticated culture of things, of institutions, of objectified ideas robs the individual of any consistent inner relationship to culture as a whole, and casts him back again on his *own* resources.

The real cultural malaise of modern man is the result of this discrepancy between the objective substance of culture, both concrete and abstract, on the one hand, and, on the other hand, the subjective culture of individuals who feel this objective culture to be something alien, which does violence to them and with which they cannot keep pace. In many quarters today there is a feeling that we are deficient in culture by comparison with the Athens of Pericles, or with Italy in the fifteenth and sixteenth centuries, or, indeed, with many less outstanding eras. But we are not lacking in any particular elements of culture. No increase in knowledge, literature, political achievements, works of art, means of communication or social manners can make good our deficiency. The possession of all these things does not, in itself, make a man cultured, any more than it makes him happy. Culture appears to me rather to lie in the relationship of the subjective spiritual energies concentrated and unified in the self to the realm of objective, historical or abstract values. A man is cultured when these objective values, of a spiritual or even of an external nature, become part of his personality in such a way that it advances beyond the 'natural' degree of perfection, that is, that which it can attain entirely by its own resources. Neither what we are purely in ourselves (be it the greatest ethical, intellectual, religious or other potential), nor the fruits of the labours of humanity by which we are surrounded (be they of overwhelming scope and perfection) can constitute the pinnacle of culture, but only the harmonious improvement of the former by the fruitful inward assimilation of the latter.

Throughout history, some eras have given greater emphasis to the task of increasing the elements of objective culture, others to that of enabling the individual to derive from that objective culture the subjective state of mind which is the ultimate purpose of culture. But the former has never been brought about by any explicit cultural policy as such, but always by the particular interests and energies of individual sections of society. On the contrary, the great eras that did have a cultural policy (even if not conceived or described as such) always concentrated on the subjective factor: the *education* of the *individual*. No cultural policy can eliminate the tragic discrepancy between objective culture, with its unlimited capacity for growth, and subjective culture, which can grow only slowly. But it can work towards reducing that discrepancy by enabling the individual to make better and more rapid use of the elements of objective culture in our lives as the raw material of subjective culture, which, when all is said and done, is the only thing that gives the former any real value.

THE CHANGE IN CULTURAL FORMS

The Marxist doctrine of economic development, according to which economic forces create a form of production in every historical period that is appropriate to them, and in which these forces grow to dimensions that no longer fit into this form, but rather destroy it and create a new one, is a doctrine that applies far beyond the economic sphere. Between life, flooding onward and expanding with ever greater energy, and the forms of its historical expression, there inevitably exists a conflict which fills the entire history of culture, even though of course it remains latent in some periods. At the present time, however, it appears to me to be fully operating in the case of a large number of cultural forms.

When artistic Naturalism had extended itself towards the end of the previous century, then this was a sign that the dominant cultural forms inherited from Classicism could no longer accommodate life as it pressed for expression. The hope emerged of being able to locate the given realities of this life in the unmediated image, if possible without the intervention of any human intention. Naturalism, however, has failed with respect to the decisive needs just as much, probably, as Expressionism does now, which has replaced the unmediated image of the object with the emotional process and its equally unmediated expression. By extending inner agitation into an external creation, without consideration, so to speak, of the latter's own form and the objective norms applicable to it, people believed they could gain a completely adequate expression for life that was not falsified by any form external to it. It seems to be the nature of inner life, however, that it always finds its expression only in forms that have a regularity, a meaning and a strength in themselves, in a certain detachment and independence with respect to the emotional dynamics that created them. Creative life constantly produces something which is not itself life, something on which it somehow peters out, something which raises its own opposing legal claim. It cannot express itself except in forms that are, and signify, something for themselves independently of life.

This contradiction is the real and constant tragedy of culture. The success of genius and of favourably endowed epochs is that, from the upwelling of inner life, creation receives a favourably harmonious form which preserves life within itself for at least a while and does not rigidify, as it were, into a hostile autonomy. In the great majority of cases, however, such a contradiction is inevitable and where the expression of life, in order to avoid this contradiction, offers itself, as it were, in a nakedness free from form, absolutely nothing that is actually comprehensible results, except an unarticulated speech but no pronouncement and, instead of the admittedly contradictory and strange obduracy of a unified form, ultimately only a chaos of atomized fragments of form. Futurism has advanced to this extreme consequence of our artistic situation: the passionate will to express itself of a life that can no longer be accommodated in the traditional forms, has not yet found new ones and hence seeks its pure possibility in the negation of form – or in an almost tendentious and abstruse form – by entering into opposition to the essence of creativity, in order to avoid the other contradiction that lies within itself. It is perhaps nowhere more completely apparent than that, in some phenomena of Futurism, the forms which life has built once more as a home for itself have become a prison.

How things stand with regard to religion can perhaps not be determined since what is decisive here does not occur in visible phenomena, but rather within the inwardness of the soul. To what extent Christianity is still the form in which religious life finds its completely adequate expression must therefore be set aside. All that can be observed is that there are indeed some circles whose religious needs turn away from Christianity. That they turn to all sorts of exotic imports or peculiar innovations seems to have no significance whatsoever. Nowhere can I detect a really viable living structure here, one that would fit religious life as an exact expression, except in totally individual combinations.

On the other hand, it is true of the general situation of culture that, here too, one frequently rejects any shaping of this life and that a supra-sectarian mysticism exerts the predominant attraction in such circles. For in mysticism the religious soul wishes to live out its life without any mediation, whether it be without the mediation of any dogma, standing naked, as it were, before God; or whether it be that even the conception of God is still experienced as a rigid entity and an inhibition, and the soul considers only its most personal, metaphysical life – no longer couched in any form of belief – to be that which is actually religious. In a manner analogous to those Futurist phenomena referred to earlier, this completely formless mysticism signifies the historical moment in which an inner life can no longer fit into the forms of its previous design, and, because it is incapable of creating other and more appropriate forms, believes it should be able to exist without any forms at all.

Within the development of philosophy this crisis seems to me to be more far-reaching than is generally admitted. The fundamental concepts and methodological functions, cultivated since classical Greek antiquity, that have been applied to the material of the world in order to form philosophical worldviews of it, in my opinion, have achieved, all that they can yield in this respect. The philosophical drive, whose expression they were, has been developed within them in directions, emotions and needs, to which those forms are no longer appropriate. If outward appearances are not deceptive, then the entire philosophical apparatus is beginning to turn into a shell from which life has been emptied.

This seems to me to be especially evident in one type of phenomenon. Each of the major categories in the history of philosophy has the task of bringing the fragmentary and chaotic fullness of existence into an absolute unity. At the same time, however, alongside each individual category there exists, or comes to exist, another one which is mutually excluded from it. Thus, these fundamental concepts appear in pairs, as alternatives demanding a decision in each case, in such a way that where one concept fails with a phenomenon, the other must apply to it, as a yes and no that leaves no room for any third option. Such are the polarities of finiteness and infiniteness of the world, mechanism and teleology of the organism, freedom and determinism of the will, phenomenon and thing-in-itself, absolute and relative, truth and error, singularity and plurality, or progress in values and constancy of values in human development. Now it seems to me that a great many of these alternatives no longer leave space for the absolute decision that assigns each questionable conceptual element to one category or the other. We sense such an inappropriate constraint in this conceptual logic; on the other hand, the breakdown of these alternatives seldom results from an already discovered third way – rather, they continue to exist as demands and unfilled gaps. This state of affairs therefore indeed betrays a far-reaching philosophical crisis which gathers the specialized problems into a general tendency, albeit one that at first would have to be characterized negatively. I shall briefly discuss some of these problems.

With regard to the determination of the life of the will by freedom or by necessity, one can probably consider the arguments for either side exhausted, without having thereby solved the problem. Alongside theoretically ascertained and natural law-like determination there is an undeniable feeling that this does not quite add up; there is the opposition of an inner reality of some type or other – which has recently concentrated itself into a theoretical assertion of freedom once again. But the latter seems to me in many ways to have the drawback of contenting itself with the simple demonstration that mechanical necessity cannot be valid for our will – and this is impartially considered to be the proof of freedom. But considering the serious reservations against the assertion of freedom as well, should this alternative really be absolute? Should the will not be able to take its course in a form that is beyond this Either–Or, a form for which, of course, we have no theoretical expression?

The great Kantian solution seems more an intellectual possibility than an expression of the real inner state of affairs from which the problem originates in the first place. In so far as Kant separates freedom and necessity into two different classes of existence – necessity to the perceivable phenomenon and freedom to the unknowable in-itself of our existence – he in fact eliminates their competition around us as subjects, but from the duality of the human subject which he accomplishes, the latter itself knows nothing at precisely the point where the problem comes up. Fundamentally, the problem is more circumvented than solved with the duality of the phenomenal self and the I-in-itself with which each of the two claims was supposed to be satisfied. For life, which finds its real expression neither by determinacy nor by freedom, is a unified entity whose problems and conflicts that arise out of it as a unity cannot in fact be solved by an *initio in partes*. For Kant's logical–conceptual interest, it was much more the concepts of freedom and necessity that were the primary problematic element than the life that gave birth to them, and that is why he divided this life in two without reservations, in order to mediate between the conflict of the concepts as such. It seems to me, however, that their seamless integration has begun to crumble and that, out of the rupture, a demand or a vague intuition arises – it is no more than that yet – namely, that the essential form of our will is something beyond both necessity and freedom, and is some third entity that does not submit to this alternative.

The opposition between unity and plurality seems to me to be equally inadequate when it undertakes to interpret the nature of an organism with a soul. The dualism of body and soul, for the crudest as well as the most refined forms of which there are ultimately always two fundamentally different 'substances', can probably be considered to have been overcome. The speculations, of course, which would draw the 'unity' of the two from the ultimate depths of profundity, have not been able to provide convincing power for any kind of positive image; that has been done only by the fact that this duality is unbearable. Perhaps one may be able to say that it is *one* life from which physical and mental existence produce themselves as its vital pulses. The fact that this life in an internal sense is a unity is no more prejudiced than is the concept of *one* world decisive as to whether the world should be conceived of as monistic or as pluralistic.

There are actually only two ultimate possibilities for solution when two strictly mutually self-exclusive concepts claim to determine any object. The objective solution discovers within the object itself a duality of existence, sides and meaning, so that each of the two contradictory concepts can find undisturbed application. The subjective solution allows the object to remain in complete unity and explains the two concepts by claiming them to be two different viewpoints from which it can be considered. Both procedures cancel out the competition of concepts, but obviously in some cases the problem is more avoided than given a real solution. And to these cases there seems to me to belong the issue as to whether the physical and mental phenomenon represents a unity or a duality.

The difficulty lies in the fact that the accentuated rejection of duality logically seems to leave only unity as an alternative, but that in so doing this does not conform to the actual picture. For we do not really gain anything if we proclaim the human being to be the unity of the mental and the physical. The visual artist may succeed in presenting the living human form as a purely unified vision. For the cognitive imagination, however, the physical and the mental ultimately lie so far apart that the concept of unity remains a mere word, a schema that is wrapped around the two, but without thereby overcoming their inner estrangement. I would therefore like to maintain that neither duality nor unity adequately expresses their relationship and that thus we still possess no conceptual formulation at all for this relationship. And this is notable because unity and duality logically contradict one another so strongly that each relationship of elements must necessarily succumb to the one if the other is negated by it. Nonetheless, even this alternative is now precarious for us; it has done its duty, as it were, and we demand for the nature of life, in so far as it is both physical and mental, an expression of form of which we have so far been unable to say anything other than that it will be a third entity beyond the apparent and hitherto compelling alternative.

Nowhere is it clearer that our means for mastering the content of life by intellectual expression are no longer sufficient than in the failure of the previously valid conceptual alternatives and the demand for a still unformulated third way. Nowhere is it clearer that what we wish to express no longer fits into these conceptual pairs, but rather bursts them asunder and seeks new forms which, for the moment, announce their secret presence only as an intimation or an uninterpreted facticity, as a desire or as difficult tentative trials.

Notes to Part II

1. I have presented them in my *Philosophy of Money* for a considerable number of historically concrete fields.

2. Life is the opposite of form, but obviously an entity can be conceptually described only if it has a form of some sort. Hence the term 'life', in the very fundamental sense meant here, is inevitably somewhat vague and logically imprecise. Life precedes or transcends all forms, and to succeed in giving a conceptual definition of it would be to deny its essence. Life can become conscious of itself only directly, by virtue of its own dynamism, not via the stratum of mediating concepts, which coincides with the realm of forms.

PART III
CULTURE OF INTERACTION

SOCIOLOGY OF THE SENSES

The current developmental stage of the social sciences appears to correspond to that of the sciences of organic life when they were characterized by the commencement of microscopic investigation. If investigation had hitherto been limited to the large and definitely separated organs, whose differences in form and function revealed themselves directly, then from that point on, the life process now revealed itself first in its ties to its smallest elements, the cells, and in its identity with the innumerable and ceaseless interactions between these cells. How they adhere to one another or destroy each other, how they assimilate or chemically influence one another – only this gradually permits one to see how the body shapes, maintains or changes its form. The major organs, in which these fundamental elements of life and their interactions group together into macroscopically perceptible special structures and functions – heart and lung, stomach and kidney, brain and organs of movement – would never have made the nexus of life comprehensible if those innumerable events, taking place between the smallest elements, which, as it were, are only held together by the macroscopic elements of life, had not been revealed as the genuine and fundamental basis of life.

Now, social science generally is still situated in this stage of being able to consider only the very large and clearly visible social structures and of trying to be able to produce insight from these into social life in its totality. States and trade unions, priesthoods and family forms, guild and factory structures, class formation and the industrial division of labour – these and similar major organs and systems appear to constitute society and to fill out the domain of the science of society. In fact, however, these are already structures of a higher order, in which or to which, as it were, from one instance to another, the real concrete life of sociated individuals is crystallized. And aside from the connecting forms that are elevated to the level of those comprehensive organizations, this pulsating life which links human beings together displays countless other ones, which, as it were, remain in a fluid, transitory condition, but are no less agents connecting individuals to social existence.

The fact that people look at and are jealous of one another, that they write each other letters or have lunch together, that they have sympathetic or antipathetic contacts, quite removed from any tangible interests, that one person asks another for directions and that people dress up and adorn themselves for one another – all the thousands of relations from person to person, momentary or enduring, conscious or unconscious, fleeting or momentous, from which the above examples are taken quite at random, continually bind us together. On every day, at every hour, such threads are spun, dropped, picked up again, replaced by others or woven together with them. Herein lie the interactions between the atoms of society, accessible only to psychological microscopy, which support the entire tenacity and elasticity, the entire variety and uniformity of this so evident and yet so puzzling life of society.

The real life of society, provided in experience, could certainly not be constructed from those large objectivized structures that constitute the traditional objects of social science. It would break apart into a number of different systems, just as if a person consisted only of the large, differentiated and immediately recognizable organs and all the innumerable, diverse and complicated cellular processes, that have only been revealed by the microscope, were missing.

In the historical as well as in the natural sciences, the effort has arisen everywhere to conceive of the gradual summation of very diverse and individually scarcely perceptible influences as the real causes of actual developments, in the place of catastrophic upheavals and comprehensive uniform forces that determine the totality of circumstances and their changes. The following investigation is based upon the belief that, in sociology too, the corresponding procedure will trace the reality of the object of investigation more exactly and profoundly than the mere treatment of large and absolutely supra-individual total structures. It aims to pursue the meanings that mutual sensory perception and influencing have for the social life of human beings, their coexistence, cooperation and opposition.

That we get involved in interactions at all depends on the fact that we have a sensory effect upon one another. While this was generally accepted as a self-evident, uniform fact that required no further discussion, a more acute observation shows that these sensory impressions, running from one person to another, in no way serve merely as the common foundation and precondition for social relationships, beyond which the contents and distinctive features of those relationships arise for quite different causes. Rather, every sense delivers contributions characteristic of its individual nature to the construction of sociated existence; peculiarities of the social relationship correspond to the nuancing of its impressions; the prevalence of one or the other sense in the contact of individuals often provides this contact with a sociological nuance that could otherwise not be produced.

The fact that we perceive our fellow human beings at all through our senses itself develops in two directions, whose cooperation is of fundamental sociological importance. Impinging on the human subject, the sensory impression of a person provokes feelings of like and dislike in us, of our own exaltation or degradation, of excitement or composure, from his or her look or the tone of his or her voice, from his or her mere physical presence in the same room. All of this does not serve the recognition or determination of the other person; I am the only one who feels good or the opposite when he or she is there and I see him or her. This reaction to the person's sensory presence leaves them, as it were, outside.

The development of the sense impression extends in the other direction as soon as it becomes a means of knowledge of the other: what I see, hear or feel of the person is now only the bridge over which I get to them as my object. The speech sound and its meaning constitute perhaps the clearest example. Just as the voice of a person has a quite directly attractive or repulsive effect on us, independently of what the person says; just as, on the other hand, what the person says helps us to attain knowledge, not only of their momentary thoughts, but also of their spiritual being, the same is probably true with regard to all sense impressions: they lead us into the human subject as its mood and emotion and out to the object as knowledge of it. With respect to non-human objects, these two tend to be widely separated. In their sensory presence we may emphasize their subjective emotional value: we experience the scent of the rose, the loveliness of a sound, the attraction of the branches swaying in the wind as a joy occurring inside our spirit. Or we want to recognize the rose or the tone or the tree – for this we employ quite different energies, often deliberately turning away from the former. What mutually alternates here, more or less out of context, is usually woven into a unity with respect to a person. Our sense impressions of them cause their emotional value, on the one hand, and, on the other, their use for an instinctive or desired knowledge of them to become co-operatively, and in practical terms inseparably, the foundation of our relationship to that person. Of course, to a very different degree, both factors – the sound of a voice and the content of what was said, the appearance and its psychological interpretation, the attractiveness or repulsiveness of the person's atmosphere, and the instinctive conclusion from all this to their spiritual coloration and sometimes their cultural level – these two developments of sense impressions, to a very different degree and in very different mixtures, build on our relationship to them.

Among the individual sensory organs, the eye is destined for a completely unique sociological achievement: the connection and interaction of individuals that lies in the act of individuals looking at one another. This is perhaps the most direct and the purest interaction that exists. Where sociological threads are spun elsewhere, they tend to have an objective content or to produce an objective form. Even the spoken and heard word has an objective meaning, which, if need be, could be transmitted in a different way. The extremely lively interaction, however, into which the look from one eye to another weaves people together, does not crystallize in any objective structure, but rather the unity that it creates between them remains directly suspended in the event and in the function. And this connection is so strong and delicate that it can only be supported by the

shortest line – the straight line between the eyes – and the smallest deviation from this line, the slightest sideways glance, destroys the uniqueness
of this connection completely. Here, to be sure, no objective trace remains
left behind, as is otherwise always the case, directly or indirectly, for all
types of relationship between human beings; the interaction dies in the
moment in which the immediacy of the function lapses. Yet the whole interaction between human beings, their empathy and antipathy, their intimacy
and their coolness, would be changed incalculably if the look from one eye
into another did not exist – which, compared with the simple seeing or
observation of the other person, signifies a new and incomparable relationship between them.

The closeness of this relationship is supported by the remarkable fact that
the look directed at the other person and perception of them is in itself
expressive, and is so precisely in the manner in which one looks at the other
person. One reveals oneself in the look that receives the other into oneself;
in the same act with which the human subject seeks to recognize its object,
it surrenders itself to the object. One cannot take through the eye without
at the same time giving. The eye reveals to the other the soul that he or she
seeks to reveal. Since this obviously occurs only during the direct look from
one eye into another, the most complete reciprocity in the entire sphere of
human relationships is achieved here.

Only from all this does it become completely comprehensible why shame
causes us to look at the ground and avoid the other's look. This is certainly
not merely the case because in this way we can at least avoid finding out
sensorily that, and to what extent, the other is watching us in such an embarrassing situation. Rather, the deeper reason is that lowering my gaze
deprives the other of the possibility of finding out about me. The look into
the eyes of the other person not only helps me to know him or her, but also
him or her to know me; along the line which connects both sets of eyes, one's
own personality, mood and impulse is carried to the other. The 'ostrich
tactic' has an actual practicality in this directly sensory and sociological
relationship: whoever does not look at the other party really does remove
him or herself to a certain extent from being seen. The human being is by
no means already totally present for the other, when the latter sees him or
her, but only when he or she also sees the former.

However, the sociological significance of the eye depends primarily upon
the expressive meaning of the *face*, which offers itself as the first object of
the gaze between one person and another. People are seldom sufficiently
aware of the extent to which even the most practical aspects of our relationships depend on reciprocal knowledge – not just in the sense of all external
things, or of the momentary intentions and mood of the other. Rather, what
we know consciously or instinctively of a person's being, of their inner foundations, of the unchangeability of their nature, all of this inevitably colours
our momentary as well as our lasting relationship to them.

The face, however, is the geometrical site of all this knowledge; it is the
symbol of everything that an individual has brought with him or her as the

prerequisite of their life. In it is deposited that which has dropped from his past to the bottom of his life and has become permanent features in the individual. In so far as we perceive the face of a person in such a significance, no matter how much it serves the purposes of practice, a supra-practical element comes into the interaction: the face brings about a situation in which a person is already being understood from his or her appearance, and not first from their actions. The face, viewed as an organ of expression is, as it were, of a completely theoretical nature. It does not *act,* like the hand, the foot or the entire body, it never supports the inner or practical behaviour of people, but rather it only *tells* others about it.

The specific sociologically significant type of 'knowing' that is mediated by the eye is determined by the fact that the face is the essential object of inter-individual seeing. This knowing (*Kennen*) is still something different from recognizing (*Erkennen*). To a certain, though very varying, extent we know with whom we are dealing from our first glance at someone. That we generally do not become conscious of this and its fundamental significance is due to the fact that we immediately direct our attention beyond this self-evident basis to the recognizability of particular features and of unique elements that determine in detail our practical behaviour towards that person. Yet if one attempts, however, to press forward this self-evidentness into consciousness, then it is astonishing how much we know about a person from the first look at them. This is nothing that can be expressed conceptually or is analysable into individual characteristics. We can perhaps not at all say whether that person seems stupid or intelligent, kind-hearted or malicious, temperamental or indolent to us. Rather, all of these qualities, recognizable in the common sense of that term, are *general* characteristics which the person shares with innumerable others. But what this first sight of that person conveys to us cannot be dissolved or transposed into such conceptual and expressible things – although it always remains the key to all subsequent knowledge of that person – rather, it is the immediate grasping of the person's individuality as betrayed by their appearance, above all their face. And here it is in principle unimportant that mistakes and adjustments also frequently occur in this process.

By offering us the visually most complete symbolism of lasting inwardness and of everything which our individual experiences have deposited in the permanent foundation of our natures, the face also gives way to the highly changeable situations of the moment. Here something emerges which is quite distinctive in the sphere of the human being: the fact that the general, supra-singular nature of the individual is always represented in the special nuancing of a momentary mood, fulfilment or impulsiveness. It is the fact that what is uniform and fixed as well as what is fluid and varied within our soul becomes visible as absolute simultaneity, as it were, the one always in the form of the other. The most extreme sociological contrast between the eye and the ear lies in the fact that the latter only offers us a revelation of the human being within the temporal form and the former only the lasting element of the person's nature, the precipitation of their past in the

substantial form of their features, so that, as it were, we see the succession
of their life in simultaneity before us.

This is the reason why the sociological mood of a blind person is quite
different from that of a deaf one. For the blind person, the other person
exists only in succession, in the temporal succession of their utterances. The
restless, disturbing simultaneity of all essential traits, the traces of all past
experience, as it lies revealed in the faces of people, elude the blind person,
and this may be the reason for the peaceful and calm mood, the uniform
friendliness towards the surroundings, which is so often observed among the
blind. It is precisely the multiplicity of what the face *can* reveal which often
makes it puzzling; in general, what we *see* of a person is interpreted by what
we *hear*, while the reverse is much more rare. That is why the person who
sees without hearing is generally much more confused, helpless and disturbed than one who hears without being able to see.

A sociologically very interesting compensation for this difference in performance is offered by our much greater ability to recall what has been
heard than what has been seen, despite the fact that what a person has said
is irredeemable as such, whereas a person presents themselves to the eye as
a relatively stable object. For this reason alone, it is much easier to lie to the
ear of a person than it is to their eye, and it is obvious that the entire nature
of human intercourse is supported by this structure of our senses and their
objects, to the extent that our fellow human beings offer such objects to
them. If the words we hear did not immediately disappear from our ear –
which it retains, however, in the form of memory – if the persistence of the
face and its meaning did not offer itself to the visual sense, which lacks the
reproductive strength of the auditory sense, then our inter-individual life
would rest on a totally different foundation. It would be idle speculation to
imagine this different being, but the fact that its possibility in principle is
realized frees us from the dogma that the human sociation which we know
is a completely self-evident one, beyond discussion, as it were, for the nature
of which there just are not any *special* causes.

Historical research has eliminated this dogma with regard to the individual major social forms. We know that our familial constitution as well as
our economic form, our law as well as our customs, are results of conditions
which were different elsewhere and therefore had other consequences. We
know that with these actualities we are by no means standing on the deepest
foundation, on which the given is the absolutely necessary, one which can
no longer be understood as a special formation from special causes. With
reference to the quite general sociological functions taking place between
one person and another, however, this question has not yet been raised. The
primary, immediate relationships, which then determine all the higher structures, appear to be so integral to the nature of society in general as to cause
one to fail to see that they are only integral to the nature of human beings;
they therefore demand an explanation drawn from the special conditions of
human beings. What I am presenting here is only one attempt of this type
to openly reveal certain form-creating factors in the mere structure of our

sensory function for the simple everyday relations as well as the complex circumstances of human beings.

The contrast between the eye and the ear, whose sociological significance has just been outlined, is clearly the extension of the dual role which the eye appears to have designated for itself. Just as all the meaning of reality always divides into the categories of being and becoming, so they also dominate what one person can perceive or wants to perceive of another. We want to know: what is this person according to his or her being, what is the lasting substance of his or her nature? What are they like at the present moment, what do they want, what are they thinking and saying?

This largely determines the division of labour between the senses. If we discount a large number of modifications, then what we see of a person is the lasting part of them; as in a section through geological strata, the history of their life and what it is based upon as the timeless dowry of nature are revealed in their face. The variations in facial expression do not correspond to the diversity of differentiation of that which we ascertain with our ears. What we hear is a person's momentary character, the flow of their nature. Only all manner of secondary knowledge and conclusions reveal to us the mood of the moment, even in a person's expressions, or their unchanging aspects in their words. In all other nature as revealed to immediate sense impressions, that which is lasting and flowing is distributed in a much more one-sided way than among human beings. The permanent stone and the flowing stream are the polar symbols of this one-sidedness. Only the human being is at the same time always something lasting and something flowing away for our senses, in which both have developed a level in the human being and where the one measures itself against the other and expresses itself in it. The formation of this duality is engaged in an interaction with that of the eye and the ear: for even though neither of them completely closes itself off from the perceptions of both categories, they are nevertheless in general constructed for mutual supplementation, for the ascertaining of the lasting and plastic nature of the human being by the eye and of the more delicately undulating utterances by the ear.

Viewed sociologically, the ear is further distinguished from the eye by the absence of that reciprocity which the look produces between one eye and another. According to its very nature, the eye cannot take without simultaneously giving, whereas the ear is the egoistic organ pure and simple, which only takes, but does not give; its external formation seems almost to symbolize this, in so far as it seems to be a somewhat passive appendage of the human appearance, and by being the most immovable organ of the human head. It pays for this egoism in that it cannot turn away or close itself, like the eye; rather, since it only takes, it is condemned to take everything that comes into its vicinity – a fact which will reveal sociological consequences. Only in conjunction with the mouth and with language, does the ear produce that inwardly uniform act of taking and giving – but even this only in alternation, since one can neither speak properly while listening nor listen properly while speaking, whereas the eye fuses both in the miracle of the 'look'.

On the other hand, the formal egoism of the ear is confronted by its peculiar relationship with respect to the objects of private property. In general, one can possess only the 'visible' whereas that which is only audible is already past in the moment of its present and provides no 'property'. A curious exception to this occurred during the seventeenth and eighteenth centuries when noble families sought to own musical pieces, which were written only for them, and were not permitted to be published. A number of Bach's concertos were produced as a result of such a commission from a prince. Owning musical pieces that were withheld from all others was considered part of the nobility of a house. There is something perverse in this for our sentiments, because hearing is by its very nature supra-individual; what happens in a room must be heard by all who are present there, and the fact that one person receives it does not deprive another of it. This is also the origin of the special, unique mental emphasis that something spoken possesses, even though it is nonetheless actually intended exclusively for a single person. Innumerable people would be able to hear physically what one person says to another, if only they were present. The fact that the content of some speech expressly excludes this formal sensory possibility thereby bestows upon every such communication an incomparable sociological coloration.

There is almost no secret that *could* be transmitted exclusively by the eyes. Transmission via the ear, however, actually incorporates a contradiction. It forces a form that is intrinsically and sensorily directed towards an unlimited number of participants to serve a content that completely excludes all of them. This is the peculiarly pointed aspect of the orally transmitted secret, of a person-to-person conversation before many eyes, namely, that it expressly denies the sensory character of the spoken word, which contains the physical possibility of countless listeners. Under normal circumstances, it is never possible for all or very many people to have one and the same facial expression, whereas an extraordinarily large number can have the same auditory impression. Let us compare a museum audience to a concert audience: the determination of an auditory impression to communicate itself uniformly and evenly to a crowd of people – a determination that is by no means only external or quantitative, but profoundly connected to its inmost nature – connects a concert audience sociologically into an incomparably closer unity and commonality of mood than is the case among the visitors to a museum.

Where, exceptionally, the eye also provides such an identity of impression for a great number of people, then the communalizing sociological effect also occurs. The fact that all people can simultaneously see the sky and the sun is, I believe, an essential element of the union which every religion implies. For each religion somehow turns, in its origin or form, to the sky or the sun and has some sort of relationship to these all-encompassing and world-dominating entities. The fact that a sense which in practical life is so exclusive as the eye, which even somehow modifies what is simultaneously seen for each person by means of the diversity of the viewpoint, nonetheless does indeed have a content – the sky, the sun, the stars – that is absolutely not exclusive, and which offers itself uniformly to everyone. This fact must foster, on the one hand, that transcendence from the narrowness and particularity of the human subject which every religion contains and, on the other, support or favour the element of a union of the faithful, which every religion likewise contains.

The diverse relationships of the eye and ear to their objects, that have been emphasized so far sociologically, foster very different relationships between individuals whose association depends on the one or the other sense. The workers in a factory workshop, the students in an auditorium, the soldiers in a battalion somehow feel themselves to be a unity. And even if their unity springs from supernatural factors, its character is still partially determined by the fact that its essential sense is the eye, that the individuals see each other during the communalizing processes but cannot speak. In this case, the consciousness of unity will have a much more abstract character than if the association also includes spoken communication. Alongside the individual aspect of a person, that is invested in their external appearance, the eye reveals that which is *alike* in all people much more than does the ear. The ear transmits the wealth of divergent moods of individuals, the flow and the momentary external expression of thoughts and impulses, the entire polarity of subjective as well as objective life. It is infinitely easier to form a general conception of human beings whom we only see than if we could speak with each of them. The general imperfection of sight also favours this difference. Only a very few people are able say with certainty even what colour the eyes of their friends are or to imagine the shape of mouth of their loved ones in visual terms. They have never really seen these things; one obviously *sees* much more of what a person has in common with others than one can *hear* this general aspect in them.

To the extent that the techniques of the senses are effective, the immediate production of very abstract, unspecific social structures is thus most favoured by visual proximity with a lack of conversational proximity. According to what was indicated above, this constellation has greatly fostered the emergence of the modern concept of the 'worker'. This enormously powerful concept, which embraces that which is common to all wage labourers, whether they make cannons or toys, was inaccessible to previous centuries, whose guilds were often much closer and more intimate, because they were essentially based on personal and spoken communication, but lacked the factory workshop or the mass meeting. Only there, where one saw innumerable people without hearing them, did there occur that high abstraction of everything that is common to all of them, which is often hampered in its growth by all the individual, concrete and variable material which the ear transmits to us.

Compared with the sociological significance of sight and hearing, that of the lower senses is of secondary importance, although not so small in the case of smell as the peculiar vagueness and undevelopment of its impressions would erroneously lead us to assume. There is no doubt that every person perfumes their surrounding layer of air in a characteristic way, and it is essential to the resulting scent impression that, of the two developments of sense impressions – towards the subject, as liking or disliking of it, and towards the object, as recognition of it – it causes the first to predominate by far over the second. Smell does not form an object on its own, as do sight and hearing, but remains, as it were, captive in the human subject, which is symbolized in the fact that there exist no independent, objectively characterizing expressions for fine distinctions. If we say, 'it smells sour', then this only means that it smells the way something smells which tastes sour.

The impressions of the sense of smell resist description with words to quite a different extent than do those of the two former senses; they cannot be projected onto the level of abstraction. And there is that much less resistance from thinking and volition to the instinctive antipathies and sympathies that are attached to the olfactory sphere surrounding people, and which, for instance, often have significant consequences for the sociological relationship of two races living in the same territory. The reception of the Negro in higher social circles of North America is out of the question by reason of the body odour of the Negro, and the often vague aversion between Germanic peoples and Jews has been ascribed to the same cause. Personal contact between educated people and workers often so vigorously advocated for the social development of the present, the *rapprochement* of the two worlds 'of which the one does not know how the other lives' also advocated by the educated classes as an ethical ideal, fails simply because of the insuperability of impressions of smell. If it were demanded as being in the moral and social interest, many members of the higher strata would certainly make considerable sacrifices in personal comfort, would forego many privileges and pleasures in favour of the dispossessed, and the fact that this is not yet happening is certainly owing to the fact that the proper forms for this have not yet been found. But people would be a thousand times likelier to tolerate such renunciations and sacrifices than physical contact with people to whom 'the sweat of honest toil' clings. The social question is not only an ethical one, but also a question of smell (*eine Nasenfrage*).

It is a fact, with a significance for social culture that has not yet been appropriately appreciated, that the perceptual acuity of all the senses evidently sinks as culture becomes more refined, whereas its emphasis upon liking and disliking rises. Indeed, I believe that the heightened sensibility in this direction generally brings much more suffering and repulsion than joys and attractions in its wake. The modern person is shocked by innumerable things, and innumerable things appear intolerable to their senses which less differentiated, more robust modes of feeling would tolerate without any such reaction. The individualizing tendency of modern human beings and the greater personalization and freedom of choice of a person's commitments must be connected to this. With his or her sometimes directly sensual and sometimes aesthetic mode of reacting, the person cannot immediately enter into traditional unions or close commitments in which no one enquires into their personal taste or their personal sensibility. And this inevitably brings with it a greater isolation and a sharper circumscribing of the personal sphere. This development is perhaps most remarkable in the sense of smell; the efforts of the present to secure greater hygiene and cleanliness are as much the cause as the effect of this.

In general, with the increase in culture, the long-distance effects of the senses become weaker and their local effects become stronger; we become not only short-sighted but short-sensed in general; yet at these short distances, we become that much more sensitive. Now, from the outset, the olfactory sense is already adapted to short distances by comparison to sight and hearing, and if we can no longer objectively perceive as much with it as do many primitive peoples, then we react that much more sensitively to its impressions. Here, too, the tendency within which this occurs is the one indicated previously, but it also does so to a higher degree than with the other senses; a person with a particularly delicate nose certainly experiences much more displeasure than joy from *this* refinement.

There is, in addition, the following, which further amplifies that isolating repulsion which we owe to the refinement of the senses. By smelling something, we draw this impression or this radiating object more deeply into ourselves, into the centre of our being: we assimilate it, so to speak, by the vital process of breathing more intimately with ourselves than is possible with respect to an object by any other sense – unless it is the case that we eat it. Smelling a person's body odour is the most intimate perception of them; they penetrate, so to speak, in a gaseous form into our most sensory inner being, and it is obvious that, with an enhanced sensitivity to olfactory impressions in general, this must lead to a selection and a distancing that to some extent creates one of the sensory foundations for the sociological reserve of the modern individual. It is characteristic that a person possessing such a fanatically exclusive individualism as Nietzsche conspicuously often says of the human types which he hates: 'They do not smell good'.

If the other senses build a thousand bridges between human beings, if they are always able to reconcile the repulsion they cause with attractions, if the interweaving of their positive and their negative emotional values gives the overall concrete relationships between human beings their particular colouring – then, by contrast, one can characterize the sense of smell as the dissociating sense. Not only because it transmits many more repulsions than attractions, not only because its decisions possess a certain radical and unappealable quality, which is very difficult to overcome with the decisions of other sensory or intellectual instances, but also because the assembly of many people never provides it with any of the attractions of the type that such situations can develop for the other senses, at least under certain conditions. Indeed, in general, shocks to the sense of smell will be directly quantitatively proportional to the mass of people in the midst of which they strike us. Already through this refinement alone, as we stated earlier, cultural refinement points to individualizing isolation, at least in cooler countries, whereas the opportunity of holding assemblies essentially outdoors, that is, without such olfactory inconveniences, has certainly influenced social intercourse in southern countries.

Although I break off my investigation at this point, I am very much conscious of its fragmentary character. Yet perhaps thereby an access is opened from one point to the stratum from which knowledge must raise up the conditions of concrete, living sociation among human beings. One will no longer be able to consider as unworthy of attention the delicate, invisible threads that are spun from one person to another if one wishes to understand the web of society according to its productive, form-giving forces – this web of which sociology hitherto was largely concerned with describing only the final finished pattern of its uppermost phenomenal stratum.

THE SOCIOLOGY OF SOCIABILITY[1]

There is an old conflict over the nature of society. One side mystically exaggerates its significance, contending that only through society is human life endowed with reality. The other regards it as a mere abstract concept by means of which the observer draws the realities, which are individual human beings, into a whole, as one calls trees and brooks, houses and meadows, a 'landscape'. However one decides this conflict, he must allow society to be a reality in a double sense. On the one hand are the individuals in their directly perceptible existence, the bearers of the processes of association, who are united by these processes into the higher unity which one calls 'society'; on the other hand, the interests which, living in the individuals, motivate such union: economic and ideal interests, warlike and erotic, religious and charitable. To satisfy such urges and to attain such purposes, arise the innumerable forms of social life, all the with-one-another, for-one-another, in-one-another, against-one-another, and through-one-another, in state and commune, in church and economic associations, in family and clubs. The energy effects of atoms upon each other bring matter into the innumerable forms which we see as 'things'. Just so the impulses and interests, which a man experiences in himself and which push him out toward other men, bring about all the forms of association by which a mere sum of separate individuals are made into 'society'.

Within this constellation, called society, or out of it, there develops a special sociological structure corresponding to those of art and play, which draw their form from these realities but nevertheless leave the reality behind them. It may be an open question whether the concept of a play impulse or an artistic impulse possesses explanatory value; at least it directs attention to the fact that in every play or artistic activity there is contained a common element not affected by their differences of content. Some residue of satisfaction lies in gymnastics, as in card-playing, in music, and in sculpture, something which has nothing to do with the peculiarities of music or sculpture as such but only with the fact that both of the latter are art and both of the former are play. A common element, a likeness of psychological reaction and need, is found in all these various things – something easily distinguishable from the special interest which gives each its distinction. In the same sense one may speak of an impulse to sociability in man. To be sure, it is for the sake of special needs and interests that men unite in economic associations or blood fraternities, in cult societies or robber bands. But, above and beyond their special content, all the associations are accompanied by a feeling for, by a satisfaction in, the very fact that one is associated with others and that the solitariness of the individual is resolved into togetherness, a union with others. Of course, this feeling can, in individual cases, be nullified by contrary psychological factors; association can be felt as a mere burden, endured for the sake of our objective aims. But typically there is involved in all effective motives for association a feeling of the worth of association as such, a drive which presses toward this form of existence and often only later calls forth that objective content which carries the particular association along. And as that which I have called artistic impulse draws its form from the complexes of perceivable things and builds this form into a special structure corresponding to the artistic impulse, so also the impulse to sociability distils, as it were, out of the realities of social life the pure essence of association, of the associative process as a value and a satisfaction. It thereby constitutes what we call sociability in the narrower sense. It is no mere accident of language that all sociability, even the purely spontaneous, if it is to have meaning and stability, lays such great value on form, on good form. For 'good form' is mutual self-definition, interaction of the elements, through which a unity is made; and since in sociability the concrete motives bound up with life-goals fall away, so must the pure form, the free-playing, interacting interdependence of individuals stand out so much the more strongly and operate with so much the greater effect.

And what joins art with play now appears in the likeness of both to sociability. From the realities of life play draws its great, essential themes: the chase and cunning; the proving of physical and mental powers; the contest and reliance on chance and the favour of forces which one cannot influence. Freed of substance, through which these activities make up the seriousness of life, play gets its cheerfulness but also that symbolic significance which distinguishes it from pure pastime. And just this will show itself more and more as the essence of sociability; that it makes up its substance from numerous fundamental forms of serious relationships among men, a substance, however, spared the frictional relations of real life; but out of its formal relations to real life, sociability (and the more so as it approaches pure sociability) takes on a symbolically playing fullness of life and a significance which a superficial rationalism always seeks only in the content. Rationalism, finding no content there, seeks to do away with sociability as empty idleness, as did the savant who asked concerning a work of art, 'What does that prove?' It is nevertheless not without significance that in many, perhaps in all, European languages, the word 'society' (*Gesellschaft*) indicates literally 'togetherness'. The political, economic, the society held together by some purpose is nevertheless, always 'society'. But only the sociable is a 'society' without qualifying adjective, because it alone presents the pure, abstract play of form, all the specific contents of the one-sided and qualified societies being dissolved away.

Sociability is, then, the play form of association and is related to the content-determined concreteness of association as art is related to reality. Now the great problem of association comes to a solution possible only in sociability. The problem is that of the measure of significance and accent which belongs to the individual as such in and as against the social milieu. Since sociability in its pure form has no ulterior end, no content, and no result outside itself, it is oriented completely about personalities. Since nothing but the satisfaction of the impulse to sociability – although with a resonance left over – is to be gained, the process remains, in its conditions as in its results, strictly limited to its personal bearers; the personal traits of amiability, breeding, cordiality, and attractiveness of all kinds determine the character of purely sociable association. But precisely because all is oriented about them, the personalities must not emphasize themselves too individually. Where real interests, cooperating or clashing, determine the social form, they provide of themselves that the individual shall not present his peculiarities and individuality with too much abandon and aggressiveness. But where this restraint is wanting, if association is to be possible at all, there must prevail another restriction of personal pushing, a restriction springing solely out of the form of the association. It is for this reason that the sense of tact is of such special significance in society, for it guides the self-regulation of the individual in his personal relations to others where no outer or directly egoistic interests provide regulation. And perhaps it is the specific function of tact to mark out for individual impulsiveness, for the ego and for outward demands, those limits which the rights of others require. A very remarkable sociological structure appears at this point. In sociability, whatever the personality has of objective importance, of features which have their orientation toward something outside the circle, must not interfere. Riches and social position, learning and fame, exceptional capacities and merits of the individual have no role in sociability or, at most, as a slight nuance of that immateriality with which alone reality dares penetrate into the artificial structure of sociability. As these objective qualities which gather about the personality, so also must the most purely and deeply personal qualities be excluded from sociability. The most personal things – character, mood, and fate – have thus no place in it. It is tactless to bring in personal humour, good or ill, excitement and depression, the light and shadow of one's inner life. Where a connection, begun on the sociable level – and not necessarily a superficial or conventional one – finally comes to centre about personal values, it loses the essential quality of sociability and becomes an association determined by a content – not unlike a business or religious relation, for which contact, exchange, and speech are but instruments for ulterior ends, while for sociability they are the whole meaning and content of the social process. This exclusion of the personal reaches into even the most external matters; a lady would not want to appear in such extreme *décolletage* in a really personal, intimately friendly situation with one or two men as she would in a large company without any embarrassment. In the latter she would not feel herself personally involved in the same measure and could therefore abandon herself to the impersonal freedom of the mask. For she is, in the larger company, herself, to be sure, but not quite completely herself, since she is only an element in a formally constituted gathering.

A man, taken as a whole, is, so to speak, a somewhat unformed complex of contents, powers, potentialities; only according to the motivations and relationships of a changing existence is he articulated into a differentiated, defined structure. As an economic and political agent, as a member of a family or of a profession, he is, so to speak, an *ad hoc* construction; his life-material is ever determined by a special idea, poured into a special mould, whose relatively independent life is, to be sure, nourished from the common but somewhat undefinable source of energy, the ego. In this sense, the man, as a social creature, is also a unique structure, occurring in no other connection. On the one hand, he has removed all the objective qualities of the personality and entered into the structure of sociability with nothing but the capacities, attractions, and interests of his pure humanity. On the other hand, this structure stops short of the purely subjective and inward parts of his personality. That discretion which is one's first demand upon others in sociability is also required of one's own ego, because a breach of it in either direction causes the sociological artefact of sociability to break down into a sociological naturalism. One can therefore speak of an upper and a lower sociability threshold for the individual. At the moment when people direct their association toward objective content and purpose, as well as at the moment when the absolutely personal and subjective matters of the individual enter freely into the phenomenon, sociability is no longer the central and controlling principle but at most a formalistic and outwardly instrumental principle.

From this negative definition of the nature of sociability through boundaries and thresholds, however, one can perhaps find the positive motif. Kant set it up as the principle of law that everyone should have that measure of freedom which could exist along with the freedom of every other person. If one stands by the sociability impulse as the source or also as the substance of sociability, the following is the principle according to which it is constituted: everyone should have as much satisfaction of this impulse as is consonant with the satisfaction of the impulse for all others. If one expresses this not in terms of the impulse but rather in terms of success, the principle of sociability may be formulated thus: everyone should guarantee to the other that maximum of sociable values (joy, relief, vivacity) which is consonant with the maximum of values he himself receives. As justice upon the

Kantian basis is thoroughly democratic, so likewise this principle shows the democratic structure of all sociability, which to be sure every social stratum can realize only within itself, and which so often makes sociability between members of different social classes burdensome and painful. But even among social equals the democracy of their sociability is a play. Sociability creates, if one will, an ideal sociological world, for in it – so say the enunciated principles – the pleasure of the individual is always contingent upon the joy of others; here, by definition, no one can have his satisfaction at the cost of contrary experiences on the part of others. In other forms of association such lack of reciprocity is excluded only by the ethical imperatives which govern them but not by their own immanent nature. This world of sociability, the only one in which a democracy of equals is possible without friction, is an *artificial* world, made up of beings who have renounced both the objective and the purely personal features of the intensity and extensiveness of life in order to bring about among themselves a pure interaction, free of any disturbing material accent. If we now have the conception that we enter into sociability purely as 'human beings', as that which we really are, lacking all the burdens, the agitations, the inequalities with which real life disturbs the purity of our picture, it is because modern life is over-burdened with objective content and material demands. Ridding ourselves of this burden in sociable circles, we believe we return to our natural-personal being and overlook the fact that this personal aspect also does not consist in its full uniqueness and natural completeness, but only in a certain reserve and stylizing of the sociable man. In earlier epochs, when a man did not depend so much upon the purposive, objective content of his associations, his 'formal personality' stood out more clearly against his personal existence: hence personal bearing in the society of earlier times was much more ceremonially rigidly and impersonally regulated than now. This reduction of the personal periphery of the measure of significance which homogeneous interaction with others allowed the individual has been followed by a swing to the opposite extreme; a specific attitude in society is that courtesy by which the strong, outstanding person not only places himself on a level with the weaker but goes so far as to assume the attitude that the weaker is the more worthy and superior. If association is interaction at all, it appears in its purest and most stylized form when it goes on among equals, just as symmetry and balance are the most outstanding forms of artistic stylizing of visible elements. Inasmuch as sociability is the abstraction of association – an abstraction of the character of art or of play – it demands the purest, most transparent, most engaging kind of interaction – that among *equals*. It must, because of its very nature, posit beings who give up so much of their objective content, who are so modified in both their outward and their inner significance, that they are sociably equal, and every one of them can win sociability values for himself only under the condition that the others, interacting with him, can also win them. It is a game in which one 'acts' as though all were equal, as though he especially esteemed everyone. This is just as far from being a lie as is play or art in all their departures from reality. But the instant the intentions and events of practical reality enter into the speech and behaviour of sociability, it does become a lie – just as a painting does when it attempts, panorama fashion, to be taken for reality. That which is right and proper within the self-contained life of sociability, concerned only with the immediate play of its forms, becomes a lie when this is mere pretense, which in reality is guided by purposes of quite another sort than the sociable or is used to conceal such purposes – and indeed sociability may easily get entangled with real life.

It is an obvious corollary that everything may be subsumed under sociability which one can call sociological play form; above all, play itself, which assumes a large place in the sociability of all epochs. The expression 'social game' is significant in the deeper sense which I have indicated. The entire interactional or associational complex among men: the desire to gain advantage, trade, formation of parties and the desire to win from another, the movement between opposition and cooperation, outwitting and revenge – all this, fraught with purposive content in the serious affairs of reality, in play leads a life carried along only and completely by the stimulus of these functions. For even when play turns about a money prize, it is not the prize, which indeed could be won in many other ways, which is the specific point of the play: but the attraction for the true sportsman lies in the dynamics and in the chances of that sociologically significant form of activity itself. The social game has a deeper double meaning – that it is played not only *in* a society as its outward bearer but that *with* the society actually 'society' is played. Further, in the sociology of the sexes, eroticism has elaborated a form of play: coquetry, which finds in sociability its lightest, most playful, and yet its widest realization. If the erotic question between the sexes turns about consent or denial (whose objects are naturally of endless variety and degree and by no means only of strictly physiological nature), so is it the essence of feminine coquetry to play hinted consent and hinted denial against each other to draw the man on without letting matters come to a decision, to rebuff him without making him lose all hope. The coquette brings her attractiveness to its climax by letting the man hang on the verge of getting what he wants without letting it become too serious for herself; her conduct swings between yes and no, without stopping at one or the other. She thus playfully shows the simple and pure form of erotic decision and can bring its polar opposites together in a quite integrated behaviour, since the decisive and fateful content, which would bring it to one of the two decisions, by definition does not enter into coquetry. And this freedom from all the weight of firm content and residual reality gives coquetry that character of vacillation, of distance, of the ideal, which allows one to speak with some right of the 'art' – not of the 'arts' – of coquetry. In order, however, for coquetry to spread as so natural a growth on the soil of sociability, as experience shows it to be, it must be countered by a special attitude on the part of men. So long as the man denies himself the stimulation of coquetry, or so long as he is – on the contrary – merely a victim who is involuntarily carried along by her vacillations

from a half-yes to a half-no – so long does coquetry lack the adequate structure of sociability. It lacks that free interaction and equivalence of the elements which is the fundamental condition of sociability. The latter appears
only when the man desires nothing more than this free moving play, in
which something definitively erotic lurks only as a remote symbol, and
when he does not get his pleasure in these gestures and preliminaries from
erotic desire or fear of it. Coquetry, as it unfolds its grace on the heights of
sociable cultivation, has left behind the reality of erotic desire, of consent
or denial, and becomes a play of shadow pictures of these serious matters.
Where the latter enter or lurk, the whole process becomes a private affair
of the two persons, played out on the level of reality; under the sociological
sign of sociability, however, in which the essential orientation of the person
to the fullness of life does not enter, coquetry is the teasing or even ironic
play with which eroticism has distilled the pure essence of its interaction
out from its substantive or individual content. As sociability plays at the
forms of society, so coquetry plays out the forms of eroticism.

In what measure sociability realizes to the full the abstraction of the
forms of sociological interaction otherwise significant because of their
content and gives them – now turning about themselves, so to speak – a
shadow body is revealed finally in that most extensive instrument of all
human common life, conversation. The decisive point is expressed in the
quite banal experience that in the serious affairs of life men talk for the
sake of the content which they wish to impart or about which they want to
come to an understanding – in sociability talking is an end in itself; in purely
sociable conversation the content is merely the indispensable carrier of the
stimulation, which the lively exchange of talk as such unfolds. All the forms
with which this exchange develops: argument and the appeals to the norms
recognized by both parties; the conclusion of peace through compromise
and the discovery of common convictions; the thankful acceptance of the
new and the parrying-off of that on which no understanding is to be hoped
for – all these forms of conversational interaction, otherwise in the service
of innumerable contents and purposes of human intercourse, here have
their meaning in themselves; that is to say, in the excitement of the play of
relations which they establish between individuals, binding and loosening,
conquering and being vanquished, giving and taking. In order that this play
may retain its self-sufficiency at the level of pure form, the content must
receive no weight on its own account; as soon as the discussion gets busi-
ness-like, it is no longer sociable; it turns its compass point around as soon
as the verification of a truth becomes its purpose. Its character as sociable
converse is disturbed just as when it turns into a serious argument. The
form of the common search of the truth, the form of the argument, may
occur, but it must not permit the seriousness of the momentary content to
become its substance any more than one may put a piece of three-dimensional reality into the perspective of a painting. Not that the content of
sociable conversation is a matter of indifference; it must be interesting,
gripping, even significant – only it is not the purpose of the conversation

that these qualities should square with objective results, which stand by definition outside the conversation. Outwardly, therefore, two conversations may run a similar course, but only that one of them is sociable in which the subject matter, with all its value and stimulation, finds its justification, its place, and its purpose only in the functional play of conversation as such, in the form of repartee with its special unique significance. It therefore inheres in the nature of sociable conversation that its object matter can change lightly and quickly; for, since the matter is only the means, it has an entirely interchangeable and accidental character which inheres in means as against fixed purposes. Thus sociability offers, as was said, perhaps the only case in which talk is a legitimate end in itself. For by the fact that it is two-sided – indeed with the possible exception of looking-each-other-over the purest and most sublimated form of mutuality among all sociological phenomena – it becomes the most adequate fulfilment of a relation, which is, so to speak, nothing but relationship, in which even that which is otherwise a pure form of interaction is its own self-sufficient content. It results from this whole complex that also the telling of tales, witticisms, anecdotes, although often a stopgap and evidence of conversational poverty, still can show a fine tact in which all the motives of sociability are apparent. For, in the first place, the conversation is by this means kept above all individual intimacy, beyond everything purely personal which would not fit into the categories of sociability. This objective element is brought in not for the sake of its content but in the interest of sociability; that something is said and accepted is not an end in itself but a mere means to maintain the liveliness, the mutual understanding, the common consciousness of the group. Not only thereby is it given a content which all can share but it is a gift of the individual to the whole, behind which the giver can remain invisible; the finest sociably told story is that in which the narrator allows his own person to remain completely in the background; the most effective story holds itself in the happy balance of the sociable ethic, in which the subjectively individual as well as the objectively substantive have dissolved themselves completely in the service of pure sociability.

It is hereby indicated that sociability is the play form also for the ethical forces of concrete society. The great problems placed before these forces are that the individual has to fit himself into a whole system and live for it: that, however, out of this system values and enhancement must flow back to him, that the life of the individual is but a means for the ends of the whole, the life of the whole but an instrument for the purposes of the individual. Sociability carries the seriousness, indeed the frequent tragedy of these requirements, over into its shadow world, in which there is no friction, because shadows cannot impinge upon one another. If it is, further, the ethical task of association to make the coming-together and the separation of its elements an exact and just expression of their inner relations, determined by the wholeness of their lives, so within sociability this freedom and adequacy are freed of their concrete and substantively deeper limitations;

the manner in which in a 'society' groups form and break up, conversation spins itself out, deepens, loosens, cuts itself off purely according to impulse and opportunity, that is a miniature picture of the social ideal that man might call the freedom of bondage.

If all association and separation shall be the strictly appropriate representation of inner realities, so are the latter here fallen by the way, and only the former phenomenon is left, whose play, obedient to its own laws, whose closed charm, represents *aesthetically* that moderation which the seriousness of realities otherwise demands of its ethical decisions.

This total interpretation of sociability is evidently realized by certain historical developments. In the earlier German Middle Ages we find knightly fraternities which were founded by friendly patrician families. The religious and practical ends of these unions seem to have been lost rather early, and in the fourteenth century the chivalrous interests and conduct remain their only specific content. Soon after, this also disappears, and there remain only purely sociable unions of aristocratic strata. Here the sociability apparently develops as the residuum of a society determined by a content – as the residuum which, because the content has been lost, can exist only in form and in the forms of with-one-another and for-one-another. That the essential existence of these forms can have only the inner nature of play or, reaching deeper, of art appears even more clearly in the court society of the *ancien régime*. Here by the falling-off of the concrete life-content, which was sucked away from the French aristocracy in some measure by the monarchy, there developed free-moving, forms, toward which the consciousness of this class was crystallized – forms whose force, definitions, and relations were purely sociable and in no way symbols or functions of the real meanings and intensities of persons and institutions. The etiquette of court society became an end in itself; it 'etiquetted' no content any longer but had elaborated immanent laws, comparable to those of art, which have validity only from the viewpoint of art and do not at all have the purpose of imitating faithfully and strikingly the reality of the model, that is, of things outside art.

With this phenomenon, sociability attains its most sovereign expression but at the same time verges on caricature. To be sure, it is its nature to shut out realities from the interactive relations of men and to build its castle in air according to the formal laws of these relations which move within themselves and recognize no purpose outside themselves. But the deep-running source, from which this empire takes its energies, is nonetheless to be sought not in these self-regulating forms but only in the vitality of real individuals, in their sensitivities and attractions, in the fullness of their impulses and convictions. All sociability is but a symbol of life, as it shows itself in the flow of a lightly amusing play; but, even so, a symbol of *life*, whose likeness it only so far alters as is required by the distance from it gained in the play, exactly as also the freest and most fantastic art, the furthest from all reality, nourishes itself from a deep and true relation to reality, if it is not to be empty and lying. If sociability cuts off completely the threads which bind it to real life and out of which it spins its admittedly stylized web, it turns from play to empty farce, to a lifeless schematization proud of its woodenness.

From this context it becomes apparent that men can complain both justly and unjustly of the superficiality of social intercourse. It is one of the most pregnant facts of mental life that, if we weld certain elements taken from the whole of being into a realm of their own, which is governed by its own laws and not by those of the whole, this realm, if completely cut off from the life of the whole, can display in its inner realization an empty nature suspended in the air; but then, often altered only by imponderables, precisely in this state of removal from all immediate reality, its deeper nature can appear more completely, more integrated and meaningful, than any attempt to comprehend it realistically and without taking distance. According as the former or the latter experience predominates, will one's own life, running its own course according to its own norms, be a formal, meaningless dead thing – or a symbolic play, in whose aesthetic charm all the finest and most highly sublimated dynamics of social existence and its riches are gathered? In all art, in all the symbolism of the religious life, in great measure even in the complex formulations of science, we are thrown back upon this belief, upon this feeling, that autonomies of mere parts of observed reality, that the combinations of certain superficial elements possess a relation to the depth and wholeness of life, which, although often not easy to formulate, makes such a part the bearer and the representative of the fundamental reality. From this we may understand the saving grace and blessing effect of these realms built out of the pure forms of existence, for in them we are released from life but have it still. The sight of the sea frees us inwardly, not in spite of but because of the fact that in its rushing up only to recede, its receding only to rise again, in the play and counter-play of its waves, the whole of life is stylized to the simplest expression of its dynamic, quite free from all reality which one may experience and from all the baggage of individual fate, whose final meaning seems nevertheless to flow into this stark picture. Just so art perhaps reveals the secret of life; that we save ourselves not by simply looking away from it but precisely in that in the apparently self-governing play of its forms we construct and experience the meaning and the forces of its deepest reality but without the reality itself. Sociability would not hold for so many thoughtful men who feel in every moment the pressure of life, this emancipating and saving exhilaration if it were only a flight from life, the mere momentary lifting of its seriousness. It can often enough be only this negative thing, a con-ventionalism and inwardly lifeless exchange of formulas; so perhaps in the *ancien régime,* where gloomy anxiety over a threatening reality drove men into pure escape, into severance from the powers of actual life. The freeing and lightening, however, that precisely the more thoughtful man finds in sociability is this; that association and exchange of stimulus, in which all the tasks and the whole weight of life are realized, here is consumed in an artistic play, in that simultaneous sublimation and dilution, in which the heavily burdened forces of reality are felt only as from a distance, their weight fleetingly in a charm.

SOCIOLOGY OF THE MEAL

It is a feature of the destiny of social existence that the essential elements that are uniformly inherent to all individuals of a certain group almost never manifest themselves as the highest, but often rather as the lowest motives and interests of these individuals. For it is not only the case that within an organic species, those forms and functions most certain to be inherited by every individual are those which were acquired earliest – that is the most primitive and not yet refined ones, which are tied to the mere necessities of life. Rather, what everyone possesses can obviously always only be the possession of the least well-endowed; and since it is always the lot of humanity that the higher can indeed sink down to the lower, but that the latter cannot so easily rise to the former, so in general the level on which *everyone* meets must lie very close to the level of the very lowest. Everything that is higher, intellectual, and significant develops not only in selected individuals, but also even where one of those individuals carries such values, they have a specific tendency in each person and diverge above the common element.

Hence, of all the things that people have in common, the most common is that they must eat and drink. And precisely this, in a remarkable way, is the most egotistical thing, indeed the one most absolutely and immediately confined the individual. What I think, I can communicate to others; what I see, I can let them see, what I say can be heard by hundreds of others – but what a single individual eats can under no circumstances be eaten by another. In none of the higher spheres is it the case that others have to forego absolutely that which one person should have. Yet because this primitive physiological fact is an absolutely general human one, it does indeed become the substance of common actions. The sociological structure of the meal emerges, which links precisely the exclusive selfishness of eating with a frequency of being together, with a habit of being gathered together such as is seldom attainable on occasions of a higher and intellectual order. Persons who in no way share any special interest can gather together at the common meal – in this possibility, associated with the primitiveness and hence universal nature of material interest, there lies the immeasurable sociological significance of the meal.

In contrast to the world religions, the cults of antiquity – which tended to appeal only to limited groups of locally connected people – were therefore able to gather together for the sacrificial meal. In Semitic antiquity, especially, this signified the fraternal relationship through the common access to

God's table. Communal eating and drinking, which can even transform a mortal enemy into a friend for the Arab, unleashes an immense socializing power that allows us to overlook that one is not eating and drinking 'the same thing' at all, but rather totally exclusive portions, and gives rise to the primitive notion that one is thereby creating common flesh and blood. Only the Christian communion, which identifies the bread with the body of Christ, was able to create the real identity of what was consumed on the foundation of this mysticism and thus an entirely unique type of connection among the participants. For here, where it is not the case that each person consumes something denied to the others, but where each person consumes the totality in its mysterious undividedness that is granted equally to everyone, the egoistic, exclusionary quality of every meal is most completely transcended.

Precisely because the shared meal elevates an event of physiological primitiveness and inevitable generality into the sphere of social interaction, and hence of supra-personal significance, it had acquired in some earlier epochs an immense social value whose most obvious manifestations are the *commandments* of the communal table. Thus, in the eleventh century the Cambridge Guild stipulated a heavy punishment for those who ate or drank with the murderer of a guild member; thus, the Vienna Council of 1267, with its strongly anti-Jewish tendency, specifically ordered that Christians should not share a table with Jews; thus, in India, contamination from eating together with someone of a lower caste occasionally has fatal consequences! The Hindu often eats alone, in order to be *absolutely* sure that he has no forbidden associate at the table. We can hardly imagine today how vitally important eating and drinking in common was throughout the medieval guild system. One might believe that this was, as it were, a visible fixed point in the insecurity and fluctuation of medieval existence, a symbol around which the security of belonging together orientated time and again.

And here the connection is revealed which permits the merely physical externality of feeding nevertheless to rest upon the principle of an infinitely higher ranking order: in so far as the meal becomes a sociological matter, it arranges itself in a more aesthetic, stylized and supra-individually regulated form. Now all the regulations concerning eating and drinking emerge, not with regard to the unessential standpoint of food as matter, but specifically with regard to the *form* of its consumption. It is here that the *regularity* of meals first appears. We know of very primitive peoples that they do not eat at set times, but rather anarchically – eating individually whenever each person gets hungry. The shared nature of the meal, however, brings about temporal regularity, for only at a predetermined time can a circle of people assemble together - the first triumph over the naturalism of eating. What one might call the hierarchy of the meal moves in the same direction, namely the fact that people no longer reach indiscriminately and unregulatedly into the dish but are instead constrained to follow a definite order in which each person serves themselves. In the English Trade Clubs, the predecessors of today's trade unions, a punishment was sometimes stipulated for someone drinking out of turn.

In all these instances, a formal norm is placed above the fluctuating needs of the individual; the socialization of the meal elevates it into an aesthetic stylization which now acts back upon the former. For where one also demands aesthetic satisfaction from a meal, over and above the goal of satiation, an additional expense is required, which it is not only easier for a community to support than the individual, but which is inwardly also more likely to be legally supported by the latter than by the former.

Finally, the regulation of table manners, and their standardization according to aesthetic principles, is a result of the socialization of the meal. Among the lower classes, where the meal is essentially centred on the food in its material sense, no typical regulations regarding table manners develop. In higher social groups, in which the attraction of being together, all the way up to its – alleged, at least – culmination in 'society', dominates the mere material of the meal, a code of rules, ranging from holding the knife and fork to the appropriate subjects of table conversation, comes into being to regulate their behaviour. Compared with the image of someone eating in a farm house or at a workers' festival, a dinner in educated circles appears to be completely schematized and regulated on a supra-individual level with regard to the participants' movements.

This strict standardization and regimentation has no external purpose at all. It signifies exclusively the transcendence or transformation which materialistically individual selfishness experiences through the transition in the social form of the meal. Even eating with a utensil has this foundation for its more aesthetic style. Eating with one's fingers has something decidedly more individualistic about it than eating with a knife and fork, since it associates the individual more directly with matter and is the expression of a more unreserved desire. In so far as the eating utensil moves this desire a certain distance away, a shared form favouring the cohesion of several persons covers the eating procedure in a manner that does not exist at all in the case of eating with one's hands. This motif is heightened in manipulating the eating utensils, in that here the generally standardized form also reveals itself to be the freer one. Grasping a knife and fork with one's whole fist is ugly because it hampers the freedom of movement. The eating gestures of the uncultured are rigid and awkward, but lacking any suprapersonal regulation; those of the cultured person possess this regulative element in so far as the appear nimble and free – like a symbol of the fact that social standardization really only gains its life from the freedom of the individual, a freedom which in this manner reveals itself to be the counterpart of naturalistic individualism.

And this synthesis is documented here once again: by comparison with the bowl, from which everyone serves themselves in primitive epochs, the plate is an individualistic product. It indicates that this portion of food has been divided out exclusively for this one person. This is emphasized by the round shape of the plate; the circular line is the most exclusive one, the one that concentrates its contents most decisively within itself – whereas the bowl intended for everyone may be angular or oval, that is, less jealously closed off. The plate symbolizes the *order*, which gives to the needs of the individual that which is coming to the individual as a part of the structured whole but, in return, does not allow the individual to encroach beyond his or her limits. But then the plate elevates this symbolic individualism onto a higher formal common ground; the plates on a table must always be completely identical, they tolerate no individuality in their midst; different plates or glasses for different people would be absolutely senseless and ugly.

Each step that leads the meal upwards towards the immediate and symbolic expression of higher, synthetic social values thereby allows it to gain a higher aesthetic value. That is why the aesthetic reconciliation of the physical fact of eating disappears at that moment in which the element of socialization disappears, despite externally preserved good form – as is apparent in the repulsiveness of the *table d'hôte*. People gather here quite exclusively merely for the purpose of eating, and togetherness is not sought as a value in its own right; on the contrary, what is presupposed here is that one does not enter into any relationship to all these people, despite sitting together with them. No amount of table decoration or good manners can here disguise the materialistic emphasis of the purpose of eating. The aversion of all finer sensibilities to the *table d'hôte* proves that it is only socialization which can lead that purpose to a higher aesthetic order. To attractions of this order there is lacking, as it were, the soul where the gathering as such has no independent meaning, and they can no longer offer any cover for the unattractiveness, indeed the ugliness, of the physical act of eating.

Yet the aesthetics of the meal must never forget *what* it is actually supposed to stylize: the satisfaction of a need located in the depths of organic life and therefore absolutely universal. If, as a result, it has something materially individualistic as its object, then it must for that very reason not be elevated to individual differentiation, but rather instead only beautify and refine a mental levelling up to the limits which the latter permits. The *individual* appearance of a meal would be incompatible with its purpose of being consumed: that would be akin to cannibalism. This is why broken, subtle, modern colours have no place on the dining table, but instead the broad, shining ones which connect with very basic sensitivities: white and silver. In the furnishing of a dining room one generally avoids very expansive, striking and challenging forms and colours and favours calm, dark and heavy ones. With regard to pictures, family portraits are preferred, that do not arouse any special attention, but rather a sense of familiarity and dependability, embedded in the breadth of the basics of life. Even in the most refined dinners, the aesthetics of the arrangement and garnishing of the dishes is guided by principles that were overcome elsewhere long ago: symmetry, very childish colour effects, primitive shaping and symbols. Even the set table must not appear as a self-enclosed work of art, such that one would not dare to destroy its form. Whereas the beauty of the work of art has its foundation in being untouched, and keeps us at a distance, the refinement of the table is such that its beauty must in fact invite us to invade it.

The strict general establishment of table manners is all the more necessary for the higher classes based on their rank, since the temptation to individualism is particularly applicable to them. Being individual in how one eats – as is common, after all, in deportment and dress, in manner of speech and all other gestures – would be completely out of place. It would constitute not only an inner contradiction, but would also be inappropriate in value terms, since something in a higher order would be applied to something of a lower order, located in a totally different dimension, in which it would find no anchor point and would therefore move in a void. Similarly, table conversation, if it wishes to retain good form, must not extend beyond general, typical subjects and ways of treating them into individual depth.

Now, all of this can also certainly be explained on the basis of physiological expediency. For this demands avoidance of distraction or excitement while eating. Yet this only expresses in the language of the body the deeper social-psychological connection, namely that its secure widespread nature has created a social realization for a very primitive need, by means of which it has been elevated into the sphere of a higher and spiritual attraction, but without having being completely detached from its basis. To complain of the banality of ordinary table conversation is therefore entirely mistaken. Table conversation, which should be gracious but always retain a certain generality and calmness, must never let that foundation become *completely* imperceptible, because the entire fragile lightness and grace of its surface play is revealed only when it is maintained.

One may recall here that, in a whole series of areas of life, the lowest phenomena and indeed even negative values are not only the gateways for the development of the higher things, but also that it is precisely their inferiority that is the reason why superior things arise. Thus Darwin noted that the physical weakness of human beings in comparison to equally large mammals is probable the impulse which led them from an isolated to a social existence; the latter, however, brought all the abilities of the intellect and the will to fruition, with which the human being was able not only to compensate for its physical inferiority, but also – precisely because of that inferiority – increase its overall strength beyond that of all its enemies.

The same form may be found among the elements of personal morality. Seducibility and seduction, evil and guilt are only one end of the moral scale which connects them, even though perhaps not even by smooth transitions, to the good and the pure: and yet the ultimate heights of morality are directly conditioned by these dark regions and depths of our existence. Who would speak of ethical merit if a battle against temptation – which even in their hagiography the saints are not spared – were not necessary, an upward struggle from weakness, sensuality and egotism? The fact that there is more joy in heaven over one repentant sinner than over ten virtuous ones actually merely expresses this inner structure, in which the negative is no mere shadow over our values, nor a contrary tendency that in its meaning only leads away from them; but rather, like the opposing energy generated by positive energy, a development from out of the values themselves. Only the dark and the evil, turning into their opposites as it were, can produce the brightest and most valuable things that we can attain.

The indifference and the banality of the field with which these remarks are concerned should not deceive us into believing that the paradoxical depth of this type is not equally alive within it. The fact that we must eat is a fact of life situated so primitively and elementarily in the development of our life-values that it is unquestionably shared by each individual with every other one. This is precisely what makes gathering together for a shared meal possible in the first place, and the transcendence of the mere naturalism of eating develops out of the socialization mediated in this way. If eating were not so elemental, it would not have found this bridge by which it is elevated to the significance of the sacrificial meal – to the stylization and aestheticization of its ultimate forms.

If it is the nature of the tragic that the noble destroys itself when its most striking forms cause ideal value to conflict precisely with ideal values, and thereby to sink back into the trivial or the negative, then the development outlined here is the absolute opposite of such a fate. For here something inferior and trivial has grown beyond itself through its own efforts; depth has risen to the heights of more spiritual and meaningful things precisely because it is depth. Here, as elsewhere, the significance of the type of life appears precisely when it does not deign to shape even insignificant things in its own image.

Note to Part III

1. "Soziologie der Geselligkeit", being the opening speech at the first meeting of the German Sociological Society *(Verhandlungen des Ersten Deutschen Soziologentages vom 19–12 Oktober, 1910, in Frankfurt A.M.* [Tübingen: J.C.B. Mohr, 1911]): 1–16.

PART IV
SPATIAL AND URBAN CULTURE

THE SOCIOLOGY OF SPACE

It is one of the most frequent abberations of the human causal impulse to take formal conditions, without which certain events cannot occur, for positive, productive results of those same things. The typical example is the power of time – a figure of speech that countless times deceives us into not searching for the *real* reasons for moderations or coldness of convictions, or for psychological healing processes or for ingrained habits. The same may hold true in many cases for the significance of space. If an aesthetic theory declares that an essential task of plastic art is to make space palpable to us, then it fails to acknowledge that our interest only applies to the particular forms of things, but not to space or spatiality in general – the latter constituting only the *conditio sine qua non* of forms, but neither their distinctive essence nor their causative factor.

If an interpretation of history emphasizes the spatial factor to such an extent that it conceives of the largeness or smallness of kingdoms, the concentration or dispersal of the population, the mobility or stability of the masses and the like as the forces of our entire historical life, radiating out from space, as it were, then here too the necessary spatial involvement of all these constellations also runs the danger of being confused with their positively effective causes. Of course, kingdoms cannot have some size or other, of course people cannot be close to or distant from each other, without space donating some of its form, no more than those events ascribed to the power of time can occur outside of time. But the contents of these forms only experience through other *contents* the distinctive nature of their fates. Space always remains the actually ineffectual form, in whose modifications real energies are manifested, but only in the way that language expresses thought processes, which occur *in* words but not *through* words. A geographical radius of so many square miles does not constitute a great kingdom; but rather this is accomplished by psychological forces from a central point which hold the inhabitants of such a region together politically. It is not the form of spatial proximity or distance that creates the special phenomena of neighbourliness or foreignness, no matter how irrefutable this might seem. Rather, these too are facts caused purely by psychological *contents*, the course of which has no different relationship to its spatial form that does a battle or a telephone call to its own – no matter how indubitably these events can also only be realized under quite definite spatial conditions. The requirement of specific psychological functions for individual historical spatial formations reflects the fact that space in general is only an activity of the mind, only the human way of connecting sensory impulses that are unrelated in themselves into uniform interpretations.

Despite this state of affairs, the emphasis on the spatial meanings of things and processes is not unjustified. For these actually often take such a course that the formal or negative condition of their spatiality stands out especially *for reflection*, and that in it we possess the clearest documentation of the real forces. Even though a chemical process or a chess game are ultimately just as connected to spatial determinations as are a military expedition or the sales of agricultural products, equally the perspective adopted by cognitive interest is so different methodologically in one group from the other that, in the first case, questions of the conditions and determinations of space and place are quite external, while in the second case they are expressly included. Kant defines space at one point as the possibility of being together; sociation has brought about quite different possibilities of being together – in the intellectual sense – among the different types of interactions of individuals; but many of these are realized in such a way that the spatial form in which this happens, as it does for all of them, justifies special emphasis. Thus, in the interest of ascertaining the forms of sociation, we enquire into the significance that the spatial conditions of a sociation possess sociologically for their other determinants and developments.

First of all there are several fundamental qualities of the spatial form upon which the structuring of communal life relies.

A.   Among these fundamental qualities is that which one could term the exclusivity of space. Just as there is only a single general space, of which all individual spaces are parts, so every portion of space possesses a kind of uniqueness, for which there is almost no analogy. To conceive of a definitely localized portion of space in the plural is a complete absurdity, and it is precisely this which makes it possible for a multitude of completely identical copies of *other* objects to exist simultaneously. For only because each occupies a different portion of space, which will never coincide with any other portion, are there *several* of these objects, although their nature is absolutely uniform. This uniqueness of space communicates itself to objects, so long as they can be conceived of merely as occupying space, and this becomes particularly important in practice for those whose spatial significance we tend to emphasize and put to spatial use.

This applies especially to land, which is the condition for fulfilling and fructifying the three-dimensional quality of space for our purposes. To the extent to which a social formation is amalgamated with or is, as it were, united with a specific extension of land, then it possesses a character of uniqueness or exclusivity that is not similarly attainable in other ways. According to their entire sociological form, certain types of association can only be realized in such a way that there is no room for a second one within the spatial area that one of its formations occupies. In contrast, with others, a certain number – all identical sociologically – can fulfil the same expanse because, as it were, they are mutually permeable. Since they possess no inner relationship to space they cannot become involved in spatial collisions.

The only example that completely coincides with the first type of association is the state. It has been said of it that it is not one association among many, but rather that one which dominates all others, and is therefore of a unique character. This notion, whose correctness for the overall character of the state is not at issue here, is true in any case with respect to the spatial character of the state. The type of association between individuals which the state creates, or which creates it, is so much connected to the territory that the concept of a second state on the same territory cannot be sustained at all.

To some extent, the municipality possesses the same character: within the boundaries of a city only this city can exist, and if there are two cities within those same borders, then they are not two cities on the same land, but rather two previously united cities which are now separated territories. This exclusivity, however, is not so absolute as is the case with the state. The sphere of significance and influence of a city – within a state – does not end at its geographical borders, but rather extends more or less noticeably over the entire country in intellectual, economic, and political waves in so far as the general state administration causes the forces and interests of each part to grow together with those of the whole. Viewed from this perspective, the community loses its excluding character and expands functionally over the entire state so that the latter becomes the general field of action, as it were, for the spiritual extensions of all the individual communities. In that each extends across its immediate boundaries, each community confronts all the others which have an effect on the entire area, so that no single community is the only one within it, and each has another region located around the exclusivity of its own territory where it is also not alone.

Within the individual city, this local form of group life can also repeat itself. When Episcopal cities developed out of German border towns, the free community was never the proprietor of the entire communal territory; rather, a bishop existed alongside the city, with a dominant group of dependent people behind him, which he ruled according to his own law. Additionally, there existed a royal feudal court in most cities, with its own specially administered court community, and finally, independent monastic orders and Jewish communities which lived according to their own laws. In earlier times, therefore, there existed communities within the city, but no genuine municipal community.

Inevitably, however, diverse reciprocal effects developed out of the spatial contact, which found expression first in the communal town precincts, before all these separate entities fused into a municipality. Thus, all inhabitants were provided with a common protective law above their particular personal rights: that is, the legal sphere of each district stretched beyond its boundaries, within which each community was the only one, extended in a uniform way for everyone into an all-encompassing total area, and thereby the local exclusivity lost its effective nature with this expansion.

This type constitutes the transition to the further stage of the spatial relationships of groups which possess no claim to exclusivity because they are not limited to a particular dimension. In this way, a large number of guilds of an identical sociological structure were able to coexist within the territory of a city. Each of these was the guild for the entire city; they shared the given expanse not in a quantitative way, but functionally; they did not collide with each other in space because, as sociological formations, they were not determined spatially even though they were determined *locally*. According to their content, they possessed the exclusivity of filling a spatial expanse, in so far as there was only one guild in the city for a given trade, and no space for a second one. But according to their form, countless formations of this type could fill up the same space without contradiction.

The most extreme pole of this series is exemplified by the church, at least if, like the Catholic Church, it raises the claim to universality and freedom from any local barrier. Nonetheless, several religions of this type, for instance, could be found together in the same city. The Catholic congregation would be the 'city's Catholic congregation' – that is, assuming a definite organization and local relationship to the city as a unit – no less than would be the congregation of any other religion. The principle of the church is non-spatial, and therefore, although it extends over every space, it does not exclude a similarly formed structure from any space.

Within the spatial realm, there is a counterpart to the contrast of the external and the timeless within the temporal realm. The latter is, by its very nature, untouched by the question of now or earlier or later and is thus of course accessible to, or present in, any moment of time. The former is precisely a concept of time, specifically, that of an endless and uninterrupted time. The corresponding distinction in the spatial realm, for which we have no simple expressions, is constituted on the one hand by the supra-spatial structures which, on the basis of their inner meaning, have no relationship to space and therefore an equal relationship to all points of space. On the other hand, there are those which enjoy this equal relationship not as an equal indifference, and therefore a mere possibility, but as a real and fundamental solidarity with space everywhere. The purest type of the first category is evidently the church, and that of the second is the state. Many intermediate phenomena interpose themselves between the two poles, some of which I have indicated. In this way, a special light is shed on the formal nature of a variety of social constructs by virtue of their position on the scale, which runs from complete territorial determinacy and includes the attendant possibility of a constellation of many similar entities over the same sector of space. The proximity or the distance, the exclusivity or the multiplicity displayed by the relationship of the group to its territory is, therefore, often the root and the symbol of its structure.

B.   A further quality of space, which has a fundamental effect on social interactions, lies in the fact that for our practical use space is divided into pieces which are considered units and are framed by boundaries – both as a cause and an effect of the division. It may be that the configurations of the earth's surface appear to prescribe for us the framework we inscribe in the boundlessness of space, or that purely imaginary lines separate pieces of ground of a similar type like a watershed, where each particle gravitates to one centre on this side and a different one on the other. We always conceive of the space which a social group fills up in some sense as a unit that expresses and supports the unity of that group, just as much as it is carried and supported by it.

The frame of a structure, its self-contained boundary, has a very similar significance for the social group as for a work of art. It performs two functions for the latter, which are really only two sides of a single function: closing the work of art off against the surrounding world and holding it together. The frame proclaims that a world is located inside of it which is subject only to its own laws, not drawn into the determinations and changes of the surrounding world. In so far as it symbolizes the self-contented unity of the work of art, the frame at the same time strengthens its reality and its impression.

Similarly, a society is characterized as inwardly homogeneous because its sphere of existence is enclosed in acutely conscious boundaries; and conversely, the reciprocal unity and functional relationship of every element to every other one gains its spatial expression in the enclosing boundary. There is perhaps nothing that demonstrates the power of state cohesion so much as the fact that this sociological centripetality, this ultimately psychological coherence of individual persons, grows into an image – as if experienced in our senses – of a solid surrounding boundary line. People seldom appreciate how marvellously the extensity of space accommodates the intensity of sociological relationships here, how the continuity of space, precisely because it nowhere contains an absolute objective border, therefore permits us to lay down anywhere such a boundary subjectively. With respect to nature, however, this demarcation is arbitrary, even in the case of an island location, because in principle one can even 'take possession' of the sea.

Once it has been laid down, the physical border's existing absolute precision illustrates particularly well the formative power of the social context and its inwardly motivated necessity in this very lack of prejudice by natural space. This is why consciousness of boundedness is not at its most precise with so-called natural boundaries (mountains, rivers, oceans or deserts) but rather with merely political boundaries which only place a geometrical line between two neighbours. And this is so, in the latter case, since shifts, expansions, contractions or fusions are much easier, because at its end the structure borders on living, psychologically active boundaries, which produce not only passive resistance, but also very active repulsions. Every boundary of this type signifies both a defensive and an offensive stance, or, more correctly perhaps, it is the spatial expression of that uniform relationship between two neighbours for which we have no completely uniform expression, and which we could term the state of indifference between the defensive and the offensive – a tension where both reside latently, regardless of whether they will develop or not.

This is obviously not to deny that the setting of a boundary, which is in any case psychological, would find an alleviation and emphasis in those natural border areas. Indeed, through the structuring of its surface, space often receives divisions which colour the relationships of the inhabitants to each other and to third parties in a unique fashion. The best known example is furnished by mountain-dwellers, with their peculiar unity of love for freedom and conservatism, of obstinacy in their behaviour towards one another, along with passionate attachment to the soil, which nonetheless creates a very strong bond between them. Conservatism in the mountain valleys is very easily explained by the difficulty of interaction with the outer world and the resultant lack of stimuli for change. Where the mountainous geography does not exercise this prohibitive effect, as in some Greek landscapes, the conservative tendency does not prevail at all. It has only negative causes, in contrast to other geographical determinacies with the same result. The Nile, for instance, offers those living alongside it, on the one hand, an extraordinary uniformity of what it provides and of the activity required for exploiting it. On the other hand, the fertility of its valley is so great that, once it has settled there, the population has no cause for restless movements. These very positive reasons impress a uniformity of ever-recurring life elements upon the region; they bind it as if to the regularity of a machine, and have often forced a conservative rigidity on the Nile Valley for centuries, such as could never have been achieved on the Aegean coast for geographical reasons alone.

The concept of a boundary is extremely important in all relationships of human beings to one another, even though its significance is not always a sociological one. For it often only indicates that the sphere of a personality has found a limit according to power or intelligence, or the ability of endurance or enjoyment. This does not mean, however, that the sphere of someone else begins at this limit and determines the boundary of the first person with its own. The latter, the sociological boundary, signifies quite special interaction. Each of the two elements affects the other by setting the boundary for it, but the substance of this interaction is the determination *not* to want or be able to exert an effect beyond this boundary. If this general concept of mutual limitation is derived from the spatial boundary, in a deeper sense the latter is still only the crystallization or spatial expression of the *psychological* limitation processes which alone are real.

It is neither countries nor plots of land, neither urban districts nor rural districts which bound one another; rather, it is their inhabitants or proprietors who exercise the reciprocal effect to which I have just alluded. Each of the spheres of two personalities or personality complexes gains an inner unity for itself, a mutual referencing of its elements, a dynamic relationship to its centre. And it is precisely this which produces what is symbolized in the spatial boundary, the supplementation of one's own positive sense of power and justice within one's own sphere by the consciousness that such power and justice do not extend into the other sphere. The boundary is not a spatial fact with sociological consequences, but a sociological fact that forms itself spatially. The idealist principle that space is our conception, or more precisely, that it comes into being through our synthetic activity with which we give form to sensory material, is specified here in such a way that the formation of space which we call a boundary is a sociological function. Of course, once it has become a spatial and sensory object that we inscribe into nature independently of its sociological and practical sense, then this produces strong repercussions on the consciousness of the relationship of the parties. Whereas this line only marks the diversity in the two relationships, that of the elements of a sphere among each other and that among those elements and the elements of another sphere, it becomes a living energy that forces the former together and will not allow them to escape their unity and pushes between them both like a physical force that emits outward repulsions in all directions.

Perhaps in the majority of all relationships between individuals as well as between groups, the concept of the boundary becomes in some way important. Everywhere, where the interests of two elements are directed at the same object, the possibility of their coexistence depends on a border line separating their spheres within the object – whether this be a legal line ending the dispute or a power boundary perhaps starting it. I recall only one case of immeasurable importance for all human social existence. All close coexistence continually depends on each person knowing more about the other through psychological hypotheses than the other person directly and consciously indicates. For if we had to rely only on what was revealed in this way, then we would only confront a few fortuitous and unconnected fragments of a mind rather than a unified person whom we can understand and upon whom we can count. Therefore we must supplement the existing fragments with conclusions, interpretations, and interpolations until a person emerges who is sufficiently complete for our inner and practical everyday needs.

This indubitably social right to pry into another person whether they desire it or not contrasts with that person's private right to their own psychological being, their right to discretion. For discretion not only means that one does not open other people's letters or listen at their doors, but also that one refrains from that pondering and conjecturing with which one could penetrate into someone's intimacies and unexposed secrets against their will. But where does the boundary lie between the permitted, and indeed necessary, reconstruction of another mind and this psychological indiscretion? And this precarious objective boundary in fact only signifies the boundary between the two personality spheres; it means that the consciousness of the one can only coincide with that of another to a limited degree, and that beyond that boundary, the domain of the other inviolably commences and that other person alone can decide on revealing it. It is obvious that the infinitely varied tracing of this line interacts in the most intimate way with the entire structure of social life. In primitive, undifferentiated times, the right to these psychological extensions of the boundary was probably greater, but interest in such extensions was perhaps less than in periods with more individualized human beings and more complex relationships. This boundary is also fixed differently in commercial transactions than in the relationship of parents and children, and is different among diplomats than among wartime comrades.

This insignificant and yet extremely important problem for the deeper analysis of social existence clearly shows how much boundary determinations of this type express the totality of interactive relationships between individuals, and indicates what an indefinable multiplicity of delimitations, and especially what a continual flux and shifting, dominates them. That is precisely why I have touched here upon this matter, which is actually quite remote from the problem of space, in order to illustrate the incomparable firmness and clarity which the social processes of demarcation receive from being spatialized. Every boundary is a psychological, more precisely, a sociological event; but through its investment in a line in space, the relationship of reciprocity attains a clarity and security in both its positive and negative sides – indeed often a certain rigidity – that tends to be denied the boundary so long as the meeting and separating of forces and rights has not yet been projected into a sensory formation, and thus as it were always remains in a *status nascens*.

Thus, if we are concerned here essentially with the interactions that result between the inside and the outside of the boundary, then those produced among the elements inside itself by the boundary as a border also deserve at least one example. The essential thing here is the breadth or narrowness of the boundary – although it is by no means the only essential thing; for also the form produced in the group by the border, its uniform or varied cohesive energy, is of unquestioned importance for the inner structure of the group. The same can be said of the issue of whether the boundary is produced everywhere by the same element (as is the case with islands, with small states in the position of San Marino or with the Indian tributary states) or from a number of related elements – even though these issues can only be alluded to here.

The breadth or narrowness of the border is by no means proportional to the size of the group. It depends instead on the tensions that develop within the group. If these find sufficient freedom of movement such that they do not collide with the boundaries, then the framework is wide, even if a relatively large number of people are grouped together inside it, as is often the constellation of Oriental kingdoms. Even for a relatively small population, on the other hand, the framework is narrow if it seems to be a constriction, which certain energies that cannot be displayed internally seek to escape over and over again.

The effect of this latter constellation on social form was unmistakably experienced by Venice, for example. The narrow restriction of its territory, which could not be directly overcome, oriented it much more towards dynamic expansion into the larger relationships of the world than to a territorial expansion of its power, which would have offered few opportunities in such a geographical position. A policy of this type – looking far out into the world and extending beyond what is immediately available – places considerable intellectual demands, which cannot be realized by the broad masses. Therefore, direct democracy was out of the question for Venice. By virtue of its spatial living conditions, it was compelled to breed an aristocracy that ruled the masses, just as, it was said, officers on a ship rule the crew.

The fact of a spatial framework for a group is by no means limited formally and sociologically to its political boundary. The framework's narrowness or breadth produces its formative consequences with the corresponding modifications whenever a number of people band together socially. The often emphasized character of an assembled crowd – its impulsiveness, its enthusiasm, its susceptibility to manipulation – is certainly connected to some degree with the fact that the crowd is in the open, or at least in a very large space, compared with the spaces that its members normally occupy. The greater breathing space gives people a feeling of freedom of movement, of an ability to venture out into the unknown, of an indefinite ability to set broader goals – which would be decidedly more difficult to achieve in enclosed rooms. The fact that such rooms are indeed often relatively too narrow, that is, they are overcrowded, can only strengthen this psychological effect, namely the growth of individual psychological momentum beyond its usual limits: for it must raise that collective feeling which fuses the individual into a unity transcending his or her individuality, sweeping the individual along like a flood past their personal directives and responsibilities.

The suggestive and stimulative effects of a great mass of people and their overall psychological manifestations, in whose form the individual no longer recognizes his or her own contribution, increase in proportion to the crowdedness and, more significantly, the size of the space that the crowd occupies. A locality that offers the individual a breathing space of an unaccustomed size through a dense crowd, necessarily favours that feeling of an expansion extending into the unknown and that heightening of powers which is so easily instilled in large masses, and which occurs only occasionally among exceptional individuals in the narrow, easily surveyed confines of an ordinary room.

This indefiniteness of the spatial frame so vividly supports the typical collective stimuli, just as in general the indistinctness and breadth of boundaries, even in the non-spatial sense, have a stimulating, seductive effect. It is this very thing which makes gatherings in the dark so dangerous, so much so that the medieval city police often attempted to prevent them by cordoning off streets with chains and the like. The darkness gives the meeting a quite special frame, which brings the significance of the narrow and the broad into a peculiar unity. By being able to survey only the most immediate environment, with an impenetrable black wall rearing up behind it, the individual feels closely pressed together with the most immediate surroundings; the delimitation against space outside the visible surroundings has reached its limiting case: this space seems simply to have disappeared. On the other hand, this very fact also causes the actually existing boundaries to disappear; fantasy expands the darkness into exaggerated possibilities; one feels surrounded by a fantastically indefinite and unlimited space. Relieving the fearfulness and insecurity that are a natural part of darkness through that tight crowding and mutual dependence of a multitude gives rise to the feared excitement and incalculability of a large gathering in the dark, as a quite unique elevation and combination of the enclosing and expanding aspects of spatial limitation.

C.   The third significance of space for social formations lies in its capacity of *fixing* their contents. Whether a group or certain of its individual elements or essential objects of its interest are completely fixed or remain spatially indeterminate must obviously affect their structure; and how much the differences in the states of mind of nomadic and settled groups are determined by this fact has been explained so frequently that it need only be alluded to here. This is by no means a schematic extension of the principle of fixed determinacy: being valid in the spatial realm, it would now manifest itself in the objective elements of life as stabilization and a firm order. In fact, this immediately comprehensible connection does not even apply universally; in very consolidated conditions which are immune to uprooting from outside, people will be able to do without some of the regulations and legal controls that are urgently required in cases of general insecurity and uneasy conditions, which are more susceptible to fragmentation.

A more special sociological significance of fixing in space can be designated by the symbolic expression 'pivot-point'. The spatial immovability of an object of interest creates certain forms of relationships that group around it. Now every immobile asset, around which negotiations or economic transactions of any kind occur, is indeed this kind of stable pivot-point for unstable conditions and interactions. Yet, at least nowadays, the spatial immovability of the object does not determine these conditions in a particularly characteristic sociological manner.

A not uninteresting variation of this may be observed in that relationship of economic individuals which is manifested in the mortgage. The reason why mortgages tend to be connected almost exclusively to immovable assets is a combination of the stationary character and the indestructibility of these assets, which can be considered as the correlate of the exclusivity that was previously discussed. In return for the uniqueness to which every part of our space is limited, one could say, it gains that immortality by reason of which land is so well suited to mortgage lending. For only in this way is it possible that the mortgaged object can remain in the hands of the debtor and yet be completely secure for the creditor: it can neither be carried away nor confused with other mortgaged objects.

Now, however, the principle of insurance has made those objects that are totally lacking in any fixed position in space eligible for mortgage lending – namely, ships. For what is of particular interest to the mortgage with respect to spatial immobility – the suitability for public registration – is easily attainable in another way with ships. Here, as in many other cases, substantive determination has actually been revealed to be functional determinacy. The fixed character, which favoured mortgaging as a rigid quality of landed property, actually achieves this in reality, at least in part, through the publicity to which it exposes people, but which is also attainable by other means. Thus the pivotal point or fulcrum of economic interaction is here overwhelmingly a spatially fixed value, but not because of its immobility, but because of certain functions attached to it.

Yet the situation was different in the Middle Ages, which in general demanded a quite different mixture of stability and mobility of the elements of life. In medieval trade and communication we find countless 'relationships' that completely escape our notions of economic or private legal action, and yet were made the objects of such action. Ruling power over territories and judicial authority within them, church patronage, and the authority to raise taxes, highways and minting privileges: all these were sold or borrowed, given as pledges or given away. By making such unstable objects, that existed only in mere interactions between people, once more the object of economic interactions would have led to even more unstable and precarious conditions if all these rights and relationships had not had the distinctive feature of *being immovably fixed at the place where they were exercised*. This was the stabilizing factor which gave so much solidity to their purely dynamic and relativistic nature that it was possible to group additional economic interactions around them. Their spatial determinacy was not like that of a substantive object, which one would always find at the same place, but akin to the abstract stability of a pivotal point, which keeps a system of elements in a specific distance, interaction and interdependence.

The significance of fixed spatiality as a pivotal point for social relationships emerges whenever the contact or union of otherwise independent elements can only occur at one particular place. I shall deal with some examples of this phenomenon, which actually represents an interaction between internal and spatial sociological determination. For churches, it is an extraordinarily astute policy to set up a chapel and pastoral centre within their Diaspora wherever even the smallest number of its congregation live in a district. This fixed point in space becomes a pivotal point for the relationships and the cohesion of the faithful, so that communal, rather than isolated, religious forces are developed. And, in addition, the forces emanating from such a visible centre also awaken a consciousness of belonging among members of the denomination, whose religious consciousness has long lain dormant in their isolation. In this respect, the Catholic Church is far superior to Protestant ones. It does not wait in the Diaspora for an actual congregation of people to undertake the spatial constitution, but rather begins with it around the smallest core, and in innumerable cases this localization has become the crystallization for an inwardly and numerically growing congregational life.

Cities serve everywhere as focal points of transactions for their immediate and wider surroundings, that is, each brings into being within itself innumerable focal points for continuing and changing trade activities. Trade expands cities all the more, the more dynamic it is, thus revealing the whole difference between *its* liveliness and the restless mobility of primitive groups. The typical contrast between forms of social dynamism is whether they merely signify a striving beyond that which exists socially and objectively, like the cycle of alternating pastures of pastoral peoples, or, on the other hand, whether they move around fixed points. Only in the latter case are they actually formed and only there do they gain a crystallization point for the commencement of lasting values, even if these only exist in the persisting form of relations and movements.

This contrast in its forms of mobility dominates external and internal life in so many ways that its spatial realization appears to be only a special case. Whether intellectual and social relationships possess a solid centre, around which interests and contrasts circulate, or whether they simply follow the linear form of time; whether two political parties share a solid centre, be it the continuous uniformity of their tendencies or a continuous opposition, or whether their relationship develops without prejudice from one issue to another; whether a strong one-sidedly nuanced sense of life predominates in the individual person – of an aesthetic nature perhaps – which ties together, harmonizes and contains all the various interests, religious and theoretical, social and erotic in a *single* sphere, or whether the person's interests are only displayed in relation to their own strength without such a continual reflection and evaluative standard – all these things obviously condition the greatest differences in patterns of life and determine the real course of our life through their constant struggles and combinations.

But all these are only individual elaborations of the same general contrast to which the sociological pivot-point belongs in the spatial realm. The real significance of trade and communication (*Verkehr*) first emerges from their actual formation of the city. For, in contrast to the simple striving into the unlimited, their significance lies in the fact that movement encounters a second equivalent power, which need not be hostile, as it always was before developed trade and communication. Now communication no longer means mutual friction, but a mutual supplementation and thereby a self-enlargement of the forces which the spatial base requires and therefore produces.

Furthermore, I wish to draw attention here to the rendezvous as a specifically sociological form, whose spatial determinacy is characterized linguistically through the ambiguity of the word: it signifies both the encounter and its location. The sociological essence of the rendezvous lies in the tension between the punctuality and fleeting quality of the relationship, on the one hand, and its temporal and spatial determinacy on the other. The rendezvous – and not merely its erotic or illegitimate forms – is distinguished psychologically from the mundane form of existence by its trait of *uniqueness* and acuteness springing from the particular occasion. Further, because it separates itself out like an island from the continuous course of life's contents, the rendezvous achieves a special hold on consciousness, precisely on the formal elements of its time and place. Because it is more vivid to the senses, place generally exhibits a greater associative effect for recollection than time. And hence, especially when one is concerned with unique and emotion-laden interactions, it is precisely the place which tends to be indissolubly linked to recollection, and thus, since this tends to occur mutually, the place remains the focal point around which remembrance weaves individuals into the web of interactions that have now become idealized.

This sociological significance of the fixed point in space already anticipates a further significant dimension, which one could designate as the individualization of place. It seems to be an indifferent, superficial fact that houses in towns were generally known by proper names in the Middle Ages and frequently even as late as the nineteenth century. Only fifty years ago, the residents of the Faubourg St. Antoine in Paris were always said to have referred to their buildings by their names (*Au roi de Siam, Étoile d'or*, and so on), despite street numbers already being in existence. Nevertheless, the difference between the individual name and the mere number of a house expresses a difference in the relationship of its owners and residents to it, and thus to their surroundings. The definiteness and indefiniteness of the act of designation intermingle here to a quite remarkable extent. The house that is called by its own name must give its inhabitants a feeling of spatial individuality, of belonging to a *qualitatively* fixed point in space. Through the name associated with it, the house forms a much more autonomous, individually nuanced existence; to our sensibility, it has a higher type of uniqueness than when designated by numbers, which are repeated in the same way in every street with only quantitative differences between them.

In contrast to the thronging and levelling of social and especially urban interaction, this type of naming documents an unmistakability and personality of existence with respect to its spatial dimension. Of course, it is paid for by an indeterminacy and a lack of objective permanency in comparison with current conditions. Therefore it must disappear once interaction exceeds a certain breadth and rapidity. The *named* house cannot be immediately located; its position cannot be constructed objectively, as is the case with current geographical designation. For all their indifference and abstractness, numbers do after all represent as ordering numbers a definite place in space, which the proper name of the locality does not. The most extreme stage is, on the one side the designation of hotel guests according to their room number, and, on the other, the fact that even the streets are no longer named, but numbered consecutively, as in some parts of New York.

This contrast in ways of naming things reveals a complete antagonism in the sociological position of the individual within the spatial sphere. The individualistic person, with their qualitative determinacy and the unmistakability of their life contents, therefore resists incorporation into an order that is valid for everyone, in which they would have a calculable position according to a consistent principle. Conversely, where the organization of the whole regulates the achievement of the individual according to an end not located within him or herself, then their position must be fixed according to an external system. It is not an inner or ideal norm but rather the relationship to the totality that secures this position, which is therefore most suitably determined by a numerical arrangement. The automatic readiness to serve on the part of the waiter or the coach driver, whose lack of individuality stands out precisely in the fact that its substance is ultimately not as mechanically uniform as that of the machine worker, is quite aptly emphasized by his being given a number rather than any more personal expression. It is this sociological distinction which the differing designations of houses represents in the relations of urban elements as projected onto space.

If, therefore, the individuality of the elements of the spatial relation cannot be united in the same symbol with the relationship to a broad and varied circle, then one can still perhaps establish a sociological scale to this same standard, conceived quite formally. This means that the individuality, the character of personal uniqueness, as it were, which the location of certain people or groups possesses, hinders or favours in the broadest combinations, the establishment of far-reaching relationships to a variety of other elements.

The most perfect unity of both determinations has been attained by the Catholic Church through its seat in Rome. On the one hand, Rome is the absolutely unique, the most incomparable historical–geographical creation and, by virtue of the fact that 'all roads lead to Rome', its position is fixed as if by a system of countless coordinates. Yet, on the other hand, it has completely lost the limitation of localization at one point by virtue of the enormous extent and substance of its past, and of the fact that it appears as a geometrical site for all the changes and contrasts in history, whose traces and significance have grown together in it, or into it, both spiritually and visibly. Precisely because it possesses Rome, the Church has a permanent spatial home with all the advantages of constant accessibility, of sensory and manifest continuity, of a secure centralization of its activities and its own institutions. But it does not need to pay for these with all the other difficulties and biases of the localization of power at a single point, because Rome is – as it were – not a single place at all. Through the breadth of the fates and significance invested within it, its psychological and sociological effects extend far beyond its fixed location, while at the same time it offers the Church the certainty of *just such* a permanency. In order to support the goals of the Church in its relationship of domination to the faithful, Rome possesses the most extreme individuality and uniqueness that was ever possessed by a single place and, at the same time, it enjoys superiority over all the limitation and contingency of an individually fixed existence. As such, great organizations require a spatial centre, for they cannot exist without subordination and domination, and, as a rule, the commander must possess a permanent place of residence, both so that he can always have his subordinates at hand and so that they know where to find him.

Yet where this remarkable unity of localization and supra-spatiality – as in Rome – is not present, it must always be paid for by certain sacrifices. The Franciscans were originally completely homeless creatures; their individualistic freedom from all earthly bonds, their poverty and their preaching mission all necessitated this. But as soon as the widespread monastic order began to require 'ministers', the latter required a permanent place of residence for the reasons just touched upon, and therefore the brothers could no longer manage without a fixed location in monasteries. No matter how much this may have served their power in the technical sense, it nonetheless reduced that incomparable serenity, that inner security of the original brothers, of whom it was said that they had nothing, but possessed everything. By sharing the fixed nature of their place of residence with all other people, their way of life was trivialized and their freedom remained only very great, but no longer infinite, because now they were tied down at least to a single point in space.

Finally, the localization of the Jewish faith in Jerusalem, comparable in some respects to that of Catholicism in Rome, had quite different effects. As long as the temple existed in Jerusalem, an invisible thread, as it were, ran out from it to each of the Jews scattered about in countless localities, with their diverse nationalities, languages, interests and even religious variations. The temple was the meeting point which mediated the partially real and partially spiritual contacts of all of Judaism. But it possesses a function through which the local individualization was strained more than in Rome and which eventually overloaded it: sacrifices could only be made in Jerusalem; Yahweh had no other sacrificial altar in any other place. Therefore, the destruction of the temple necessarily broke this bond. The specific power and distinctive nuance of the Yahweh cult, which had emerged as a result of that singular spatialization, then gave way to a more colourless deism. For this reason, the separation of Christianity occurred more easily and powerfully; the place of the centre in Jerusalem was taken by the autonomous synagogues; the effective cohesion of the Jews retreated more and more from the religious to the racial dimension. These were the consequences of that local concentration, which confronted the sociological bond with a rigid choice: here or nowhere.

D. A fourth type of external circumstances, which translate themselves into the liveliness of sociological interactions, is offered by space through the sensory proximity or distance between people who stand in some relationship or other to one another. The first glance will convince us that two organizations that are held together by the very same interests, forces and convictions change their character according to whether their participants have spatial contact with each other, or are separated from one another. And this is not only true in the above sense of a difference in the overall relationship because other inwardly independent ones created by physical proximity are added to the overall relationship. Rather, it is also true that the spatially based interactions can also fundamentally modify the primary relationship, even from a distance. An economic cartel or a friendship, a stamp collectors' association or a religious community can do without personal contact permanently or for a period of time, but at the very moment when there is no distance to overcome, the possibility of innumerable quantitative and qualitative modifications of the cohesive bond immediately appears.

But before entering into this aspect, let us note the principle that the difference in both types of connection is more relative than the sharp logical contrast between proximity and separation would lead one to suspect. The psychological effect of proximity can actually be replaced very closely by means of indirect communication and even more by fantasy. The opposing poles of human associations in the psychological sense – those that are purely objective and impersonal, and those completely dependent on the intensity of emotions – are precisely the ones which succeed most easily in this endeavour. The first group, such as certain economic or scientific transactions, can succeed because their elements can be completely expressed in logical forms and thus in written form. The same is true of the other category, such as religious and certain romantic associations, because the power of fantasy and the devotion of the feelings can overcome the conditions of time and space in a manner that quite often seems almost mystical.

To the extent that these two extremes lose their purity, spatial proximity becomes more necessary: if those logically grounded relationships display gaps that can only be filled by imponderables that cannot be grasped by logic, or if the purely inward ones cannot do without a certain complement of sensual desires. Perhaps the totality of social interactions could be arranged on a scale from this viewpoint, according to what degree of spatial proximity or distance a sociation either demands or tolerates from given forms and contents. The manner in which one could combine the criteria for such a scale will be illustrated further in what follows.

Under identical conditions with respect to emotions and interests, the spatial tension capacity of any sociation is dependent upon the amount of capacity for abstraction that is available. The more primitive is consciousness, the more incapable it is of conceiving the unity of what is spatially separated or the non-unity of that which is spatially proximate. At this point, the type of forces creating sociation goes back directly to the ultimate foundations of mental life, and specifically to the fact that the naive uniformity of the untrained imagination does not yet distinguish properly between the self and its surroundings. On the one hand, the ego still floats without any individualistic emphasis among the images of things and other people, as the lack of an ego in the child and the semi-communistic lack of differentiation of early social conditions demonstrate. On the other hand, at this level objects are not yet accorded any being-for-themselves; the naive egoism of the child and of the primitive person wishes to take immediately everything it desires – and it desires almost everything with which it comes into sensory proximity. It thus extends the dominion of the ego over things almost to the same degree as occurs theoretically through the subjectivism of thinking and the ignorance of objective laws.

It therefore becomes obvious how decisive sensory proximity must be for the consciousness of belonging together in this psychological state. Since this proximity is not at issue as an objective spatial fact but rather as the psychological superstructure above that fact, it can occasionally be replaced even at this level, as already mentioned earlier, by other psychological constellations, for example by common membership of a totem group which, among the Australian Aborigines creates close relationships among individuals living widely separated, so that they spare each other during a war between their respective groups.

In general, however, for primitive consciousness, only the external contacts support the internal ones – no matter how different in character they may be – and an undifferentiated imagination is actually unable to distinguish the two. In a similar way, even today in the backwardness of small town conditions the relationship to one's neighbours in a building plays a very different role than in the metropolis where, in the complexity and confusion of the external image of city life, one grows accustomed to continual abstractions, to indifference towards that which is spatially closest and to an intimate relationship to that which is spatially very far removed.

During epochs in which abstraction capable of transcending space is demanded by objective conditions, but is hampered by psychological underdevelopment, sociological tensions accordingly arise with considerable consequences for the form of the relationship. For instance, the patronage of the Anglo-Saxon king over the Church has been justly attributed to the considerable remoteness from the See of Rome. At that time, personal presence was still considered too major a condition for the exercise of authority for such authority to be willingly turned over to such a distant agency. In passing, I would also like to take up a historical repercussion within this context. Where the intellectual superiority of a single part or the force of circumstances makes unavoidable a relationship over a distance which consciousness is not mature enough to overcome, then this must have contributed greatly to the training of abstraction, to the elasticity of the mind as it were. Sociological necessity had to generate its own individual psychological organ. Thus, in the Middle Ages, the relationship of Europe to Rome – where it did not fail because of spatial distance – became for that very reason the school for the ability to engage in abstraction, the ability to feel beyond the sensorily immediate. It became the triumph of the powers that were effective only because of their content over those that depended upon spatial presence.

Accordingly, if relationships over a distance primarily presume a certain degree of intellectual development, so, conversely, the more sensory nature of local proximity is revealed in the fact that being on a friendly or hostile footing with close neighbours – in short, a decidedly positive footing – and mutual indifference tend to be mutually exclusive to the extent of the proximity. The dominant intellectuality always implies a reduction of the emotional extremes. By virtue of its objective content as well as its psychological function, intellectuality places itself beyond the opposite extremes between which feeling and the will oscillate. Intellectuality is the principle of impartiality, so that neither individuals nor historical epochs of a decidedly intellectual nature tend to be distinguished by the one-sidedness or the intensity of love and hate.

This correlation also applies to the individual relationships between people. Intellectuality, no matter how much it provides a basis for general understanding, also creates a certain distance between people through this very activity itself. Because it facilitates *rapprochement* and harmony between the most remote parties, it fosters a cool and often alienating objectivity between neighbours. If relationships to spatially distant people tend to display a certain calmness, reticence and lack of passion, then this appears to naive consciousness just as much an immediate consequence of distance as that same naive consciousness views the weakening of a throwing motion according to the amount of spatial distance passed through as a *success* of the mere spatial distance. In reality, the significance of the spatial interval is merely that it eliminates the stimulations, frictions, attractions and repulsions which sensory proximity calls forth, and thus produces a majority for the intellectual forces within the complex of sociating psychological forces.

With respect to a spatially close person, with whom one has contact in the most mutually varied situations and moods without the possibility of caution or choice, there tend to be only decisive emotions, so that this proximity can be the basis both for the most effusive joy and the most unbearable constraint. It is a very old observation that residents of the same building can only stand on a friendly or a hostile footing. The exceptions to this rule confirm its foundation. On the one hand, in the case of a very high level of education or, on the other, in the modern metropolis, complete indifference and the exclusion of all emotional reactions can occur even between next door neighbours. In the first case, this happens because the overwhelming intellectuality relegates emotional reactions, as it were, to the status of contact stimuli, and in the second because the incessant contacts with countless people produce the same effect through the dulling of the senses. Here the indifference to that which is spatially close is simply a protective device without which one would be mentally ground down and destroyed in the metropolis.

Where excessively lively temperaments oppose this weakening consequence of metropolitan life, other protective devices have occasionally been sought. In Alexandria during the imperial period, two of the five quarters of the city were inhabited primarily by Jews, through which segregation people sought to prevent conflicts between neighbours as much as possible by mutually uniform national origins. If, therefore, the peacemaker attempts above all things to spatially separate passionately conflicting parties, then this does not at all contradict his attempting to bring them together when they were far apart. For in some personalities the fantasy which is effective at a distance releases an untrammelled exaggeration of feeling, by comparison with which the irritating consequences of sensory proximity, no matter how great they may be, seem somehow both limited and infinite.

Alongside the obvious practical effects of spatial proximity and the sociologically highly important consciousness of having those effects available at all times – even if one has no desire to make use of them at the moment – the result of proximity for the form of sociation is composed of the significance of the individual senses with which individuals mutually perceive one another. This achievement of the senses for the connection of people with one another must be the topic of special investigations, which cannot be included here because of their very comprehensive foundations of a physiological and psychological nature. I shall list only a few aspects by way of example.

If contact is such that individuals see each other constantly, but can only speak to each other relatively infrequently – like workers in a factory building, the students in a lecture or soldiers of a usually undivided battalion – then the consciousness of unity will have a more abstract character than when that contact also includes oral communication. In comparison to the optical image of a person or persons, which always shows only a relatively stable content that can only be varied within narrow limits, the ear transmits an infinite variety of the most divergent moods, emotions and thoughts – in short the entire polarity of subjective and objective life.

Conversational proximity creates a much more individual relationship than does visual closeness, and not only because it supplements the latter, but also quite directly: only very few people have an accurate visual image even of their closest contacts, who they daily have before their very eyes, and few would be able to list confidently the colour of their eyes or the shape of their mouth from memory. By contrast, recollection of what has been said is infinitely richer and firmer, and it alone actually sets down the image of the personality as something truly unique and personal. Where only the sense of sight exploits proximity, more of a feeling of a general-conceptual and unspecific unity or of a mechanical concurrence will result, whereas the possibility of speaking and hearing will produce individual, animated, organic feelings of unity.

Of much greater significance for the association or repulsion among human beings is the sense of smell, forming a scale here with the other two senses to the extent that it connects the most inarticulate, instinctive and exclusively emotional condition of these relationships to physical proximity. The sense of sight on its own provides lighter, more conscious and differentiated motifs of unification or its opposite. The sense of hearing really binds people together; only this sense is the lasting carrier of associations that have a history, whereas the former senses only allow the more or less undeveloped aspects of people to be touched. The sense of smell and, especially, its stimuli remain below the threshold of consciousness and cannot be expressed in words (since we have concepts only for the crude

and non-individual nuances of smell); and it is these to which we may probably ascribe a share in those elementary sympathies and antipathies, often
beyond any comprehensibility, that are formed unilaterally or mutually
between persons.

The sense of smell has a great influence at least on the sociological
relationship of different races living in the same territory. The reception of
Negroes into the higher social circles in American is excluded simply
because of the odour of the Negro; the often instinctive aversion between
Germans and Jews has been ascribed to the same factor. Personal contact
between the educated class and the workers, often so vigorously advocated
for modern social development, that *rapprochement* of the two social worlds
'of those who do not know how the other half lives', which is also recognized as an ethical ideal by the educated, fails simply because of the insuperability of the sensory impressions in this area. The average educated
person would rather endure all sorts of deprivations than physical contact
with the people to whom the aroma of 'the honest sweat of their brow'
clings. In this way, physical proximity influences social formation quite considerably, at least in a negative sense, and probably more and more as
culture increases, because that reduces the acuity of perception for all the
senses, not least for the sense of smell, just as it increases the emphasis on
pleasure and displeasure.

One could characterize the sense of smell as the dissociating sense, since
the gathering of many people never provides it with any attractions, as the
same situation might do, at least under certain conditions, for the other
senses. Already through this physical–psychological mediation, cultural
refinement points towards individual isolation, at least in the colder countries, whereas the opportunity to arrange meetings essentially in the open,
and hence without having to bring about that unpleasantness, must have
influenced to a considerable degree all social interaction in the southern
countries, although naturally in competition or collaboration with a
hundred other causes.

Alongside these psychological consequences of proximity or distance in
the narrow sense for social interactions, there are also those of a more
logical or at least rational nature, which have nothing to do with the sensory,
irrational immediacy just outlined. The changes, for example, which a
relationship undergoes through the transition of its elements from distance
to spatial proximity do not consist exclusively in a rising intensity of ties, but
also in their weakening, in reserve or even in repulsion.

As well as these direct antipathies that sensory proximity may provoke,
what takes effect here is more or less the absence or disavowal of the ideal-
izations in which – more or less abstractly conceived – we have clothed our
fellow human beings. Here one sees the effects of the necessary emphasis
upon an inner distance, the delimitation of the personal spheres, the repulsion of improper intimacy, in short, of all those dangers that are not at all an
issue with spatial distance. A certain precaution and indirectness is at work
here which communication must make in cases of personal immediacy,

because a greater objectivity, an alleviation of personal conflicts, a lesser probability of haste and intensity tends to be a part of indirect relationships or with those at a distance.

Among the most subtle sociological tasks of the art of living is that of preserving the values and affections that develop between people at a certain distance for a close relationship. One may involuntarily conclude that the warmth and inwardness of a relationship must increase in proportion to the degree of personal closeness. What could develop in this way under the best of conditions is anticipated from the beginning in the tone and intensity of interaction, only to feel then often enough that one has demanded too much of the mere form of a spatial relationship. We search in vain, because the suddenness of the physical proximity has deceived us about the slowness with which the psychological proximity develops to match it. In this way, setbacks and periods of coolness arise, which not only take back this illusionary 'too much' but also carry away the values of love or friendship or mutual interests that had been achieved previously. This situation is one of the not uncommon confusions among people, which probably could have been avoided from the outset by an instinctive sense of tact but, once they have come into being, can no longer be put right again by that alone, but only with the assistance of conscious closer attention and reflection.

I wish to draw a second example from relationships that are far removed from the intimacy of those just discussed, in order to pursue the sociological differences of spatial distances with regard to their calculable results. Where a minority that is held together by common interests is found within a larger group, it is generally quite decisive for the behaviour of the minority towards the totality as to whether it lives compactly together or dispersed in small units within the majority group. It cannot be generally determined which of these two forms is the more favourable for the power position of such a minority under otherwise equal circumstances. If the subgroup in question finds itself in a defensive posture *vis-à-vis* the majority, then the extent of the minority's forces decides that question. If they are very minimal, so that the only option is evasion, hiding or avoidance of devastating attacks, then, as is immediately obvious, the greatest dispersal would be advisable. With considerably more forces, especially larger numbers of people, for whom the chance of resisting an attack already exists, then, conversely, the greatest possible concentration will favour preservation. Just as even schools of herring protect themselves through their compactness by thus offering a smaller surface to attack and less free space for invading enemies, so living closely together similarly provides exposed minorities with the greater probability of successful resistance, mutual assistance, and an effective consciousness of solidarity.

The spatial distribution of the Jews has made use of both possibilities. In so far as their Diaspora distributed them throughout the entire civilized world, no persecution could affect *all* their sections, and if life was made impossible for them at one place, there was always the possibility of joining others elsewhere for protection and support. On the other hand, because they generally lived in a ghetto or otherwise mostly densely located together in a particular place, they also enjoyed the defensive advantages and strength that solid, air-tight cohesion offered.

Once the energies have reached the proportion from which they can proceed on to attacks, to gaining advantages and power, then the relationship is inverted. At this stage, a concentrated minority will be able to accomplish as much as one that cooperates from a number of different points. Thus, whereas the ghetto was a decided benefit and a strengthening factor for the Jews in that earlier stage of weaker forces that were generally dependent upon defence, it seems extraordinarily disadvantageous now that the strengths and energies of Judaism have grown, and their dispersal throughout the population has increased their collective power most effectively. This is one of the not too rare instances in which the absolute increase of a quantity directly reverses the relationships within it.

If one no longer views the minority as the element that is variable with respect to its structure, but rather enquires of this given spatial dispersion or concentration as to the constitution of the surrounding totality, then the following necessary tendency will result. A small subgroup, if it is living together compactly within a surrounding group that is held together by a central power, will favour an individualizing form of government granting the autonomy of constituent parts. For where such a group cannot take care of its own interests, cannot live its life by its own norms, then it has no technical possibility at all of protecting itself from violation by the majority. A parliamentary regime, for instance, which consistently subjects the personal life of the constituent parts to mere majority decisions, will simply majoritize such a minority. But if this minority lives dispersed, so that it is denied any possibility of independent development, direct power or autonomous institutions, then the autonomy of local parts of the whole will now be of value to it, since it will not attain a majority in any of them. Rather, considering its fragmented strength, it will be of a centralist frame of mind, because the consideration from which it can still hope to gain something can most readily be expected to come from a uniform, indeed even an absolutist, central authority. With such a diffuse structure, it will only achieve power through the individual outstanding personalities that it produces, and the best opportunities for this form of power also exist with a rule that is as personal and as powerful as possible. The local remoteness of the members points them towards a central authority; their compactness leads them away from it.

The success of this spatial situation is quite different when it does not affect the section of a group but rather a whole group. A community, all of whose elements live dispersed, is not so likely to have centralist leanings, unless other factors are very influential. When the rural Swiss farming communities banded together into governmental polities in the Middle Ages, they essentially repeated the basic outlines of the city constitutions. The farmers' association, however, was totally subsumed in the institutions it created, as was that of the city. Instead, the original assembly of the people remained the most important agency for jurisprudence and the direction of all public affairs. A certain mistrust seems to be at work here, because the permanent monitoring of the central authorities is impossible from a distance and because social interactions are less intensive than those of the compact urban population. For the latter, objective structures are necessary as fixed points in the ebbs and flows that urban life produces, both through continual contacts as well as through the strong, but continuously graduated social differentiations of its elements. These consequences of local conditions will also approximate to a certain rigidity of centralization, even on a democratic foundation of the city population.

A truly direct democracy, however, requires a spatially narrow limitation of its circle, as the classical document of the *Federalist* proclaims: 'The natural limit of a democracy is that distance from the central point which will but just permit the most remote citizens to assemble as often as their public functions demand'. And Greek antiquity would have considered it as a form of exile to be so far removed from the locus of political assemblies that one could not regularly participate in them. Democracy and aristocracy coincide in this interest in direct autonomy if their spatial conditions are identical. The history of Sparta reveals this conditionality in a very interesting combination. People there knew very well that dispersed living in the flat countryside favoured the aristocracy because, under these local spatial conditions, even democracies acquire a type of aristocratic character because of their self-sufficiency and independence from predominant central powers, as the history of the Germanic tribes very frequently demonstrates. Therefore, when the Spartans wished to overthrow democracy in Mantinea they dissolved the city into a multitude of smaller settlements. They themselves, however, found a solution to the conflict between the agrarian character of their state, in which the spatial distance always remained quite palpable and which, in that respect, was quite suited to their aristocratic character, and the energetic centralization demanded by their militarism – they left their agriculture to be conducted by dependent peoples, while they themselves lived quite close together in Sparta.

The fate of the nobility in the French *ancien régime* took a course that was outwardly rather similar. It had been highly autonomous in its agrarian-extensive mode of life until the increasingly centralizing government, with its evident apex in the court life of Louis XIV, on the one hand undermined the legal and administrative independence of the gentry while at the same time attracting them more and more to Paris. In contrast to the oppositional minorities, the correlation here is the following: the spatial concentration of a group corresponds to centralist tendencies, whereas spatial dispersion corresponds to autonomist tendencies. And since this relationship appears in complete opposition to the social tendency of life, both in its democratic and aristocratic forms, then it follows that the spatial factor of proximity or distance influences the sociological group form decisively, or at least is one of the decisive factors.

E.   All the sociological formations previously considered retraced, to a
certain extent, the static configuration of space: the boundary and distance,
a fixed position and neighbourhood are like continuations of spatial configurations into the structure of humanity, which is divided in this space.
This latter facet adds quite new consequences to the possibility that people
move from place to place. The spatial conditions of their existence thereby
become fluid, and just as humanity in general only gains the existence that
we know through mobility, so, in the same way, innumerable special consequences for their interactions result from changes of place in the narrower
sense, from migration. A few of these will be sketched out here. The fundamental division of such phenomena from the sociological point of view is
this: what forms of sociation appear in the case of a wandering group in contrast to a spatially fixed one? Likewise: what forms result for the group itself
and the migrating people when it is not the group as a whole but certain elements of it which migrate?

1.   The major formations of the first type are nomadism and those movements known as migrations of people. For the former, wandering is part of
the substance of life, as marked by the endlessness and the circularity of the
return to the same place again and again. For the mass migrations of
peoples, it is considered more an intermediate state between two different
forms of life – whether it be that of a fixed abode or whether it be that the
previous of the two is nomadic.
     To the extent that the sociological viewpoint only enquires into the
effects of wandering as such, it need not separate the two types. For its
effect on the social form is typically the same in both cases: suppression or
elimination of the inner differentiation of the group, and hence a lack of
real political organization, which, however, is often quite compatible with
despotic autocracy. For the latter constellation, the relationship of patri-
archal conditions to nomadism should be recalled. Where the necessity
grows for hunting peoples to disperse themselves and roam, the husband
removes his wife from the proximity of her family and deprives her of its
support, therefore acquiring a greater power over her. Thus the mass
migrations among American Indians have been held directly responsible
for the transition from a matrilineal to a patrilineal kinship organization.
In addition, among actual nomads, herding takes the place of hunting and,
as everywhere, this is the business of men. The despotism of the man is
developed among nomads from this masculine direction of the most
important or even the exclusive acquisition of food. Familial and state despotism, however, not only generally produce each other, but also nomads
must of necessity favour the latter since the individual has no support from
his land.
     The same situation that makes nomads everywhere the subjects as well
as the objects of robbery – namely, the mobility of their possessions – makes
life in general something so unstable and rootless that the resistance against
powerful, uniting personalities is certainly not so strong as when the

existence of each individual is concentrated on his own native land. This is especially true because the farmer does not have that opportunity to leave, which was such a distinctive weapon for itinerant tradesmen against centralizing tendencies. And, in addition, these despotic concentrations of power will usually occur for military purposes, to which the adventurous and savage nomad is more disposed than the farmer.

Of course, as was said, nomadic groups generally lack the strict and firm organization which otherwise forms part of the techniques of military despots. And as a result of the broad dispersal and mutual independence of individual nomadic families, there is no disposition present for such organization, since every more subtle and comprehensive organization presupposes divisions of labour, whereas they, in turn, presume a close spatial or dynamic contact among the elements. Yet the despotic concentration in those mass migrations of nomadic peoples that have driven their way through European history, no less than that of China, Persia and India, was obviously not an organized synthesis. Rather, its impetus depended on the mechanical aggregation of quite undifferentiated elements that poured out with the uniform and solid pressure of a stream of mud.

The plains and steppes, which appeal to a nomadic life on the one hand, and, on the other are the source of the great tribal migrations – those of eastern Europe, northern and central Asia or the American plains – therefore least of all reveal developed racial types, and this ethnographic levelling is probably no less the consequence than the cause of a sociological levelling. A deeply grounded relationship exists between movement in space and the differentiation of social and personal elements of existence. Both constitute merely different satisfactions of the *one* side of the contrasting psychological tendencies whose other side tends toward rest, uniformity and substantive unity in the feeling and image of life.

The struggles and compromises, the mixtures and alternating predominance of the two sides, can be used as a pattern to register all the contents of human history. The extent to which we require stimulation through differing, changing impressions can be fulfilled on both sides: either through the alternating impressions, demands and adventures of migratory life or through the differentiation of stable relationships. This not only shows the mind, when it looks around, all those alternations in the form of immanence, of the juxtaposition of social factors but also satisfies the mind's need for difference in the consciousness of its difference against all others – and a distinct type of difference from each individual. From this it becomes clear, on the one hand, how the extraordinary increase in the need for difference among modern people simultaneously reaches for both forms, but also how in certain cases they can stand in for each other, so that societies which are stable in space are strongly differentiated internally. Migratory ones, on the other hand, have from the very beginning concealed the feelings of difference that are necessary for their nervous constitution, and they require a social levelling for the simultaneous tendency of life under unstable circumstances.

The technique of wandering becomes the supporter of this primary relationship. The members of a wandering society are especially dependent upon one another. Their common interests have a more momentary form by comparison to those of sedentary groups, and for that reason they conceal individual differences with the specific energy of the momentary, which so often triumphs over that which is objectively more essential. Individual difference has a double sense: as qualitative or social diversity and as conflict and quarrel. For nomadic peoples, the impulses of spatial expansion and contraction confront each other very abruptly; nutritional conditions lead the individuals as far apart as possible (and the spatial separation must lead to a psychological–qualitative one), whereas the need for protection forces them together again and again and neglects the differentiation.[1] Livingstone says of the divisions of African clans, who obviously do not feel themselves terribly close in other respects, that they stick closely together during migrations of the entire tribe and support one another. From the Middle Ages, it is frequently reported that itinerant merchants introduced completely communistic orders for themselves while travelling. And it is merely a continuation of this that the mercantile guilds and Hanseatic associations, which were created in foreign countries, often formed complete living communities, characteristically enough, precisely at the very beginning of their development.

Alongside the levelling factor of migration, the despotic element was probably not entirely lacking even in such cases. At least, it is stressed in describing the troops of itinerant merchants from Palmyra, who travelled through the Euphrates region in the period of the Roman Empire, that their leaders were the most noble men from the old aristocracy, to whom the caravans' participants often erected commemorative columns. It is therefore to be assumed that their authority during the journey was a discretionary one, just as is that of the ship's captain during a voyage, and under quite analogous circumstances.

Precisely because wandering individualizes and isolates in its own right, because it makes people rely on themselves, it drives them towards a tight cohesion, over and above otherwise existing differences. By taking the support of home away from people, and alongside of this its firm gradations, it suggests that they add the tightest possible cohesion to the fate of itinerants – isolation and lack of support – to form a supra-individual unity.

This basic sociological trait of wandering betrays itself as the formally invariant element in phenomena that have no substantive connection to those touched upon so far. As acquaintanceship made while travelling, as long as it is only that and does not assume a different character independently of how it was formed, often develops an intimacy and openness for which no inner reason can actually be found. Three factors appear to me to work together here: the separation from one's accustomed milieu, the momentary impressions and encounters held in common, and the consciousness of an imminent and definitive separation once more. The second of these factors is immediately obvious in its tendency to produce a unification, a kind of intellectual communism, just so long as the identity of experience persists and dominates consciousness, but the other two factors are only accessible to more difficult sociological considerations.

With respect to the first, one must keep clearly in mind how few people know purely from within and through secure instincts where the immovable boundary of their psychological private property is actually located, and what reserves their individual existence demands in order that it remain unscathed. Only through impulses and rejections, disappointments and adaptations, do we tend to learn what we can betray of ourselves to others without risking embarrassing situations, feelings of indiscretion or actual damage. The fact that the inner sphere of the individual cannot at all be so clearly delimited in advance from that of the others, as can the sphere of one's body; or that this boundary never totally loses its relativity, even after it has overcome the hesitations of its initial formation – all this is easily revealed when we leave our accustomed relationships behind, in which we have staked out a fairly definite area for ourselves through gradually expanding rights and duties, through the understanding of others and being understood, and by testing our powers and our emotional reactions. In this way, we know for certain here what we may say and what we must keep quiet, and through what measure of the two we can produce and maintain the proper image of our personality in others.

Now, since this relative degree of exposure, fixed by our relationship to our environment, solidifies for many people as if it were something absolute and correct in itself, so, as a rule, in a totally new environment they lose any standard of how much of themselves to reveal when confronted with a total stranger. On the one hand, they become subject to suggestions that they cannot resist due to their current rootlessness and, on the other hand, they lapse into inner insecurities, in which they can no longer restrain the intimacy or confession to which they are stimulated, but instead allow this process to roll on until it stops, as if they were on an inclined plane.

In addition, there is the third factor: that we drop our accustomed reserve all the more easily when confronted with someone with whom we will have nothing more to do after a mutual or unilateral disclosure. All sociations are most decisively influenced in the character of their form and content by the notion of the temporal duration for which one considers them intended. This is one of the sociological insights whose truth is quite obvious for the crudest cases, but is all the more frequently ignored in the case of more subtle ones.

The fact that the qualitative essence of a relationship between a man and a woman is different in a life-long marriage than in a fleeting association, and the fact that a professional soldier has a different relationship to the army than someone serving for one or two years, is obvious to anyone. But the conclusion that these macroscopic effects of quantities of time must also appear in less crass cases – on a pro rata basis and, as it were, microscopically – does not appear to have been acknowledged anywhere. Whether a contract has been made for one or ten years; whether a social gathering is calculated to last a few hours in the evening or, like a country outing, for an entire day; whether one gets together at a *table d'hôte* of a hotel which changes guests every day or in a guest-house which is meant for longer stays – all this is essential for the nuancing of the course of a gathering, despite the otherwise quite identical nature of the material, attitudes and character of the people at a gathering. Of course the direction in which it takes effect cannot be seen from the quantity of time itself, but rather depends upon the totality of circumstances. A longer duration of time sometimes leads to a *négligence*, as it were, to a letting-go of the connecting bond, because one feels sure of it and does not find it necessary to further strengthen through new efforts a commitment that is irrevocable anyway. Sometimes, again, the consciousness of this very indissolubility will move us to mutual adaptation and a more or less resigned compliance in order to make the compulsion we have adopted at least as tolerable as possible. The brevity of time will occasionally lead to the same intensity in utilizing a relationship as does its length for other temperaments, who can endure a merely superficial or 'half-hearted' relationship for a short while, but not as a permanent state of affairs. This indication of the effect that can be exerted by the consideration of the duration of a relationship upon every aspect of it, is here merely meant to indicate the sociological nature of a short-term encounter as belonging to a broad and fundamental context.

Because of the feeling that it creates no obligations, and that one is actually anonymous with respect to someone whom one will separate from forever in a few hours time, an acquaintanceship made during travel often tempts us to quite peculiar confidences – indeed to the unreserved indulgence of our drive to express ourselves which, from our experiences of its consequences, we have learned to restrict in our normal long-term relationships. In this way, people have attributed the erotic opportunities of the military stratum to the fact it lacks the sedentary character of most other classes, so that for a woman the relationship with a soldier possesses the nuances of a fleeting dream that not only makes no commitments but is also attractive precisely because its brevity tempts one into the greatest intensity in exploiting and yielding to it. Similarly, the successes of the mendicant friars, who came today and left tomorrow and had the right to hear confessions anywhere, were explained in part by the fact that people were able to confess more openly to them than to their actual father confessor who constantly had his penitents under his own gaze.

Here, as so often, the extremes seem to share a certain uniform meaning that is denied to the intermediate sphere: people reveal themselves to those who are closest to them as well as those farthest removed, whereas the strata in between form the location of real reserve. Even in these very diverse phenomena, the formal basic context is discernible: the peculiarly relaxed mood of a person as a wanderer or with travellers and, by virtue of this, an abandon beyond the usual boundaries of individualization. This is what I earlier characterized as something approaching intellectual communism;

existing in innumerable transformations that may be difficult to recognize, this sociological theme pushes toward a levelling, a depersonalizing uniformity within the wandering group.

2. Quite separately from this, it should be observed how the migration of part of a group has an effect upon the whole and otherwise sedentary group. From out of the multiplicity of relevant phenomena, I shall mention here only two, one of which is to trace that effect on the uniformity of the group, the second precisely on the other side of its duality. In order to hold together dynamically the spatially remote elements of a group that is spatially broadly dispersed, highly developed epochs work out a system of varied means, above all, that everything is uniform in objective culture, accompanied by the consciousness that it is the same here as at each point of the same circle: the uniformity of language, law, general ways of life, the style of buildings and objects. In addition, there are the functionally unifying elements: the centralized, and at the same time, universally extending administration of the state and the church, more selective – but still transcending all local divisions – associations of employers and industrial workers, and commercial connections between wholesale and retail merchants, as well as the more subjective, but still very powerful, associations of students, veterans, teachers, university professors and collectors of all sorts. In short, a tangle of threads leading to absolute or partial centres holds all portions of a highly cultivated state together – of course, with quite unevenly distributed energy since neither the substantive culture is sufficiently uniform in degree and type, nor do the functional connections draw all elements to their centres with the same interest and the same force.

Nonetheless, in so far as these unifications take effect, they require to only a slight extent and accidentally, as it were, movement of people over large distances. Modern life is able to bring about the consciousness of social unity, first, by means of those objective regularities and the knowledge of the common points of contact; second, through the institutions which are permanently fixed; and third, through written communication. But as long as this objective organization and technique is missing, a different means of unification, which later recedes, has priority: namely, travel which, of course, because of its purely personal character, can never cover the breadth of the spatial area as the preceding means do, and can never substantively centralize an equivalent spatial expanse.

The merchant and the scholar, the civil servant and the craftsman, the monk and the artist, the élite as well as the lowest elements of society, were all frequently more mobile in the Middle Ages and the Early Modern period than now. What we gain in a consciousness of homogeneity through letters and books, bank accounts and branch offices, through mechanical reproduction of the same model and through photography, all in those days had to be brought about through people travelling. This was as expensive to accomplish as it was deficient in results, because where one is only concerned with merely objective transfers, the journey of a person is an

extreme, awkward and undifferentiated process, since the person must drag
along as additional baggage all the external and internal aspects of his or
her personality, which have nothing to do with the issue in question. And
even if this journey yielded a good many personal and emotional relationships as a by-product, still it did not serve the end in question here: that of
making the unity of the group palpable and effective.

Objective relationships, which completely exclude the personal element
and therefore can lead from each element to an unlimited number of others,
are much more capable of making people aware of a unity that extends
beyond individuals. It is precisely the emotional relationship that often not
only excludes all others, but also exhausts itself in its immediate vicinity, to
such an extent that its yield for the consciousness of unity of the circle to
which both parties belong is minimal. It is characteristic of this subjective
character of connections, and yet at the same time of their importance as
well, that in the Middle Ages the maintenance of the roads and bridges was
considered a *religious* duty. The fact that so many relationships, which are
now mediated objectively, only came about through the travels of persons
in earlier eras seems to me to be a reason for the relative weakness of the
consciousness of unity in the extended groups of prehistory.

At any rate, travels were frequently the only, often at least one of the
comparatively strongest, carriers of centralization, especially in the political sense. In some cases, the king took the various parts of the kingdom personally into his possession in the form of a single tour of the realm, as is
reported of the Frankish kings and as was the practice of the earlier kings
of Sweden. In other instances, this occurred by the king travelling around
in the realm either periodically or continually – the former was the case with
the oldest Russian rulers, who travelled to all their cities every year, while
the latter prevailed among the German emperors of the First Empire. The
Russian custom is supposed to have served the cohesion of the empire. The
German custom, which arose from the lack of an imperial capital, was for
that very reason the sign of a worrying decentralization, but was the best
that the king personally could do under those circumstances for the unity
of the various parts of the empire. In fact, one of the causes of this touring
by German princes, namely, the lack of means of transportation which
required that taxes in kind be consumed on the spot, itself created a kind of
very personal relationship between each district and the king. The establishment of the itinerant justices by Henry II in England served a similar
purpose. Considering the imperfections of centralization and communication, the administration of the counties by the high sheriffs had been
subject to considerable abuses from the very outset. These itinerant justices
were the first to bring the highest court of the state – by means of the distance they had as outsiders to all individual parts of the country and by the
substantive uniformity of their legal decisions – in relationship to all parts
of the realm and to the distant unity of law and administration centralized
in the king. As long as supra-local means that are effective over a long distance are still lacking to infuse even local officials with this unity, the

travelling of officials will provide the most effective possibility of centralizing the distant localities into the ideal political unity.

The impression upon the senses of people who are known to come from that centre of the totality and are to return to it again also tends in this direction. Such immediacy and visibility contains an advantage for an organization supported by mobile elements over one that is held together by more abstract means, which occasionally compensate for its greater contingency and isolation. For its propaganda among rural workers, a semi-socialistic English organization, the English Land Restoration League uses 'red vans', in which their speakers live, which travel from place to place and constitute the focal point of meetings and agitation. Despite its mobility, such a wagon is psychologically a stationary element by virtue of its characteristic appearance that is known everywhere. Its coming and going creates a stronger consciousness of unity across space among the scattered party members than a stationary party branch office would achieve under otherwise similar circumstances, with the result that other parties have already begun to imitate this van-propaganda.

The principle of travelling can serve religious as well as state and party unity. The English Christians only adopted parish churches relatively late. At least until well into the seventh century, bishops travelled around in the diocese with their assistants in order to perform their religious duties. Just as certainly as the unity of the *individual community* received an incomparable fixity and concreteness through the construction of a church, so this could tend toward a particularistic closure of the congregation, while the unity of the entire diocese, indeed of the Church as a whole, must have been brought to consciousness much more effectively by the travels of its representatives. To this day, the Baptists of North America conduct their proselytization in the remoter regions by means of special wagons, 'gospel cars', which are said to be furnished as chapels. This mobilization of the religious service must be especially favourable to such propaganda, because it graphically demonstrates to the scattered adherents that they are not left in isolated, lost outposts, but rather belong instead to a unified totality that is held together by continually functioning ties.

Finally, it is the ethical behaviour of groups towards their wandering elements that occasionally makes them points of meeting and unification. Because the indispensability of travel for all intellectual and economic exchange in the Middle Ages was matched by its dangers and difficulties, and the poor, who were the object of public charity in any case, were almost continually itinerant, it could transpire that the Church would commend travellers to the daily prayers of the pious, along with the ill and the imprisoned. And the Koran similarly ordains that one-fifth of the bounty belongs to God, his representatives, the orphans, the beggars and the travellers. Direct charity for travellers later became differentiated according to a general historical developmental norm into the objective easing of travelling through roads, protection, institutions of diverse types, and the subjective independence and self-reliance of individuals. This general religious

obligation to travellers was the ethical reflection of the continuing sociological interaction and functional unity which the wanderers produced.

Alongside this unifying effect of travel on the fixed group, which strives
to overcome its spatial dispersion functionally through the travel back and
forth of its individual elements, there is another effect, which particularly
serves the antagonistic forces of the group. This results when one part of a
group is basically settled, whereas another is characterized by its mobility,
and this difference in formal spatial behaviour becomes the bearer, the
instrument and the amplifying element of an already existing, latent or open
hostility. The most marked type here is the vagabond and the adventurer,
whose perpetual roving projects the unrest and the *rubato* character of their
inner rhythm of life into space. In themselves, the differences between those
who are by nature sedentary and those whose inclination is towards mobility provide infinite possibilities for variation in the structure and development of society.

Each of these two dispositions senses its natural and implacable enemy
in the other. For where society, through a delicate differentiation of occupations, does not manage to provide the born vagabond with an activity suitable to his nature – and this is seldom the case, because even the required
regularity in time is inwardly all too closely related to permanence in space
– such a person will exist as a parasite upon the settled elements. But the
settled elements do not persecute the vagabond solely because they hate
him, but they also hate him because they must persecute him for the sake
of their own self-preservation. And the very same thing which puts the
vagabond in that exposed and vulnerable position – his impulse for a continuous change of scene, the ability and desire to 'disappear' – is, at the same
time, his protection against persecution and ostracism: it is at once his attack
and his defensive weapon. Just as his relationship to space is the adequate
expression of his subjective inwardness and its oscillations, so equally the
same is true for his relationship to his social group.

We are concerned here exclusively with singular elements, who are constrained by their restlessness and mobility, but are also capable of declaring
war on the entire society. Associations of vagabonds are extremely rare, at
least compared with their interpenetration through the whole of society. In
these, distinguished sociologically, we would be dealing with communities
of migrants rather than migrating communities like those of the nomads.
The adventurer's entire principle of life would conflict with such an organization, since an organization can hardly escape some type of permanence. In
any case, there are the beginnings of such associations, which one could
term fluid sociations, but these obviously can regulate and integrate into
themselves only a minor part of the inner and outer life of their members.
One such homeless association was that of the wandering minstrels of the
Middle Ages. It required the entire cooperative spirit of the times for these
itinerant people to create a type of inner order for themselves. By rising as
high as the establishment of 'masters' and other titles, the latter muted at
least the formal intensity of its antagonism with the rest of society.

This occurs even more uncompromisingly with a different type of physical motion as the agent of a social antagonism: namely, where two subgroups are brought into sharper hostility by such movement. Here the travels of journeymen, especially in the Middle Ages, provide the best example. The organizations upon which the journeymen depended, in making their claims against the cities and the master craftsmen, considered travelling a prerequisite. Or put another way, the two were linked in an indissoluble interaction. Travelling would not have been possible without an institution that gave the newly arrived journeyman an initial base, and inevitably, his fellows, who had been or might be in a similar position, had to provide this. Since it was the journeymen's associations which took care of providing employment, the journeyman was actually at home anywhere in Germany (and similarly for other countries). A network for transmitting news among the journeymen equalized supply of, and demand for, work relatively quickly, and thus at first it was this very tangible advantage which brought into existence journeymen's associations that spanned the entire realm. Travelling meant that the journeymen's guilds enjoyed a much more active communication than those of the masters, with their immobile residences, so that a uniformity of law and custom grew up among the journeymen which provided the individual or small groups with extraordinarily strong support in their struggles for wages, standard of living, honour and social position.

In addition to the socializing effect of its members' travels, the position of the journeymen class was also strengthened by its mobility; for the latter enabled them to carry out hirings and boycotts in a manner that the master craftsmen could not immediately counter. They were evidently only able to do so after they had compensated for the disadvantages of their sedentariness by means of alliances encompassing the entire area that would be open to the travels of the journeymen. Thus, we hear of alliances of cities and guilds in solidarity against the journeymen, alliances which tended to encompass a single self-contained geographical zone, which would constitute the normal region within which a journeyman would travel.

Hence, two different forms of dominating the same space were in conflict here. The mobility, with which the group sends its members back and forth offensively and defensively, choosing on each occasion the point of least resistance and highest utility, confronted the theoretical domination of the same space by the agreements of the other group distributed throughout it. Those agreements were supposed to eliminate the inner differences of the group of master craftsmen, from which the mobility of the others profited. Only after the establishment of uniform behaviour and powers for all elements of the master craftsmen's group did the opportunity arising from the opposing group's mobility prove to be illusory. Correspondingly, in the seventeenth and eighteenth centuries the state was also able to dominate the master guilds, who had to be stationary, much more easily than it could those of the journeymen, since the latter could escape from any territory and limit the influx, thereby severely damaging the workings of the guilds.

For that reason, even states were only able to be effective against the journeymen's associations when a large part of the realm took action *simultaneously* against them in the eighteenth century.

The character of human sociations is thus determined to a great extent by how often their members meet. Between the masters and the journeymen, this category is distributed here in such a peculiar way that the one group meets frequently and in general as often as needed, because of their rootedness, but for that same reason only within the locally limited circle. The others, by contrast, meet less frequently, less completely and more by chance, but in the broader environs, which encompass several guild districts. Whereas, for instance, a journeyman who broke his contract was generally punished severely in the Middle Ages, it was conceded to the journeymen weavers in Berlin in 1331 that everyone could receive immediate dismissal and payment of wages, *if he intended to leave the city*.

An instance of the opposite situation is to be found where the frequent travels and migrations of the workers always prevented a certain part of them from taking part in a movement for more wages, and thus placed them at a disadvantage with respect to the settled entrepreneurs. Among those categories of workers who are mobilized by the nature of their occupation, such as seasonal agricultural labourers and seamen, the disadvantage of impermanence can often increase to the point of a complete lack of rights, since, for instance, in a legal claim to damages against the employer, they are unable to locate their witnesses and keep them together during the long-drawn-out legal proceedings.

It seems in general, as if the closer one comes to the present, the greater the advantages of the settled person against his mobile opponent become. And this is understandable from the increased ease of moving from one place to another. For this means that even the fundamentally settled person can be anywhere at any time, so that alongside his sedentariness, he increasingly comes to enjoy all the advantages of mobility, whereas the restless, fundamentally mobile person does not gain the advantages of sedentariness to the same extent.

BRIDGE AND DOOR

The image of external things possesses for us the ambiguous dimension that in external nature everything can be considered to be connected, but also as separated. The uninterrupted transformations of materials as well as energies brings everything into relationship with everything else and make *one* cosmos out of all the individual elements. On the other hand, however, the objects remain banished in the merciless separation of space; no particle of matter can share its space with another and a real unity of the diverse does not exist in spatial terms. And, by virtue of this equal demand on self-excluding concepts, natural existence seems to resist any application of them at all.

Only to humanity, in contrast to nature, has the right to connect and separate been granted, and in the distinctive manner that one of these activities is always the presupposition of the other. By choosing two items from the undisturbed store of natural things in order to designate them as 'separate', we have already related them to one another in our consciousness, we have emphasized these two together against whatever lies between them. And conversely, we can only sense those things to be related which we have previously somehow isolated from one another; things must first be separated from one another in order to be together. Practically as well as logically, it would be meaningless to connect that which was not separated, and indeed that which also remains separated in some sense. The formula according to which both types of activity come together in human undertakings, whether the connectedness or the separation is felt to be what was naturally ordained and the respective alternative is felt to be our task, is something which can guide all our activity. In the immediate as well as the symbolic sense, in the physical as well as the intellectual sense, we are at any moment those who separate the connected or connect the separate.

The people who first built a path between two places performed one of the greatest human achievements. No matter how often they might have gone back and forth between the two and thus connected them subjectively, so to speak, it was only in visibly impressing the path into the surface of the earth that the places were objectively connected. The will to connection had become a shaping of things, a shaping that was available to the will at every repetition, without still being dependent on its frequency or rarity. Path-building, one could say, is a specifically human achievement; the animal too continuously overcomes a separation and often in the cleverest and most ingenious ways, but its beginning and end remain unconnected, it does not accomplish the miracle of the road: freezing movement into a solid structure that commences from it and in which it terminates.

This achievement reaches its zenith in the construction of a bridge. Here the human will to connection seems to be confronted not only by the passive resistance of spatial separation but also by the active resistance of a special configuration. By overcoming this obstacle, the bridge symbolizes the extension of our volitional sphere over space. Only for us are the banks of a river not just apart but 'separated'; if we did not first connect them in our practical thoughts, in our needs and in our fantasy, then the concept of separation would have no meaning. But natural form here approaches this concept as if with a positive intention; here the separation seems imposed between the elements in and of themselves, over which the spirit now prevails, reconciling and uniting.

The bridge becomes an aesthetic value in so far as it accomplishes the connection between what is separated not only in reality and in order to fulfil practical goals, but in making it directly visible. The bridge gives to the eye the same support for connecting the sides of the landscape as it does to the body for practical reality. The mere dynamics of motion, in whose particular reality the 'purpose' of the bridge is exhausted, has become something visible and lasting, just as the portrait brings to a halt, as it were, the physical and mental life process in which the reality of humankind takes place and gathers the emotion of that reality, flowing and ebbing away in time, into a single timelessly stable visualization which reality never displays and never can display. The bridge confers an ultimate meaning elevated above all sensuousness, an individual meaning not mediated by any abstract reflection, an appearance that draws the practical purposive meaning of the bridge into itself, and brings it into a visible form in the same way as a work of art does with its 'object'. Yet the bridge reveals its difference from the work of art, in the fact that despite its synthesis transcending nature, in the end it fits into the image of nature. For the eye it stands in a much closer and much less fortuitous relationship to the banks that it connects than does, say, a house to its earth foundation, which disappears from sight beneath it. People quite generally regard a bridge in a landscape to be a 'picturesque' element, because through it the fortuitousness of that which is given by nature is elevated to a unity, which is indeed of a completely intellectual nature. Yet by means of its immediate spatial visibility it does indeed possess precisely that aesthetic value, whose purity art represents when it puts the spiritually gained unity of the merely natural into its island-like ideal enclosedness.

Whereas in the correlation of separateness and unity, the bridge always allows the accent to fall on the latter, and at the same time overcomes the separation of its anchor points that make them visible and measurable, the door represents in a more decisive manner how separating and connecting are only two sides of precisely the same act. The human being who first erected a hut, like the first roadbuilder, revealed the specifically human capacity over against nature, in so far as he or she cut a portion out of the continuity and infinity of space and arranged this into a particular unity in accordance with a *single* meaning. A piece of space was thereby brought together and separated from the whole remaining world. By virtue of the fact that the door forms, as it were, a linkage between the space of human beings and everything that remains outside it, it transcends the separation between the inner and the outer. Precisely because it can also be opened, its closure provides the feeling of a stronger isolation against everything outside this space than the mere unstructured wall. The latter is mute, but the door speaks. It is absolutely essential for humanity that it set itself a boundary, but with freedom, that is, in such a way that it can also remove this boundary again, that it can place itself outside it.

The finitude into which we have entered somehow always borders somewhere on the infinitude of physical or metaphysical being. Thus the door becomes the image of the boundary point at which human beings actually always stand or can stand. The finite unity, to which we have connected a part of infinite space designated for us, reconnects it to this latter; in the unity, the bounded and the boundaryless adjoin one another, not in the dead geometric form of a mere separating wall, but rather as the possibility of a permanent interchange – in contrast to the bridge which connects the finite with the finite. Instead, the bridge removes us from this firmness in the act of walking on it and, before we have become inured to it through daily habit, it must have provided the wonderful feeling of floating for a moment between heaven and earth. Whereas the bridge, as the line stretched between two points, prescribes unconditional security and direction, life flows forth out of the door from the limitation of isolated separate existence into the limitlessness of all possible directions.

If the factors of separateness and connectedness meet in the bridge in such a way that the former appears more as the concern of nature and the latter more the concern of humankind, then in the case of the door, both are concentrated more uniformly in human achievement *as* human achievement. This is the basis for the richer and livelier significance of the door compared to the bridge, which is also revealed in the fact that it makes no difference in meaning in which direction one crosses a bridge, whereas the door displays a complete difference of intention between entering and exiting. This completely distinguishes it from the significance of the window which, as a connection of inner space with the external world, is otherwise related to the door. Yet the teleological emotion with respect to the window is directed almost exclusively from inside to outside: it is there for looking out, not for looking in. It creates the connection between the inner and the outer chronically and continually, as it were, by virtue of its transparency; but the one-sided direction in which this connection runs, just like the limitation upon it to be a path merely for the eye, gives to the window only a part of the deeper and more fundamental significance of the door.

Of course, the particular situation can also emphasize one direction of the latter's function more than the other. When the masonry openings in Gothic or Romanesque cathedrals gradually taper down to the actual door and one reaches it between rows of semi-columns and figures that approach each other more and more closely, then the significance of these doors is obviously meant to be that of a leading into but not a leading out of somewhere – the latter existing rather as an unfortunately unavoidable accidental property. This structure leads the person entering with certainty and with a gentle, natural compulsion on the right way. (This meaning is extended, as I mention for the sake of analogy here, by the rows of pillars between the door and the high altar. By perspectively moving closer together, they point the way, lead us onwards, permit no wavering – which would not be the case if we actually observed the real parallelism of the pillar; for then the end point would display no difference from that of the beginning, there would be no marking to indicate that we must start at the one point and end up at the other. Yet no matter how wonderfully perspective is used here for the inner orientation of the church, it ultimately also lends itself to the opposite effect and allows the rows of pillars to direct us to the door with the same narrowing from altar to door as the one that leads us to its main point.) Only that external conical form of the door makes entering in contrast to exiting its completely unambiguous meaning. But this is in fact a totally unique situation which it symbolizes, namely, that the movement of life, which goes equally from inside to outside and from outside to inside, terminates at the church and is replaced by the only direction which is necessary. Life on the earthly plane, however, as at every moment it throws a bridge between the unconnectedness of things, likewise stands in every moment inside or outside the door through which it will lead from its separate existence into the world, or from the world into its separate existence.

The forms that dominate the dynamics of our lives are thus transferred by bridge and door into the fixed permanence of visible creation. They do not support the merely functional and teleological aspect of our movements as tools; rather, in their form it solidifies, as it were, into immediately convincing plasticity. Viewed in terms of the opposing emphases that prevail in their impression, the bridge indicates how humankind unifies the separatedness of merely natural being, and the door how it separates the uniform, continuous unity of natural being. The basis for their distinctive value for the visual arts lies in the general aesthetic significance which they gain through this visualization of something metaphysical, this stabilization of something merely functional. Even though one might also attribute the frequency with which painting employs both to the artistic value of their mere form, there does indeed still exist here that mysterious coincidence with which the purely artistic significance and perfection of an object at the same time always reveals the most exhaustive expression of an actually nonvisible spiritual or metaphysical meaning. The purely artistic interest in, say, the human face, only concerned with form and colour, is satisfied in the highest degree when its representation includes the ultimate in inspiration and intellectual characterization.

Because the human being is the connecting creature who must always separate and cannot connect without separating – that is why we must first conceive intellectually of the merely indifferent existence of two river banks as something separated in order to connect them by means of a bridge. And the human being is likewise the bordering creature who has no border. The enclosure of his or her domestic being by the door means, to be sure, that they have separated out a piece from the uninterrupted unity of natural being. But just as the formless limitation takes on a shape, its limitedness finds its significance and dignity only in that which the mobility of the door illustrates: in the possibility at any moment of stepping out of this limitation into freedom.

THE METROPOLIS AND MENTAL LIFE

The deepest problems of modern life derive from the claim of the individual to preserve the autonomy and individuality of his existence in the face of overwhelming social forces, of historical heritage, of external culture, and of the technique of life. The fight with nature which primitive man has to wage for his *bodily* existence attains in this modern form its latest transformation. The eighteenth century called upon man to free himself of all the historical bonds in the state and in religion, in morals and in economics. Man's nature, originally good and common to all, should develop unhampered. In addition to more liberty, the nineteenth century demanded the functional specialization of man and his work; this specialization makes one individual incomparable to another, and each of them indispensable to the highest possible extent. However, this specialization makes each man the more directly dependent upon the supplementary activities of all others. Nietzsche sees the full development of the individual conditioned by the most ruthless struggle of individuals; socialism believes in the suppression of all competition for the same reason. Be that as it may, in all these positions the same basic motive is at work: the person resists being levelled down and worn out by a social-technological mechanism. An enquiry into the inner meaning of specifically modern life and its products, into the soul of the cultural body, so to speak, must seek to solve the equation which structures like the metropolis set up between the individual and the supra-individual contents of life. Such an enquiry must answer the question of how the personality accommodates itself in the adjustments to external forces. This will be my task today.

The psychological basis of the metropolitan type of individuality consists in the *intensification of nervous stimulation* which results from the swift and uninterrupted change of outer and inner stimuli. Man is a differentiating creature. His mind is stimulated by the difference between a momentary impression and the one which preceded it. Lasting impressions, impressions which differ only slightly from one another, impressions which take a regular and habitual course and show regular and habitual contrasts – all these use up, so to speak, less consciousness than does the rapid crowding of changing images, the sharp discontinuity in the grasp of a single glance, and the unexpectedness of onrushing impressions. These are the psychological conditions which the metropolis creates. With each crossing of the street, with the tempo and multiplicity of economic, occupational and social life, the city sets up a deep contrast with small town and rural life with reference to the sensory foundations of psychic life. The metropolis exacts from man as a discriminating creature a different amount of consciousness than does rural life. Here the rhythm of life and sensory mental imagery flows more slowly, more habitually, and more evenly. Precisely in this connection the sophisticated character of metropolitan psychic life becomes understandable – as over against small town life which rests more upon deeply felt and emotional relationships. These latter are rooted in the more unconscious layers of the psyche and grow most readily in the steady rhythm of uninterrupted habituations. The intellect, however, has its locus in the transparent, conscious, higher layers of the psyche; it is the most adaptable of our inner forces. In order to accommodate to change and to the contrast of phenomena, the intellect does not require any shocks and inner upheavals; it is only through such upheavals that the more conservative mind could accommodate to the metropolitan rhythm of events. Thus the metropolitan type of man – which, of course, exists in a thousand individual variants – develops an organ protecting him against the threatening currents and discrepancies of his external environment which would uproot him. He reacts with his head instead of his heart. In this an increased awareness assumes the psychic prerogative. Metropolitan life, thus, underlies a heightened awareness and a predominance of intelligence in metropolitan man. The reaction to metropolitan phemomena is shifted to that organ which is least sensitive and quite remote from the depth of the personality. Intellectuality is thus seen to preserve subjective life against the overwhelming power of metropolitan life, and intellectuality branches out in many directions and is integrated with numerous discrete phenomena.

The metropolis has always been the seat of the money economy. Here the multiplicity and concentration of economic exchange gives an importance to the means of exchange which the scantiness of rural commerce would not have allowed. Money economy and the dominance of the intellect are intrinsically connected. They share a matter-of-fact attitude in dealing with men and with things; and, in this attitude, a formal justice is often coupled with an inconsiderate hardness. The intellectually sophisticated person is indifferent to all genuine individuality, because relationships and reactions result from it which cannot be exhausted with logical operations. In the same manner, the individuality of phenomena is not commensurate with the pecuniary principle. Money is concerned only with what is common to all: it asks for the exchange value, it reduces all quality and individuality to the question: How much? All intimate emotional relations between persons are founded in their individuality, whereas in rational relations man is reckoned with like a number, like an element which is in itself indifferent. Only the objective measurable achievement is of interest. Thus metropolitan man reckons with his merchants and customers, his domestic servants and often even with persons with whom he is obliged to have social intercourse. These features of intellectuality contrast with the nature of the small circle in which the inevitable knowledge of individuality as inevitably produces a warmer tone of behaviour, a behaviour which is beyond a mere objective balancing of service and return. In the sphere of the economic psychology of the small group it is of importance that under primitive conditions production serves the customer who orders the good, so that the producer and the consumer are acquainted. The modern metropolis, however, is supplied almost entirely by production for the market, that is, for entirely unknown purchasers who never personally enter the producer's actual field of vision. Through this anonymity the interests of each party acquire an unmerciful matter-of-factness; and the intellectually calculating economic egoism of both parties need not fear any deflection because of the imponderables of personal relationships. The money economy dominates the metropolis; it has displaced the last survivals of domestic production and the direct barter of goods; it minimizes, from day to day, the amount of work ordered by customers. The matter-of-fact attitude is obviously so intimately interrelated with the money economy, which is dominant in the metropolis, that nobody can say whether the intellectualistic mentality first promoted the money economy or whether the latter determined the former. The metropolitan way of life is certainly the most fertile soil for this reciprocity, a point which I shall document merely by citing the dictum of the most eminent English constitutional historian: throughout the whole course of English history, London has never acted as England's heart but often as England's intellect and always as her moneybag!

In certain seemingly insignificant traits, which lie upon the surface of life, the same psychic currents characteristically unite. Modern mind has become more and more calculating. The calculative exactness of practical life which the money economy has brought about corresponds to the ideal of natural science: to transform the world into an arithmetic problem, to fix every part of the world by mathematical formulas. Only money economy has filled the days of so many people with weighing, calculating, with numerical determinations, with a reduction of qualitative values to quantitative ones. Through the calculative nature of money a new precision, a certainty in the definition of identities and differences, an unambiguousness in agreements and arrangements has been brought about in the relations of life elements – just as externally this precision has been effected by the universal diffusion of pocket watches. However, the conditions of metropolitan life are at once cause and effect of this trait. The relationships and affairs of the typical metropolitan usually are so varied and complex that without the strictest punctuality in promises and services the whole structure would break down into an inextricable chaos. Above all, this necessity is brought about by the aggregation of so many people with such differentiated interests, who must integrate their relations and activities into a highly complex organism. If all clocks and watches in Berlin would suddenly go wrong in different ways, even if only by one hour, all economic life and communication of the city would be disrupted for a long time. In addition, an apparently mere external factor – long distances – would make all waiting and broken appointments result in an ill-afforded waste of time. Thus, the technique of metropolitan life is unimaginable without the most punctual integration of all activities and mutual relations into a stable and impersonal time schedule. Here again the general conclusions of this entire task of reflection become obvious, namely, that from each point on the surface of existence – however closely attached to the surface alone – one may drop a sounding into the depth of the psyche so that all the most banal externalities of life finally are connected with the ultimate decisions concerning the meaning and style of life. Punctuality, calculability, exactness are forced upon life by the complexity and extension of metropolitan existence and are not only most intimately connected with its money economy and intellectualistic character. These traits must also colour the contents of life and favour the exclusion of those irrational, instinctive, sovereign traits and impulses which aim at determining the mode of life from

within, instead of receiving the general and precisely schematized form of
life from without. Even though sovereign types of personality, characterized
by irrational impulses, are by no means impossible in the city, they are,
nevertheless, opposed to typical city life. The passionate hatred of men like
Ruskin and Nietzsche for the metropolis is understandable in these terms.
Their natures discovered the value of life alone in the unschematized existence which cannot be defined with precision for all alike. From the same
source of this hatred of the metropolis surged their hatred of money
economy and of the intellectualism of modern existence.

The same factors which have thus coalesced into the exactness and
minute precision of the form of life have coalesced into a structure of the
highest impersonality; on the other hand, they have promoted a highly personal subjectivity. There is perhaps no psychic phenomenon which has been
so unconditionally reserved to the metropolis as has the blasé attitude. The
blasé attitude results first from the rapidly changing and closely compressed
contrasting stimulations of the nerves. From this, the enhancement of
metropolitan intellectuality, also, seems originally to stem. Therefore,
stupid people who are not intellectually alive in the first place usually are
not exactly blasé. A life in boundless pursuit of pleasure makes one blasé
because it agitates the nerves to their strongest reactivity for such a long
time that they finally cease to react at all. In the same way, through the
rapidity and contradictoriness of their changes, more harmless impressions
force such violent responses, tearing the nerves so brutally hither and
thither that their last reserves of strength are spent; and if one remains in
the same milieu they have no time to gather new strength. An incapacity
thus emerges to react to new sensations with the appropriate energy. This
constitutes that blasé attitude which, in fact, every metropolitan child shows
when compared with children of quieter and less changeable milieus.

This physiological source of the metropolitan blasé attitude is joined by
another source which flows from the money economy. The essence of the
blasé attitude consists in the blunting of discrimination. This does not mean
that the objects are not perceived, as is the case with the half-wit, but rather
that the meaning and differing values of things, and thereby the things themselves, are experienced as insubstantial. They appear to the blasé person in
an evenly flat and gray tone; no one object deserves preference over any
other. This mood is the faithful subjective reflection of the completely
internalized money economy. By being the equivalent to all the manifold
things in one and the same way, money becomes the most frightful leveller.
For money expresses all qualitative differences of things in terms of 'how
much?' Money, with all its colourlessness and indifference, becomes the
common denominator of all values; irreparably it hollows out the core of
things, their individuality, their specific value, and their incomparability. All
things float with equal specific gravity in the constantly moving stream of
money. All things lie on the same level and differ from one another only in
the size of the area which they cover. In the individual case this coloration,
or rather discoloration, of things through their money equivalence may be

unnoticeably minute. However, through the relations of the rich to the objects to be had for money, perhaps even through the total character which the mentality of the contemporary public everywhere imparts to these objects, the exclusively pecuniary evaluation of objects has become quite considerable. The large cities, the main seats of the money exchange, bring the purchasability of things to the fore much more impressively than do smaller localities. That is why cities are also the genuine locale of the blasé attitude. In the blasé attitude the concentration of men and things stimulate the nervous system of the individual to its highest achievement so that it attains its peak. Through the mere quantitative intensification of the same conditioning factors this achievement is transformed into its opposite and appears in the peculiar adjustment of the blasé attitude. In this phenomenon the nerves find in the refusal to react to their stimulation the last possibility of accommodating to the contents and forms of metropolitan life. The self-preservation of certain personalities is bought at the price of devaluating the whole objective world, a devaluation which in the end unavoidably drags one's own personality down into a feeling of the same worthlessness.

Whereas the subject of this form of existence has to come to terms with it entirely for himself, his self-preservation in the face of the large city demands from him a no less negative behaviour of a social nature. This mental attitude of metropolitans toward one another we may designate, from a formal point of view, as reserve. If so many inner reactions were responses to the continuous external contacts with innumerable people as are those in the small town, where one knows almost everybody one meets and where one has a positive relation to almost everyone, one would be completely atomized internally and come to an unimaginable psychic state. Partly this psychological fact, partly the right to distrust which men have in the face of the touch-and-go elements of metropolitan life, necessitates our reserve. As a result of this reserve we frequently do not even know by sight those who have been our neighbours for years. And it is this reserve which in the eyes of the small-town people makes us appear to be cold and heartless. Indeed, if I do not deceive myself, the inner aspect of this outer reserve is not only indifference but, more often than we are aware, it is a slight aversion, a mutual strangeness and repulsion, which will break into hatred and fight at the moment of a closer contact, however caused. The whole inner organization of such an extensive communicative life rests upon an extremely varied hierarchy of sympathies, indifferences, and aversions of the briefest as well as of the most permanent nature. The sphere of indifference in this hierarchy is not as large as might appear on the surface. Our psychic activity still responds to almost every impression of somebody else with a somewhat distinct feeling. The unconscious, fluid and changing character of this impression seems to result in a state of indifference. Actually this indifference would be just as unnatural as the diffusion of indiscriminate mutual suggestion would be unbearable. From both these typical dangers of the metropolis, indifference and indiscriminate suggestibility, antipathy protects us. A latent antipathy and the preparatory stage of practical antagonism effect the distances and aversions without which this mode of life could not at all be led. The extent and the mixture of this style of life, the rhythm of its emergence and disappearance, the forms in which it is satisfied – all these, with the unifying motives in the narrower sense, form the inseparable whole of the metropolitan style of life. What appears in the metropolitan style of life directly as dissociation is in reality only one of its elemental forms of socialization.

This reserve with its overtone of hidden aversion appears in turn as the form or the cloak of a more general mental phenomenon of the metropolis: it grants to the individual a kind and an amount of personal freedom which has no analogy whatsoever under other conditions. The metropolis goes back to one of the large developmental tendencies of social life as such, to one of the few tendencies for which an approximately universal formula can be discovered. The earliest phase of social formations found in historical as well as in contemporary social structures is this: a relatively small circle firmly closed against neighbouring, strange, or in some way antagonistic circles. However, this circle is closely coherent and allows its individual members only a narrow field for the development of unique qualities and free, self-responsible movements. Political and kinship groups, parties and religious associations begin in this way. The self-preservation of very young associations requires the establishment of strict boundaries and a centripetal unity. Therefore they cannot allow the individual freedom and unique inner and outer development. From this stage, social development proceeds at once in two different, yet corresponding, directions. To the extent to which the group grows – numerically, spatially, in significance and in content of life – to the same degree the group's direct, inner unity loosens, and the rigidity of the original demarcation against others is softened through mutual relations and connections. At the same time, the individual gains freedom of movement, far beyond the first jealous delimitation. The individual also gains a specific individuality to which the division of labour in the enlarged group gives both occasion and necessity. The state and Christianity, guilds and political parties, and innumerable other groups have developed according to this formula, however much, of course, the special conditions and forces of the respective groups have modified the general scheme. This scheme seems to me distinctly recognizable also in the evolution of individuality within urban life. The small-town life in antiquity and in the Middle Ages set barriers against movement and relations of the individual toward the outside, and it set up barriers against individual independence and differentiation within the individual self. These barriers were such that under them modern man could not have breathed. Even today a metropolitan man who is placed in a small town feels a restriction similar, at least, in kind. The smaller the circle which forms our milieu is, and the more restricted those relations to others are which dissolve the boundaries of the individual, the more anxiously the circle guards the achievements, the conduct of life, and the outlook of the individual, and the more readily a quantitative and qualitative specialization would break up the framework of the whole little circle.

The ancient *polis* in this respect seems to have had the very character of a small town. The constant threat to its existence at the hands of enemies from near and afar effected strict coherence in political and military respects, a supervision of the citizen by the citizen, a jealousy of the whole against the individual whose particular life was suppressed to such a degree that he could compensate only by acting as a despot in his own household. The tremendous agitation and excitement, the unique colourfulness of Athenian life, can perhaps be understood in terms of the fact that a people of incomparably individualized personalities struggled against the constant inner and outer pressure of a de-individualizing small town. This produced a tense atmosphere in which the weaker individuals were suppressed and those of stronger natures were incited to prove themselves in the most passionate manner. This is precisely why it was that there blossomed in Athens what must be called, without defining it exactly, 'the general human character' in the intellectual development of our species. For we maintain factual as well as historical validity for the following connection: the most extensive and the most general contents and forms of life are most intimately connected with the most individual ones. They have a preparatory stage in common, that is, they find their enemy in narrow formations and groupings, the maintenance of which places both of them into a state of defence, against expanse and generality lying without and the freely moving individuality within. Just as in the feudal age, the 'free' man was the one who stood under the law of the land, that is, under the law of the largest social orbit, and the unfree man was the one who derived his right merely from the narrow circle of a feudal association and was excluded from the larger social orbit – so today metropolitan man is 'free' in a spiritualized and refined sense, in contrast to the pettiness and prejudices which hem in the small-town man. For the reciprocal reserve and indifference and the intellectual life conditions of large circles are never felt more strongly by the individual in their impact upon his independence than in the thickest crowd of the big city. This is because the bodily proximity and narrowness of space makes the mental distance only the more visible. It is obviously only the obverse of this freedom if, under certain circumstances, one nowhere feels as lonely and lost as in the metropolitan crowd. For here as elsewhere it is by no means necessary that the freedom of man be reflected in his emotional life as comfort.

It is not only the immediate size of the area and the number of persons which, because of the universal historical correlation between the enlargement of the circle and the personal inner and outer freedom, has made the metropolis the locale of freedom. It is rather in transcending this visible expanse that any given city becomes the seat of cosmopolitanism. The horizon of the city expands in a manner comparable to the way in which wealth develops; a certain amount of property increases in a quasi-automatical way in ever more rapid progression. As soon as a certain limit has been passed, the economic, personal, and intellectual relations of the citizenry, the sphere of intellectual predominance of the city over its hinterland, grow as in geometrical progression. Every gain in dynamic extension becomes a step, not for an equal, but for a new and larger extension. From every thread spinning out of the city, ever new threads grow as if by themselves, just as within the city the unearned increment of ground rent, through the mere increase in communication, brings the owner automatically increasing profits. At this point, the quantitative aspect of life is transformed directly into qualitative traits of character. The sphere of life of the small town is, in the main, self-contained and autarchic. For it is the decisive nature of the metropolis that its inner life overflows by waves into a far-flung national or international area. Weimar is not an example to the contrary, since its significance was hinged upon individual personalities and died with them; whereas the metropolis is indeed characterized by its essential independence even from the most eminent individual personalities. This is the counterpart to the independence, and it is the price the individual pays for the independence, which he enjoys in the metropolis. The most significant characteristic of the metropolis is this functional extension beyond its physical boundaries. And this efficacy reacts in turn and gives weight, importance, and responsibility to metropolitan life. Man does not end with the limits of his body or the area comprising his immediate activity. Rather is the range of the person constituted by the sum of effects emanating from him temporally and spatially. In the same way, a city consists of its total effects which extend beyond its immediate confines. Only this range is the city's actual extent in which its existence is expressed. This fact makes it obvious that individual freedom, the logical and historical complement of such extension, is not to be understood only in the negative sense of mere freedom of mobility and elimination of prejudices and petty philistinism. The essential point is that the particularity and incomparability, which ultimately every human being possesses, be somehow expressed in the working out of a way of life. That we follow the laws of our own nature – and this after all is freedom – becomes obvious and convincing to ourselves and to others only if the expressions of this nature differ from the expressions of others. Only our unmistakability proves that our way of life has not been superimposed by others.

Cities are, first of all, seats of the highest economic division of labour. They produce thereby such extreme phenomena as in Paris the renumerative occupation of the *quatorzième*. They are persons who identify themselves by signs on their residences and who are ready at the dinner hour in correct attire, so that they can be quickly called upon if a dinner party should consist of thirteen persons. In the measure of its expansion, the city offers more and more the decisive conditions of the division of labour. It offers a circle which through its size can absorb a highly diverse variety of services. At the same time, the concentration of individuals and their struggle for customers compel the individual to specialize in a function from which he cannot be readily displaced by another. It is decisive that city life has transformed the struggle with nature for livelihood into an inter-human struggle for gain, which here is not granted by nature but by other men. For specialization does not flow only from the competition for gain but also from the underlying fact that the seller must always seek to call forth new and differentiated needs of the lured customer. In order to find a source of income which is not yet exhausted, and to find a function which cannot readily be displaced, it is necessary to specialize in one's services. This process promotes differentiation, refinement, and the enrichment of the public's needs, which obviously must lead to growing personal differences within this public.

All this forms the transition to the individualization of mental and psychic traits which the city occasions in proportion to its size. There is a whole series of obvious causes underlying this process. First, one must meet the difficulty of asserting his own personality within the dimensions of metropolitan life. Where the quantitative increase in importance and the expense of energy reach their limits, one seizes upon qualitative differentiation in order somehow to attract the attention of the social circle by playing upon its sensitivity for differences. Finally, man is tempted to adopt the most tendentious peculiarities, that is, the specifically metropolitan extravagances of mannerism, caprice, and preciousness. Now, the meaning of these extravagances does not at all lie in the contents of such behaviour, but rather in its form of 'being different', of standing out in a striking manner and thereby attracting attention. For many character types, ultimately the only means of saving for themselves some modicum of self-esteem and the sense of filling a position is indirect, through the awareness of others. In the same sense a seemingly insignificant factor is operating, the cumulative effects of which are, however, still noticeable. I refer to the brevity and scarcity of the inter-human contacts granted to the metropolitan man, as compared with social intercourse in the small town. The temptation to appear 'to the point', to appear concentrated and strikingly characteristic, lies much closer to the individual in brief metropolitan contacts than in an atmosphere in which frequent and prolonged association assures the personality of an unambiguous image of himself in the eyes of the other.

The most profound reason, however, why the metropolis conduces to the urge for the most individual personal existence – no matter whether justified and successful – appears to me to be the following: the development of modern culture is characterized by the preponderance of what one may call the 'objective spirit' over the 'subjective spirit'. This is to say, in language as well as in law, in the technique of production as well as in art, in science as well as in the objects of the domestic environment, there is embodied a sum of spirit. The individual in his intellectual development follows the growth of this spirit very imperfectly and at an ever increasing distance. If, for instance, we view the immense culture which for the last hundred years has been embodied in things and in knowledge, in institutions and in comforts, and if we compare all this with the cultural progress of the individual during the same period – at least in high status groups – a frightful disproportion in growth between the two becomes evident. Indeed, at some points we notice a retrogression in the culture of the individual with reference to spirituality, delicacy, and idealism. This discrepancy results essentially from the growing division of labour. For the division of labour demands from the individual an ever more one-sided accomplishment, and the greatest advance in a one-sided pursuit only too frequently means dearth to the personality of the individual. In any case, he can cope less and less with the overgrowth of objective culture. The individual is reduced to a negligible quantity, perhaps less in his consciousness than in his practice and in the totality of his obscure emotional states that are derived from this practice. The individual has become a mere cog in an enormous organization of things and powers which tear from his hands all progress, spirituality, and value in order to transform them from their subjective form into the form of a purely objective life. It needs merely to be pointed out that the metropolis is the genuine arena of this culture which outgrows all personal life. Here in buildings and educational institutions, in the wonders and comforts of space-conquering technology, in the formations of community life, and in the visible institutions of the state, is offered such an overwhelming fullness of crystallized and impersonalized spirit that the personality, so to speak, cannot maintain itself under its impact. On the one hand, life is made infinitely easy for the personality in that stimulations, interests, uses of time and consciousness are offered to it from all sides. They carry the person as if in a stream, and one needs hardly to swim for oneself. On the other hand, however, life is composed more and more of these impersonal contents and offerings which tend to displace the genuine personal colorations and incomparabilities. This results in the individual's summoning the utmost in uniqueness and particularization, in order to preserve his most personal core. He has to exaggerate this personal element in order to remain audible even to himself. The atrophy of individual culture through the hypertrophy of objective culture is one reason for the bitter hatred which the preachers of the most extreme individualism, above all Nietzsche, harbour against the metropolis. But it is, indeed, also a reason why these preachers are so passionately loved in the metropolis and why they appear to the metropolitan man as the prophets and saviours of his most unsatisfied yearnings.

If one asks for the historical position of these two forms of individualism which are nourished by the quantitative relation of the metropolis, namely, individual independence and the elaboration of individuality itself, then the metropolis assumes an entirely new rank order in the world history of the spirit. The eighteenth century found the individual in oppressive bonds which had become meaningless – bonds of a political, agrarian, guild, and religious character. They were restraints which, so to speak, forced upon man an unnatural form and outmoded, unjust inequalities. In this situation the cry for liberty and equality arose, the belief in the individual's full freedom of movement in all social and intellectual relationships. Freedom would at once permit the noble substance common to all to come to the fore, a substance which nature had deposited in every man and which society and history had only deformed. Besides this eighteenth-century ideal of liberalism, in the nineteenth century, through Goethe and Romanticism, on the one hand, and through the economic division of labour, on the other hand, another ideal arose: individuals liberated from historical bonds now wished to distinguish themselves from one another. The carrier of man's values is no longer the 'general human being' in every individual, but rather man's qualitative uniqueness and irreplaceability. The external and internal history of our time takes its course within the struggle and in the changing entanglements of these two ways of defining the individual's role in the whole of society. It is the function of the metropolis to provide the arena for this struggle and its reconciliation. For the metropolis presents the peculiar conditions which are revealed to us as the opportunities and the stimuli for the development of both these ways of allocating roles to men. Therewith these conditions gain a unique place, pregnant with inestimable meanings for the development of psychic existence. The metropolis reveals itself as one of those great historical formations in which opposing streams which enclose life unfold, as well as join one another with equal right. However, in this process the currents of life, whether their individual phenomena touch us sympathetically or antipathetically, entirely transcend the sphere for which the judge's attitude is appropriate. Since such forces of life have grown into the roots and into the crown of the whole of the historical life in which we, in our fleeting existence, as a cell, belong only as a part, it is not our task either to accuse or to pardon, but only to understand.[2]

Notes to Part IV

1. The unequal juxtaposition of these two necessities, which do not find a harmony, organization or supplementation in any higher aspect dominating the two, is perhaps the reason for the minimal and difficult development of tribes at the nomadic level.

2. The content of this lecture by its very nature does not derive from a citable literature. Argument and elaboration of its major cultural–historical ideas are contained in my *Philosophie des Geldes* [The Philosophy of Money].

PART V

FASHION, ADORNMENT AND STYLE

THE PHILOSOPHY OF FASHION

Our manner of apprehending the phenomena of life causes us to feel a number of forces at every point of our existence, and in such a way that each of these forces actually strives beyond the real phenomenon, suffusing its infinity with the others and being transformed into mere tension and longing. For the human being is a dualistic creature from the very beginning, but this does not affect the unit of his or her actions; in fact, they only prove to be powerful as the result of a multiplicity of elements. A phenomenon which lacked this branching of its root forces would be impoverished and empty to us. Only if every inner energy pushes outwards beyond the measure of its visible expression does life gain that wealth of inexhaustible possibilities which enhances its fragmentary reality. Only in this manner do its phenomena give a hint of deeper forces, more unresolved tensions, struggle and peace of a more comprehensive kind than those betrayed by its immediate facticity.

This dualism cannot be described directly, but only in the individual antagonisms that are typical of our existence, and are felt to be its ultimate, structuring form. The first hint is provided by the physiological foundation of our nature: the latter requires motion as well as rest, productivity as well as receptivity. Continuing this analysis into the life of the mind, we are directed, on the one hand, by the striving for the general, as well as by the need to grasp the particular; the general provides our mind with rest, while the particular causes it to *move* from case to case. And it is no different in emotional life: we seek calm devotion to people and things just as much as energetic self-assertion against them both.

The whole history of society is reflected in the conflict, the compromise, the reconciliations, slowly won and quickly lost, that appear between adaptation to our social group and individual elevation from it. Whether the oscillation of our inner life between these two poles is expressed philosophically in the antagonism between cosmotheism and the doctrine of the inherent differentiation and separate existence of every cosmic element, or whether it is grounded in practical conflict as the partisan antagonisms between socialism and individualism, it is always one and the same fundamental form of duality which is finally manifested biologically in the contrast between heredity and variation. The former of these represents the idea of generality, of uniformity, of inactive similarity of the forms and contents of life; the latter stands for motion, for the differentiation of separate elements producing the restless development of one individual aspect of life into another. Within its own sphere, every essential form of life in the history of our species represents a unique way of unifying the interest in duration, unity and equality, and similarity with that in change, particularity and uniqueness.

Within the social embodiment of these oppositions, one side is usually maintained by the psychological tendency towards *imitation*. Imitation could be characterized as a psychological inheritance, as the transition of group life into individual life. Its attraction is first of all that it also permits purposive and meaningful action even where nothing personal or creative is in evidence. We might define it as the child of thought and thoughtlessness. Imitation gives the individual the assurance of not standing alone in his or her actions. Instead, it elevates itself over the previous practice of that activity as if on a solid foundation, which now relieves the present practice of it from the difficulty of maintaining itself. Whenever we imitate, we transfer not only the demand for creative activity, but also the responsibility for the action from ourselves to another. Thus the individual is freed from choosing and appears simply as a creature of the group, as a vessel of social contents. The drive to imitate as a principle characterizes a level of development upon which the wish for purposive personal activity is alive, but the ability to gain individual contents from it is not yet present. The progress we have made beyond this level is that thinking, action and feeling are no longer determined only by what exists, by the past and by tradition, but also by the *future*: the teleological human being is the opposite of the imitative one.

Thus we see that imitation in all the instances where it is a constitutive factor, represents *one* of the fundamental directions of our nature, namely, that which contents itself with the absorption of the individual into the general, and emphasizes the permanent element in change. Conversely, wherever change is sought in permanence, wherever individual differentiation and self-elevation above generality are sought, imitation is here the negating and restraining principle. And precisely because the longing to abide by that which is given, to act and be like others, is the irreconcilable enemy of those striving to advance to new and individual forms of life, social life appears to be the battleground upon which every inch is stubbornly contested by both sides, and social institutions may be seen as the – never permanent – reconciliations, in which the continuing antagonism of both principles has taken on the external form of cooperation.

The vital life conditions of fashion as a universal phenomenon in the history of our species are circumscribed by these factors. Fashion is the imitation of a given pattern and thus satisfies the need for social adaptation; it leads the individual onto the path that everyone travels, it furnishes a general condition that resolves the conduct of every individual into a mere example. At the same time, and to no less a degree, it satisfies the need for distinction, the tendency towards differentiation, change and individual contrast. It accomplishes the latter, on the one hand, by the change in contents – which gives to the fashions of today an individual stamp compared with those of yesterday and of tomorrow – and even more energetically, on the other hand, by the fact that fashions are always class fashions, by the fact that the fashions of the higher strata of society distinguish themselves from those of the lower strata, and are abandoned by the former at the moment when the latter begin to appropriate them. Hence fashion is nothing more than a particular instance among the many forms of life by the aid of which we seek to combine in a unified act the tendency towards social equalization with the desire for individual differentiation and variation. If we were to study the history of fashions – which hitherto have been examined only from the viewpoint of the development of their *contents* – with regard to their significance for the form of the social process, then we would find that it is the history of attempts to adjust the satisfaction of these two opposing tendencies more and more perfectly to the conditions of the prevailing individual and social culture. The individual psychological traits that we observe in fashion all conform to this basic essence of fashion.

Catwalks

Fashion is, as I have said, a product of class division and operates – like a number of other forms, honour especially – the double function of holding a given social circle together and at the same time closing it off from others. Just as the frame of a picture characterizes the work of art inwardly as a coherent, homogeneous, independent entity and, at the same time, outwardly severs all direct relations with the surrounding space; just as the uniform energy of such forms cannot be expressed unless we analyse the double effect, both inwards and outwards, so honour owes its character and above all its moral rights for us – rights, however, that are frequently considered to be unjust from the standpoint of those standing outside a social class – to the fact that the individual, in his or her personal honour, at the same time represents and maintains that of their social circle and their class. Thus, on the one hand, fashion signifies a union with those of the same status, the uniformity of a social circle characterized by it, and, in so doing, the closure of this group against those standing in a lower position which the higher group characterizes as not belonging to it.

Connection and differentiation are the two fundamental functions which are here inseparably united, of which one of the two, although or because it forms a logical contrast to the other, becomes the condition of its realization. That fashion is such a product of social needs is perhaps demonstrated by nothing stronger than the fact that, in countless instances, not the slightest reason can be found for its creations from the standpoint of an objective, aesthetic or other expediency. Whereas in general our clothing, for instance, is objectively adapted to our needs, there is not a trace of expediency in the method by which fashion dictates, for example, whether wide or narrow skirts, short or long hair styles, or coloured or black ties should be worn. Judging from the ugly and repugnant things that are sometimes modern, it would seem as though fashion were desirous of exhibiting its power by getting us to adopt the most atrocious things for its sake alone. The complete indifference of fashion to the material standards of life is illustrated by the arbitrary manner in which it recommends something appropriate in one instance, something abstruse in another, and something materially and aesthetically quite indifferent in a third. This indicates that fashion is concerned with other motivations, namely solely with formal social ones. Of course, it may occasionally adopt objectively justified elements but, as fashion, it is only effective when its independence from any other motivation becomes positively palpable, just as our dutiful action is only considered completely moral when we are not motivated by its external content and goal, but solely by the fact that it simply is our duty. This is the reason why the domination of fashion is most unbearable in those areas which ought to be subject only to objective decisions: religiosity, scientific interests, and even socialism and individualism have all been the subject of fashions. But the motives which alone should lead to the adoption of these contents of life stand in absolute opposition to the complete lack of objectivity in the developments of fashion.

If the social forms, the clothes, the aesthetic judgements, the whole style in which human beings express themselves are conceived in the constant transformation through fashion, so fashion – that is, the latest fashion – in all these things affects only the upper strata. Just as soon as the lower strata begin to appropriate their style – and thereby overstep the demarcation line which the upper strata have drawn and destroy the uniformity of their coherence symbolized in this fashion – so the upper strata turn away from this fashion and adopt a new one, which in its turn differentiates them from the broad masses. And thus the game goes merrily on. Naturally, the lower strata look and strive towards the upper, and they encounter the least resistance in those fields which are subject to the whims of fashion, because it is here that mere external imitation is most readily accessible. The same process is at work – although not always as visible here as it is, for example, between mistress and maid – between the different strata within the upper classes. Indeed, we may often observe that the more closely one stratum has approached the other, the more frantic becomes the hunt for imitation from below and the flight towards novelty above. The prevalence of the money economy is bound to hasten this process considerably and render it visible, because the objects of fashion, embracing as they do the externalities of life, are particularly accessible to the mere possession of money, and therefore through these externalities conformity to the higher stratum is more easily acquired here than in fields which demand an individual proof of worthiness that money cannot secure.

The extent to which this element of demarcation – alongside the element of imitation – forms the essence of fashion is especially apparent wherever the social structure does not possess any layered hierarchy of social strata, in which case fashion asserts itself in neighbouring strata. Among some primitive peoples it is reported that closely connected groups living under exactly similar conditions sometimes develop sharply differentiated fashions, by means of which each group establishes uniformity within itself, as well as differentiation from outsiders. On the other hand, there exists a widespread predilection for importing fashions from outside, and such foreign fashions assume a greater value within a particular social circle, simply because they did not originate there. Even the prophet Zephaniah expressed his indignation at the aristocrats in foreign clothing. As a matter of fact, the exotic advantage of fashions seems to favour especially strongly the exclusiveness of the groups which adopt them. Precisely because of their external origin, these imported fashions create a special and significant form of socialization, which arises through the mutual relationship to a point located outside the circle. It sometimes appears as though social elements, just like the axes of vision, converge best at a point that is not too near. Thus, among primitive peoples, money – and thus economic value itself – is the object of the most intense general interest, and often consists of objects that are brought in from outside. In some areas (on the Solomon Islands, and in Ibo on the Niger, for example) there exists a kind of industry for the production of shells, or other monetary symbols that are not employed as a medium of exchange in the place of production itself, but in neighbouring districts, to which they are exported – just as the fashions in Paris are frequently created with the sole intention of them becoming a fashion elsewhere. In Paris itself, fashion displays the greatest tension and reconciliation of its dualistic elements. Individualism, the adaptation to what is personally flattering stylewise, is much deeper than in Germany, but at the same time a certain very broad framework of general style – the current fashion – is strictly observed, so that the individual appearance never *clashes* with the general style, but always *stands out* from it.

If one of the two social tendencies essential to the establishment of fashion, namely, the need for integration on the one hand and the need for separation on the other, should be absent, then the formation of fashions will not occur and its realm will end. Consequently, the lower strata possess very few fashions and those they have are seldom specific; for this reason the fashions of primitive peoples are much more stable than ours. By virtue of their social structure, they lack that danger of mixing and blurring which spurs on the classes of civilized peoples to their differentiations of clothing, manners, taste, etc. Through these very differentiations, the sections of groups interested in separation are held together internally: the pace, tempo and rhythm of gestures is fundamentally determined by clothing and similarly dressed people behave in relatively similar ways. For modern life, with its individualist fragmentation, this is particularly valuable. And this is why fashions among primitive peoples will also be less numerous, that is more stable, because the need for the newness of impressions and forms of life – quite apart from its social effects – is much less acute among them. Changes in fashion reflect the extent of dullness of nervous impulses: the more nervous the age, the more rapidly its fashions change, simply because the need for the appeal of differentiating oneself, one of the most important elements of all fashion, goes hand in hand with the weakening of nervous energy. This fact in itself is one of the reasons why the real seat of fashion is found among the upper strata.

With regard to the purely social motives of fashion, two neighbouring primitive peoples provide very telling examples of its goals of integration and differentiation. The Kaffirs have a very rich structured and stratified social order, and although clothing and jewelry are subject to certain legal restrictions, one finds a quite rapid change of fashions among them. The bushmen, on the other hand, among whom no class formation whatsoever has occurred, have not developed any fashions at all, that is no interest has been noted among them with regard to changes in clothing and jewelry.

The same negative reasons have occasionally also prevented the formation of fashions at the heights of culture, but in a completely conscious manner. It is said that around the year 1390 in Florence there was no prevailing fashion in men's clothing because each one wished to present himself in his own special way. Thus, in this instance, one of the elements of fashion – the desire for integration – was absent, and without it there can be no fashion. On the other hand, it is reported that the Venetian *nobili* had no fashion since they were all required by a specific law to wear black, so as not to make their small numbers all too obvious to the lower strata. Here there was no fashion since the other constitutive element was missing, because differentiation from their social inferiors was to be deliberately avoided.

The essence of fashion consists in the fact that it should always be exercised by only a part of a given group, the great majority of whom are merely on the road to adopting it. As soon as a fashion has been universally adopted, that is, as soon as anything that was originally done only by a few has really come to be practised by all – as is the case in certain elements of clothing and in various forms of social conduct – we no longer characterize it as fashion. Every growth of a fashion drives it to its doom, because it thereby cancels out its distinctiveness. By reason of this play between the tendency towards universal acceptance and the destruction of its significance, to which this general adoption leads, fashion possesses the peculiar attraction of limitation, the attraction of a simultaneous beginning and end, the charm of newness and simultaneously of transitoriness. Fashion's question is not that of being, but rather it is simultaneously being and non-being; it always stands on the watershed of the past and the future and, as a result, conveys to us, at least while it is at its height, a stronger sense of the present than do most other phenomena.

If the momentary concentration of social consciousness upon the point which fashion signifies is also the one in which the seeds of its own death and its determined fate to be superceded already lie, so this transitoriness does not degrade it totally, but actually adds a new attraction to its existing ones. At all events, an object does not suffer degradation by being called 'fashionable', unless we reject it with disgust or wish to debase it for other material reasons; in which case, of course, fashion becomes a concept of value. In the practice of life, anything else that is similarly new and suddenly disseminated in the same manner will not be characterized as fashion, if we believe in its continuance and its *objective* justification. If, on the other hand, we are convinced that the phenomenon will vanish just as rapidly as it came into existence, then we call it fashion. Hence, among the reasons why nowadays fashion exercises such a powerful influence on our consciousness there is also the fact that the major, permanent, unquestionable convictions are more and more losing their force. Consequently, the fleeting and fluctuating elements of life gain that much more free space. The break with the past which, for more than a century, civilized human kind has been labouring unceasingly to bring about, concentrates consciousness more and more upon the present. This accentuation of the present is evidently, at the same time, an emphasis upon change and to the extent to which a particular strata is the agent of this cultural tendency, so to that degree will it turn to fashion in all fields, and by no means merely with regard to clothing. Indeed, it is almost a sign of the *increased* power of fashion that it has overstepped the bounds of its original domain, which comprised only externals of dress, and has acquired an increasing influence over taste, theoretical convictions, and even the moral foundations of life in their changing forms.

From the fact that fashion as such can never be generally in vogue, the individual derives the satisfaction of knowing that, as adopted by him or her, it still represents something special and striking; while at the same time the individual feels inwardly supported by a broad group of persons who are striving for the same thing, and not, as is the case for other social satisfactions, by a group that is doing the same thing. Therefore the feelings which the fashionable person confronts are an apparently agreeable mixture of approval and envy. We envy the fashionable person as an individual, but approve of them as a member of a group. Yet even this envy here has a peculiar nuance. There is a nuance of envy which includes a sort of ideal participation in the envied objects. An instructive example of this is furnished by the conduct of the worker who is able to get a glimpse of the feasts of the rich. In so far as we envy an object or a person, we are no longer absolutely excluded from them, and between both there now exists some relation or other, and between both the same psychological content now exists, even though in entirely different categories and forms of sensation. This quiet personal usurpation of the envied property – which is also the pleasure of unrequited love – contains a kind of antidote, which occasionally counteracts the worst degenerations of the feeling of envy. The elements of fashion afford an especially good chance for the development of this more conciliatory shade of envy, which also gives to the envied person a better conscience because of his or her satisfaction with regard to their good fortune. This is due to the fact that, unlike many other psychological contents, these contents of fashion are not denied *absolutely* to anyone, because a change of fortune, which is never entirely out of the question, may play them into the hands of an individual who had previously been confined to the state of envy.

From all this we see that fashion is the genuine playground for individuals with dependent natures, but whose self-consciousness, however, at the same time requires a certain amount of prominence, attention, and singularity. Fashion elevates even the unimportant individual by making them the representative of a totality, the embodiment of a joint spirit. It is particularly characteristic of fashion – because, by its very essence, it can be a norm which is never satisfied by everyone – that it renders possible a social obedience that is at the same time a form of individual differentiation. In slaves to fashion (*Modenarren*) the social demands of fashion appear exaggerated to such a high degree that they completely acquire a semblance of individuality and particularity. It is characteristic of the slave to fashion that he carries the tendency of a particular fashion beyond the otherwise self-contained limits. If pointed shoes are in style, then he wears shoes that resemble spear tips; if pointed collars are all the rage, he wears collars that reach up to his ears; if it is fashionable to attend scholarly lectures, then he is never seen anywhere else, and so on. Thus he represents something totally individual, which consists in the quantitative intensification of such elements as are qualitatively common property of the given social circle. He leads the way, but all travel the same road. Representing as he does the most recently conquered heights of public taste, he seems to be marching at the head of the general process. In reality, however, what is so frequently true of the relation between individuals and groups also applies to him: that actually, the leader is the one who is led.

Democratic times obviously favour such a condition to a remarkable degree, so much so that even Bismarck and other very prominent party leaders of constitutional governments have emphasized the fact that, inasmuch as they are leaders of a group, they are bound to follow it. Such times cause persons to seek dignity and the sensation of command in this manner; they favour a confusion and ambiguity of sensations, which fail to distinguish between ruling the mass and being ruled by it. The conceit of the slave to fashion is thus the caricature of a democratically fostered constellation of the relations between the individual and the totality. Undeniably, however, the hero of fashion, through the conspicuousness gained in a purely quantitative way, but clothed in a difference of quality, represents a genuinely original state of equilibrium between the social and the individualizing impulses. This enables us to understand the outwardly so abstruse devotion to fashion of otherwise quite intelligent and broad-minded persons. It furnishes them with a combination of relations to things and human beings that, under ordinary circumstances, tend to appear separately. What is at work here is not only the mixture of individual distinctiveness and social equality, but more practically, as it were, it is the mingling of the sensation of domination and subordination. Or, formulated differently, we have here the mixing of a male and a female principle. The very fact that this mixing process only occurs in the sphere of fashion as in an ideal dilution that, as it were, only realizes the form of both elements in a content that is in itself indifferent, may lend a special attraction to fashion, especially for sensitive natures that do not care to concern themselves with robust reality. From an objective standpoint, life according to fashion consists of a mixture of destruction and construction; its content acquires its characteristics by destruction of an earlier form; it possesses a peculiar uniformity, in which the satisfaction of the destructive impulse and the drive for positive elements can no longer be separated from each other.

Because we are dealing here not with the significance of a single content or a single satisfaction, but rather with the play between both contents and their mutual distinction, it becomes evident that the same combination which extreme obedience to fashion acquires can also be won by opposition to it. Whoever consciously clothes or deports themselves in an unmodern manner does not attain the consequent sensation of individualization through any real individual qualification of his or her own, but rather through the mere negation of the social example. If modernity is the imitation of this social example, then the deliberate lack of modernity represents a similar imitation, yet under an inverted sign, but nonetheless one which offers no less a testimony of the power of the social tendency, which makes us dependent upon it in some positive or negative manner. The deliberately unmodern person accepts its forms just as much as does the slave to fashion, except that the unmodern person embodies it in another category: in that of negation, rather than in exaggeration.

Indeed, it occasionally becomes decidedly fashionable in whole circles of a large-scale society to clothes oneself in an unmodern manner. This constitutes one of the most curious social–psychological complications, in which the drive for individual conspicuousness primarily remains content, first, with a mere inversion of social imitation and, secondly, for its part draws its strength again from approximation to a similarly characterized narrow circle. If a club or association of club-haters were founded, then it would not be logically more impossible and psychologically more possible than the above phenomenon. Just as atheism has been made into a religion, embodying the same fanaticism, the same intolerance, the same satisfaction of emotional needs that are embraced in religion proper; and just as freedom too, by means of which a tyranny has been broken, often becomes no less tyrannical and violent; so this phenomenon of tendentious lack of modernity illustrates how ready the fundamental forms of human nature are to accept the total antithesis of contents in themselves and to show their strength and their attraction in the negation of the very thing to whose acceptance they still seemed a moment earlier to be irrevocably committed. Thus, it is often absolutely impossible to tell whether the elements of personal strength or of personal weakness have the upper hand in the complex of causes of such lack of modernity. It may result from the need not to make common cause with the crowd, a need that has as its basis, of course, not in independence from the crowd, but rather in an inner sovereign stance with respect to the latter. However, it may also be due to a weak sensibility, which causes individuals to fear that they will be unable to maintain their little piece of individuality if they adopt the forms, tastes and customs of the general public. Such opposition to the latter is by no means always a sign of personal strength. On the contrary, personal strength will be so conscious of its unique value, which is immune to any external connivance, that it will be able to submit without any unease to general forms up to and including fashion. Rather, it is precisely in this obedience that it will become conscious of the *voluntariness* of its obedience and of that which transcends obedience.

If fashion both gives expression to the impulse towards equalization and individualization, as well as to the allure of imitation and conspicuousness, this perhaps explains why it is that women, broadly speaking, adhere especially strongly to fashion. Out of the weakness of the social position to which women were condemned throughout the greatest part of history there arises their close relationship to all that is 'custom', to that which is 'right and proper', to the generally valid and approved form of existence. For those who are weak steer clear of individualization; they avoid dependence upon the self, with its responsibilties and the necessity of defending oneself unaided. Those in a weak position find protection only in the typical form of life, which prevents the strong person from exercising his exceptional powers. But resting on the firm foundation of custom, of the average, of the general level, women strive strongly for all the relative individualization and general conspicuousness that thus remains possible. Fashion offers them this very combination to the most favourable extent, for we have here, on the one hand, a sphere of general imitation, the individual floating in the broadest social current, relieved of responsibility for their tastes and their actions, and yet, on the other hand, we have a certain conspicuousness, an individual emphasis, an individual ornamentation of the personality.

It seems that there exists for each class of human beings, indeed probably for each individual, a definite quantitative relationship between the impulse towards individualization and the drive for immersion in the collectivity, so that if the satisfaction of one of these drives is denied in a certain field of life, it seeks another, in which it then fulfils the amount that it requires. Thus, it seems as though fashion were the valve, as it were, through which women's need for some measure of conspicuousness and individual prominence finds vent, when its satisfaction is more often denied in other spheres.

During the fourteenth and fifteenth centuries, Germany displayed an extraordinarily strong development of individuality. To a great extent, the collectivistic regulations of the Middle Ages were breached by the freedom of the individual person. Within this individualistic development, however, women still found no place and the freedom of personal movement and self-improvement was still denied them. They compensated for this by adopting the most extravagant and exaggerated fashions in dress. Conversely, we see that in Italy during the same epoch, women were given free play for individual development. The women of the Renaissance possessed extensive opportunities for culture, external activity, and personal differentiation such as were not offered to them again for many centuries. In the upper classes of society, especially, education and freedom of expression were almost identical for both sexes. Yet it is also reported that no particularly extravagant Italian female fashions emerged from that period. The need to exercise individuality and gain a kind of distinction in this sphere was absent, because the impulse embodied therein found sufficient satisfaction in other spheres. In general, the history of women in their outer as well as their inner life, in the individual aspect as well as in their collectivity, exhibits such a comparatively great uniformity, levelling and similarity, that they require a more lively activity at least in the sphere of fashions, which is nothing more nor less than variety, in order to add an attraction to themselves and their lives – for their own feeling as well as for others.

Just as in the case of individualism and collectivism, so there exists between the uniformity and the variety of the contents of life a definite proportion of needs, which is tossed to and fro in the different spheres and seeks to balance the refusal in the one by consent, however acquired, in the other. On the whole, we may say that the woman, compared to the man, is a more faithful creature. Now fidelity, expressing the uniformity and regularity of one's nature only according to the side of one's feelings, demands a more lively change in the outward surrounding spheres in order to establish the balance in the tendencies of life. The man, on the other hand, who in his essence is less faithful and who does not ordinarily maintain an emotional relationship that he has entered into with the same absoluteness and concentration of all his vital interests, is consequently in less need of external variation. Indeed, the lack of acceptance of changes in external fields, the indifference towards fashions in outward appearance are specifically a male quality, not because a man is more uniform, but because he is the more many-sided creature, and for that reason, can exist without external changes. Therefore the emancipated woman of the present, who seeks to approach towards the whole differentiation, personality and activity of the male sex, lays particular stress on her indifference to fashion. In a certain sense, fashion also gives women a compensation for their lack of social position in a professional group. The man who has become absorbed in a vocation has thereby entered into a relatively uniform social circle, in which he resembles many others within this stratum, and is thus often only an exemplar of the concept of this stratum or occupation. On the other hand, and as if to compensate him for this absorption, he is invested with the full importance and the objective as well as the social power of this stratum. To his individual importance is added that of his stratum, which often can cover over the defects and deficiencies of purely personal existence.

Fashion accomplishes this identical process by other means. Fashion too supplements a person's lack of importance, their inability to individualize their existence purely by their own unaided efforts, by enabling them to join a group characterized and singled out in the public consciousness by fashion alone. Here too, to be sure, the personality as such is adapted to a general formula, yet this formula itself, from a social standpoint, possesses an individual colouring, and this makes up by a socially roundabout way for precisely what is denied to the personality in a purely individual way. The fact that the *demi-monde* is so frequently the pioneer of new fashion is due to its distinctively uprooted form of life. The pariah existence to which society condemns the *demi-monde* produces an open or latent hatred against everything that has the sanction of law, against every permanent institution, a hatred that still finds its relatively most innocent expression in the striving for ever new forms of appearance. In this continual striving for new, previously unheard-of fashions, in the ruthlessness with which the one that is most opposed to the existing one is passionately adopted, there lies an aesthetic form of the destructive urge that seems to be an element peculiar to all who lead this pariah-like existence, so long as they are not inwardly completely enslaved.

And if we seek to gaze into the final and most subtle movements of the soul, which are difficult to express in words, so we find that they too exhibit this antagonistic play of the fundamental human tendencies, which seek to regain their continually lost balance by means of ever new proportions. It is in fact fundamental to fashion that it makes no distinction at all between all individualities alike, and yet it is always done in such a way that it never affects the whole human being; indeed it always remains somewhat external to the individual – even in those spheres outside mere clothing fashions. For the form of mutability in which it is presented to the individual is under all circumstances a contrast to the stability of the sense of self, and indeed the latter must become conscious of its relative duration precisely through this contrast. The changeableness of the elements of fashion can express itself as mutability and develop its attraction only through this enduring element of the sense of self. But for this very reason fashion always stands, as I have pointed out, at the very periphery of the personality, which regards itself as a *pièce de résistance* to fashion, or at least can be experienced as such in an emergency.

It is this significant aspect of fashion that is adopted by refined and special persons, in so far as they use it as a kind of mask. They consider blind obedience to the standards of the public in all externals as the conscious and desired means of reserving their personal feelings and their taste, which they are eager to keep to themselves alone; indeed, so much to themselves that they do not care to allow their feelings and tastes to be seen in a form that is visible to all. It is therefore precisely a refined feeling of modesty and reserve which, seeking not to resort to a peculiarity in externals for fear perhaps of betraying a peculiarity of their innermost soul, causes many a delicate nature to seek refuge in the masking levelling of fashion. Thereby a triumph of the soul over the given nature of existence is achieved which, at least as far as form is concerned, must be considered one of the highest and finest victories: namely, that the enemy himself is transformed into a servant, that precisely that which seemed to violate the personality is seized voluntarily, because the levelling violation is here transferred to the external strata of life in such a way that it furnishes a veil and a protection for everything that is innermost and now all the more free. The struggle between the social and the individual is resolved here in so far as the strata for both are separated. This corresponds exactly to the triviality of expression and conversation through which very sensitive and retiring people, especially women, often deceive one about the depth of the individual soul behind these expressions.

All feeling of shame rests upon the conspicuousness of the individual. It arises whenever a stress is laid upon the self, whenever the attention of a social circle is drawn to an individual, which at the same time is felt to be in some way inappropriate. For this reason retiring and weak natures are particularly inclined to feelings of shame. The moment they step into the centre of general attention, the moment they make themselves conspicuous in any way, a painful oscillation between emphasis upon and withdrawal of the sense of the self manifests itself. In so far as this individual conspicuousness, as the source of the feeling of shame, is quite independent of the particular content on the basis of which it occurs, so one is actually frequently ashamed of good and noble things. If in society, in the narrower sense of the term, banality constitutes good form, then this is due not only to a mutual regard, which causes it to be considered bad taste to stand out through some individual, singular expression that not everyone can imitate, but also to the fear of that feeling of shame which forms a self-inflicted punishment for those departing from the form and activity that is similar for, and equally accessible to, everyone.

By reason of its distinctive inner structure, fashion furnishes a conspicuousness of the individual which is always looked upon as proper, no matter how extravagant its form of appearance or manner of expression may be; as long as it is fashionable it is protected against those unpleasant reflections which the individual otherwise experiences when he or she becomes the object of attention. All mass actions are characterized by the loss of the feeling of shame. As a member of a mass, the individual will do many things which would have aroused uncontrollable repugnance in their soul had they been suggested to them alone. It is one of the most remarkable social–psychological phenomena, in which this characteristic of mass action is well exemplified, that many fashions tolerate breaches of modesty which, if suggested to the individual alone, would be angrily repudiated. But as dictates of fashion they find a ready acceptance. The feeling of shame is eradicated in matters of fashion, because it represents a mass action, in the same way that the feeling of responsibility is extinguished in participants in mass criminality, who if left to themselves as individuals would shrink from such deeds. As soon as the individual aspects of the situation begin to predominate over its social and fashionable aspects, the sense of shame immediately commences its effectiveness: many women would be embarrassed to confront a single male stranger alone in their living room with the kind of low necklines that they wear in society, according to the dictates of fashion, in front of thirty or a hundred men.

Fashion is also only one of the forms through which human beings seek to save their inner freedom all the more completely by sacrificing externals to enslavement by the general public. Freedom and dependency also belong to those pairs of opposites, whose ever-renewed struggle and endless mobility give to life much more piquancy, and permit a much greater breadth and development than could a permanent, unchangeable balance of the two. Just as, according to Schopenhauer, to each person a certain amount of joy and sorrow is given, whose measure can neither remain empty nor be filled to overflowing, but in all the diversity and vacillations of internal and external circumstances only changes its form, so – much less mystically – we may observe in each period, in each class, and in each individual either a really permanent proportion of dependency and freedom, or at least the longing for it, whereas we can only change the fields over which they are distributed. And it is the task of the higher life, to be sure, to arrange this distribution in such a way that the other values of existence thereby acquire the most favourable development. The same quantity of dependency and freedom may help, at one time, to increase moral, intellectual and aesthetic values to the highest point and, at another time, without any change in quantity but merely in distribution, it may bring about the exact opposite result. As a whole, one could say that the most favourable result for the total value of life will be obtained when all unavoidable dependency is transferred more and more to the periphery of life, to its externalities. Perhaps Goethe, in his later period, is the most eloquent example of a wholly great life, for by means of his adaptability in all externals, his strict regard for form, his willing obedience to the conventions of society, he attained a maximum of inner freedom, a complete saving of the centres of life from the unavoidable quantity of dependency. In this respect, fashion is also a social form of marvellous expediency, because, like the law, it affects only the externals of life, and hence only those sides of life which are turned towards society. It provides human beings with a formula by means of which we can unequivocally attest our dependency upon what is generally adopted, our obedience to standards established by our time, our class, and our narrower circle, and enables us to withdraw the freedom given us in life and concentrate it more and more in our innermost and fundamental elements.

Within the individual soul these relations of equalizing unification and individual demarcation are, to a certain extent, actually repeated. The antagonism of the tendencies which produce fashion is transferred, as far as form is concerned and in an entirely similar manner, even to those inner relations of some individuals who have nothing whatever to do with social obligations. The phenomenon to which I am referring exhibits the often emphasized parallelism with which the relations between individuals are repeated in the correlation between the psychological elements of individuals themselves. More or less intentionally, the individual often establishes a mode of conduct or a style for him or herself which, by the rhythm of its rise, its sway and decline, becomes characterized as fashion. Young people especially often display a sudden singularity in their behaviour; an unexpected, objectively unfounded interest arises that governs their whole sphere of consciousness, only to disappear in the same irrational manner. We might characterize this as a personal fashion, which forms a limiting case of social fashion. The former is supported, on the one hand, by the individual demand for differentiation and thereby attests to the same impulse that is active in the formation of social fashion. The needs for imitation, similarity, and for the blending of the individual into the mass, are here satisfied purely within the individuals themselves: namely through the concentration of the personal consciousness upon this one form or content, through the uniform shading his or her nature receives from that concentration, through the imitation, as it were, of their own self, where here replaces the imitation of others.

A certain intermediate stage is often realized within close social circles between individual style and personal fashion. Ordinary persons frequently adopt some expression, which they apply at every opportunity – in common with as many others as possible in the same social circle – to all manner of suitable and unsuitable objects. In one respect this is a group fashion, yet in another it is really individual, for its express purpose consists in having the *individual* make the *totality* of his or her circle of ideas subject to this formula. Brutal violence is hereby committed against the individuality of things – all nuances are blurred by the curious supremacy of this one category of expression, for example, when we designate all things that we like for any reason whatever as 'chic', or 'smart' – even though the objects in question may bear no relation whatsoever to the fields to which these expressions belong. In this manner, the inner world of the individual is made subject to fashion, and thus repeats the form of the group dominated by fashion. And this also occurs chiefly by reason of the objective absurdity of such individual manners, which illustrate the power of the formal, unifying element over the objective, rational element. In the same way, many persons and social circles only ask that they be uniformly governed, and the question as to how qualified or valuable is this domination plays a merely secondary role. It cannot be denied that, by doing violence to objects treated in this way, and by clothing them all uniformly in a category that we apply to them, the individual exercises an authority over them, and gains an individual feeling of power, an emphasis of the self over against these objects.

The phenomenon that appears here in the form of a caricature is noticeable to lesser degrees everywhere in the relationship of people to objects. It is only the most noble human beings who find the greatest depth and power of their ego precisely in the fact that they respect the individuality inherent in things. The hostility which the soul bears to the supremacy, independence and indifference of the universe continuously gives rise, as it were – beside the loftiest and most valuable strivings of humanity – to attempts to oppress things externally. The self prevails against them not by absorbing and moulding their powers, not by recognizing their individuality in order to make them serviceable, but by forcing them outwardly to subjugate themselves to some subjective formula. To be sure, in reality the self has not gained control of the things themselves, but only of its own falsified fantasy image of them. However, the feeling of power, which originates from this, reveals its lack of foundation and its illusory nature by the rapidity with which such expressions of fashions pass away. It is just as illusory as the feeling of the uniformity of being, that springs for the moment out of this schematization of all expressions.

We have seen that in fashion, as it were, the different dimensions of life acquire a peculiar convergence, that fashion is a complex structure in which all the leading antithetical tendencies of the soul in one way or another are represented. This makes it abundantly clear that the total rhythm in which individuals and groups move will also exert an important influence upon their relationships to fashion; that the various strata of a group, quite aside from their different contents of life and external possibilities, will exhibit different relationships to fashion simply because their contents of life are evolved either in a conservative or in a rapidly varying form. On the one hand, the lower masses are difficult to set in motion and are slow to develop. On the other hand, it is the highest strata, as everyone knows, who are the most conservative, and who are frequently enough quite archaic. They frequently dread every movement and transformation, not because they have an antipathy to the contents or because the latter are injurious to them, but simply because it is transformation as such and because they regard every modification of the whole, which after all provides them with the highest position, as suspicious and dangerous. No change can bring to them any additional power; at most they have something to fear from each change, but nothing more to hope for from any transformation.

The real variability of historical life is therefore vested in the middle classes and, for this reason, the history of social and cultural movements has taken on an entirely different pace since the *tiers état* assumed power. This is why fashion, itself the changing and contrasting form of life, has since then become much broader and more animated. This is also because of the transformations in immediate political life, for people require an ephemeral tyrant the moment they have rid themselves of an absolute and permanent one. The frequent changes in fashion constitute a tremendous subjugation of the individual and in that respect form one of the necessary complements to increased social and political freedom. A class which is inherently so much more variable, so much more restless in its rhythms than the lowest classes with their silently unconscious conservatism, and the highest classes with their consciously desired conservatism, is the totally appropriate location for a form of life in which the moment of an element's triumph marks the beginning of its decline. Classes and individuals who demand constant change – because precisely the rapidity of their development secures them an advantage over others – find in fashion something that keeps pace with their own inner impulses. And social advancement must be directly favourable to the rapid advance of fashion, because it equips the lower strata so much more quickly to imitate the upper strata and thus the process characterized above – according to which every higher stratum throws aside a fashion the moment a lower one adopts it – acquires a breadth and vitality never dreamed of before.

This fact has an important bearing upon the content of fashion. Above all, it creates a situation in which fashions can no longer be so expensive and, therefore, obviously can no longer be so extravagant as they were in earlier times, where there was a compensation in the form of the longer duration of their domination for the costliness of the first acquisition or the difficulties in transforming conduct and taste. The more an article becomes subject to rapid changes of fashion, the greater the demand for *cheap* products of its kind. This is not only because the larger and therefore poorer classes nevertheless have enough purchasing power to regulate industry and demand objects which at least bear the outward and precarious semblance of modernity, but rather also because even the higher strata of society could not afford to adopt the rapid changes in fashion forced upon them by the pressure of the lower classes if its objects were not relatively cheap. The speed of development is of such importance in genuine articles of fashions that it even withdraws them from certain economic advances that have been won gradually in other fields. It has been noticed, especially in the older branches of production in modern industry, that the speculative element gradually ceases to play an influential role. The movements of the market can be better observed, requirements can be better foreseen and production can be more accurately regulated than before, so that the rationalization of production makes greater and greater inroads upon the fortuitousness of market opportunities and upon the unplanned fluctuations of supply and demand. Only pure articles of fashion seem to be excluded from this. The polar fluctuations, which in many cases the modern economy knows how to avoid and from which it is visibly striving towards entirely new economic orders and formations, still predominate in the fields immediately subject to fashion. The form of feverish change is so essential here that fashion stands, as it were, in a logical contradiction to the developmental tendencies of modern societies.

In contrast to this characteristic, however, fashion possesses the quite remarkable quality that each individual fashion to a certain extent makes its appearance as though it wished to live forever. Whoever purchases furniture today that should last a quarter of a century, countless times purchases according to the newest fashion and no longer considers articles that were in vogue even two years earlier. Yet is evident that, after a couple of years, the attraction of fashion will desert the present article in precisely the same way as it left the earlier one, and satisfaction or dissatisfaction with both forms will then be determined by other, objective criteria. A distinctive psychological process seems to be at work here, in addition to the mere bias of the moment. A fashion always exists and it is therefore, as a general concept, as a fact of fashion as such, indeed immortal; and this seems to reflect in some manner or other upon each of its manifestations, although the essence of each individual fashion is precisely that of *not* being immortal. In this instance, the fact that change itself does not change endows each of the objects which it affects with a psychological shimmer of permanency.

This permanency within change is actually realized in the individual contents of fashion in the following distinctive manner. Fashion, to be sure, is concerned only with change, yet like all phenomena it has the tendency to conserve energy; it endeavours to attain its objects as completely as possible, but nevertheless with the relatively most economical means. For this very reason, fashion repeatedly returns to old forms – as is illustrated particularly in the fashion for clothes – so that the course of fashion has been likened to that of a cyclical course. As soon as an earlier fashion has been partially expunged from memory there is no reason why it should not be allowed to return to favour and why the charm of difference, which constitutes its very essence, should not be exercised against that very fashion which derived its attraction when it came onto the scene from its contrast to the style now being revived.

In all events, the power of the form of motion from which fashion lives is not strong enough to dominate every content uniformly. Even in the spheres governed by fashion, all forms are not equally suited to become fashion, for the peculiar character of many of them furnishes a certain resistance. This may be compared with the unequal relation that the objects of external perception bear to the possibility of their being transformed into works of art. It is a very tempting, but hardly a profound or tenable view, that every object of reality is equally suited to become the object of a work of art. The forms of art, as they have developed historically – determined by a thousand fortuitous events, frequently one-sided and affected by technical perfections and imperfections – are by no means equally elevated above all the contents of reality. On the contrary, the forms of art possess a closer relationship to some of these contents than they do to others. Some of these contents assume artistic form without apparent effort, as though nature had created them for that very purpose, while others, as though wilful and created differently by nature, avoid all transformation into the given forms of art. The sovereignty of art over reality by no means implies, as naturalism and many theories of idealism so steadfastly maintain, the ability to draw all the contents of existence uniformly into its sphere. None of the formations with which the human mind masters the material of existence and adapts it to its purpose is so general and neutral that all objects, indifferent to their own structure, should uniformly conform to it.

Thus fashion can absorb to all appearances and *in abstracto* any chosen content: any given form of clothing, art, conduct, or opinion can become fashionable. And yet there lies within the inner essence of some forms a special disposition to live themselves out as fashion, just as others put up an inward resistance. Thus, for example, everything that may be termed 'classic' is comparatively far removed from fashion and alien to it, although occasionally, of course, the classic also falls under the sway of fashion. For the essence of the classical is a concentration of appearance around a sublime middle point; the classical possesses something collective, which does not offer so many points of attack, as it were, from which modification, disturbance and destruction of the balance might emanate. What is characteristic of classical sculpture is the total concentration of the limbs: the whole is absolutely governed from within the spirit and the feeling of life governing the whole uniformly embraces every part, because of the visible unity of the object. That is the reason why we speak of the 'classical repose' of Greek art. It is due exclusively to the concentration of the object, which permits no part to bear any relation to any extraneous powers and fortunes, and thereby incites the feeling that this formation is exempt from the changing influences of general life. In contrast to this, everything eccentric, immoderate and extreme will be drawn to fashion from within: fashion does not take hold of things characterized in this way as an external fate, but rather, as it were, as the historical expression of their objective peculiarities. The widely projecting limbs of the Baroque statue are, as it were, always in perpetual danger of being broken off, since the inner life of the figure does not exercise complete control over them, but lays them open to the fortuitous elements of external life. Baroque forms already possess within themselves the unrest, the character of fortuitousness, the subjugation to the momentary impulse which fashion realizes as a form of social life. An additional factor confronts us here: namely, that we soon grow tired of eccentric, bizarre or fanciful forms and thus, from a purely psychological standpoint, long for the change that fashion outlines for us. Here too lies one of the deep relationships between the classical and the 'natural' composition of things that people have claimed to discover. No matter how weakly delimited and erroneous in general the concept of the 'natural' may often be, one can at least make the negative statement that certain forms, tendencies and viewpoints have *no* claim to this title, and that these are the very ones that succumb especially quickly to the change of fashions, precisely because they lack a relation to the abiding centre of things and life which would justify their claim to a lasting existence. Thus, Elizabeth Charlotte of the Palatinate, a sister-in-law of Louis XIV, who was an exceedingly masculine personality, inspired the fashion at the French court of women deporting themselves like men and being addressed as such, while men conducted themselves as women. It is self-evident that such behaviour can only become a fashion, because it is so far removed from the inalienable substance of human relations to which the form of life will eventually and, in some way or other have to return. Just as little as we can say that all fashion is somewhat unnatural – not least because fashion as a form of life is itself natural to the human being as a social being – so conversely one can indeed say of the absolutely unnatural that it can at least exist in the form of *fashion*.

To sum up the whole issue, the peculiarly piquant and stimulating attraction of fashion lies in the contrast between its extensive, all-embracing distribution and its rapid and complete transitoriness, in the right to be unfaithful to it. Furthermore, the charm of fashion lies no less in the tightness with which it draws a given social circle together – the intimate connection of which it expresses as both cause and effect – than it does upon the decisiveness with which it separates the given social circle from others. Finally, the appeal of fashion also lies in its being supported by a social circle, which demands mutual imitation from its members and thereby releases the individual from all responsibility – both ethical and aesthetic – as well as in the possibility of producing within these original nuances, whether it be through exaggeration or even through rejection, the elements of fashion. Thus fashion reveals itself to be only a single, particularly characteristic example among those manifold structures in which social expediency has objectivized the antagonistic tendencies of life on equal terms.

ADORNMENT[1]

Man's desire to please his social environment contains two contradictory tendencies, in whose play and counterplay in general, the relations among individuals take their course. On the one hand, it contains kindness, a desire of the individual to give the other joy; but on the other hand, there is the wish for this joy and these 'favours' to flow back to him, in the form of recognition and esteem, so that they be attributed to his personality as values. Indeed, this second need is so intensified that it militates against the altruism of wishing to please: by means of this pleasing, the individual desires to *distinguish* himself before others, and to be the object of an attention that others do not receive. This may even lead him to the point of wanting to be envied. Pleasing may thus become a means of the will to power: some individuals exhibit the strange contradiction that they need those above whom they elevate themselves by life and deed, for they build their own self-feeling upon the subordinates' realization that they *are* subordinate.

The meaning of adornment finds expression in peculiar elaborations of these motives, in which the external and internal aspects of their forms are interwoven. This meaning is to single the personality out, to emphasize it as outstanding in some sense – but not by means of power manifestations, not by anything that externally compels the other, but only through the pleasure which is engendered in him and which, therefore, still has some voluntary element in it. One adorns oneself for oneself, but can do so only by adornment for others. It is one of the strangest sociological combinations that an act, which exclusively serves the emphasis and increased significance of the actor, nevertheless attains this goal just as exclusively in the pleasure, in the visual delight it offers to others, and in their gratitude. For, even the envy of adornment only indicates the desire of the envious person to win like recognition and admiration for himself; his envy proves how much he believes these values to be connected with the adornment. Adornment is the egoistic element as such: it singles out its wearer, whose self-feeling it embodies and increases at the cost of others (for, the same adornment of all would no longer adorn the individual). But, at the same time, adornment is altruistic: its pleasure is designed for the others, since its owner can enjoy it only in so far as he mirrors himself in them; he renders the adornment valuable only through the reflection of this gift of his. Everywhere, aesthetic formation reveals that life orientations, which reality juxtaposes as mutually alien, or even pits against one another as hostile, are, in fact, intimately interrelated. In the same way, the aesthetic phenomenon of adornment indicates a point within sociological interaction – the arena of man's being-for-himself and being-for-the-other – where these two opposite directions are mutually dependent as ends and means.

Adornment intensifies or enlarges the impression of the personality by operating as a sort of radiation emanating from it. For this reason, its materials have always been shining metals and precious stones. They are 'adornment' in a narrower sense than dress and coiffure, although these, too, 'adorn'. One may speak of human radioactivity in the sense that every individual is surrounded by a larger or smaller sphere of significance radiating from him; and everybody else, who deals with him, is immersed in this sphere. It is an inextricable mixture of physiological and psychic elements: the sensuously observable influences which issue from an individual in the direction of his environment also are, in some fashion, the vehicles of a spiritual fulguration. They operate as the symbols of such a fulguration even where, in actuality, they are only external, where no suggestive power or significance of the personality flows through them. The radiations of adornment, the sensuous attention it provokes, supply the personality with such an enlargement or intensification of its sphere: the personality, so to speak, *is* more when it is adorned.

Inasmuch as adornment usually is also an object of considerable value, it is a synthesis of the individual's having and being; it thus transforms mere possession into the sensuous and emphatic perceivability of the individual himself. This is not true of ordinary dress which, neither in respect of having nor of being, strikes one as an individual particularity; only the fancy dress, and above all, jewels, which gather the personality's value and significance of radiation as if in a focal point, allow the mere *having* of the person to become a visible quality of its *being*. And this is so, not *although* adornment is something 'superfluous', but precisely *because* it is. The necessary is much more closely connected with the individual; it surrounds his existence with a narrower periphery. The superfluous 'flows over', that is, it flows to points which are far removed from its origin but to which it still remains tied: around the precinct of mere necessity, it lays a vaster precinct which, in principle, is limitless. According to its very idea, the superfluous contains no measure. The free and princely character of our being increases in the measure in which we add superfluousness to our having, since no extant structure, such as is laid down by necessity, imposes any limiting norm upon it.

This very accentuation of the personality, however, is achieved by means of an impersonal trait. Everything that 'adorns' man can be ordered along a scale in terms of its closeness to the physical body. The 'closest' adornment is typical of primitive peoples: tattooing. The opposite extreme is represented by metal and stone adornments, which are entirely unindividual and can be put on by everybody. Between these two stands dress, which is not so inexchangeable and personal as tattooing, but neither so unindividual and separable as jewelry, whose very elegance lies in its impersonality. That this nature of stone and metal – solidly closed within itself, in no way alluding to any individuality; hard, unmodifiable – is yet forced to serve the person, this is its subtlest fascination. What is really elegant avoids pointing to the specifically individual; it always lays a more general, stylized, almost abstract sphere around man – which, of course, prevents no finesse from connecting the general with the personality. That new clothes are particularly elegant is due to their being still 'stiff'; they have not yet adjusted to the modifications of the individual body as fully as older clothes have, which have been worn, and are pulled and pinched by the peculiar movements of their wearer – thus completely revealing his particularity. This 'newness', this lack of modification by individuality, is typical in the highest measure of metal jewelry: it is always new; in untouchable coolness, it stands above the singularity and destiny of its wearer. This is not true of dress. A long-worn piece of clothing almost grows to the body; it has an intimacy that militates against the very nature of elegance, which is something for the 'others', a social notion deriving its value from general respect.

If jewelry thus is designed to enlarge the individual by adding something supra-individual which goes out to all and is noted and appreciated by all, it must, beyond any effect that its material itself may have, possess *style*. Style is always something general. It brings the contents of personal life and activity into a form shared by many and accessible to many. In the case of a work of art, we are the less interested in its style, the greater the personal uniqueness and the subjective life expressed in it. For, it is with these that it appeals to the spectator's personal core, too – of the spectator who, so to speak, is alone in the whole world with this work of art. But of what we call handicraft – which because of its utilitarian purpose appeals to a diversity of men – we request a more general and typical articulation. We expect not only that an individuality with its uniqueness be voiced in it, but a broad, historical or social orientation and temper, which make it possible for handicraft to be incorporated into the life systems of a great many different individuals. It is the greatest mistake to think that, because it always functions as the adornment of an individual, adornment must be an individual work of art. Quite the contrary: *because* it is to serve the individual, it may not itself be of an individual nature – as little as the piece of furniture on which we sit, or the eating utensil which we manipulate, may be individual works of art. The work of art cannot, in principle, be incorporated into another life – it is a self-sufficient world. By contrast, all that occupies the larger sphere around the life of the individual, must surround it as if in ever wider concentric spheres that lead back to the individual or originate from him. The essence of stylization is precisely this dilution of individual poignancy, this generalization beyond the uniqueness of the personality – which, nevertheless, in its capacity of base or circle of radiation, carries or absorbs the individuality as if in a broadly flowing river. For this reason, adornment has always instinctively been shaped in a relatively severe style.

Besides its formal stylization, the *material* means of its social purpose is its *brilliance*. By virtue of this brilliance, its wearer appears as the centre of a circle of radiation in which every close-by person, every seeing eye, is caught. As the flash of the precious stone seems to be directed at the other – like the lightning of the glance the eye addresses to him – it carries the social meaning of jewels, the being-for-the-other, which returns to the subject as the enlargement of his own sphere of significance. The radii of this sphere mark the distance which jewelry creates between men – 'I have something which you do not have'. But, on the other hand, these radii not only let the other participate: they shine in *his* direction; in fact, they exist only for his sake. By virtue of their material, jewels signify, in one and the same act, an increase in distance and a favour.

For this reason, they are of such particular service to vanity – which needs others in order to despise them. This suggests the profound difference which exists between vanity and haughty pride: pride, whose self-consciousness really rests only upon itself, ordinarily disdains 'adornment' in every sense of the word. A word must also be added here, to the same effect, on the significance of 'genuine' material. The attraction of the 'genuine', in all contexts, consists in its being more than its immediate appearance, which it shares with its imitation. Unlike its falsification, it is not something isolated; it has its roots in a soil that lies beyond its mere appearance, while the unauthentic is only what it can be taken for at the moment. The 'genuine' individual, thus, is the person on whom one can rely even when he is out of one's sight. In the case of jewelry, this more-than-appearance is its *value*, which cannot be guessed by being looked at, but is something that, in contrast to skilled forgery, is *added* to the appearance. By virtue of the fact that this value can always be realized, that it is recognized by all, that it possesses a relative timelessness, jewelry becomes part of a supra-contingent, supra-personal value structure. Talmi-gold and similar trinkets are identical with what they momentarily *do* for their wearer; genuine jewels are a value that goes beyond this; they have their roots in the value ideas of the whole social circle and are ramified through all of it. Thus, the charm and the accent they give the individual who wears them, feed on this supra-individual soil. Their genuineness makes their aesthetic value – which, too, is here a value 'for the others' – a symbol of general esteem, and of membership in the total social value system.

There once existed a decree in medieval France which prohibited all persons below a certain rank to wear gold ornaments. The combination which characterizes the whole nature of adornment unmistakably lives in this decree: in adornment, the sociological and aesthetic emphasis upon the personality fuses as if in a focus; being-for-oneself and being-for-others become reciprocal cause and effect in it. Aesthetic excellence and the right to charm and please, are allowed, in this decree, to go only to a point fixed by the individual's social sphere of significance. It is precisely in this fashion that one adds, to the charm which adornment gives one's whole appearance, the *sociological* charm of being, by virtue of adornment, a representative of one's group, with whose whole significance one is 'adorned'. It is as if the significance of his status, symbolized by jewels, returned to the individual on the very beams which originate in him and enlarge his sphere of impact. Adornment, thus, appears as the means by which his social power or dignity is transformed into visible, personal excellence.

Centripetal and centrifugal tendencies, finally, appear to be fused in adornment in a specific form, in the following information. Among primitive peoples, it is reported, women's private property generally develops later than that of men and, originally, and often exclusively, refers to adornment. By contrast, the personal property of the male usually begins with weapons. This reveals his active and more aggressive nature: the male enlarges his personality sphere without waiting for the will of others. In the case of the more passive female nature this result – although formally the same in spite of all external differences – depends more on the others' good will. Every property is an extension of personality; property is that which obeys our wills, that in which our egos express, and externally realize, themselves. This expression occurs, earliest and most completely, in regard to our body, which thus is our first and most unconditional possession. In the *adorned* body, we possess *more*; if we have the adorned body at our disposal, we are masters over more and nobler things, so to speak. It is, therefore, deeply significant that bodily adornment becomes private property above all: it expands the ego and enlarges the sphere around us which is filled with our personality and which consists in the pleasure and the attention of our environment. This environment looks with much less attention at the unadorned (and thus as if less 'expanded') individual, and passes by without including him. The fundamental principle of adornment is once more revealed in the fact that, under primitive conditions, the most outstanding possession of women became that which, according to its very idea, exists only for others, and which can intensify the value and significance of its wearer only through the recognition that flows back to her from these others. In an aesthetic form, adornment creates a highly specific synthesis of the great convergent and divergent forces of the individual and society, namely, the elevation of the ego through existing for others, and the elevation of existing for others through the emphasis and extension of the ego. This aesthetic form itself stands above the contrasts between individual human strivings. They find, in adornment, not only the possibility of a reciprocal organization that, as anticipation and pledge of their deeper metaphysical unity, transcends the disharmony of their appearance.

THE PROBLEM OF STYLE

It has long been said that the practical existence of humanity is absorbed in the struggle between individuality and generality, that at almost every point of our existence the obedience to a law valid for everyone, whether of an inner or an outer nature, comes into conflict with the purely internal determination of our existence, with the individuality of the person who obeys only his own vital sense. But it might seem paradoxical that in these collisions of the political, economic and moral fields only a much more general form of contrast expresses itself, which is no less able to bring the nature of artistic style to its fundamental expression.

I begin with a very simple experience from the psychology of art. The deeper and more unique the impression of a work of art is on us, the less the question of style tends to play a role in this impression. On viewing any of the countless, rather ungratifying statues of the seventeenth century, we are above all aware of their baroque character; with the neo-classical portraits from around 1800 we think mainly of the style of their times; nothing about numerous quite indifferent pictures from the present excites our attention, except perhaps that they display the naturalistic style. Facing a statue by Michelangelo, however, a religious painting by Rembrandt, or a portrait by Velasquez, the question of style becomes completely irrelevant; the work of art takes us utterly prisoner in the unified wholeness with which it confronts us, and whether it additionally belongs to some temporal style or other is a question which will not occur, at least not to the merely aesthetically interested observer. When a foreignness of sensibility does not permit us to grasp the real individuality in the work of art, so that we can only penetrate to its more general and typical features – as is often the case for instance with oriental art – only then does our consciousness of style remain active and especially effective even with regard to great works. For the decisive thing is this: style is always that type of artistic arrangement which, to the extent it carries or helps to carry the impression of a work of art, negates its quite individual nature and value, its uniqueness of meaning. By virtue of style, the particularity of the individual work is subjugated to a general law of form that also applies to other works; it is, so to speak, relieved of its absolute autonomy. Because it shares its nature or a part of its design with others it thus points to a common root that lies beyond the individual work – in contrast to the works that grow purely out of themselves, that is, from the mysterious, absolute unity of the artistic personality and its uniqueness. And just as the stylization of a work contains the note of a generality, a law of perception and feeling that applies beyond the specific artistic individuality, the same can be said with respect to the *subject* of the work of art. A stylized rose is supposed to represent the general character of a rose, the style of a rose, not the individual reality of a specific rose. Different artists attempt to achieve this through quite different constructions, just as for different philosophers that which appears as common to all realities is quite different, even opposite. For an Indian artist, a Gothic artist, or one from the Empire period, such stylization will therefore lead to quite heterogeneous phenomena. But the meaning of each is nonetheless not to make the rose perceptible, but rather its law of formation, the root of its form, which is universally active as the unifying force in all the multiplicity of its forms.

Here, however, an objection seems unavoidable. We do speak after all, of Botticelli's or Michelangelo's style, of Goethe's or Beethoven's. The right to do so is the following: that these great figures have created a mode of expression flowing from their very individual genius, which we now sense as the general character in all their individual works. Then such a style of an individual master may be adopted by others so that it becomes the shared property of many artistic personalities. In these others it expresses its destiny as a style, of being something over or beside the expression of personality, so that we quite rightly say, 'These have Michelangelo's style', just as we have a possession that has not grown from us ourselves, but been acquired externally and only subsequently incorporated into the sphere of our ego.

Michelangelo, by contrast, is this style himself, it is identical to Michelangelo's own being, and by virtue of that it is also that general character which is expressed in and colours all artistic utterances of Michelangelo, but only because it is the root-force of these works and these works only. Therefore, it can only be distinguished logically, so to speak, and not objectively from what is unique to the individual work as such. In this case, saying that style is the man himself is well justified, even more clearly in the sense that the man is the style. In the cases of a style coming from outside, on the other hand, shared with others and the period, that maxim has at best the meaning that it shows where the limits of the originality of the individual lie.

From this general theme – that style is a principle of generality which either mixes with the principle of individuality, displaces it or represents it – all the individual features of style as a psychic and artistic reality are developed. It displays in particular the fundamental distinction between applied arts and fine art. The essence of the work of applied art is that it exists many times; its diffusion is the quantitative expression of its usefulness, for it always serves a need that is shared by many people. The essence of the work of fine art, on the other hand, is uniqueness. A work of art and its copy are something totally different from a model and its realization, something different from the copies of a fabric or a piece of jewelry manufactured according to a pattern. The fact that innumerable fabrics and pieces of jewelry, chairs and book bindings, candelabras and drinking glasses are manufactured without distinction from a single model, is the symbol that each of these things has its law outside itself. Each such object is only the chance example of something general, in short, its sense of form is style and not the singularity with which a psyche is expressed according to its uniqueness in precisely this one object.[2] This is by no means a denigration of applied art, no more than the principle of generality and the principle of individuality possess a ranking among themselves. Instead, they are the poles of the human creative ability, neither of which could be dispensed with, and each of which determines every point of life, inward and outward, active and enjoying, only in cooperation with the other, although in an infinite variety of mixtures. And we will become acquainted with the vital needs which can only be satisfied by the stylized, not the artistic individual object.

Just as previously the concept of artistic individual design was disputed by the fact that even great artists have a style – namely, their own, which is a law, and therefore a style, of their own – the corresponding objection comes up here. We also observe, especially today, how the objects of applied art are individually designed, by definite personalities with the unmistakable cachet of such; we often see only one copy of an individual object, perhaps manufactured for only one user. But there is a peculiar situation, which can be pointed out here, that keeps this from being a counterexample. To say of some things that they are unique, and of others that they are one individual thing out of many, often has only a symbolic meaning, and certainly that is the case here. With that we refer to a certain quality which is characteristic of the thing and gives its existence the meaning of singularity or repetitiveness, without some contingent exterior fate always having to realize this quantitative expression of its nature. We have all had the experience that a sentence we hear disgusts us with its banality, without being able to maintain that we have often heard it, or even ever heard it at all. It is just inwardly, qualitatively old hat, even if no one else has ever actually used it; the sentence is banal because it deserves to be banal.

And conversely we have the irrefutable impression that certain works and certain people are unique – even if chance combinations of existence actually produce another or many other exactly identical personalities or objects. That doesn't affect any of these, because they have the right, one could say, to be unique, or rather, this numerical designation is only the expression of a qualitative nobility of nature, whose basic nature is incomparability. And such is the situation with the singularities of applied art: because their essence is style, because the general artistic substance of which their particular shape is formed always remains tangible in them, it is their *meaning* to be reproduced, they are internally constituted for multiplicity, even though expense, caprice or jealous exclusivity only permit them by chance to become reality once.

Matters are different with those artistically formed objects of use which actually refuse this style-meaning through their design and wish to have or do indeed have the effect of individual works of art. I should like to lodge the strongest protest possible against this tendency of the applied arts. Those objects are destined to be incorporated into life, to serve an externally given end. In this they contrast completely with the work of art, which is imperiously closed within itself. Each work is a world unto itself, it is its own end, symbolizing by its very frame that it refuses any participation as a servant in the movements of a practical life outside itself. A chair exists so that one can sit on it, a glass in order that one can fill it with wine and take it in one's hand; if due to their design these two give the impression of that self-satisfied artistic nature which follows only its own laws and expresses the autonomy of its psyche totally within itself, then the most repulsive conflict arises. Sitting on a work of art, working with a work of art, using a work of art for the needs of practice – that is cannibalism, it is the degradation of the master to the status of slave, and this is not a master who occupies that status by the contingent favour of fate, but inwardly, in accordance with the law of his nature. The theoreticians, whom one hears pronouncing in the same breath that the piece of applied art should be a work of art and that its highest principle is practicality, do not seem to sense this contradiction: that the practical is a means – which therefore has its end outside itself – while the work of art is never a means, but a work closed in itself, one that unlike the 'practical' never borrows its law from anything that is not itself. The principle that if possible every object of use should be a work of art like Michelangelo's *Moses* or *Jan Six* by Rembrandt is perhaps the most common misunderstanding of modern individualism. It would give to things that exist for other people and purposes the form of those whose meaning resides in the pride of being-for-themselves; to the things that are used and used up, moved and handed around it would give the form of those which outlast the bustle of practical life unmoved, like a blessed island; finally to those things that appeal because of their utilitarian end to the general in us, to that which we share with others, it would give the form of those objects which are unique because an individual soul has embodied its uniqueness in them, so that they gravitate towards the point of uniqueness in us, where each man is alone with himself.

And here finally lies the reason why all this conditionality of the applied arts does not signify a denigration. Instead of the character of individuality, applied art is supposed to have the character of style, of broad generality – which of course does not mean absolutely broad, open to every philistine and all tastes – and thus it represents in the aesthetic sphere a different principle of life than actual art, but not an inferior one. We must not be deluded into thinking that the subjective achievement of its creator can display the same refinement and nobility, the same depth and imagination as that of the painter or the sculptor. The fact that style also appeals to the observer at levels beyond the purely individual, to the broad emotional categories subject to the general laws of life, is the source of the calming effect, the feeling of security and serenity with which the strictly stylized object provides us. From the stimulation points of individuality to which the work of art so often appeals, life descends with respect to the stylized object into the more pacified levels, where one no longer feels alone. There – or so at least these unconscious events can be interpreted – the supra-individual law of the objective structure before us find its counterpart in the feeling that we too are reacting with the supra-individual part of ourselves, which is subject to universal laws. Thus we are saved from absolute responsibility, from balancing on the narrowness of mere individuality.

This is the reason why the things that surround us as the basis or background of daily life should be stylized. For in his own rooms, a person is the main thing, the point, so to speak, which must rest on broader, less individual, subordinate layers and distinguish himself from them, in order to bring about an organic and harmonious overall feeling. The work of art hanging in its frame on the wall, resting on its pedestal, or lying in a portfolio, shows by this external demarcation alone that it does not intervene in direct life, like tables and glasses, lamps and rugs, that it cannot serve people as a 'necessary extra'. The principle of calm, which the domestic surrounding of a person must support, has led with miraculous instinctive practicality to the stylization of this environment: of all the objects we use, it is probably furniture which most consistently carries the cachet of some 'style'. This becomes most evident in the dining-room, which even for physiological reasons is supposed to favour relaxation, the descent from the surging excitements of the day into a broader comfort shared with others. Without being aware of this reason, the aesthetic tendency has always encouraged that the dining-room be especially stylized, and the 'style movement', beginning in Germany in the 1870s, concentrated initially on the dining-room.

Just as the principle of style as well as that of the uniqueness of form have everywhere tended to display some sort of a mixture and reconciliation with their respective opposite, a higher power also rectifies the exemption of home furnishings from individual artistic design with the demand for their stylization. Oddly enough this demand for style only exists – for modern man at least – for the individual objects of his surroundings, but not for the surroundings as a whole. The residence, as furnished by the individual in accordance with his taste and needs, can by all means have the personal, unmistakable tone that flows from the special nature of this individual, which would nonetheless be unbearable if every single object in it betrayed the same individuality. This might seem paradoxical at first glance. But assuming that it is true, it would first of all explain why living in rooms that are kept strictly in a certain historical style has a peculiarly unpleasant, strange and cold quality for us, while those that are composed of pieces in different but no less strict styles according to individual taste, which must of course be firm and consistent, seem most liveable and warm to us.

An environment consisting entirely of objects in *one* historical style coalesces into a closed unity which excludes the individual who lives there, so to speak; he finds no gap where his personal life, free from any past style, could enter into it or join it. This becomes quite different, oddly, as soon as the individual constructs his environment of variously stylized objects; by his doing the objects receive a new centre, which is not located in any of them alone, but which they all manifest through the particular way they are united. This centre is a subjective unity, an experience by a personal psyche and an assimilation to it which becomes tangible in the objects. This is the irreplaceable attraction which leads us to furnish our rooms with objects from past times, and especially those which bear the calm happiness of a style, that is, a supra-individual law of form, to create a new whole, whose synthesis and overall form are of a thoroughly individual nature and suited to one and only one specially attuned personality.

What drives modern man so strongly to style is the unburdening and concealment of the personal, which is the essence of style. Subjectivism and individuality have intensified to breaking-point, and in the stylized designs, from those of behaviour to those of home furnishing there is a mitigation and a toning down of this acute personality to a generality and its law. It is as if the ego could really no longer carry itself, or at least no longer wished to show itself and thus put on a more general, a more typical, in short, a stylized costume. There is a very delicate shame in the fact that a supra-individual form and law are placed between the subjective personality and its objective environment. Stylized expression, form of life, taste – all these are limitations and ways of creating a distance, in which the exaggerated subjectivism of the times finds a counterweight and concealment. The tendency of modern man to surround himself with antiquities – that is, things in which the style, the character of their times, the general mood that hovers around them are essential – this tendency is certainly not a contingent snobbery. Instead it goes back to that deeper need to give the individually excessive life an addition of calm breadth and typical lawfulness. Earlier times, which only had one style which was therefore taken for granted were situated quite differently in these difficult questions of life. Where only one style is conceivable, every individual expression grows organically from it; it has no need to search first for its roots; the general and the personal go together without conflict in a work. The unity and lack of problems we envy in Greek antiquity and many periods of the Middle Ages are based on such an unproblematic general foundation for life, that is to say, on the style, which arranged its relationship to the individual production much more simply and freer of contradictions than is possible for us, who have a variety of styles at our disposal in all areas, so that individual work, behaviour and taste have a loose optional relation to the broad foundation, the general law, which they do require after all. That is the reason why the products of earlier times often seem to have so much more style than those of our own age. For we say an object is devoid of style if it appears to have sprung from a momentary, isolated, temporary sentiment, without being based on a more general feeling, a non-contingent norm. This necessary fundamental aspect can very well be what I term the individual style. In great and creative people, the individual work flows from such an all-encompassing depth of being that it is able to find there the firmness and the foundation, the transcendence of here and now, which comes to the work of the lesser artist from an external style. Here the individual is the case of an individual law; anyone who is not that strong must adhere to a general law; if he fails to, his work fails to have style – which, as is now easily understood, can only happen in periods with multiple style possibilities.

Finally, style is the aesthetic attempt to solve the great problem of life: an individual work or behaviour, which is closed, a whole, can simultaneously belong to something higher, a unifying encompassing context. The distinction between the individual style of the very great and the general style of the lesser expresses that broad practical norm: 'and if you cannot become a unity yourself, then join a unity as a serving partner'. It expresses this in the language of art, which grants even the most modest achievement at least a ray of the splendour and unity that shine in the practical world only on the very great.

Notes to Part V

1. In the original, this section, printed in smaller type, is called '*Exkurs über den Schmuck*' (Note on Adornment). – According to the context, '*Schmuck*' is translated as 'adornment', 'jewels', or 'jewelry'. – translator's note.

2. Therefore, *material* also has such a great importance for style. The human form, for instance, demands quite a different type of expression if it is presented in porcelain or in bronze, in wood or in marble. For the material is in fact the *general* substance, which offers itself equally to an arbitrary number of different forms, and thus determines these as their general prerequisite.

PART VI
LEISURE CULTURE

THE ALPINE JOURNEY

A process which has been in the making for decades in the Swiss transport system has recently been completed. It is something more than an economic analogy to call it the wholesale opening-up and enjoyment of nature. Destinations that were previously only accessible by remote walks can now be reached by railways, which are appearing at an ever-increasing rate. Railways have been built where the gradients are too steep for roads to be constructed, as in the Muerren or Wanger Alps. The railway-line up the Eiger appears to have been finalized, and the same number of climbers who have scaled this difficult peak can now be brought up in a single day by rail. The Faustian wish, 'I stand before you, nature, a solitary individual' is evermore rarely realized and so increasingly rarely declared. Alpine journeys had a pedagogic value in that they were a pleasure that could only be had by a self-reliance that was both external and internal to oneself. Now there is the lure of the ease of an open road, and the concentration and convergence of the masses – colourful but therefore as a whole colourless – suggesting to us an average sensibility. Like all social averages this depresses those disposed to the higher and finer values without elevating those at the base to the same degree.

All in all I accept that the advantages of this socialistic wholesale opening up of the Alps outweigh the reliance on the efforts of the individual. Countless people who previously were barred because of their lack of strength and means are now able to enjoy nature. I disagree with that foolish romanticism which saw difficult routes, prehistoric food and hard beds as an irremovable part of the stimulus of the good old days of alpine travel; despite this it is still possible for those who wish, to find solitude and quiet in the Alps. But the increased accessibility of alpine travel does cause us to question the benefit our civilization draws from it; since alpine travel has already to be seen as an important element of the psychic life (*Seelenleben*) of our upper strata and as such as a matter of social psychology (*Volkerpsychologie*).

It is said that it is part of one's education (*Bildung*) to see the Alps, but not education alone for its twin sister is 'affluence' (*Wohlhabenheit*). The power of capitalism extends itself to ideas as well; it is capable of annexing such a distinguished concept as education as its own private property. Furthermore, profound and spiritual (geistige) human beings believe they are cultivating their inner depths and spirituality when they visit the Alps. Alongside the physical act of climbing and the temporary pleasure it creates is a certain moral element and spiritual satisfaction which appears to be located outside egoistic pleasure. By distancing their own spiritual and educational values from other sensual pleasures, it seems to me that these people employ one of those easy self-deceptions whereby their own culture, which would find egoism shocking, retains a subjectivity despite its lofty sentiments and seeks shamelessly to cloak its own pleasures with objective justifications. I think that the educative value of alpine travel is very small. It gives the feeling of tremendous excitement and charge in its incomparable merging of forbidding strength and radiant beauty, and at the time the contemplation of those things fills us with an unrivalled intensity of feeling, prompting undisclosed inner feelings as if the high peaks could uncover the depths of our soul. Strangely this excitement and euphoria, which drive the emotions to a level more intense than normal, subside remarkably quickly. The uplift which a view of the high Alps gives is followed very quickly by the return to the mood of the mundane. In particular compared to travel in Italy this is very pronounced. The difference between the strength and depth of that momentary rapture and the lasting value on the formation and mood of the soul, encourages comparison between the Alps and music. In this way I also believe that music is given an exaggerated educational value. It also takes us into fantastic regions of the life of the senses, whose riches are so to speak tied to those areas; we take little or nothing from them to adorn other areas of our inner life. All of the verve and heightening that music brings out in us and which we claim as our own, fades away with the notes and leaves the state of one's soul exactly at the point where it was before. Like a talent for music, the effect of music belongs to something beyond the other faculties for learning (Bildungssphaeren). The magnificence of music should be as accessible as that of the Alps; I think that the idea that the value of both to education in its deepest sense, in its effect upon the integrity of the soul, is in need of revision.

The clearest expression of this error is the confusion of the egoistic enjoyment of alpine sports with educational and moral values. In alpine clubs there is the idea that the surmounting of life-endangering difficulties is morally commendable, a triumph of the spirit over the resistance of the material, and a consequence of moral strength: of courage, will-power and the summoning of all abilities for an ideal goal. One forgets that the forces deployed are a means to goals which have no moral claim and indeed are often unethical; as a means for momentary enjoyment, which comes from the exertion of all one's energies, from playing with danger and the emotion of the panoramic view. Indeed, I would place this enjoyment as the highest that life can offer. The less settled, less certain and less free from contradiction modern existence is the more passionately we desire the heights that stand beyond the good and evil whose presence we are unable to look over and beyond. I do not know anything in visible nature that bears the character of the materially transcendent as a snowscape that expresses 'the summits' in its colour and form. Whoever has once enjoyed this will yearn for the release in something that is simply other than the 'I' – the 'I' with its melancholy disquiet, full of the life of the plains, choking the exercise of the will. This is so more with respect to the mountains than the sea, which, with its foam waiting to drain away only to come flooding back in, with the purposeless *circulus vitiosus* of its movement, reminds us only too painfully of our own inner life. Admittedly many are attracted by this. Since not only the addition to the 'I' through its opposite releases us, but also the sea as symbol and picture, shorn of all incidentals, mirrors our destiny and unhappiness, rather like a secret homeopathy, and discloses a reconciliation and a healing elevation over life. Nevertheless, this is only a soothing, a forgetting and a reverie and, as such, merely a passive enjoyment. From the loneliness of the icy wilderness, however, bursts out the sensation of a desire for action, that feeling of joy and being beyond life that can be derived from perhaps no other external situation, even though this is admittedly only the temporary delusion of aesthetic stimulation.

But this pleasure remains completely egoistic and, therefore, the risking of life as mere enjoyment is unethical; indeed even more unethical since for the hire of a guide for fifty or hundred francs one risks another's life through possible accident. An alpinist would be indignant if one wanted to compare him or her to a gambler. And yet both wish to place their existence at risk as a purely subjective excitation and gratification. Frequently the gambler does not look for material profit but the excitement of risk and the gripping combination of the cold-bloodedness and passion of one's own skill and the incalculability of fate. The alpinist plays for a stake which from an ethical viewpoint should be wagered for only the highest objective values and not for the sake of selfish and immediate gratification. Only a romantic excitation can delude itself that every voluntary risking of life is part of tradition when social and religious commitments could supposedly only be gained at the price of life, thereby conferring on their goals the veneer of ethical dignity.

THE ADVENTURE

Each segment of our conduct and experience bears a twofold meaning: it revolves about its own centre, contains as much breadth and depth, joy and suffering, as the immediate experiencing gives it, and at the same time is a segment of a course of life – not only a circumscribed entity, but also a

component of an organism. Both aspects, in various configurations, characterize everything that occurs in a life. Events which may be widely divergent in their bearing on life as a whole may nonetheless be quite similar to
one another; or they may be incommensurate in their intrinsic meanings but
so similar in respect to the roles they play in our total existence as to be
interchangeable.

One of two experiences which are not particularly different in substance,
as far as we can indicate it, may nevertheless be perceived as an 'adventure'
and the other not. The one receives the designation denied the other
because of the difference in the relation to the whole of our life. More precisely, the most general form of adventure is its dropping out of the continuity of life. 'Wholeness of life', after all, refers to the fact that a consistent
process runs through the individual components of life, however crassly and
irreconcilably distinct they may be. What we call an adventure stands in contrast to that interlocking of life-links, to that feeling that those counter-
currents, turnings, and knots still, after all, spin forth a continuous thread.
An adventure is certainly a part of our existence, directly contiguous with
other parts which precede and follow it; at the same time, however, in its
deeper meaning, it occurs outside the usual continuity of this life. Nevertheless, it is distinct from all that is accidental and alien, merely touching
life's outer shell. While it falls outside the context of life, it falls, with this
same movement, as it were, back into that context again, as will become
clear later; it is a foreign body in our existence which is yet somehow connected with the centre; the outside, if only by a long and unfamiliar detour,
is formally an aspect of the inside.

Because of its place in our psychic life, a remembered adventure tends to
take on the quality of a dream. Everyone knows how quickly we forget
dreams because they, too, are placed outside the meaningful context of life-
as-a-whole. What we designate as 'dreamlike' is nothing but a memory
which is bound to the unified, consistent life-process by fewer threads than
are ordinary experiences. We might say that we localize our inability to
assimilate to this process something experienced by imagining a dream in
which it took place. The more 'adventurous' an adventure, that is, the more
fully it realizes its idea, the more 'dreamlike' it becomes in our memory. It
often moves so far away from the centre of the ego and the course of life
which the ego guides and organizes that we may think of it as something
experienced by another person. How far outside that course it lies, how
alien it has become to that course, is expressed precisely by the fact that we
might well feel that we could appropriately assign to the adventure a subject
other than the ego.

We ascribe to an adventure a beginning and an end much sharper than
those to be discovered in the other forms of our experiences. The adventure is freed of the entanglements and concatenations which are characteristic of those forms and is given a meaning in and of itself. Of our ordinary
experiences, we declare that one of them is over when, or because, another
starts; they reciprocally determine each other's limits, and so become a

means whereby the contextual unity of life is structured or expressed. The adventure, however, according to its intrinsic meaning, is independent of the 'before' and 'after'; its boundaries are defined regardless of them. We speak of adventure precisely when continuity with life is thus disregarded on principle – or rather when there is not even any need to disregard it, because we know from the beginning that we have to do with something alien, untouchable, out of the ordinary. The adventure lacks that reciprocal interpenetration with adjacent parts of life which constitutes life-as-a-whole. It is like an island in life which determines its beginning and end according to its own formative powers and not – like the part of a continent – also according to those of adjacent territories. This factor of decisive boundedness, which lifts an adventure out of the regular course of a human destiny, is not mechanical but organic: just as the organism determines its spatial shape not simply by adjusting to obstacles confining it from right and left but by the propelling force of a life forming from inside out, so does an adventure not end because something else begins; instead, its temporal form, its radical being-ended, is the precise expression of its inner sense.

Here, above all, is the basis of the profound affinity between the adventurer and the artist, and also, perhaps, of the artist's attraction by adventure. For the essence of a work of art is, after all, that it cuts out a piece of the endlessly continuous sequences of perceived experience, detaching it from all connections with one side or the other, giving it a self-sufficient form as though defined and held together by an inner core. A part of existence, interwoven with the uninterruptedness of that existence, yet nevertheless felt as a whole, as an integrated unit – this is the form common to both the work of art and the adventure. Indeed, it is an attribute of this form to make us feel that in both the work of art and the adventure the whole of life is somehow comprehended and consummated – and this irrespective of the particular theme either of them may have. Moreover, we feel this, not although, but because, the work of art exists entirely beyond life as a reality; the adventure, entirely beyond life as an uninterrupted course which intelligibly connects every element with its neighbours. It is because the work of art and the adventure stand over against life (even though in very different senses of the phrase) that both are analogous to the totality of life itself, even as this totality presents itself in the brief summary and crowdedness of a dream experience.

For this reason, the adventurer is also the extreme example of the ahistorical individual, of the man who lives in the present. On the one hand, he is not determined by any past (and this marks the contrast between him and the aged, of which more later); nor, on the other hand, does the future exist for him. An extraordinarily characteristic proof of this is that Casanova (as may be seen from his memoirs), in the course of his erotic-adventurous life, every so often seriously intended to marry a woman with whom he was in love at the time. In the light of his temperament and conduct of life, we can imagine nothing more obviously impossible, internally and externally. Casanova not only had excellent knowledge of men but also rare knowledge of himself. Although he must have said to himself that he could not stand marriage even two weeks and that the most miserable consequences of such a step would be quite unavoidable, his perspective on the future was wholly obliterated in the rapture of the moment. (Saying this, I mean to put the emphasis on the moment rather than on the rapture.) Because he was entirely dominated by the feeling of the present, he wanted to enter into a future relationship which was impossible precisely because his temperament was oriented to the present.

In contrast to those aspects of life which are related only peripherally – by mere fate – the adventure is defined by its capacity, in spite of its being isolated and accidental, to have necessity and meaning. Something becomes an adventure only by virtue of two conditions: that it itself is a specific organization of some significant meaning with a beginning and an end; and that, despite its accidental nature, its extra-territoriality with respect to the continuity of life, it nevertheless connects with the character and identity of the bearer of that life – that it does so in the widest sense, transcending, by a mysterious necessity, life's more narrowly rational aspects.

At this point there emerges the relation between the adventurer and the gambler. The gambler, clearly, has abandoned himself to the meaninglessness of chance. In so far, however, as he counts on its favour and believes possible and realizes a life dependent on it, chance for him has become part of a context of meaning. The typical superstition of the gambler is nothing other than the tangible and isolated, and thus, of course, childish, form of this profound and all-encompassing scheme of his life, according to which chance makes sense and contains some necessary meaning (even though not by the criterion of rational logic). In his superstition, he wants to draw chance into his teleological system by omens and magical aids, thus removing it from its inaccessible isolation and searching in it for a lawful order, no matter how fantastic the laws of such an order may be.

The adventurer similarly lets the accident somehow be encompassed by the meaning which controls the consistent continuity of life, even though the accident lies outside the continuity. He achieves a central feeling of life which runs through the eccentricity of the adventure and produces a new, significant necessity of his life in the very width of the distance between its accidental, externally given content and the unifying core of existence from which meaning flows. There is in us an eternal process playing back and forth between chance and necessity, between the fragmentary materials given us from the outside and the consistent meaning of the life developed from within.

The great forms in which we shape the substance of life are the syntheses, antagonisms, or compromises between chance and necessity. Adventure is such a form. When the professional adventurer makes a system of life out of his life's lack of system, when out of his inner necessity he seeks the naked, external accidents and builds them into that necessity, he only, so to speak, makes macroscopically visible that which is the essential form of every 'adventure', even that of the non-adventurous person. For by adventure we always mean a third something, neither the sheer, abrupt event whose meaning – a mere given – simply remains outside us nor the consistent sequence of life in which every element supplements every other toward an inclusively integrated meaning. The adventure is no mere hotchpotch of these two, but rather that incomparable experience which can be interpreted only as a particular encompassing of the accidentally external by the internally necessary.

Occasionally, however, this whole relationship is comprehended in a still more profound inner configuration. No matter how much the adventure seems to rest on a differentiation within life, life as a whole may be perceived as an adventure. For this, one need neither be an adventurer nor undergo many adventures. To have such a remarkable attitude toward life, one must sense above its totality a higher unity, a super-life, as it were, whose relation to life parallels the relation of the immediate life totality itself to those particular experiences which we call adventures.

Perhaps we belong to a metaphysical order, perhaps our soul lives a transcendent existence, such that our earthly, conscious life is only an isolated fragment as compared to the unnameable context of an existence running its course in it. The myth of the transmigration of souls may be a halting attempt to express such a segmental character of every individual life. Whoever senses through all actual life a secret, timeless existence of the soul, which is connected with the realities of life only as from a distance, will perceive life in its given and limited wholeness as an adventure when compared to that transcendent and self-consistent fate. Certain religious moods seem to bring about such a perception. When our earthly career strikes us as a mere preliminary phase in the fulfilment of eternal destinies, when we have no home but merely a temporary asylum on earth, this obviously is only a particular variant of the general feeling that life as a whole is an adventure. It merely expresses the running together, in life, of the symptoms of adventure. It stands outside that proper meaning and steady course of existence to which it is yet tied by a fate and a secret symbolism. A fragmentary incident, it is yet, like a work of art, enclosed by a beginning and an end. Like a dream, it gathers all passions into itself and yet, like a dream, is destined to be forgotten; like gaming, it contrasts with seriousness, yet, like the *va banque* of the gambler, it involves the alternative between the highest gain and destruction.

Thus the adventure is a particular form in which fundamental categories of life are synthesized. Another such synthesis it achieves is that between the categories of activity and passivity, between what we conquer and what is given to us. To be sure, their synthesis in the form of adventure makes their contrast perceptible to an extreme degree. In the adventure, on the one hand, we forcibly pull the world into ourselves. This becomes clear when we compare the adventure with the manner in which we wrest the gifts of the world through work. Work, so to speak, has an organic relation to the world. In a conscious fashion, it develops the world's forces and materials toward their culmination in the human purpose, whereas in adventure we have a non-organic relation to the world. Adventure has the gesture of the conqueror, the quick seizure of opportunity, regardless of whether the portion we carve out is harmonious or disharmonious with us, with the world, or with the relation between us and the world. On the other hand, however, in the adventure we abandon ourselves to the world with fewer defences and reserves than in any other relation, for other relations are connected with the general run of our worldly life by more bridges, and thus defend us better against shocks and dangers through previously prepared avoidances and adjustments. In the adventure, the interweaving of activity and passivity which characterizes our life tightens these elements into a coexistence of conquest, which owes everything only to its own strength and presence of mind, and complete self-abandonment to the powers and accidents of the world, which can delight us, but in the same breath can also destroy us. Surely, it is among adventure's most wonderful and enticing charms that the unity towards which at every moment, by the very process of living, we bring together our activity and our passivity – the unity which even in a certain sense *is* life itself – accentuates its disparate elements most sharply, and precisely in *this* way makes itself the more deeply felt, as if they were only the two aspects of one and the same, mysteriously seamless life.

If the adventure, furthermore, strikes us as combining the elements of certainty and uncertainty in life, this is more than the view of the same fundamental relationship from a different angle. The certainty with which – justifiably or in error – we know the outcome, gives our activity one of its distinct qualities. If, on the contrary, we are uncertain whether we shall arrive at the point for which we have set out, if we know our ignorance of the outcome, then this means not only a quantitatively reduced certainty but an inwardly and outwardly unique practical conduct. The adventurer, in a word, treats the incalculable element in life in the way we ordinarily treat only what we think is by definition calculable. (For this reason, the philosopher is the adventurer of the spirit. He makes the hopeless, but not therefore meaningless, attempt to form into conceptual knowledge an attitude of the soul, its mood toward itself, the world, God. He treats this insoluble problem as if it were soluble.) When the outcome of our activity is made doubtful by the intermingling of unrecognizable elements of fate, we usually limit our commitment of force, hold open lines of retreat, and take each step only as if testing the ground.

In the adventure, we proceed in the directly opposite fashion: it is just on the hovering chance, on fate, on the more-or-less that we risk all, burn our bridges, and step into the mist, as if the road will lead us on, no matter what. This is the typical fatalism of the adventurer. The obscurities of fate are certainly no more transparent to him than to others; but he proceeds as if they were. The characteristic daring with which he continually leaves the solidities of life underpins itself, as it were, for its own justification with a feeling of security and 'it-must-succeed', which normally only belongs to the transparency of calculable events. This is only a subjective aspect of the fatalist conviction that we certainly cannot escape a fate which we do not know: the adventurer nevertheless believes that, as far as he himself is concerned, he is certain of this unknown and unknowable element in his life. For this reason, to the sober person adventurous conduct often seems insanity; for, in order to make sense, it appears to presuppose that the unknowable is known. The prince of Ligne said of Casanova, 'He believes in nothing, except in what is least believable'. Evidently, such belief is based on that perverse or at least 'adventurous' relation between the certain and the uncertain, whose correlate, obviously, is the scepticism of the adventurer – that he 'believes in nothing': for him to whom the unlikely is likely, the likely easily becomes unlikely. The adventurer relies to some extent on his own strength, but above all on his own luck; more properly, on a peculiarly undifferentiated unity of the two. Strength, of which he is certain, and luck, of which he is uncertain, subjectively combine into a sense of certainty.

If it is the nature of genius to possess an immediate relation to these secret unities which in experience and rational analysis fall apart into completely separate phenomena, the adventurer of genius lives, as if by mystic instinct, at the point where the course of the world and the individual fate have, so to speak, not yet been differentiated from one another. For this reason, he is said to have a 'touch of genius'. The 'sleepwalking certainty' with which the adventurer leads his life becomes comprehensible in terms of that peculiar constellation whereby he considers that which is uncertain and incalculable to be the premises of his conduct, while others consider only the calculable. Unshakeable even when it is shown to be denied by the facts of the case, this certainty proves how deeply that constellation is rooted in the life conditions of adventurous natures.

The adventure is a form of life which can be taken on by an undetermined number of experiences. Nevertheless, our definitions make it understandable that one of them, more than all others, tends to appear in this form: the erotic – so that our linguistic custom hardly lets us understand by 'adventure' anything but an erotic one. The love affair, even if short-lived, is by no means always an adventure. The peculiar psychic qualities at whose meeting point the adventure is found must be added to this quantitative matter. The tendency of these qualities to enter such a conjuncture will become apparent step by step.

A love affair contains in clear association the two elements which the form of the adventure characteristically conjoins: conquering force and unextortable concession, winning by one's own abilities and dependence on the luck which something incalculable outside ourselves bestows on us. A degree of balance between these forces, gained by virtue of his sense of their sharp differentiation, can, perhaps, be found only in the man. Perhaps for this reason, it is of compelling significance that, as a rule, a love affair is an 'adventure' only for men; for women it usually falls into other categories. In novels of love, the activity of woman is typically permeated by the passivity which either nature or history has imparted to her character; on the other hand, her acceptance of happiness is at the same time a concession and a gift.

The two poles of conquest and grace (which manifest themselves in many variations) stand closer together in woman than in man. In man, they are, as a matter of fact, much more decisively separated. For this reason, in man their coincidence in the erotic experience stamps this experience quite unambiguously as an adventure. Man plays the courting, attacking, often violently grasping role: this fact makes one easily overlook the element of fate, the dependence on something which cannot be predetermined or compelled, that is contained in every erotic experience. This refers not only to dependence on the concession on the part of the other, but to something deeper. To be sure, every 'love returned', too, is a gift which cannot be 'earned', not even by any measure of love – because to love, demand and compensation are irrelevant; it belongs, in principle, in a category altogether different from a squaring of accounts – a point which suggests one of its analogies to the more profound religious relation. But over and above that which we receive from another as a free gift, there still lies in every happiness of love – like a profound, impersonal bearer of those personal elements – a favour of fate. We receive happiness not only from the other: the fact that we do receive it from him is a blessing of destiny, which is incalculable. In the proudest, most self-assured event in this sphere lies something which we must accept with humility. When the force which owes its success to itself and gives all conquest of love some note of victory and triumph is then combined with the other note of favour by fate, the constellation of the adventure is, as it were, preformed.

The relation which connects the erotic content with the more general form of life as adventure is rooted in deeper ground. The adventure is the exclave of life, the 'torn-off' whose beginning and end have no connection with the somehow unified stream of existence. And yet, as if hurdling this stream, it connects with the most recondite instincts and some ultimate intention of life as a whole – and this distinguishes it from the merely accidental episode, from that which only externally 'happens' to us. Now, when a love affair is of short duration, it lives in precisely such a mixture of a merely tangential and yet central character. It may give our life only a momentary splendour, like the ray shed in an inside room by a light flitting by outside. Still, it satisfies a need, or is, in fact, only possible by virtue of a need which – whether it be considered as physical, psychic, or metaphysical – exists, as it were, timelessly in the foundation or centre of our being. This need is related to the fleeting experience as our general longing for light is to that accidental and immediately disappearing brightness.

The fact that love harbours the possibility of this double relation is reflected by the twofold temporal aspect of the erotic. It displays two standards of time: the momentarily climatic, abruptly subsiding passion; and the idea of something which cannot pass, an idea in which the mystical destination of two souls for one another and for a higher unity finds a temporal expression. This duality might be compared with the double existence of intellectual contents: while they emerge only in the fleetingness of the psychic process, in the forever moving focus of consciousness, their logical meaning possesses timeless validity, an ideal significance which is completely independent of the instant of consciousness in which it becomes real for us. The phenomenon of adventure is such that its abrupt climax places its end into the perspective of its beginning. However, its connection with the centre of life is such that it is to be distinguished from all merely accidental happenings. Thus 'mortal danger', so to speak, lies in its very style. This phenomenon, therefore, is a form which by its time symbolism seems to be predetermined to receive the erotic content.

These analogies between love and adventure alone suggest that the adventure does not belong to the life-style of old age. The decisive point about this fact is that the adventure, in its specific nature and charm, is a *form of experiencing*. The *content* of the experience does not make the adventure. That one has faced mortal danger or conquered a woman for a short span of happiness; that unknown factors with which one has waged a gamble have brought surprising gain or loss; that physically or psychologically disguised, one has ventured into spheres of life from which one returns home as if from a strange world – none of these are necessarily adventure. They become adventure only by virtue of a certain experiential tension whereby their substance is realized. Only when a stream flowing between the minutest externalities of life and the central source of strength drags them into itself; when the peculiar colour, ardour, and rhythm of the life process become decisive and, as it were, transform its substance – only then does an event change from mere experience to adventure. Such a principle of accentuation, however, is alien to old age. In general, only youth knows this predominance of the process of life over its substance; whereas in old age, when the process begins to slow up and coagulate, substance becomes crucial; it then proceeds or perseveres in a certain timeless manner, indifferent to the tempo and passion of its being experienced. The old person usually lives either in a wholly *centralized* fashion, peripheral interests having fallen off and being unconnected with his essential life and its inner necessity; or his centre atrophies, and existence runs its course only in isolated petty details, accenting mere externals and accidentals. Neither case makes possible the relation between the outer fate and the inner springs of life in which the adventure consists; clearly, neither permits the perception of contrast characteristic of adventure, namely, that an action is completely torn out of the inclusive context of life and that, simultaneously, the whole strength and intensity of life stream into it.

In youth, the accent falls on the process of life, on its rhythm and its antinomies; in old age, it falls on life's substance, compared to which experience more and more appears relatively incidental. This contrast between youth and age, which makes adventure the prerogative of youth, may be expressed as the contrast between the romantic and the historical spirit of life. Life in its immediacy – hence also in the individuality of its form at any one moment, here and now – counts for the romantic attitude. Life in its immediacy feels the full strength of the current of life most of all in the pointedness of an experience that is torn out of the normal run of things but which is yet connected with the heart of life. All such life which thrusts itself out of life, such breadth of contrast among elements which are penetrated by life, can feed only on that overflow and exuberance of life which exists in adventure, in romanticism, and in youth. Age, on the other hand – if, as such, it has a characteristic, valuable, and coherent attitude – carries with it a historical mood. This mood may be broadened into a worldview or limited to the immediately personal past; at any rate, in its objectivity and retrospective reflectiveness, it is devoted to contemplating a substance of life out of which immediacy has disappeared. All history as depiction in the narrower, scientific sense originates in such a survival of substance beyond the inexpressible process of its presence that can only be experienced. The connection this process has established among them is gone, and must now, in retrospect, and with a view to constructing an ideal image, be re-established by completely different ties.

With this shift of accent, all the dynamic premise of the adventure disappears. Its atmosphere, as suggested before, is absolute presentness – the sudden rearing of the life process to a point where both past and future are irrelevant; it therefore gathers life within itself with an intensity compared with which the factuality of the event often becomes of relatively indifferent import. Just as the game itself – not the winning of money – is the decisive motive for the true gambler; just as for him, what is important is the violence of feeling as it alternates between joy and despair, the almost touchable nearness of the demonic powers which decide between both – so the fascination of the adventure is again and again not the substance which it offers us and which, if it were offered in another form, perhaps would receive little heed, but rather the adventurous form of experiencing it, the intensity and excitement with which it lets us feel life in just this instance. This is what connects youth and adventure. What is called the subjectivity of youth is just this: The material of life in its substantive significance is not as important to youth as is the process which carries it, life itself. Old age is 'objective'; it shapes a new structure out of the substance left behind in a peculiar sort of timelessness by the life which has slipped by. The new structure is that of contemplativeness, impartial judgement, freedom from that unrest which marks life as being present. It is all this that makes adventure alien to old age and an old adventurer an obnoxious or tasteless phenomenon. It would not be difficult to develop the whole essence of adventure from the fact that it is the form of life which in principle is inappropriate to old age.

Notwithstanding the fact that so much of life is hostile to adventure, from the most general point of view adventure appears admixed with all practical human existence. It seems to be an ubiquitous element, but it frequently occurs in the finest distribution, invisible to the naked eye, as it were, and concealed by other elements. This is true quite aside from that notion which, reaching down into the metaphysics of life, considers our existence on earth as a whole, unified adventure. Viewed purely from a concrete and psychological standpoint, every single experience contains a modicum of the characteristics which, if they grow beyond a certain point, bring it to the 'threshold' of adventure. Here the most essential and profound of these characteristics is the singling out of the experience from the total context of life. In point of fact, the meaning of no single part of life is exhausted by its belonging in that context. On the contrary, even when a part is most closely interwoven with the whole, when it really appears to be completely absorbed by onflowing life, like an unaccented word in the course of a sentence – even then, when we listen more closely, we can recognize the intrinsic value of that segment of existence. With a significance which is centred in itself, it sets itself *over against* that total development to which, nevertheless, if looked at from another angle, it inextricably belongs.

Both the wealth and the perplexity of life flow countless times from this value-dichotomy of its contents. Seen from the centre of the personality, every single experience is at once something necessary which comes from the unity of the history of the ego, and something accidental, foreign to that unity, insurmountably walled off, and coloured by a very deep-lying incomprehensibility, as if it stood somewhere in the void and gravitated toward nothing. Thus a shadow of what in its intensification and distinctness constitutes the adventure really hovers over every experience. Every experience, even as it is incorporated into the chain of life, is accompanied by a certain feeling of being enclosed between a beginning and an end – by a feeling of an almost unbearable pointedness of the single experience as such. This feeling may sink to imperceptibility, but it lies latent in every experience and rises from it – often to our own astonishment. It is impossible to identify any minimal distance from the continuity of life short of which the feeling of adventurousness could not emerge – as impossible, to be sure, as to identify the maximal distance where it must emerge for everyone. But everything could not become an adventure if the elements of adventure did not in some measure reside in everything, if they did not belong among the vital factors by virtue of which a happening is designated a human experience.

Similar observations apply to the relation between the accidental and the meaningful. In our every encounter there is so much of the merely given, external, and occasional that we can, so to speak, decide only on a quantitative basis whether the whole may be considered as something rational and in some sense understandable, or whether its insolubility as regards its reference to the past, or its incalculability as regards its reference to the future, is to stamp its whole complexion. From the most secure civic undertaking to the most irrational adventure there runs a continuous line of vital phenomena in which the comprehensible and the incomprehensible, that which can be coerced and that which is given by grace, the calculable and the accidental, mix in infinitely varied degrees. Since the adventure marks one extreme of this continuum, the other extreme must also partake of its character. The sliding of our existence over a scale on which every point is simultaneously determined by the effect of our strength and our abandonment to impenetrable things and powers – this problematic nature of our position in the world, which in its religious version results in the insoluble question of human freedom and divine predetermination, lets all of us become adventurers. Within the dimensions into which our station in life with its tasks, our aims, and our means place us, none of us could live one day if we did not treat that which is really incalculable as if it were calculable, if we did not entrust our own strength with what it still cannot achieve by itself but only by its enigmatic cooperation with the powers of fate.

The substance of our life is constantly seized by interweaving forms which thus bring about its unified whole. Everywhere there is artistic forming, religious comprehending, the shade of moral valuing, the interplay of subject and object. There is, perhaps, no point in this whole stream where every one of these and of many other modes of organization does not contribute at least a drop to its waves. But they become the pure structures which language names only when they rise out of that fragmentary and confused condition where the average life lets them emerge and submerge and so attain mastery over life's substance. Once the religious mood has created its structure, the god, wholly out of itself, it is 'religion'; once the aesthetic form has made its content something secondary, by which it lives a life of its own that listens only to itself, it becomes 'art'; once moral duty is fulfilled simply because it is duty, no matter how changing the contents by means of which it is fulfilled and which previously in turn determined the will, it becomes 'morality'.

It is no different with adventure. We are the adventurers of the earth; our life is crossed everywhere by the tensions which mark adventure. But only when these tensions have become so violent that they gain mastery over the material through which they realize themselves – only then does the 'adventure' arise. For the adventure does not consist in a substance which is won or lost, enjoyed or endured: to all this we have access in other forms of life as well. Rather, it is the radicalness through which it becomes perceptible as a life tension, as the rubato of the life process, independent of its materials and their differences – the quantity of these tensions becoming great enough to tear life, beyond those materials, completely out of itself: this is what transforms mere experience into adventure. Certainly, it is only one segment of existence among others, but it belongs to those forms which, beyond the mere share they have in life and beyond all the accidental nature of their individual contents, have the mysterious power to make us feel for a moment the whole sum of life as their fulfilment and their vehicle, existing only for their realization.

PART VII

MONEY AND COMMODITY CULTURE

ON THE PSYCHOLOGY OF MONEY

In the content of knowing as well as that of acting close observation discovers the continuous separation of a relatively solid from a relatively fluid component. The first is formed by the individual sensory facts of our experience and by the ultimate goals of our will; the second by the causal connections with which, separating and connecting, we descend beneath the phenomenal side of those facts, and on the other hand by the means with which we seek to achieve our already formulated purposes more and more thoroughly, but also more and more indirectly. The fact, as it presents itself to our eyes, may have originated from an infinitude of causes, and while the mind captures it, the conception of its causes and of the causes of its causes is caught up in a continuing flow and a continuing deepening; and thus the transformation of our higher goals is an extremely slow one, since these goals seem to be stationary compared with the inevitable motion in acquiring the means and in the continuing work on foundation building as well as on the elevation of the teleological construction.

It is clear that the theoretical and practical movements are ultimately one and the same, and only take on opposing directions according to differences of interest and viewpoint. I recognize the means to an end when I have recognized what causes will produce this end. The purposive consciousness of humanity, therefore, is deepened hand in hand with its causal consciousness; and what we call cultural progress is based upon this very deepening, perhaps to the same degree as on the discovery of new facts or the changing of our ultimate volitional goals.

The difference between primitive and cultivated conditions is measured by the number of links that lie between the immediate action and its ultimate end. Where the chain of cause and effect is short and known only fragmentarily, then, in order to realize an end, it is necessary to bring about an event which directly realizes it. Now it is obvious, however, that this event will very often not be directly attainable, and while the less cultivated person must renounce his or her goal in this case, the more advanced one will adopt a procedure which does not bring about the end itself, but some other event, which in turn leads to the desired one. The progress of the public spirit therefore indicates the increase of institutions through which the individual can achieve, at least indirectly, those ends which it is difficult or improbable for him or her to attain directly. Every tool which allows the strength of the human hand to achieve an effect in an indirect manner and through transformations which would be denied it through direct impact on the object to be shaped, every legal institution which guarantees to the declared will of a person a consequence which he or she would never have been able to achieve through his or her own strength, every religious congregation which prepares a way inward and upward to the religious sentiment which the individual does not believe he or she is able to find by him or herself – all of these are instances of the deepening of the teleological process outlined above, as the public spirit creates this process when the disproportion between that which the individual wants and that which he or she can achieve as an individual requires detours which only the general community can make passable. Every uniform and generally recognized means of exchange offers an instance of the lengthening of the teleological chain. If all economic transactions are based upon the fact that I want to have something which another person possesses at the moment and that the other will transfer it to me if I transfer something to them which I possess and which they want to possess, then it is obvious that the second link in this two-sided process will not always occur when the first appears. There are innumerable times when I will desire object a that is in the possession of person A, while the object or service b which I am willing to give for it is totally unattractive to A; or perhaps the mutually offered goods are desired by each side, but the quantities with which they correspond to each other does not permit an immediate agreement through direct equivalence. Therefore it is of the greatest value for the attainment of our goals that an intermediate link be inserted in the teleological chain, one into which I can convert b at any time and which can, in turn, be converted into a – roughly in the same way that any particular force, for instance, falling water, heated gas, or windmill sails, can be converted into any particular type of energy once it is introduced into the dynamo. The generally recognized means of exchange becomes the transit point for all bilaterally binding transactions, and thus reveals itself, like the examples mentioned above, to be an extension of purposive action, in the sense that it is a means to obtain the desired objects, indirectly and through a public institution, that would be unattainable through my efforts aimed directly at them. Just as my thoughts must take on the form of the generally understood language in order to advance my practical ends by that roundabout way, so my services and possessions must enter into the form of monetary value in order to serve my continuing volition.

This characteristic of money causes the following psychological trait in it to take effect. It is one of the most significant qualities of the human mind that merely indifferent means to an end become for it ends in their own right, if only they have stood long enough before our consciousness, or if the end to be achieved with them is very remote. The value that they originally held only in trust from the end to be achieved becomes autonomous and clings to them in psychological immediacy rather than indirectly. All external customs, for instance, gain the power to appear in their own right as moral regulations solely through this process, since they were originally only the means or the condition for more distant social ends. Many a philologist remains trapped throughout his life in the investigation of the least important trivialities, whereas the actual end of this mediating effort – the understanding of the intellectual nature of an epoch or of an individual – does not enter his consciousness at all. For countless people, the perfection of technology in their activities has become such an end in itself that they completely forget the higher ends which all technology is only supposed to serve. This is one of the most practical institutions of the intellectual organism. If at every moment we had to have our eye on the entire teleological series which justifies an action, then consciousness would fragment in an intolerable manner. Perhaps the principle of conserving energy has the consequence that instrumental consciousness is concentrated upon the immediately present step of the teleological process, while the more remote ultimate end sinks away from consciousness. In order to have collected strength for the initially necessary implementation of the means, the latter must first of all dominate consciousness to the exclusion of all else.

In the entire fabric of human purposive action there is perhaps no intermediate link in which this psychological trait of the growth of the means to an end appears so purely as with money; never has a value which an object possesses only through its convertibility into others of definitive value been so completely transferred into a value itself.

It is interesting, therefore, to see how this psychological interruption of the teleological series appears not only in direct greed and miserliness, but also in its apparent opposite, the pleasure in simply spending money as such, and finally in pleasure in the possession of as many things as possible from whose specific usefulness and the reason for which they are produced, one does not profit, but which one just wishes to 'have'. Ordinary people compare this type of disposition to that of hamsters. Herein are the stages of the teleological process: the rational ultimate goal is, indeed, only the enjoyment from the use of the object; the means to it are: first, that one have money, second that one spend it, and third that one possess the object. Purposive consciousness can stop at any one of these three stages and constitute it as an end in itself; and in fact, so forcibly, that each of its three components can degenerate into manias.

At the stage in which money grows to become an end in itself, it can display differing degrees of psychological independence in that capacity. From the necessity that exists throughout life to focus on the acquisition of money as the immediate goal of one's efforts, there can arise the belief that all happiness and all definitive satisfaction in life are connected with the possession of a certain sum of money. Only when that instrumental character of money has taken on a definite substantial amount of solidity, however, does this belief become confirmed and the blissful feeling from having a great deal of money remains in the consciousness. If the belief comes to a halt below this crystallization point, then the phenomenon of deadly boredom and disappointment sets in, which can be observed so often among business people when they have gone into retirement after saving up a certain sum of money. They no longer know what to do with their considerable sum of money, and after the circumstances cease which concentrated the consciousness of value upon money, it reveals its true character as a mere means, which becomes useless and unsatisfying as soon as life must rely upon it alone.

A condition of simple respite often appears to be the highest ideal in the midst of the troubles and anxieties of the world; we forget that it is not the respite itself which we miss, but only the respite from certain things and for certain things, and only as a precondition of the positive satisfaction which we are lacking. And thus the majority of people soon feel an intolerable emptiness and pointlessness of existence when they have attained this supposedly ultimate goal. In exactly the same manner, the misunderstanding of the merely relative and conditional character of money, the error which the mercantile system displayed 'writ large', as it were, wreaks its vengeance. However, where the psychological metamorphosis by which money became an end in itself was decisive enough to survive throughout one's entire life, the conditions for perfect happiness are given. For the miser is spared the disappointments which always follow real enjoyment, those deficiencies which we immediately encounter when we go beyond the preparatory stages of acquiring things; the miser's joys must be psychologically similar to aesthetic ones, which confine themselves to the pure, precious form of things and are independent of the impurities and imperfections of their contingent reality. Here too, however, one can detect a subtle difference between the miser who will not separate himself for anything from the money once acquired, despite attractive opportunities for profit, and the one who willingly throws it away with both hands if he hopes thereby to make usurious profits: in the first case the teleological process has ossified even earlier than in the latter.

The psychologically opposite phenomenon is exhibited by those peculiar, but all too rare people who will give someone 100 Marks without a second thought, but will part with a sheet of paper or the like from their stationery stock only after exercising genuine will-power. While the miser forgoes acquiring things for the sake of the means of acquisition and is therefore indifferent to the value of things, in this case consciousness is focused entirely on the object without thinking of the means by which one can re-acquire it at any moment. People of this type are concerned only with the value of the *thing*, whereas misers are concerned only with the *value* of the thing.

It has been established in the historical development of money that it originally had to be a value existing in its own right. For so long as governmental minting did not yet guarantee individuals the ability to resell the compensation they received for their commodity, no one would have been so foolish as to give up the latter. The less secure the actual function of a means of exchange is, the less it will be able to be merely a means of exchange and the more people will demand instead that it have an intrinsic value; the inherently existing value of a means of exchange can decrease in the same proportion as its exchange power increases. If the latter achieves its maximum, through legitimation by public power, then the former can become a minimum. In contrast, it has been emphasized that money is only a measure of *values* and only as such could it be a means of exchange for them. Yet one could only measure quantitatively determinable objects by objects of a similar nature: spatial quantities only by spatial values, weights only by weights, etc. This is why money must on all accounts be a value itself in order to measure values, and therefore it could never diminish to a merely fictitious standard, to a mere 'symbolic money' separated from any relationship to a real commodity.

This entire controversy over whether money is itself a value or only the symbol of a value; a pure intersection point for commodities, without itself being a commodity, and if it still is such, whether it must remain so, seems to me – as long as it remains confined to principles and theories – to exhibit an astonishing neglect of crucial psychological factors. For opponents of symbolic money – to condense the entire tendency down to a single word – forget that the values for which money is to serve as a measure are in the end only psychologically valuable, that value does not exist objectively at all in the absolute sense, but only by virtue of the fact that the human will desires the object in question, which no more has an inherent objective quality than sunshine inherently has the feeling of well-being that it produces in nervous systems organized a certain way. But then every object *has* the value that is ascribed to it, and if only a sufficient agreement were attainable in the ascription of the value, then there would be no obvious reason why a piece of stamped paper, not backed up by any more tangible value, should not have a certain exchange value for all eternity – not as if it were being granted thereby a certain quality of objective value which would make it equal to objects qualified in the same way, but because these too have become values through no other process than that of the human will. Neither food nor shelter, neither clothing nor precious metals, are values in and of themselves – as demonstrated by cases when asceticism or other states of mind make us completely indifferent to them. Rather, they become values only in the psychological process of our assessment of them.

If one is unwilling to recognize the monetary value of symbolic money, even when its exchange value is universally accepted, then one makes the same mistake as does that type of economic idealism which is willing to accept as a 'good' only that which corresponds to a *true* need, but not that which satisfies superfluous or disapproved needs: a view which also fails to recognize that all granting of value is only a psychological fact and nothing else, and therefore simply must be recognized as such wherever it occurs. There are sufficient reasons available that make tying monetary value to a precious metal desirable and indispensable, and there are enough causes that make the conditions for a symbolic money unfulfillable. In principle, however, there is not the slightest reason why an arbitrary symbol such as money should not perform the same services as gold and silver as a measure of value and means of exchange, providing only that the transfer of the value consciousness to the symbol has been fully completed, which is quite possible through the process of the psychological elevation of the means to the rank of an ultimate end – something which occurs hundreds of times in other areas.

It is obvious that this process had to be completed first and most thoroughly with a means such as money, which is the necessary intersecting point for a *large number* of ends. To the extent that many ends require the same means, such a fact is emphasized for our consciousness in such a way that its value appears to grow beyond that of a mere means. And this success will be more likely to occur if the ends to be achieved with it are very multifarious and diverse, because they are then reciprocally neutralized in their variation, and the only thing they have in common – the means for acquiring them all – stands out in that much brighter a light. This has many consequences for the psychology of money. The stinginess of advanced age, for instance, is simply explained from the fact that the means which is common to so many ends striven for in life must receive correspondingly more emphasis and dominance in consciousness in proportion to a longer life. In addition, in this context, many goals and attractions of life wither away for old age, whereas the value with which their previous attraction also enclosed the means associated with them has now gained an independence that causes it to live on after the disappearance of the earlier goals.

Furthermore, if money is the common intersection of various series of ends, then the plenitude and diversity of the latter must increasingly fade; and this is indeed money's fate, since with an increasing level of culture, one can purchase with it more and more quite different things. Just as very versatile people, active in a great many directions, easily give the impression of a certain lack of character, a lack of any definite coloration, which is more appropriate instead to a one-sided and pronounced nature, so a kind of psychological interference effect also enters in the case of money, because the qualitative plenitude of the ends that are gathered together in it place it somehow between all qualities, and thereby deprive it of any specific psychological coloration, which always possesses a somewhat one-sided trait. And this reflects back upon the objects of monetary transactions by means of an easily understandable process.

The blasé character of our prosperous strata is connected to this. If money thus becomes the common denominator for all values of life, if the question is no longer what they are worth but how much they are worth, then their individuality is diminished. Through the possibility of being compared against an indifferent standard, and one accessible to all, they lose the interest tied to the specific and the unique. To the blasé person, there exists nothing which seems to him or her to be priceless, and conversely, anyone who believes that they are able to buy everything with money must necessarily become blasé. If this character of the universal validity of the psychological ultimate end repeatedly makes only *those* objects appear valuable which cost a great deal of money, then one can see from the same process that for some personality types only that which cannot be had for money has value. This is not an inversion but a heightening of this psychological consequence of monetary transactions.

The valuelessness of money in the higher sense probably has, as a consequence, the result that the treatment of women is the worst among uncultivated peoples in those places where they are purchased, and improves somewhat where they are acquired by personal achievement of the suitor to the bride's parents rather than through a definite payment. This is also the reason why a present of money is the lowest thing and the one which debases the personality the most. In any case, it remains an astonishing phenomenon that people are willing to accept the greatest sacrifices of another person – life, suffering, honour and everything else – without damaging their honour, but not a present of money. Here, that emotional activity may also play a part which, when applied positively, can make a virtue of necessity. Because of its lack of qualities, money *can* be given back under any conditions, which is often simply impossible with other things – for example, personal sacrifices of time and effort. The feeling of honour has adapted itself sufficiently to unalterable circumstances to be able to accept as a gift anything which cannot be directly given back. Because the value of money exists exclusively in its quantity, it can assume a specific character only from an extraordinary accumulation that can only be granted to a few. This is why, according to common sentiment, accepting money debases honour less, the more money there is in question. And deceit with money – especially in small amounts – is seen as a particularly low crime which degrades the perpetrator socially much more than deeds which indicate a much worse moral degradation.

Money is 'common' because it is the equivalent for everything and anything; only that which is individual is distinguished; that which is equivalent to many things is equivalent to the least among them and therefore pulls even the highest thing down to the level of the lowest. Coincidence, of course, occasionally allows even that offsetting of higher things by money to rebound to the advantage of the totality – as when, for instance, the sale of offices by the Bourbons opened access to state administration for the bourgeois strata; just as, conversely, the institution of salaries for positions makes it possible for talent without affluence to serve in the right place. If the classical world up to the period of the Sophists or to the Empire had, or claimed to have, no compensation for intellectual and governmental services, then that closed off the path to service for innumerable talents.

The impersonality of money also makes a wide expansion of charity possible. One is less concerned with to whom one donates money than when what is at issue is more personal acts of charity; the frequent anonymity of charitable donations also follows this tendency. For its part, this can have a corresponding unifying and conciliating effect upon the donors. The successes of the Gustavus Adolphus Society[1] would have been impossible if the objective character of the monetary contributions had not blurred the sectarian differences between the contributors. Since, in this way, a common effort of the Lutheran, Reformed and United Churches became possible, it served as an ideal bonding agent and tended to strengthen the feelings of all of these people that they belonged together after all.

It is interesting to note how the seductive character of money, which can be transformed into everything possible at any time, can come into conflict with the charitable consequence of this impersonality. St. Francis allowed his order to beg for food and clothing, but never for money, not even to support the sick and the needy. It is a feature of the greater cosmopolitanism and sophistication of St. Thomas of Aquinas, however, that he draws the opposite conclusion from the same property of money. He does indeed consider usury despicable, but he adds that money already gained from another's usury is still usable capital, which may be rightfully employed for purposes of charity to the poor, because, in his words, we ought to be allowed to imitate God at least to that extent of making the sins of people useful for one's own good ends.

Finally, however, the impersonal character of money has another psychological consequence, which the immense expansion and intensification of transactions, due to the reduction of all values of money, helps to transmit. Money's lack of quality brings in its wake the lack of qualities among people as payers and receivers of money. What is given away in return for money goes to the person who offers the most for it, without regard for who or what he might otherwise be; but where other equivalents are at stake, where property is relinquished in return for honour, service or gratitude, the nature of the person to whom one is giving is taken into consideration. Conversely, where I myself make a purchase with money, it is a matter of indifference to me from whom I buy something which is desirable to me and worth the price. However, where I acquire something in return for a service, for personal obligation in the inner and outer sense, I first examine closely the person with whom I am dealing, because there is nothing other than money which I am willing to give to just anyone else. The statement on vouchers that their value will be surrendered to the bearer 'without checking for legitimacy' is characteristic of the nature of money in general. The fact that in financial transactions one person is worth as much as any other has its basis in the fact that no person is worth anything; only money has worth. That is why it is quite true that pleasantness stops where financial matters start; money is the absolutely objective entity, where everything personal comes to an end. And this is also why it has no history of the type that gives every other possession the broadest variety of positive and negative values, which often cannot be compensated by anything else. Hence, the idea that a certain sum of money is 'bloodstained' or 'accursed' is an unjustified sentimental projection, and is becoming more and more rare as financial dealings increase; the phrase *non olet* could not be more true of money.

How many psychological obstacles to trade are removed by this particular character of the general means of transaction requires no further discussion.

The indifference of money, which has grown so much in our times, whose consequence is also the indifference of objects, is well displayed in those commodity dealings that are characterized by the fact that all the commodities involved in them have the same price. Here the decisive aspect is the fact that what motivates the buyer and contains the purpose of the transaction from the outset is not the distinctiveness of the commodity, but the definiteness of the price that is to be paid for it. The specific quality increasingly recedes in the face of the quantity, which is the only thing that is asked about. The understandable consequence of this is that more and more things are purchased without regard for their quality, but only because they are cheap. The very same psychological essence of money also brings about the opposite phenomenon, namely, that many things are treasured and sought after only because they cost a large amount of money. For many people, the mere fact that the object can only be had for a certain price provides it with value. This frequently results in a circular determination of value: if the seller allows the price to decline, then the valuation of the commodity also declines, and this pushes the price even lower.

Even earlier, however, this character of money produced the peculiar phenomenon that those classes, to whom many goals of personal aspiration were denied from the very outset on the grounds of their civic position, turned to the acquisition of money with particular success. This was the case with the freed slaves of Ancient Rome, the Huguenots in France and the Jews all over the world. Even though the channels to other types of success are closed to them, money is the neutral area which is harder to close off from them than any other, since, because of its unspecific character, there are many channels through which it may run to them. On the other hand, it is clear that it is precisely such subjugated classes who concentrate all their efforts on acquiring money, since, as a result of money's indifferent position above the specific elements of life, such classes can now attain influence and enjoyment, the direct and specific means to which are closed off to them.

In one respect, however, the omnipotence of money is weaker than in earlier times; the money fine now no longer has such a broad scope. It is known that ancient Germanic law allowed even the severest misconduct to be punished by money payment and that already in the seventh century the Church's Lent penance could be replaced by monetary donations. The separation from money was considered to be something so essential that everything could be compensated with it – perhaps this is even based on the moral merit that had already been ascribed in the Gospels to giving away wealth. The value of money has declined as atonement both for violating the human as well as the divine order. But the following apparent exception proves the rule. Precisely because more and more things could be had for money, because it advanced to become the equivalent for most elements of life, it ceased to be an equivalent for very exceptional and special relationships. The fact that virtually everything can be had for money does not stand in contradiction to its inability to settle moral and religious obligations any longer; in reality, it explains this state of affairs. The lowering of the status of money and the elevation of moral consciousness cooperated in the disappearance of the fine for such purposes.

On the other hand, the fact that so many values of life may be expressed in terms of money has at least allowed criminal law to establish the general concept of fraud – the damaging of others by means of false pretences – for its own purposes, that is, in the sense that only those who have damaged the *assets* of another are punished as frauds. Yet this also indicates very clearly that, although money is an equivalent expression for many things, it does not possess that function for everything. The worst kind of fraudulent pretence, which completely destroys another person's joy in life, and would certainly demand criminal prosecution according to its character, remains unpunishable (apart perhaps from Paragraph 179 of the German Code of Criminal Law) if the damage affects purely personal individual circumstances to such an extent that it cannot be estimated according to the impersonal standard of money. The sense of the impersonality of money is also one of the reasons for which surrendering female honour in return for money appears so particularly despicable to us. The latter is something so personal that the only equivalent response would be the same surrender of the entire personality, but certainly not that which is the most unindividual thing of all and the one most remote from the specific content of the personality. Thus, the woman who nevertheless surrenders her virtue for money thereby commits the worst imaginable degradation of her personality and reveals it to everyone.

All in all, one can say that the peculiar psychological coloration – or better, decoloration – to which things are subjected by their equivalence to a completely colourless means of exchange brings, as it were, a certain smoothness, a grinding down of their sharp corners and, by easing and accelerating the circulation of things in that way, this is a side of the cultural process which transforms both ideals and realities from the form of stability, something unchangeably fixed and existing forever, into that of motion, the eternal flow of things and continuous development. If now experience is being increasingly stressed as the only means of knowing, rather than the absolute and a priori knowledge that was striven for in previous times, then this implies the transformation of a cognitive substance that was required to be valid for all times into one which is capable of continual modification, increase and correction. If the species of organisms are conceived only as transitional points of an evolution continuing into infinity, rather than as eternal creative thoughts of God; and if therefore the adaptation to changing developmental conditions emerges as an ideal, rather than uniform and unchanging forms of behaviour; if the metaphysical belief in certain supreme ideas, to the subjective and objective eternity of which people adhered, is recognized as the changeable result of purely psychological processes; if the firm delineations within the respective social group become more and more fluid and the rigidities of the caste system, compulsory guild membership and ties to tradition are being broken down, so that the personality can circulate through a diversity of ways of life – then all of these are symptoms of one and the same ethnopsychological transformation, which money also serves by virtue of its direct and indirect easing of giving and taking.

Just as in the *panta rei* of phenomena there is still *one* that persists: the law; just as in the continuing change of factors the relation among them remains constant, so one could characterize money as the steady pole in the flight of economic phenomena, as the constant value of a fraction whose numerators and denominators continually change by the same multiple. Just as it is precisely the greatest variety of phenomena which exemplify the law most clearly, so money reveals the persistence of its value that much more clearly, the more impersonal and varied the things are between which it creates an equivalence. Money removes the material aspect and its variations that much more and raises itself as *akineton kinoun* above everything individual, quite comparable epistemologically to the law, which exists all the more purely and firmly the more colourful and changeable are the individual cases that it governs.

Now if it has been proclaimed, elegaically or sarcastically, that money is the god of our times, then significant psychological relationships can in fact be detected between these two notions that seem so opposite. The concept of God has its deeper nature in the fact that all the diversity in the world comes to a unity in Him, that He is, in the important phrase of Nicholas Cusanus, the *coincidentia oppositorum*. This idea that all the antagonisms and irreconcilable elements of the world find an equalization and unification in Him engenders the peace and security, but also the plenitude of accompanying notions which we find in the idea of God. The psychological similarity between the latter and the idea of money should be clear from the preceding discussion. The *tertium comparationis* is the feeling of peace and security, which is particularly provided by the possession of money, in contrast to any other kind of possession, and which corresponds psychologically to the feeling the pious person finds in his or her God. In both cases, it is the elevation above the individual element which we find in the desired object, the trust in the omnipotence of the highest principle to secure for us at any moment this individual and lower element, to be able as it were to transform itself into the latter. Just as God in the form of faith, so money in the form of the concrete object is the highest abstraction to which practical reason has risen.

MONEY IN MODERN CULTURE

If sociology wished to capture in a formula the contrast between the modern era and the Middle Ages, it could try the following. In the Middle Ages a person was a member bound to a community or an estate, to a feudal association or a guild. His personality was merged with real or local interest groups, and the latter in turn drew their character from the people who directly supported them. This uniformity was destroyed by modernity. On the one hand, it left the personality to itself and gave it an incomparable mental and physical freedom of movement. On the other hand, it conferred an unrivalled objectivity on the practical content of life. Through technology, in organizations of all kinds, in factories and in the professions, the inherent laws of things are becoming increasingly dominant and are being freed from any coloration by individual personalities, just as our image of nature is striving to eradicate its anthropomorphic traits and we impose an objective regularity on it. Thus modernity has made subject and object mutually independent, so that each can more purely and completely find its own development. How the two sides of this differentiation process are affected by the money economy is what I consider here.

Until the high Middle Ages in Germany, the relationship between a person and their property appears in two forms. In primeval times we encounter ownership of land as an authority to which the individual personality is entitled; it flows from the individual's personal affiliation to his market community. By the tenth century personal land ownership had disappeared, and all personal rights had become dependent on the ownership of real property.

In both forms, however, a tight local connection was maintained between person and property. For instance, in the fellowship of vassal farmers, where feudal tenure to a hide of land gave one full membership of the association, someone who owned a hide outside of the farmers' association *to which he personally belonged* was considered landless. Conversely, someone who owned a property within the socage community without belonging to it personally (free citizens, burghers, guilds and so on) was required to appoint a representative, who *personally* owed allegiance to the feudal lord and would take over the rights and duties of a member.

This interdependence of personality and material relationships, which is typical of the barter economy, is dissolved by the money economy. At every moment it interposes the perfectly objective and inherently qualityless presence of money and monetary value between the person and the particular object. It fosters a distance between personality and property by mediating between the two. Thus it has differentiated the formerly intimate association of the personal and the local elements to such a degree that today I can receive income in Berlin from American railroads, Norwegian mortgages and African gold mines. This form of long-distance ownership, which we take for granted today, has only become possible since money has moved between owner and possession, both as a connecting and a separating factor.

In this way, money produces both a previously unknown impersonality in all economic ownership and an equally enhanced independence and autonomy of the personality, and the relationship of personality to associations develops similarly to that with property. The medieval guild included the entire person; a weavers' guild was not an association of individuals that only pursued the mere interests of weaving. Instead, it was a *living community* in occupational, social, religious, political and many other respects. No matter how objective the interests around which the medieval association grouped, it still existed directly through its members and the latter were absorbed in it without rights of their own.

In contrast to this unity, the money economy has now produced innumerable associations which either only demand financial contributions from their members or proceed merely in terms of monetary interest. In this way, on the one hand, the pure objectivity of the purposes of the organization, their purely *technical* character, their lack of any personal coloration are made possible, while, on the other hand, the subject is freed from restrictive commitments, because it is no longer connected to the totality as an entire person, but principally by spending and receiving money. Since the interest of the individual participant in an association is expressible in money, directly or indirectly, money has slipped like an insulating layer between the objective totality of the association and the subjective totality of the personality, just as it has come between owner and property. This has allowed both a new possibility of development and a new independence from one another. The pinnacle of this development is represented by the joint-stock company, whose business is completely objective to, and uninfluenced by the individual shareholder, while the company has absolutely nothing to do with him personally except that he holds a sum of money in it.

By virtue of this impersonality and colourlessness – which is peculiar to money in contrast to all specific values, and which must continually increase if we follow this course of cultural development – money comes to compensate an ever-increasing number and variety of things, it has performed incalculable services. This brings into existence a community of action of those individuals and groups who stress their separation and reserve at all other points. Hence, an entirely new line is drawn through the elements of life susceptible to associations. I shall mention only two examples that seem to me to demonstrate nicely how money is able on the one hand to unify interests and on the other hand to maintain a separateness of interests.

In France after 1848, syndicates of workers' associations from particular trades were formed in such a way that each association delivered all its funds to the association and thus a joint-savings bank was formed. This was supposed to make retail purchasing possible, provide loans, etc. These syndicates, however, were certainly not intended to unite the participating associations into a single, large one; rather, each was supposed to retain its particular organization. This case is illustrative because at that time workers were seized by a veritable passion to found associations. If they expressly rejected the unification that seemed so natural, they must have had particularly strong grounds for their reluctance – yet at the same time they were able to effect the unity of their interests which nevertheless existed through the common possession of a fund of money.

Furthermore, the successes of the Gustavus Adolphus Society, the great society for the support of Protestant congregations, would have been impossible if the objective character of the monetary contributions had not blurred the denominational differences of the contributors. But because money enabled this to be a common creation of the Lutheran, Reformed and Unitarian churches, who could not have been moved to any other type of common organization, it served as an ideal adhesive and strengthened the feeling of community among all these sects.

Generally one can say that the trade union and all its enormous successes, a type of organization virtually unknown in the Middle Ages, which one could say unites individuals impersonally for a course of action, has only become possible by virtue of money. Money offers us the only opportunity to date for a unity which eliminates everything personal and specific, a form of unification that we take completely for granted today, but which represents one of the most enormous changes and advances of culture.

Thus when one laments the alienating and separating effect of monetary transactions, one should not forget the following. Through the necessity of exchanging it and receiving definitive concrete values for it, money creates an extremely strong bond among the members of an economic circle. Precisely because it cannot be consumed directly, it refers people to others, from whom one can obtain what is actually to be consumed. In that way, the modern person is dependent on infinitely more suppliers and supply sources than was the ancient Germanic freeman or the later serf; his existence depends at any moment on a hundred connections fostered by monetary interests, without which he could no more exist than could the limb of an organic creature cut off from the circulation of its vital fluids.

What brings about this intertwining and growing together of modern life more than anything else is our division of labour, which could not develop beyond the roughest beginnings under the system of bartering. For how was one to measure the values of various products against one another so long as there was no common standard of measurement for the most different things and qualities? How could exchange proceed smoothly and easily as long as there was no medium of exchange that could even up every difference, no medium into which one could convert every product and which one could convert into any product? And by making the division of production possible, money inevitably ties people together, for now everyone is working for the other, and only the work of all creates the comprehensive economic unity which supplements the one-sided production of the individual.[2] Thus it is ultimately money which establishes incomparably more connections among people than ever existed in the days of feudal associations or the arbitrary unifications most highly praised by the guild romantics.

Finally, money has produced a comprehensive common level of interests for all people such as could never have been produced in the days of the barter economy. Money provides a common basis of direct mutual understanding and an equality of directives which contributed an extraordinary amount to producing that dissimulation of the generally human which played such an important part in the cultural and social history of the preceding century. A similar phenomenon appeared in the history of the Roman Empire when the money economy had completely established itself.

But, just as money in general has brought into being an entirely new relation between freedom and dependence – this should be clear from what has already been said – similarly the pronounced closeness and inevitability of the integration that it brings about has the peculiar consequence of opening up a particularly wide scope to individuality and the feeling of personal independence. The person in those earlier economic epochs was mutually dependent on far fewer people, but those few were and remained individually determined, while today we are much more dependent on suppliers in general, but frequently and arbitrarily change the individuals with whom we interact; we are much more independent of any *particular* supplier. It is precisely these types of relationship which must produce a strong individualism, for what alienates people from one another and forces each one to rely only on himself is not isolation from others. Rather, it is the anonymity of others and the indifference to their individuality, a relationship to them without regard to who it is in any particular instance. In contrast to times when every external relationship to others simultaneously bore a personal character, in modernity the money economy makes possible a cleaner separation between the objective economic activity of a person and his individual coloration, his actual ego, which now completely retreats from those external relationships and in that way can concentrate more than ever on its inmost strata.

The streams of modern culture rush in two seemingly opposing directions: on the one hand, toward levelling, equalization, the production of more and more comprehensive social circles through the connection of the remotest things under equal conditions; on the other hand, towards the elaboration of the most individual matters, the independence of the person, the autonomy of its development. Both tendencies are supported by the money economy, which makes possible, first, a completely general interest and a means of connection and communication which is equally effective everywhere. Second, it permits the most pronounced reserve, individualization and freedom for the personality.

The later point still requires evidence. The expressibility and redeemability of services by means of money has always been felt to be a means and support of personal freedom. Thus, classical Roman law provided that someone who was obliged to make a certain payment could refuse to fulfil it in kind and could settle it with money, even against the will of the recipient. That provided a guarantee that one could pay off all personal obligations in money, and in that respect, this provision has been deemed the *Magna Charta* of personal freedom in the arena of civil law.

The emancipation of serfs often proceeded in the same direction. The dependent artisans of a medieval manor, for instance, often attained freedom by a process where their services were first limited, then specified and finally transformed into a monetary tax. Thus it was considered a great advance toward freedom when the English counties were permitted, from the thirteenth century on, to substitute monetary payments for their obligations to provide soldiers and labourers. Similarly, one of the most important regulations with which Joseph II sought to introduce the emancipation of peasants was the provision that they were allowed, and in fact required, to redeem their socage labour and their payments in kind through monetary taxes. The substitution of a monetary tax for service immediately releases the person from the specific bondage that was imposed by that service. The other no longer has any claim to direct personal action, but only to the impersonal result of such action. By paying money the person no longer offers himself, but only something without any personal relationship to the individual.

But for that very reason, the substitution of a monetary payment for a service can also have a degrading character. The deprivation of the rights of the Athenian allies began when they substituted monetary payments for their previous contingents of ships and crews. This apparent liberation from their personal obligation, after all, contained the renunciation of any political activity of their own, of the importance which can only be claimed for the employment of a specific service, for the deployment of concrete forces. This is so often overlooked as the money economy expands: in the duties that are bought off with money there often lie less apparent rights and significances which are also abandoned.

This same double meaning attached to the payment of money is also connected with its receipt, with selling. On one hand, one senses the conversion of a possession into money as a liberation. With the assistance of money, we can now pour the value of the possession into any arbitrary form, while it was previously captured in that one particular form. With money in our pocket, we are free, whereas previously, the object made us dependent on the conditions of its conservation and fructification. But how often does this very freedom simultaneously mean a vapidity of life and a loosening of its substance! For that reason, the same legislation that prescribed the monetary settlement of peasant service also prohibited the compulsory enclosure of the peasants. It seemed of course, no injustice was being done to the latter if his master bought his rights to the land for a proper price (in order to add it to his estate's holdings). In the soil, however, there is much more for the peasant than the value of the property. For him it was the possibility of useful action, a centre of interests, a practical reality giving life direction which he lost as soon as he lost possession of the land and had only its value in money. The frequent enclosures of the farmers in the previous century did indeed give them a monetary freedom, but deprived them of the priceless thing which gives value to freedom: the steady object of personal activity.

That in turn is the questionable thing about a culture oriented to money, like that of late Athens, of late Rome, or of the modern world. Because more and more things are paid for with money and become attainable through it, and money accordingly stands out as the constant in the flow of activity, one overlooks all too often that even the objects of economic exchange still have aspects that cannot be expressed in monetary terms. It is all too easy to believe that one has their exact and complete equivalent in their monetary value. This is certainly a deep reason for the problematic character, the restlessness and the dissatisfaction of our times. The qualitative nature of objects lose their psychological emphasis through the money economy; the continuously required estimation according to monetary value eventually causes this to seem the only valid one; more and more, people speed past the specific value of things, which cannot be expressed in terms of money. The revenge for this is that very modern sensibility that the core and meaning of life slips through our fingers again and again, that definitive satisfactions become ever rarer, that all the effort and activity is not actually worthwhile. I do not wish to assert that our epoch is already entirely caught up in that state of mind, but where we are approaching it is certainly connected with the progressive obscuring of the qualitative values by a merely quantitative one, by an interest in a pure more-or-less, since after all it is only the qualitative values which ultimately satisfy our needs.

Indeed objects themselves are devalued of their higher significance through their equivalence with this means of exchange which can apply to anything at all. Money is 'common' because it is the equivalent for anything and everything. Only that which is unique is distinguished; whatever is equal for many is the same even for the lowest among them, and for that reason it pulls even the highest down to the level of the lowest. That is the tragedy of every levelling process: it leads directly to the position of the *lowest* element. For the higher can always descend to the lowest, but anything low seldom ascends to the highest level. Thus the innermost value of things suffers under the uniform convertibility of the most heterogeneous elements into money, and popular language is therefore justified in calling the very special and distinguished 'priceless'.

The 'blasé attitude' of our prosperous classes is only the psychological reflection of this fact. Because they now possess a means with which, despite its colourless uniformity, they can purchase the most varied and special things, and because therefore the question of what something is worth is increasingly displaced by the question of how much it is worth, the delicate sensibility for the specific and most individual charms of things must necessarily atrophy more and more. And that is just what a blasé attitude is: no longer reacting to the gradations and peculiarities of things with a corresponding nuance of sensibility, but rather valuing them within a uniform and thus dull coloration, no longer distinguished by variation.

Through this very character, however, which money increasingly assumes, the more things it compensates for – within a rising culture – it loses the significance it previously possessed. The monetary fine, for instance, has its sphere limited. Ancient Germanic law punished the severest crimes, including murder, with fines. From the seventh century, it was possible to substitute money for religious penance, while modern legal systems limit monetary penalties to relatively minor misdemeanours. This is not a sign against, but rather for, the increased importance of money; precisely because it now compensates for so many more things and has therefore become that much more characterless and colourless, it is said to be unsuitable to serve for compensation in very special and exceptional cases, in which the most inward and essential aspects of the personality are affected. It is not despite the fact that one can get everything with money, but precisely because of it, that it has ceased to settle the moral and religious requirements on which penance was based.

Characteristically, two major currents of historical development meet at this point. If murder could be atoned for in primitive society by money, then that meant on the one hand, that the individual and his value was not yet so recognized, that it was not yet felt to be so incomparable and irreplaceable as in later times when it stood out from the group more decisively and individually. On the other hand, it meant that money had not yet become so indifferent, that it had not yet transcended any qualitative significance. The increasing differentiation of people and the equally increasing indifference of money converge to make the punishment of murder by monetary penalties impossible.

A second extremely important consequence of the prevailing monetary system runs in a similar direction to this grinding down and deterioration of money by the growth of its equivalents. This is the tendency to perceive money, a mere means to acquire other goods, as an independent good, whereas it has its entire meaning only as a transition, a link in a series that leads to a definitive purpose and enjoyment. If the series is broken off psychologically at this level, then our consciousness of the end stops at money. Because the majority of modern people must focus on the acquisition of money as their proximate goal for most of their lives, the notion arises that all happiness and all definitive satisfaction in life is firmly connected to the possession of a certain sum of money; it grows inwardly from a mere means and a presupposition to an ultimate purpose. But when this goal has been attained, then frequently deadly boredom and disappointment set in which are most conspicuous among business people who retreat into retired life after having saved up a certain sum. After the loss of the circumstances which caused the consciousness of value to concentrate on it, money reveals itself in its true character a mere means that becomes useless and unnecessary, as soon as life is concentrated on it alone – it is only the bridge to definitive values, and one cannot live on a bridge.

The colonization of ends by means is one of the major features and main problems of any higher culture. The latter has its essence in the fact that, by contrast to primitive circumstances, the intentions of people can no longer be achieved through simple, obvious, direct actions. Instead, they are gradually becoming so difficult, complicated and remote that one requires a multi-part construction of means and apparatus, a multi-level detour of preparatory steps for them. The first step can hardly ever lead to the goal in higher cultures, and not only is a means required, but this itself cannot often enough be achieved directly, but there is a multiplicity of means, one of which often supports the others, which finally flow into the definitive end. The greater danger is of getting stuck in the labyrinth of means and thereby forgetting the ultimate goal. Thus, the more intertwined, artificial and structured the technique of all areas of life becomes – that means after all the system of mere means and tools – it is felt increasingly as an intrinsically satisfying ultimate purpose, beyond which one can no longer enquire.

That is the origin of the stability of all external customs, which were originally only means to certain social ends, but continue to exist as intrinsic values, as self-supporting demands, while the ends have long been forgotten or become illusory. A feeling of tension, expectation and unresolved insistence runs through modernity, in particular as it seems, through its most recent stages – as if the main event, the definitive one, the actual meaning and the central point of life and things were yet to come. That is certainly the emotional outcome of that excess of means, of the compulsion of our complicated technique of life to build one means on top of another, until the actual end which they were supposed to serve recedes further and further towards the horizon of consciousness and ultimately sinks beneath it. But no element has a broader share in this process than money, never has an object which only has value as a means grown with such energy, such completeness and such success for the overall situation of life, into a – really or apparently – satisfying goal of aspiration.

The importance that money has been given through the enormous growth of the range of objects that can be acquired by it radiates out into many individual character traits of modern life. Money has moved the complete satisfaction of an individual's wishes into a much greater and more tempting proximity. It gives the possibility of obtaining at a single stroke, as it were, whatever appears at all desirable. Between the human being and his wishes it inserts a mediating stage, a relieving mechanism and, because everything else becomes attainable with the acquiring of this one thing, it stimulates the illusion that all these other things are more easily obtained. But as one comes closer to happiness, the longing for it grows, for it is not that which is absolutely distant and denied us which inflames the greatest longing and passion, but rather that which is not owned, but seems to be becoming nearer and nearer.

The enormous desire for happiness of modern man, as expressed in Kant no less than in Schopenhauer, in social democracy no less than in the growing Americanism of the times, has obviously been nourished on this power and this result of money. The specifically modern 'covetousness' of classes and individuals, which one may condemn or welcome as a stimulus to the development of culture, was able to develop because there is now a slogan that concentrates everything desirable in itself, a central point one need only acquire, like the magic key in a fairy tale, in order to attain all the joys of life.

Thus – and this is very important – money becomes that absolute goal which it is possible in principle to strive for at any moment, in contrast to the constant goals, not all of which may be wanted or can be aspired to all the time. This provides the modern person with a continuing spur to activity; he now has a goal which appears as the *pièce de résistance* as soon as other goals give it space; it is potentially always there. That is the reason for the restlessness, feverishness, the unrelenting character of modern life, which is provided by money with the unremovable wheel that makes the machine of life a *perpetuum mobile*. Schleiermacher emphasizes that Christianity was the first to make piety, the desire for God, into a permanent state of the psyche, whereas earlier times connected religious moods to particular times and places.

Thus the desire for money is the permanent disposition that the mind displays in an established money economy. Accordingly, the psychologist simply cannot ignore the frequent lament that money is the God of our times. Of course, he can only linger on it and discover significant relationships between the two ideas because it is the privilege of psychology not to commit blasphemy. The concept of God has its deeper essence in the fact that all the varieties and contrasts of the world reach unity in it, that it is the *coincidentia oppositorum*, in the beautiful phrase of Nicholas of Cusa, that peculiarly modern spirit of the waning Middle Ages. It is in this idea that all the strange and irreconciled aspects of being find unity and harmony, from which stem the peace, the security and the all-encompassing richness of feeling, which are part of the idea of God and of the idea that we possess Him.

The feelings stimulated by money have a psychological similarity to this in their own arena. By increasingly becoming the absolutely sufficient expression and equivalent of all values, it rises in a very abstract elevation over the whole broad variety of objects; it becomes the centre in which the most opposing, alien and distant things find what they have in common and touch each other. Thus money actually does grant us that elevation over the individual, that trust in its own omnipotence as in that of a supreme principle which can provide us these individual and lower elements at any moment, as if it could transform itself into these. This feeling of security and calm which the possession of money provides, this conviction of possessing the intersection of all values in the form of money, thus contains in a purely psychological sense, formally one could say, the equalization point which gives the deeper justification to that complaint about money as the God of our times.

Other, more remote character traits of modern mankind, directed differently, flow from the same source. The money economy brings along with it the necessity for continuous mathematical operations in everyday life. The life of many people is filled out with determining, weighing up, calculating and reducing of qualitative values to quantitative ones. This certainly contributes to the rational, calculating nature of modern times against the more impulsive, holistic, emotional character of earlier epochs. Thus much greater accuracy and sharper demarcations had to enter into the elements of life through monetary valuation, teaching people to determine and specify every value down to the penny. Where things are conceived of in their direct relationships to one another – thus not reduced to the common denominator of money – then much more rounding off and comparison of one unit to another occurs. The exactness, sharpness and precision in the economic relationships of life, which of course fade into its other elements, keep pace with the spread of the money economy, but not, of course, to the benefit of grand style in living.

The ever-growing use of smaller monetary units has the same effect, and heralds the spread of the money economy. Until 1759, the Bank of England did not issue notes under £20 sterling, but since then it has gone down to £5. And, more revealingly, until 1844 its notes circulated an average of fifty-one days before being broken into smaller change, while by contrast they circulated only thirty-seven days in 1871 – in twenty-seven years, then, the need for small change increased by near 25 per cent. The fact that people carry around small denominations of money in their pockets, with which they can immediately purchase all sorts of small articles, often on a whim, must encourage industries that thrive from this possibility. This and in general the divisibility of money into the tiniest sums certainly contributes to the frivolous style of the external, and particularly the aesthetic areas of modern life, as well as to the growing number of trivialities with which we furnish our life.

The punctuality and exactness – somewhat analogous to that of pocket watches – which the spreading of the monetary system has conferred on the external relationships of people, is by no means accompanied by an equivalent increased inner conscientiousness in the ethical sphere. Rather, through the quite objective and indifferent character with which it offers itself equally and unrelatedly to the highest and the lowest actions, money tempts us to a certain laxity and thoughtlessness of action, which would be inhibited in other cases by the particular structure of the exchange objects and the individual relationship of the agent to them. Thus persons who are otherwise honest may participate in deceitful 'promotions', and many people are likely to behave more unconscientiously and with more dubious ethics in money matters than elsewhere. The result that is ultimately achieved, money, bears few traces of its origins, while other possessions and situations, because they are more individual and have distinctive qualities, carry their origins within themselves, either objectively or psychologically; they are visible in those things and the things recall their origins. But once the act has flowed into the great ocean of money, by contrast, then it can no longer be recognized, and what flows out no longer bears any resemblance to that which flowed in.

Returning from these individual consequences of the circulation of money, I close with a general remark on its relationship to the deeper traits and motifs of our culture. If one would venture to summarize the character and greatness of modern life into a formula, then it could be this: that the contents of knowledge, of action and of the formation of ideals are being transformed from their solid, substantial and stable form into a state of development, movement and instability. Every look at the fates of those elements of life, which are occurring under our very eyes, unmistakably shows this line of formation: we are dispensing with the absolute truths that would be contrary to all development, and gladly sacrificing our knowing to continual reshaping, duplication and correction – for this is exactly what the continual emphasis on empiricism means.

The species of organisms are no longer considered eternal thoughts of Creation, but transitional points of an Evolution striving towards infinity. The same tendency extends to the lowest inanimate and to the highest spiritual formations; modern natural science is teaching us to dissolve the rigidity of material into the restless turmoil of the tiniest particle. We now recognize that the uniform ideals of earlier times, once considered to be founded beyond any change and contradiction, are dependent on and adaptations to historical conditions. The fixed boundaries of social groups are dissolving more and more. The rigidity of caste and class ties and traditions is being increasingly broken – whether this be a benefit or a disadvantage – and the personality can circulate through a changing variety of situations, reflecting, as it were, the fluidity of things.

The rule of money takes its place in this great and uniform process of life, which the intellectual and social culture of modernity put in such decisive contrast to the Middle Ages as well as antiquity, supporting the process and supported by it. By finding their equivalent in a completely colourless means of exchange beyond any specific determinacy, by being able to be exchanged into such a means at any moment, things become worn down and smoothed, in a sense, their rough surfaces are reduced, and continual equalization processes occur between them. Their circulation, giving and taking occur at a quite different pace than in the days of the barter economy; more and more things that appeared to be beyond exchange are pulled down into its restless flow. I recall only, as one of the simplest examples, the fluctuating value of real property since the dominance of money. Since the advent of the money economy, the same transformation of stability to instability that characterizes the entire modern philosophy has also seized the economic cosmos, whose destinies, as they form a part of that movement, are also a symbol and reflection of its entirety.

Here we can only point out that a phenomenon like the money economy, no matter how much it appears to follow its own purely internal laws, nevertheless follows the same rhythm that regulates all contemporaneous movements in culture, even the most remote of them. Unlike historical materialism, which makes the entire cultural process dependent on economic conditions, the consideration of money can teach us that far-reaching effects on the entire psychic and cultural state of the period do indeed emanate from the formation of economic life. That formation itself, on the other hand, receives its character from the great uniform trends of historical life, whose ultimate sources and motives remain a divine secret.

But if these similarities and deep connections reveal the monetary system to us as a branch from the same root that produces all the other flowers of our culture, then one can take consolation from this against the complaints raised particularly by the preservers of spiritual and emotional values against the *auri sacra fames* and the devastation wrought by the financial system. For the more knowledge nourishes itself from that root, that much more clearly must the relationships of the money economy appear, both to the dark sides and to the subtlest and highest aspects of our culture. Thus, like all great historical forces, the money economy might resemble the mythical spear that is itself capable of healing the wounds it inflicts.

THE BERLIN TRADE EXHIBITION

In his *Deutsche Geschichte* Karl Lamprecht relates how certain medieval orders of knights gradually lost their practical purpose but continued as sociable gatherings. This is a type of sociological development that is similarly repeated in the most diverse fields. The double meaning of the word 'society' symbolizes this twin sense. Alongside the very process of sociation there is also, as a by-product, the sociable meaning of society. The latter is always a meeting-point for the most diverse formation of interest groups, thus remaining as the sole integrating force even when the original reasons for consocation have lost their effectiveness. The history of world exhibitions, which originated from annual fairs, is one of the clearest examples of this most fundamental type of human sociation. The extent to which this process can be found in the Berlin exhibition alone allows it to be placed in the category of world exhibitions. In the face of the richness and diversity of what is offered, the only unifying and colourful factor is that of amusement. The way in which the most heterogeneous industrial products are crowded together in close proximity paralyses the senses – a veritable hypnosis where only one message gets through to one's consciousness: the idea that one is here to amuse oneself. Through frequency of repetition this impression overwhelms countless no less worthy impressions, which because of their fragmentation fail to register. The sense of amusement emerges as a common denominator due to a petty but psychologically subtle arrangement: every few steps a small entry fee is charged for each special display. One's curiosity is thus constantly aroused by each new display, and the enjoyment derived from each particular display is made to seem greater and more significant. The majority of things which must be passed creates the impression that many surprises and amusements are in store. In short, the return to the main motif, amusement, is more effectively achieved by having to make a small sacrifice, which overcomes one's inhibitions to indulge, than if a higher entry price, giving unrestricted access, was charged, thereby denying that continuous small stimulation.

Every fine and sensitive feeling, however, is violated and seems deranged by the mass effect of the merchandise offered, while on the other hand it cannot be denied that the richness and variety of fleeting impressions is well suited to the need for excitement for overstimulated and tired nerves. While

increasing civilization leads to ever greater specialization and to a more frequent one-sidedness of function within an evermore limited field, in no way
does this differentiation on the side of production extend to consumption.
Rather the opposite: it appears as though modern man's one-sided and
monotonous role in the division of labour will be compensated for by consumption and enjoyment through the growing pressure of heterogeneous
impressions, and the ever faster and more colourful change of excitements.
The differentiation of the active side of life is apparently complemented
through the extensive diversity of its passive and receiving side. The press
of contradictions, the many stimuli and the diversity of consumption and
enjoyment are the ways in which the human soul – that otherwise is an im-
patient flux of forces and denied a complete development by the differentiations within modern work – seeks to come alive. No part of modern life
reveals this need as sharply as the large exhibition. Nowhere else is such a
richness of different impressions brought together so that overall there
seems to be an outward unity, whereas underneath a vigorous interaction
produces mutual contrasts, intensification and lack of relatedness.

Now this unity of the whole creates a stronger impression and becomes
more interesting when one considers the impossibility of surveying the
objects produced in a single city. It is only as a floating psychological idea
that this unity can be apprehended since in its origins the styles and emerging trends receive no clear expression. It is a particular attraction of world
fairs that they form a momentary centre of world civilization, assembling
the products of the entire world in a confined space as if in a single picture.
Put the other way round, a single city has broadened into the totality of cultural production. No important product is missing, and though much of the
material and samples have been brought together from the whole world
they have attained a conclusive form and become part of a single whole.
Thus it becomes clear what is meant by a 'world city' and that Berlin, despite
everything, has become one. That is, a single city to which the whole world
sends its products and where all the important styles of the present cultural
world are put on display. In this sense perhaps the Berlin exhibition is
unique, perhaps it has never been so apparent before how much the form
of modern culture has permitted a concentration in one place, not in the
mere collection of exhibits as in a world fair, but how through its own production a city can represent itself as a copy and a sample of the manufacturing forces of world culture.

It is a point of some cultural historical interest to follow how a particular
style for such exhibitions has developed. The specific exhibition style is seen
at its clearest in the buildings. An entirely new proportion between permanence and transience not only predominates in the hidden structure but also
in the aesthetic criteria. In doing this the materials and their intrinsic properties have achieved a complete harmony in their external design, so
satisfying one of the most fundamental demands of all art. The majority of
the buildings, in particular the main ones, look as if they were intended for
temporary purposes; because this lack of permanence is unmistakable they

are absolutely ineffective as unsolid buildings. And the impression of lack of solidity works only where the temporary can claim permanence and durability. In the exhibition style the imagination of the architect is freed from the stipulation of permanence, allowing grace and dignity to be combined in their own measure. It is the conscious denial of a monumental style that has produced a new and positive shape. Elsewhere it is the meaning of art to incorporate the permanence of form in transient materials, and the ideal of architecture is to strive to give expression to the permanent, whereas here the attraction of the transient forms its own style and, even more characteristically, does this from material that doesn't appear as if it was intended for temporary use. And in fact the architects of our exhibition have succeeded in making the opposition to the historical ideal of architecture not a matter of absurdity or lack of style; rather they have taken the point last reached in architecture as their starting-point, as if only this arrangement would allow its meaning to emerge fully against a differently coloured background and yet be seen as part of a single tradition.

It is on the architectural side that this exhibition reaches its acme, demonstrating the aesthetic output of the exhibition principle. From another point of view its productivity is at least as high: and here I refer to what could be termed the shop-window quality of things, a characteristic which the exhibition accentuates. The production of goods under the regime of free competition and the normal predominance of supply over demand leads to goods having to show a tempting exterior as well as utility. Where competition no longer operates in matters of usefulness and intrinsic properties, the interest of the buyer has to be aroused by the external stimulus of the object, even the manner of its presentation. It is at the point where material interests have reached their highest level and the pressure of competition is at an extreme that the aesthetic ideal is employed. The striving to make the merely useful visually stimulating – something that was completely natural for the orientals and Romans – for us comes from the struggle to render the graceless graceful for consumers. The exhibition with its emphasis on amusement attempts a new synthesis between the principles of external stimulus and the practical functions of objects, and thereby takes this aesthetic superadditum to its highest level. The banal attempt to put things in their best light, as in the cries of the street trader, is transformed in the interesting attempt to confer a new aesthetic significance from displaying objects together – something already happening in the relationship between advertising and poster art.

Indeed it strikes one as curious that the separate objects in an exhibition show the same relationships and modifications that are made by the individual within society. On the one side, the depreciation of an otherwise qualified neighbour, on the other, accentuation at the expense of the same; on the one side, the levelling and uniformity due to an environment of the same, on the other, the individual is even more accentuated through the summation of many impressions; on the one side, the individual is only an element of the whole, only a member of a higher unity, on the other, the claim that the same individual is a whole and a unity. Thus the objective relation between social elements is reflected in the impression of things in unison within a single frame yet composed of interactively excited forces, and of contradictions, yet also their confluence. Just as in the exhibition the contours of things in their interactive effects, their moving to and fro undergoes an aesthetic exploitation, so in society the corresponding patterns allow an ethical use.

German, in particular north German, exhibitions could compete only with difficulty with French ones where the ability to accentuate by all means possible the stimulus of appearance has a much longer history and wider applicability. Nevertheless this exhibition shows the attempt, often successful, to develop aesthetic opportunities which through display can contribute to their attractiveness. Certainly the qualities of taste are mostly lacking in the individual items of the exhibition. Aside from the practical motive of Berlin's exhibition, it is to be hoped at the least that the aesthetic impulse is encouraged beyond the exhibition itself and becomes part of the way products are presented.

Notes to Part VII

1. Translator's note: This society, founded in 1832, was intended to provide material and spiritual assistance to isolated Protestant congregations.

2. Monetary payment advances the division of labour, because as a rule only a one-sided service is paid for with money; this abstract, amorphous equivalent corresponds only to the objective individual product divorced from the personality. Money does not buy the entire person – except in the case of slavery – but only the atomized product of the division of labour. That is why the development of the latter must proceed hand in hand with the spread of the money economy. The deficiencies and contradictions in the modern condition of domestic servants are explained by this fact, for here an entire person is still being purchased with money.

PART VIII

POLITICS OF CULTURE

INFELICES POSSIDENTES!
(UNHAPPY DWELLERS)[1]

On the walls of the Berlin entertainment establishments there stands the *mene mene tekel*; the marble and the paintings, the gold and the satin that cover them seek in vain to cover the writing, it penetrates through the nervous splendour just as the future penetrates through the present, and today's seers know how to interpret it. As if the evolution of the human species, which led from sensuality to reason, were going in reverse, so now no stimulus seems worth enjoying other than titillation of the senses and intoxication of the nerves. Who still wishes to know anything about serious, quiet art that must be sought with the soul, which the person enjoying it must first acquire, in order to possess it? The pleasures required today are those which thrust themselves upon the nerves the way the streetwalker thrusts herself forward and thus caricatures the natural, healthy relationship of the sexes in its opposite. Splendour for the eyes is called for, and the establishments breathlessly compete to outdo one another in this respect, while the bourgeois sits there contentedly, like a spectator of the gladiators' match or a harem owner, and waits to see which of his pleasure slaves will prove most amusing and, at the same time, comfortable. The removal of any deeper content is needed so that the mind not be asked to break through a shell or cut a path for itself in order to reach the core. That is why all that may be offered is what can be offered on the surface, and that is why sensations predominate rather than reflections.

And yet the tragedy does not begin with the satyr play, but even before it starts. A terrible seriousness will not only replace this gleaming intoxication, in fact it is already there; it is its cause just as it will be its consequence. A healthy, happy person does not succumb to alcoholism, but rather it is the impoverished and the unfortunate who seek intoxication. And just as one must abstain from condemning with moralizing indignation the ragged drunkard who was chased by his misfortune into the blissful forgetfulness of a bottle of spirits, so too the modern Jeremiah for his part would remain trapped in superficiality if he had only a curse and condemnation for the superficiality, the sensual frenzy and the hollow splendour of modern amusements and did not see what poverty and pain forces the popular mind into this intoxication, causing it to flee to the highest levels of emotional life, because terror prevails in the lower ones.

There may have been a time when one could encapsulate the relationship of reality and play in the harmless antithesis, that life is serious, but art is cheerful. But just as increasing development magnifies the antitheses everywhere, driving asunder into opposition what was uniformly joined in the embryonic state, so too life has also become terrible, fearful and tragic, and it is merely the extension of this – the unavoidable reverse of this state of affairs – if recreation and play become satyr-like, orgiastic and sensually intoxicated.

It was a master stroke of Wagner to have created a Bayreuth, in which those who are to enjoy his art spend the day unoccupied, or at least separated from the toils and fears of real life. He realized that modern life is not the place from which a serious and profound art can be understood and appreciated. That is why he characterized his ideal as the converse of Schiller's famous phrase: life should be cheerful and art serious. The quieter and more contented is the seriousness of life, the more strength and opportunity for deepening play remains.

Now, however, play has become feverishly excited, tensing all the nervous forces to the utmost – we not only expend the strength we have but also live, to a certain extent, on our future resources, consuming for the demands of the moment what should suffice for the future; hence, the thousandfold bankruptcy of strength. The modern person is driven back and forth between the passion to win everything and the fear of losing everything. The competition of individuals, races and classes stages the feverish chase of daily work and also draws the person who does not work into that restless rhythm and self-consumption and into the fear, more or less clear, that those from whose labour he lives might not always be inclined to trade his coupons for the sweat of their brows.

If this is how the day looks, then what does the evening look like? What emotional forces still remain after the day has used up what was available in activity, tension and concentration? The Ronacher and Apollo Theatres answer the question as to what capacities the urbanite of our days still brings to the theatre. Because life uses up his strength completely, all that may be offered him as relaxation is something that requires absolutely no effort. Exhausted by the haste and worries of the day, the nerves no longer react to stimuli, except those which are directly physiological, so to speak, those to which the organism responds even when all the more refined sensibilities have become blunted: light and gleaming colours, light music, and finally – and principally – sexual feelings.

Just as it has been said that the peculiar thing about the history of women is that it is not the history of women but that of men, so one can say that the history of recreation, games and amusements, when viewed more closely, is the history of work and serious things. After the peaceful day's work of earlier times it may have been possible that, whoever visited a theatre at all, would be refreshed by Goethe or Shakespeare. The economic and social wear and tear in which we find ourselves and which transfers its restlessness, its sapping of strength and its passion even into individual circumstances, no longer leaves us with as much strength for recreation; things must be made comfortable for us.

The terrible and tragic aspect of such domination by the shallow and the common is that it not only takes hold of those of a bad or base disposition, who would give in to it in any case, but also the better and more noble ones. The more profoundly the latter are affected by the seriousness of reality, the more violently they are shaken by the powers of everyday life, the more easily even they slide into the lower depths, where people 'just want to amuse themselves' – and the entire misery of our amusement industry lies in these words: 'just amuse oneself'. The element of more noble emotional forces which the way of life of earlier ages still left available to pleasure has been removed by the pressure of the times, and we are now called upon to amuse ourselves according to the principle of energy conservation. Since the upper ten thousand has become aware of the misery of the masses, since the distress – internal or external – of our own existence has been further burdened with the predominance of social misery, so the life of the better-off and higher strata has also experienced the kind of impediment which, on the one hand, leaves only the lower emotional energies for enjoyment, while on the other, if one is to enjoy oneself, tends to seek out the wildest intoxication, the most dazzling effects, so that one's own inner premonitions and admonitions may be drowned out.

Of course one would search in vain in the consciousness of individuals for such foundations of their behaviour. Everyone swims comfortably and uninhibitedly in the great river of amusement, and the tragic cause of the mindless addiction to entertainment, against which the moral sermonizer can merely inveigh, reveals itself only to the sociologist. The frivolity of the individual is merely the external manifestation of the deeply serious social background; and that which is separated out into antagonisms for the individualistic viewpoint is, from the social perspective, brought together as the two necessary sides of a historical unity for which the individual bears both the essence and fate of his class within himself. The proletarian observing the pleasure palaces from the outside may feed his resentment on the idea of *beati possidentes*; yet if he could see deeper then he would recognize that the more sparkling, noisy and intoxicating is the hubbub inside, the more wretched is the exhaustion and the more tormenting is the obsession to lose oneself that brought it into existence. The time of *beati possidentes* is past and Ronacherism was never a sign of the happiness of the propertied class, but rather of its wretchedness, even though the individual may carry this only in his dim subconscious. A happy person does not reach for such pleasures, just as little as he would reach for a bottle of liquor or a morphine syringe. And perhaps the demand for more just and sensible conditions of social stratification and property distribution will rise up some day not only from the hunger of the dispossessed but from the Midas-like thirst of the upper classes as well. For them, the wild race of competition and the awakening social conscience are increasingly tending to vitiate the pleasures which make it worth while to be propertied, and this drives that class into the intoxication of the senses and the coarsening of refinement – the final refuge of those who no longer really know how to enjoy themselves. And for these reasons, the temples of the most licentious pleasures ought to inscribe above their doors: *infelices possidentes*!

SOME REMARKS ON PROSTITUTION IN THE PRESENT AND IN FUTURE[2]

The moral outrage which 'good society' displays towards prostitution gives cause for puzzlement in more than one respect. As if prostitution were not the inevitable consequence of the conditions which none other than 'good' society is attempting to force upon the entire people! As if it were completely the free will of the girls,[3] as if it were a pleasure to prostitute oneself! Certainly, between the first time, where poverty or helpless isolation or the lack of any moral education or the bad example in her environment motivate a girl to surrender herself for money, and the indescribable misery with which the career ends – between these two boundaries there is usually a period of pleasure and frivolity. But how dearly paid and how short! There is no more false term than calling these poor creatures 'women of pleasure' and thereby assuming that they live for pleasure; this may be true for the pleasure of others, but certainly not for their own. Or do people think it is enjoyable to chase around the streets night after night in heat or rain or cold in order to serve some man, perhaps a repulsive one, as an ejaculation mechanism? Do people believe that this life, threatened on the one side by the most unpleasant diseases, on the other by poverty and hunger and on a third by the police, is really something chosen with the free will which alone can justify moral outrage?

The higher and unregulated type of prostitution is better off for a greater period of time. If the girl is pretty and understands the art of refusal, or is perhaps even involved with the theatre, then she can pick and choose among her admirers, perhaps even among diamond bracelets. It is not so much that the fall tends to be all the more deeper, when the charms with which she paid for a life *in dulci jubilo* have faded, but rather that society is much more lenient towards this more refined prostitution – which is better off overall than street or brothel prostitution – than towards the very base kind of prostitution, which after all, if it is a sin, is certainly much more harshly punished than the finer sort by the misery of its existence.

The actress who is not a bit more moral than the streetwalker, indeed perhaps even more calculating and grasping, is welcomed in salons from which streetwalkers would be expelled with the dogs. The fortunate person is in the right, and the terrible law, 'to he who has, to him much is given', is nowhere enforced more strictly than in '*good*' society. Just as it always hangs only the petty thieves, so it heaps the full measure of its virtuous outrage over the miserable street prostitutes; it withholds that outrage to the same extent in so far as the prostitutes are better off. Society simply views an unfortunate person as an enemy – and certainly not without justification. The unfortunate person, the one who came out on the wrong end of things with or without any guilt on his or her own part and suffers the just or unjust verdict of expulsion, will hold the totality responsible for the fact he or she has not achieved a better station in life. Such persons will hate it and it will hate them and push them even further down. Just as the prosperous and fortunate person receives a good fortune bonus in addition to the direct fortunate consequences of his or her situation by being honoured and elevated by society, so the unfortunate one is further punished for his or her misfortune by being treated by society as its born enemy. One can observe every day how a prosperous person *angrily* chases away a beggar – as if being poor were a moral wrong that justifies moral outrage. Here, as so often, the bad conscience of the wealthy person *vis-à-vis* the poor one takes refuge behind the mask of a moral justification, something which occurs so widely and with such striking pseudo-justification that the person affected ultimately ends up believing it themselves. The difference in the judgement and treatment made by society between elegant and impoverished prostitution is one of the most shining – or better, darkest – examples of the justice of a society, which makes the unfortunate person even more unfortunate by persecuting her for her misfortune as if for a sin committed against it, perhaps even from the dim anticipation that this person is very likely to commit a sin against society.

This relationship is the basis for the fact that prostitution, which is as old as cultural history, can nevertheless be characterized in its present form as a product of our particular social conditions. Less advanced cultures find nothing offensive in prostitution, and quite understandably so, because it is not as harmful to them as it is under more developed conditions. Herodotus says of the ancient Lydians that their girls offered themselves for money in order to gain a dowry; the same custom applies in some parts of Africa even today, and it neither diminishes respect for the girls – often including even royal princesses – nor does it prevent them from marrying and becoming thoroughly respectable women. As a residue of ancient, unregulated sexual conditions, we find the widespread notion that every woman actually belongs to the tribe as a whole and, as it were, evades a social duty in marrying *one* man; in any case, she must fulfil this social duty before marriage by giving herself to everyone. And this idea extends so far up into the sphere of morality that a cult of prostitution frequently appears – a sacrifice, the proceeds from which flow into the temple treasury, as Strabo reports of the Babylonian girls.

All of this is only possible where there is as yet no permanent money economy. For where money becomes the standard for everything and anything, where, with money, one can have a universe of the most various things, money takes on a colourlessness and a lack of qualities that, in a certain sense, devalues everything for which it can be an equivalent. Money is the most impersonal thing that exists in practical life,[4] and is therefore completely unsuited to serve as a means of exchange for such a personal value as the devotion of a woman. If this nevertheless occurs, then money drags this individual and uniquely valuable thing down to its own level, and the woman concerned thereby shows that she does not value her most personal and private nature any higher than the thousands of lower-valued things for which this means of exchange is also an equivalent.

Where money has not yet become the standard for almost all values of life to the extent it has for us, and where it is still something rare and less refined, giving up oneself for it is not yet so degrading. And in addition, the lower is the position of women, the more they are subsumed under a general type, and the less this incompatibility between commodity and price strikes us. In more primitive cultures, in which women in particular are less individualized, their human dignity does not suffer to such a high degree because their favours are compensated by such an unindividual value as money. In our more developed circumstances, however, in which money is becoming increasingly impersonal because one can buy more and more things with it, the purchasing of this most personal thing with money is becoming increasingly degrading and constitutes one of the essential causes of the arrogance of capitalists and for the depth of the abyss between possession and supply. It should be possible to acquire what is most personal and sacred in a person only by giving one's own person and its innermost values in return – as is the case in a good marriage. Where one knows, however, that one need only give money in order to enjoy this, then this quite understandably leads to a contempt for, and an ignorance of, the value of personalities of the dispossessed who give away everything so cheaply. The naiveté of this attitude among our higher strata often surprises us – or rather does not surprise us. Just as the gap between upper and lower all too often not only merely pushes the lower further and further down but also morally drags down the higher strata, just as slavery not only degrades the slave but also the slaveholder, so this incongruity between commodity and price, which is inherent in prostitution today, implies not only the demoralization of those who offer themselves, but also of those who make use of it. Every time a man buys a woman for money, a piece of respect for humanity is lost, and in the prosperous strata, where this is a daily practice, it is without doubt a strong lever of that arrogance which comes from the possession of money, that fatal self-deception by which this possession grants some kind of value or inner significance to one's own personality. This complete displacement of values, which deepens and makes it increasingly difficult to cross the gulf between the affluent person and the person who must submit to being bought by him – this is the moral syphilis that follows in the wake of prostitution and which, like its physical counterpart, ultimately infects even those who are not involved with its direct causation.

These considerations point towards the only perspective from which prostitution can be correctly judged for the present and the future, that is to say, in connection with the general social and cultural circumstances. Whenever one considers it in isolation, whenever one does not trace it down to its roots, which extend beneath the entire ground on which society stands, one runs the risk of measuring it by the standards of an 'absolute ethics' and thus condemning it in an uncomprehended manner, either in a shallow manner or unjustly. The necessity of prostitution in higher cultures is based upon the temporal difference between the onset of sexual maturity among men on the one hand and, on the other, their intellectual, economic maturity, as well as that of their character. This latter, after all, is quite justly required before society will permit him to establish a household of his own. The intensified struggle for existence, however, increasingly tends to postpone economic independence; the complex demands of occupational training and of making a living do not permit the complete development of the mind until later and later in life. The character must work its way through steadily growing difficulties of situations, temptations and experiences in order to be entrusted with the responsibility for other people's existence, for the rearing of children.

Thus, the time when a man may legitimately have a woman grows later and later, and since the physical constitution has not yet adapted to this situation, and the sexual drive awakes at a relatively early age, a growing need for prostitution must arise as culture develops. We may leave aside here the issue of whether a strengthened morality might be able to suppress these premarital drives, since we know for the present that this is simply not happening and we only wish to reason with facts here. The associations for promoting morality do indeed claim that such a suppression is not only possible, but even desirable in the interests of health. Nature, however, is unlikely to be sufficiently kind as to leave the neglect of such a strong drive unpunished merely because the fortuitous cultural circumstances do not allow it any legitimate satisfaction.

In short, the need for persons to satisfy this drive is present in society. On the other hand, this society is aware of how much it loses through such existences lost in this way, and of the fact that these girls are simply slaughtered as sacrifices for the drives of others. It is touching that 'good' society feels this way; but how odd that it is so delicate in precisely this respect and has such a sensitive conscience for the sacrifices that its preservation costs! Without a second thought, it sends thousands of workers into the mines, to a life that barely knows the sun and, day for day and year for year, is a sacrifice for society. It is seemingly only a sacrifice of certain services, but in reality it involves the entire life, because the service rendered here – as is

the case with prostitutes, though completely different in substance – determines the level of the rest of their existence and narrowly circumscribes its
attractions and freedoms. Technical or scientific achievement, viewed with
regard to the worker, may not be considered merely as what it has cost him
in momentary effort, but necessarily also contains *implicitly* his entire
previous training, his entire past. Similarly, the work of countless workers
and that of prostitutes contains all its consequences and relationships, the
entire attitude toward life and the entire future of the worker, which is connected just as necessarily to that attitude as the technical or scientific
achievement was to the past. The same false individualism that separates
individuals from their social ties in order to consider them purely 'for themselves' also isolates their achievement from its interconnection with the rest
of their life and fails to see that society, which seemingly only demands the
sacrifice of individual efforts, actually demands the sacrifice of their entire
lives from coal miners and countless others. The worker in the arsenic mine,
in the mirror-coating factory and in all the directly dangerous or slowly
poisoning manufacturing plants – are they not all just sacrifices which
society imposes on others or for that matter, itself, in order to secure its continued existence? And it demands or produces them without getting excited
about it any further. Why not sacrifice a few thousand girls in order to make
a normal sexual life possible for unmarried men and to protect the chastity
of other girls and women? Is the necessity or desire to own mirrors more
urgent and important than sexual needs? I consider it all well and good
when people do not watch cold-bloodedly as so many girls are forced onto
the wayside, into physical and spiritual ruin, but then one should also be
consistent enough to be outraged over these other sacrifices, which are so
often much more cruel. People are measuring with a peculiar double standard here, although the reasons for this are not difficult to discover. On the
one hand, people do not openly admit the necessity of prostitution in the
current order of things and, on the other hand, they are just as ready to view
the existence of those other workers as a sacrifice in and for society. The
equivalence of the social response to both categories is made invisible by
both of these tendencies and by the difficulty of recognizing the similarity
of form through the enormous substantive and ethical differences in the
cases.

About one thing, however, there should be no illusions: as long as marriage exists, so prostitution will exist as well. Only with completely free love,
where the contrast between legitimate and illegitimate has generally
become untenable, will there no longer be a need for special people devoted
to the sexual satisfaction of the masculine sex. In order not to be frivolous
and ruinous to both spouses, monogamous marriage, with the obligation –
or at least a self-imposed obligation – to fidelity should only be entered into
at an age when the sexual drive has already existed for several years. To be
sure, the limit for marriage will be lowered in a socialist society because the
individual will be relieved of the responsibility for individual economic
support of the wife and children; but then a certain further maturity will be

all the more important, so that this external alleviation does not lead to marriages that are hastily and frivolously entered into. And even though improved education may accelerate the attainment of this maturity, it is opposed by the fact that a refinement of the species in all of nature, and among people as well, is connected to a retardation of complete development and, as experience shows, children whose parents are both too young tend to be weak or degenerate. Given the polygamous impulses which indeed lie within the masculine nature, monogamy as an erotic and moral institution, even after elimination of the economic difficulties, demands a *man* who has had the opportunity to test and know himself, and not a budding youth, even though the sensual impulses may already reveal their strength in him. If one cannot permit this man to make a lifetime commitment to a woman, neither can one deny him the expression of those natural impulses. But how is he supposed to satisfy them? Only two forms remain. Either the form we find among may primitive peoples where the girls have a completely free choice of lovers before marriage, but are not thereby hindered legally or emotionally in subsequently entering into a monogamous marriage; or prostitution, which designates certain people for this purpose in order to relieve all others of it. I cannot believe in the former option. The more developed and noble humanity becomes, the more individual the relationships between men and women become. Precisely when marriage is no longer a matter of purchase or compulsion, but intended to rely solely on purely inner mutual sympathy, a prior life of promiscuity cannot be the ground from which it can arise. Under more primitive circumstances, in which the highest emotional interactions between the sexes do not yet exist at all, the earlier life of the wife can be irrelevant to the marriage; the more intimate and personal marriage becomes, the less possible it becomes to leap to it from polyandry. Now the same appears to apply to the husband, although it will not restrain men from premarital satisfaction of their physical drives to the same degree as women, because women as a result of their physical and psychological sexual character, become sufficiently mature for marriage at an earlier age than men, and can therefore marry at an earlier age. Economic reasons will no longer prevent this, as they do now, and consequently the entire issue will thus more or less fall by the wayside.

If, then, free love will not be universal, there will have to be a certain number of girls who carry out the functions of today's prostitutes. The objection that no more girls will be willing to do this if poverty did not compel them is obvious, though not completely sound. Strong social needs, after all, create functionaries for themselves, no matter what the cost. Social expediency creates the organs it needs, not only by breaking individual reluctance externally, but also by overcoming it within people. But of course, the necessary precondition – and the only one under which prostitution can exist in a humane society – is that the position of the prostitutes be elevated. If one adheres to marriage on the one hand, if one concedes on the other that it can only be entered into well after the appearance of sexual maturity among men, and if finally, one neither wishes to suppress premarital drives (if only because it cannot be done), nor to make all the girls subject to those drives, then it follows that some kind of prostitution arrangement is necessary – but it would be thoroughly unjust to make the girls who are subjected to this social demand suffer because of it. Present day bourgeois society does this consistently: prostitutes are the scapegoats who are punished for the sins committed by the men of 'society'. It is as if some peculiar kind of ethical shift provides an atonement for the bad conscience of society by casting the victims of its sins fundamentally further and further away and thus into deeper and deeper corruption; thereby granting itself the right to treat them as criminals.

It is a pervasive trait of our society that it raises the highest demands for firmness of character and strength of resistance to temptation precisely on those to whom it most consistently denies the foundations of morality. It demands a greater respect for the possessions of others from the starving worker than from the stock market baron or the noble scoundrel. It demands the greatest modesty of the worker even as it daily tempts him with the sight of the luxury of those he has made wealthy. Society is more outraged, however, over the criminality of prostitutes than of any other class, and does not consider how much more difficult it must be for the outcast to overcome the urge to do wrong than it is for those with a warm place in the lap of society. In short, it insists on duty all the more strenuously the more difficult it makes the fulfilment of that duty.

A more ethical social formation will change this. It will recognize that no one ought to be given reason to feel like the enemy of society. It will have realized that on countless occasions it is not punishment which follows the crime, but rather that society first punished unjustly and thereby first provoked the crime. If it admits at all that there is such a thing as prostitution – and as long as it clings to monogamy it must do this – then it will have to raise the social position of such women and thereby remove the really noxious aspects of this phenomenon. For just as prostitution is a secondary evil, so too are the secondary phenomena resulting from it – the immorality, the general corruption of convictions and the criminality of prostitutes – in fact, all phenomena that are not necessarily connected with it, but today only arise out of their exceptional position which the character of exclusively monetary transactions, the arrogance of the *possidentes vis-à-vis* the have-nots and the hypocrisy of our society causes. If these victims of circumstances no longer have to pay for the sins of others, then they will no longer be tempted to earn this punishment, in a certain sense, by sins of their own.

What makes the construction of that which lies in the future so difficult here, as in all other respects, is the fact that we can only calculate with the current psychological constitution of humanity. The standard for pleasure and sorrow, for emotional reactions in general, which is supposed to result from future conditions, and which we will use to measure their value, is only available to us by imagining the effect of these conditions upon *ourselves*; we, however, are the products of our past and our entire way of feeling is determined by circumstances that may subsequently be completely changed. The position of prostitution depends upon the social feelings that it arouses, and we cannot know how much the elimination of capitalism and it consequences will shift those feelings. Although one can also assume with certainty that the current contempt for and ostracism of fallen women – which in a terrible interaction produces progressive moral degradation – will come to an end, it is still probable that a woman living monogamously will arouse feelings of being a more highly valued person, as long as monogamy persists, than will a woman who gives herself to many men. Similarly, if marriage is the definitive goal for relationships between the sexes, prostitution will continue to be considered a necessary evil. That is the consequence of the conflict between the demands of sexual maturity and the requirements of maturity for marriage – a consequence whose tragedy cannot be eliminated, but only ameliorated, by no longer considering the victims as the subjects of individual guilt, but instead as the objects of social guilt.

Furthermore, this entire consideration will be modified if yet another of the presumptions adopted from present-day circumstances should change. We have assumed that in the future women will still be mature enough for marriage at a younger age than men, so that all the difficulties do not exist for them which ensue for men from the later attainment of this level. Yet what if this earlier individual development were only the result of the lack of development of sexuality? We see throughout nature that creatures develop later and reach the summit of their development later the more refined and complete they are, the higher they stand on the scale of organisms; the lowest animals are the first to be completely developed. It could be possible that the repression of women, which has caused them to appear to be inferior for millennia, has had this result. The fewer demands are placed on an organism, the simpler the functions for which it must develop, and the earlier its development is complete. Now if the pressure on women is removed, if they are called out of immaturity to prove themselves based on their own forces, to develop the broadest variety of tendencies, then perhaps that difference with respect to men will also disappear and the age of individual maturity will occur just as late in them as in men. The development of the mind and character which is required by marriage will also last much longer for them than that of the physiological functions and drives. If the latter also strive for expression, then women will also face the alternative of asceticism or premarital physical satisfaction. The consequences of such a uniformity of conditions for both sexes cannot be predicted without getting lost in fantastic combinations. We have too little ability to survey the simultaneous changes in all other aspects of the constitution of society that are of at least equal importance for the shaping of sexual relations. The ultimate ideal of this entire development is that harmonic adaptation of the physical–sensual and the mental–character development in which the two are no longer temporally separate. If under the lowest social circumstances, maturity in both respects actually occurs simultaneously, and the regulation of sexual circumstances is therefore simple for them, then a developed culture has torn the two apart and thereby created the difficulties of these circumstances. It is a task of the increasing efficiency of our organization to readapt the two on a higher level, according to the major rules of development, which so often repeats the forms of its earliest, embryonic circumstances at its culmination in a spiritualized, perfected and purified form.

THE WOMEN'S CONGRESS AND SOCIAL DEMOCRACY

The interests of the Berlin Women's Congress have acquired their sharpest critical development in the antagonism of the bourgeois and the social democratic women's movement. In every major field of interests there is a fundamental problem towards which every discussion moves as if under a kind of logical gravitational attraction and which consumes every special question, if the most extreme intellectual self-control does not hold us firmly to it. The Women's Congress has demonstrated once again how much the issue of socialism is the 'secret king' of all individual social issues today, and how inevitably the latter, left to their own devices as it were, flow into the former.

The Congress had issued an invitation to the Organization of Social Democratic Working Women to participate in the work of the Congress. The invitation was declined. Two leaders of the working women's movement, Frau Zetkin and Frau Braun, nevertheless took part in the discussions, even though only to emphasize the worthlessness of the bourgeois women's movement to the interests of working women. They emphasized that they did not need to support explicitly efforts for economic, legal and cultural equality for women with men because the Social Democratic Party – and it alone of all others – had already been advocating the same demands in its programme for years. In addition, they claimed, the subjects under deliberation at the Congress and the circle interested in them were *quantités négligeables* in comparison to the mass of working women and the shameful misery among them. Nor was there any hope of improvement for working women on the basis of the existing social order, within which the bourgeois women's movement operates. For all these reasons, they claimed the proletarian women's movement viewed 'the ladies' movement' partly with indifference and partly with hostility.

The main response to this was that the movement represented in the Congress was moving in parallel with the proletarian one on a series of points; it too was oriented towards the protection of women workers, the achievement of better working conditions, the hiring of female factory inspectors, a reform of the laws relating to domestic servants and so on. It would not be deterred from these efforts, regardless of whether the work were done together with social democratic organizations or not. 'Fight who you will', said Frau Schwerin in so many words, 'there will not be a fight between you and us, because *we* are not fighting against *you*'.

If one expresses the standpoints addressed in this manner in terms of their common denominator, then a very clear alternative emerges. If social democracy insists upon its official standpoint that by an internal revolution it can bring about the socialization of the means of production, and by this one means – the one and only means possible – it can remove all the social ills, all the injustice and all the repression of the present day, then it is a completely correct consequence of this that it should reject all attempts to cure by other means a proportion of these ills as an obstacle and a treacherous palliative. Thus, given this assumption that only the totality as totality can be healed, and that this will result in the healing of every individual problem, then it would be an erroneous attempt for the current women's movement to seek any connection with the social democratic movement.

The case is quite the reverse, however, if one expects the healing of the whole to come as the result and summation of gradually raising the parts to better and ever better conditions. This version of the methodical conviction would not need to transform either the starting point or the endpoint of socialist efforts. For the misery of the proletariat can be felt in its entire depth and its amelioration can be conceived as the highest and most noble task of the times, whereas one can no more be able to believe in the radical means of a revolutionary change of the entire social situation than, say, in a sudden miracle from heaven. One of the most malevolent allegations of the Social Democratic Party – actually, of all parties – is to accuse those who deviate from it in their choice of means of not feeling the whole magnitude of the sufferings that must be remedied.

But even those for whom it is necessary to believe in that absolute goal, in the complete elimination of class distinctions and the private ownership of capital, do not betray themselves by considering the goal achievable only through reforms to be introduced gradually, as it were from the bottom up. Modern socialism, from its genetic connection with philosophical speculation, has received in trust, the trait of wishing to solve all riddles and difficulties of things with a single formula or a single stroke. Yet just as the shibboleth of Hegelian philosophy has been replaced by the patient work of gaining knowledge from the individual elements of the world, whose gradual constellation can first solve the riddle of the totality, so the unitary formula of socialism can be replaced by practical work upon the individual aspects of social conditions – as it were deduction replaced by induction – in order that, in this way, the whole might grow together from the sum of the parts. In the world of history and the humanities, in contrast to the physical world, the foundational base often only emerges from the perfection of the individual elements, which linguistic usage confusingly refers to as a superstructure over the former. An unceasing expansion of worker protection and worker insurance, general and unrestricted higher education, gradual work towards a standard working day and a minimum wage – are all these not a 'socialization of the means of production', a gradual levelling of social distinctions? Here it can remain purely a matter of belief as to whether the path taken in such a direction will actually lead to these endpoints or whether it might turn off at a certain point in a different direction.

Unless I am deceived, this sober tendency towards a – relatively – slowly progressing evolution, which does not call for the improvement of individual conditions out of radically changed overall circumstances, but conversely for the radical change of the overall circumstances as the sum of improved individual conditions, has already taken root in broad socialist groups. Perhaps here, as so often, it is precisely women who pursue the direction, once taken, all the way to its most radical consequences, a fact which may well be connected with the greater lack of differentiation and the greater uniformity and impulsiveness of feminine emotional life. Yet if that programmatic interpretation of social progress is possible at all, then the rejection on principle of the efforts of the bourgeois women's movement by social democrats appears to be simply an expression of blind hatred, which rejects every reform coming from bourgeois circles *a limine*, in order that agitation will not be able to find any bridges at any point over class-based divisions, the elimination of which is indeed the whole purpose of social democracy itself.

The Congress itself completely skipped over the question of the kind of overall constitution of society into which its goals could or should be incorporated. To the extent that I followed it, all the German female speakers displayed a strict objectivity towards, and concentration upon, the problem at hand, whether it might be the reform of women's clothing, the position of the woman in financial law, prostitution or university study. This stamped the entire congress with the tendency of providing only building blocks, in the conviction that if only these stones were properly formed and internally strong and supportive, they could be incorporated into any construction of society without themselves thereby prejudicing its style.

Now it cannot be denied that the tendency of the bourgeois women's movement is initially directly opposite to the proletarian one. The division of labour between the sexes as indicated by nature, according to which the woman is reliant upon activity for and within the family, and in which, apart from well-justified exceptions, she best fulfils her cultural mission, is the starting point for two completely distinct malformations. The industrial development of this century has torn the proletarian woman away from this natural calling. The girl goes to work in the factory at an age in which she urgently requires the protective atmosphere of her family; the married woman is not only taken away by the factory from her direct duties to home and children; the influences of that work also sap her of the physiological conditions for bearing healthy children. Thus the economic independence of the proletarian woman is the source of the greatest evils both for her and for the community, so that what is at stake is to surround her with protective and limiting regulations. The proletarian woman has too much, not too little, social freedom – no matter how poor her individual freedom may be.

The situation is quite the reverse in the higher strata. Here, the modern division of labour has relieved the woman of so many previous household functions that, for a very large number of women, society no longer offers an adequate challenge to their abilities. This is true for young women, old maids, childless women as well as those with a few or already grown children. They are nonetheless tied into this situation and countless valuable abilities must either remain undeveloped or, turning back on themselves, cause all sorts of breakdowns. The foolish old maid, the mannish emancipated woman or the hyperaesthetic, sensitive woman verging on perversity are all victims of a culture that has limited or taken the capacities of women from their historically fortified sphere of activity, without opening others up for them.

This, together with the increased difficulty of supporting a person not earning money, is the source of the bourgeois women's movement. The house is felt to be an intolerable barrier, not – at least not in the better cases – because the world outside is more beautiful or more comfortable, but rather because that world promises a solution and a sense of accomplishment to unused energies. The bourgeois woman seeks new rights as the way to new duties; she seeks economic and social freedom as the starting point for fulfilling activity. Thus her efforts display the exact opposite image to those of the proletarian woman. The house from which the proletarian woman has been violently expelled is a violent restraint for her; independent economic activity, which becomes a curse for one, would be a blessing for the other. Yet if there is an indubitable and direct antagonism between bourgeois and proletarian women here, then it is important that here too one guard against letting linguistic expression mistakenly intensify the contrast. The difference between the two sets of interests is not such as would cause a hostile working of the one against the other; the advantages that the one class achieves for itself by no means imply a disadvantage for the other. Rather, it is the same economic social order which produces such different reactions, depending only upon the different circumstances into which it permeates. The present-day industrial mode of production, on the one hand has torn the proletarian woman away from household activity and, on the other, impoverished the domain of the bourgeois woman which is limited to that same sphere. Thus, both phenomena belong equally to those typical cases which probably represent the entire suffering of the present day: the fact that the development of objective conditions has progressed faster than the development and adaptation of individuals. The culture and technology of things poses requirements and develops consequences that no longer coincide with the historically evolved living conditions of the people.

Perhaps this is the deeper foundation of the interpretation Goethe already gave to our contemporary illness:

The heavy secret of our illness
Wavers between excessive haste
And omission.

The content of life finds its form for every creature in a certain proportion between obligation and freedom, between being determined and belonging to oneself. The dimensions of both, which historical adaptation has fixed for women as the appropriate ones corresponding to their personal circumstances and needs, have been overtaken and uprooted by the hypertrophic development of our production. It is this same disintegration between the personal and human disposition and its social possibilities of satisfaction that is responsible for the misery of the proletarian woman and the atrophy of so many bourgeois women: the only difference is that it concerns different sides of that vital proportion in the two cases.

It is not my duty to make prognoses here on a future social development that would permit us to regain the lost adaptation on a higher level. The intention was only to show that the bourgeois and the proletarian women's question, despite or because of their apparent divergence, are only different sides of the same total social phenomenon. A more deeply penetrating look reveals the total economical and ethical constitution as the centre from which the intensification has proceeded equally towards both sides, and therefore the only one from which its solution can be expected.

Notes to Part VIII

1. Published in *Die Zukunft* (1893) 3: 82–5, under the pseudonym Paul Liesegang.

2. We are glad to publish the present essay because of its stimulating and original ideas. The fact that the viewpoint of the anonymous author deviates in essential points from those that have hitherto prevailed in our party scarcely need be argued to our readers. It might nevertheless be good to point it out in order to prevent misunderstandings. Another essay on prostitution from our point of view has been promised us. We reserve the right to speak up ourselves if need be. The editors.

3. Translator's note: Simmel's use of *Mädchen* ('girl') has been retained, since it seemed to reflect, no doubt unconsciously on his part, precisely the conventional condescension he addresses in the article.

4. I take this from an essay by G. Simmel, 'Zur Psychologie des Geldes' (On the psychology of money) in *Schmollers Jahrbuch* XIII, 4.

PART IX
BELIEFS AND CULTURE

ON THE SOCIOLOGY OF RELIGION

The ambivalent twilight that for us surrounds the origin and the nature of religion will not disperse as long as we persist in seeing only *one* problem there, which needs only *one* solution. No one has so far been able to provide a definition that would tell us, without vague generalization and yet encompassing all its phenomena, what 'religion' is, a definition that could state the ultimate determinacy of its nature which is common to the religions of the Christians and the South Sea Islanders, to Buddha and [the Aztec] Uitzlopochtli. Religion is clearly demarcated neither with respect to mere metaphysical speculation on the one hand, nor with respect to superstition on the other, nor even sufficiently so that its purest and deepest manifestations would be immune from being scrutinized for admixtures of these two.

Such indeterminacy of religion's essence is matched by the multiplicity of psychological motives from which reflection causes it to spring forth. One can view fear or love, reverence for ancestors or self-idolization, the moral impulses or a feeling of dependency as the inner root of religion – any of these theories is completely erroneous only if it claims to present *the* origin of religion, while it is justified if it claims to present *a single* origin. That is why we can only approach a solution to the problem if we take an inventory of all the impulses, ideas and circumstances that take effect in this area, but with a specific renunciation of widening the meaning of individual motives beyond their already identified instances into general laws of the essence of religion. And we need more than this reservation for the attempt to gain an understanding of religion from expressions of social life that lie far removed from it; rather, it must be strongly emphasized that, no matter in what extremely worldly or empirical manner the origin of the ideas of the supernatural and superempirical may be explained, neither the subjective emotional value of the resultant idea nor the issue of its objective truth value are in any way affected. The realm of both values lies beyond the boundaries at which our purely genetic or psychological investigation has its endpoint.

If we attempt in this way to find the starting points for the essence of religion in the relationships of human beings to one another, which in themselves are not yet religion at all, then we are only following a method already recognized in other areas. With reference to science, it has long been conceded that it is merely an enhancement, structuring and refinement of all those means of knowledge, whose lower and more obscure levels also assist us in gaining the insights and experiences of everyday practical life. We will only achieve a genetic understanding of art once we have analysed the aesthetic elements in those structures of life which in themselves are not yet art: in concrete feeling, in practical action, and in social formations. All such high and pure structures first enter tentatively and incipiently, as it were, into an interweaving with other forms and contents. Yet we must seek them in these undeveloped stages in order to understand them in their highest and most independent ones. The psychological understanding of them relies on our finding their position in a series, whose elements by gradual development turn into one another, by means of a kind of organic growth, through a multitude of stages, so that the new and distinctive in each one appears to be the development of the seeds in the preceding one.

Thus we may be assisted in understanding the origin and persistence of religion if we discover, in all sorts of relationships and interests, certain religious elements which may lie beyond – or better, fall short of – religion, elements which represent starting points to that which has achieved independence and coherence as 'religion'. I do not believe that religious feelings and impulses are expressed only in religion; rather, that they are found in many sorts of constellations, as one element participating on many different occasions, in whose culmination and isolation only religion exists as an independent element of life, as an area of the strictest limitation. Now, in order to find the points where fragments of the religious nature emerge within the interactions between human beings – religion before it is religion, as it were – one requires a detour through some phenomena which at first glance might seem to lie totally in another direction.

It has long been known that the social form of life in lower cultural circumstances is custom. The very same living conditions of society which, on the one hand, were later codified as law and enforced by state power, and, on the other, were left to the freedom of the cultivated and disciplined individual, are guaranteed in narrower and primitive groups by that distinctive, direct supervision of the individual by the surroundings which is known as custom. Custom, law and free morality of the individual are different types of combinations of the social elements, which can all have as their content the absolutely same precepts, and in fact do have the same content among quite different peoples and at different times.[1] Thus, many norms and results of public life can be borne equally well by the free play of competing forces and by the regimentation of the lower elements by higher ones; hence, many social interests are protected at times by the organization of the family, only to be taken over later by professional organizations or state administration.

Stated in general terms, the interrelationships which constitute life in society are always raised on the basis of definite purposes, causes and interests; and in so far as the latter – the material of social life, as it were – persist, the forms of relationship in which they are realized can be quite diverse, just as, on the other hand, the same form and type of social interaction can accommodate within itself the most varied contents. It seems to me as if, among these forms which the relationships of human beings to one another assume, and which can be the bearers of very diverse contents, there is one which one can only characterize as the religious form – a designation, of course, which anticipates the name of the mature structure from its beginnings and preconditions. For it is not the case that the coloration that justifies its name radiates from already existing religion onto those relationships; but rather, in their contacts, in the purely psychological aspect of their interactions, human beings develop that certain tone, whose intensified development, separated and matured to take on its own being, is known as religion.

We can indeed ascertain that many types of relations of people to one another contain an element of the religious. The relationship of the devoted child to its father, of the enthusiastic patriot to his homeland or of the enthusiastic cosmopolitan to humanity; the relationship of the worker to his class struggling upwards or that of the proud feudal lord to his peers; the relationship of the subject to the ruler under whose influence he stands, or of the good soldier to his army – all these relationships, with such an infinitely varied content, if viewed from the form of their spiritual side can yet have a common tone which one must identify as religious.

All religiosity contains a distinctive mixture of selfless devotion and eudemonistic desire, of humility and revolt, of sensory immediacy and transcendental abstraction. Thereby, there comes into being a definite degree of tension of the emotions, a specific intensity and solidity of the inner relationship and the insertion of the subject into a higher order, which is simultaneously felt as something inward and personal. This religious aspect seems to me to be contained in the aforementioned relationships and in many others as well; it bestows upon them a note which distinguishes them from relationships based on pure egoism or pure suggestion, or purely external or even purely moral forces. This element obviously appears with a greater or lesser strength. It may simply accompany those relationships like a light overtone, or it may provide their decisive coloration. In many important cases, a developmental stage of relationships is characterized by it; that is, one and the same content, which was previously and will later be supported by other types of relationships between human beings, takes on the form of a religious relationship in a given period. This becomes clearest in the case of legislation, which at certain times shows a theocratic character, completely subject to religious sanction, only to be guaranteed elsewhere by state power or custom. Indeed, it seems that the necessary order of society may have started in many cases from a completely undifferentiated form, in which the moral, religious and juridicial sanctions were still an undivided unity – hence the *dharma* of the Indians, the *themis* of the Greeks, or the *fas* of the Romans – and that subsequently, according to the diverse historical circumstances, one or the other cultural form made itself the bearer of such orders.

We also note such changes in the relationship of the individual to the whole group: in periods of excited patriotism, this relationship assumes a consecration, intensity and devotion which we characterize as religious, whereas in other periods it is directed by convention or the laws of the state. The important point for us is that one is concerned here in all cases with relationships between human beings, and that it is a change only of the aggregate state of these relationships, so to speak, if they make the transition from the purely conventional to the religious, from the religious to the legal and from the legal to the condition of free morality. Similarly, a number of socially harmful types of immorality have found a place in the Code of Criminal Law only by way of punishment within the religious community; or, as anti-Semitism shows us, a socioeconomic or racial relationship between certain subdivisions of the group can be elevated into the religious category, without being in substance anything other than a social relationship; or, as many suspect, cult prostitution was only the religious formation of an ordering of sexual life supported elsewhere by pure convention.

Now, in the light of these examples, we can argue in greater detail against a misunderstanding to which we previously alluded. The significance of the theory being set forth here is not that certain social interests and events are ascribable to a religious nature, which already existed in its own right. This does occur, often enough, creating combinations of the greatest historical importance and also has importance for the examples mentioned earlier. What I mean, however, is precisely the converse connection, much less spectacular, of course, and more difficult to separate out: namely, the fact that, in those relationships of social elements, the coloration that we subsequently call religious or term religious by analogy to existing religiosity, actually appears spontaneously as a purely social psychological constellation – one of the possible modes in which human beings can behave towards others. Religion as an independent area, attached to the idea of unique substances and interests, is by contrast only something that is derivative, in roughly the way as the state in the Roman or the modern sense, as an objective and existing entity, is something secondary compared with the original interactions, commitments and orders that prevailed among the social elements, and which have only gradually projected or transferred protection and executive power over their contents to a special structure outside themselves – namely, the state.

The whole history of social life is permeated by this process, namely that the immediate reciprocal determinations of individuals, with which their communal life begins, grow into separate and independent organs. Thus, from the modes of behaviour necessary for the self-preservation of the group, there arises, on the one hand, the law that codifies them and, on the other, the judicial stratum whose obligation in accord with the division of labour is to apply the law. Similarly, out of the socially necessary labour, which was at first performed with the direct cooperation of everyone and according to the crude empirical knowledge of the day, there emerges, on the one hand, technology as an ideal system of knowledge and rules and, on the other, the working class, which now becomes the differentiated agent of the corresponding achievements.

A similar process may also obtain for religion – although in these infinitely complicated matters, analogy is always surrounded by countless deviations. The individual in a community behaves toward the others or the totality in the way described above; their relationship has that characteristic degree of rebellion, devotion, dedication and inwardness. On the one hand, an ideal content can develop out of this: namely, gods who are the protectors of the relationships described in this way, who appear to be the stimulators of these emotional states, who present in separated form what had previously existed only in the mere form of a relationship and in a fusion with more concrete elements of life. And this complex of ideas or fantastic notions now acquires in the priesthood, as it were, an executive and an exponent within the division of labour, like the law in the judiciary or the cognitive interests in the learned profession. Once this autonomization and substantialization of religion has occurred, it then reflects back on its own upon the immediate psychological circumstances of human beings among themselves and now gives them the conscious and identified coloration of religiosity. But in so doing it merely returns to them what it itself owes them in the first place. And one can perhaps say that often so strange and abstruse religious ideas would never have been able to achieve their powers in human relations if they were not the mere formulas or embodiments of previously existing forms of relationships, for which consciousness simply had not yet found a more felicitous expression.

The intellectual motif of this discussion is a very general one and may be expressed as a broad rule, of which the materialist interpretation of history represents an individual case. In so far as the latter, by deriving all the total contents of historical life from the forms of the economy and having customs and law, art and religion, scientific institutions and the social structure determined by the way in which the group produces its material conditions of existence, thereby exaggerates a partial phenomenon of a very comprehensive process into its sole content. The development of the forms and contents of social life, through all the multiplicity of its areas and modes of presentation, in fact takes place in such a manner that the same content appears in many different types of forms, and the same form expresses itself with many types of content.

The events of history are ordered in such a manner *as if* the tendency prevailed within it to make do as long as possible with any given sum of elements. This is evidently the reason why history does not disintegrate into a sum of aphoristic elements, a reason, rather, which connects by affinity both coexistence and succession. The fact that the individual form of life – social, literary, religious or personal – outlives its connection to an individual content and lends itself unchanged to the new; that the individual content can preserve its essential existence through a multitude of successive forms

– all these processes are what keeps the continuity in historical events from breaking off, and prevents the occurrence of an incomprehensible leap, an interruption of the connection with everything that took place previously. Now since the development of the species in general proceeds from the sensory and the external to an emphasis upon the spiritual and the internal – and then, in fact, often to reverse this direction of influence once again – so aspects of economic life will frequently be elevated to the form of abstraction and spirituality, and the forms which economic interests have created will extend into contents of life of a quite different nature. But this is still only *one* of the cases in which continuity and the economizing principle present themselves in history. If the form of state rule, for instance, is repeated in the constitution of the family; if the dominant religion provides artistic achievements with their mood and ideas; if frequent wars make the individual brutal and aggressive even in peacetime; if the line that separates the political parties extends as well through quite unpolitical areas and distributes the divergent tendencies of political life to those parties – then all these are expressions of the prominent character of all historical life, only one side of which is illuminated by the materialist theory of history.

This very character typifies the development which occupies us here: forms of social relationships coalesce or spiritualize themselves into a religious world of imagination or add new elements to those already existing. Or, viewed another way, a specific emotional content, originating in the form of inter-individual interaction, transfers itself from the relationship into a transcendental idea. The latter forms the new category upon which forms or contents, which have their origin in the relationships between human beings, live themselves out. I shall attempt to demonstrate this general hypothesis in a number of specific sides of the religious life. *Faith*, which has been called the essential element and substance of religion, first appears as a relationship *between people*: for we are concerned with *practical* faith, which is by no means *merely* a lower stage or a weakening of theoretical conviction. If I say, 'I believe in God.', then this belief means something quite different than is expressed in the assertions that I believe in the existence of the other, in life on the moon or the immutability of human nature. It not only means that I accept the existence of God, even though it is not strictly provable; it implies at the same time a certain inner relationship to Him, an emotional devotion to Him and an orientation of life to Him. In all of this, there is a unique mixture of faith, in the sense of a way of knowing, with practical impulses and emotional states. And now the analogy to this in the sociation of human beings. We by no means build up our mutual relationships merely on what we know for certain of one another. Instead, our feelings and suggestions are expressed in certain conceptions that one can only characterize as based on faith and which, in turn, impact back on practical circumstances. It is a very specific, difficult to define, psychological fact which we characterize with the words that we believe in someone: the child in its parents, the friend in a friend, the individual in his people, the subject in his prince.

The social role of this faith has not yet been investigated at all, but it is certain that without it society would disintegrate. It is very often the basis, for example, of obedience. On innumerable occasions, the relationship of obedience does not rely on the certain knowledge of justice and superiority, nor on mere love or suggestion, but rather on that hybrid psychological object which we call faith in a person or faith in a collectivity of people. People have often stressed the incomprehensibility of the fact that individuals and entire classes allow themselves to be oppressed and exploited even though they have sufficient power to free themselves. This is precisely what is caused by well-meaning, uncritical *faith* in the power, the merit, superiority and kindness of a superior stratum, which does not present itself by any means merely as an unfounded theoretical assumption, but also as a unique structure grown together out of knowledge, instinct and feeling – which one can uniformly and simply characterize as faith in those people. The fact that we cling to faith in a person, contrary to all intellectual evidence – contrary to all appearances no matter how emphatic – is one of the strongest bonds that holds human society together.

Now this faith is of a decidedly religious character. I do not mean this in the sense that a religion exists from which these sociological circumstances borrow their character. Rather, I believe that this character originates without any regard for religious data, as a purely inter-individual psychological form of relationship which is then represented in a pure and abstract form in religious faith. One could say that the pure process of believing has been embodied in faith in a divine entity, set free from its connection to a social counterpart; here, on the contrary, the object only grows out of the subjective process of believing. Faith, which lives from the relations of human beings as a social necessity, now becomes an independent, typical function of human beings, which demonstrates itself spontaneously, from inside to the outer world. Similarly, it is by no means a rare phenomenon that a certain object first produces a certain psychological process in us, but later, this process, having become independent, itself forms a corresponding object. The practice of human interaction in its everyday, as well as its highest contents so often displays the psychological form of faith as its agent, that the need to 'believe' in general grows up in it and proves itself with objects of its own – created in and for that process. This is a process roughly similar to the way in which the impulse of love or admiration can throw itself at objects which, in and of themselves, would not be able to arouse such feelings at all; their qualification for this purpose is only reflected onto them from the need of the subject. Conversely, viewed from the other side, the world-creating God has been called the product of the human need for causality. With the latter assertion, there is of course no denial that this idea might also possess objective reality, that a reality might correspond to it; only the motivation from which it inwardly arose as an idea is at issue. One assumes that the infinitely frequent application of causality to its original, empirical and relative sphere ultimately made the need for it the only predominating one, so that it was able to get the satisfaction, which was actually denied to it in the sphere of the absolute, with the idea of the absolute being that created the world. The same process may elevate faith beyond its original social sphere into an organic need, as it were, and may create its absolute object for it in the idea of the divine.

A second dimension of the social nature that develops into a corresponding dimension within religious nature lies in the concept of *unity*. The fact that we do not simply remain satisfied with the unconnected multiplicity of the impressions of things, but instead look for their connections and interactions which would hold them together as a unity; indeed, that we actually presume the presence of higher unities and centres of individual phenomena in order to find our way through the phenomena – this is certainly a quality which has matured out of social realities and necessities. Nowhere is a totality created so directly and so tangibly from individual elements, nowhere is the detachment and free mobility of the latter so energetically controlled by the nevertheless existent centralization as occurs in the *gens*, in the family, in the state or in every practical association. If primitive associations are often organized as groups of ten, then this tangibly indicates that the relationship of the elements in the group resembles that of the fingers: a relative freedom and ability of the individual elements to move independently, which is nevertheless combined in a unity of cooperation and indivisibility of existence.

Since all of social life is interaction, it is for this very same reason unity; for what else does unity mean other than that the multiplicity is reciprocally connected and the fate of each element does not leave any other one unaffected? Precisely the fact that there is occasional opposition to the unity of society, that the freedom of the individual attempts to withdraw itself, and that this freedom does not establish itself so self-evidently, even in the strongest and most naive connections, as does the unity of an organism in its components – it is precisely this which must have forced it to the surface in human consciousness, as a special form and a special value of existence. The unity of things and interests, which is presented to us first in the social sphere, finds its pure representation, one detached from anything material, as it were, in the idea of the divine – most perfectly of course in the monotheistic one, but also relatively in the lower religions. The deepest essence of the divine idea is that the diversity and contradictoriness of things finds connection and unity within it, be it the absolute unity of the *one* God, or the partial unities of polytheism, which are related to the individual provinces of being. Thus, for instance, the social form of life of the ancient Arabs, with its all-dominating influence of the tribal unit, already prefigured monotheism; among Semitic peoples, such as the Jews, the Phoenicians and the Canaanites, the nature of their social unification and its changes are clearly reflected in the character of their divine principle. As long as the family unit was the prevailing form of life, Baal signified only the father, to whom people belong like children. In so far as the social community includes foreign branches not related by blood, Baal becomes the ruler enthroned objectively on high; as soon as the *social* unity loses the character of kinship, the same happens to the religious unity, so that the latter appears as the purely detached form of the former.

Indeed, even the unification which rises above the differentiation of the sexes forms a special religious type. The psychological blurring of sexual differences, which appeared significantly in the life of the Syrians, Assyrians and Lydians, was perfected in the conception of divinities which comprise these in a unified manner within themselves: the half-masculine Astarte, the male-female Sandon, the sun god Malkart who exchanges the symbol of gender with the moon goddess.

We are not concerned here with the trivial statement that human beings paint themselves in their gods, which is so general as not to require an argument, but rather with searching for the individual human traits, the development and heightening of which beyond the human scale creates the gods. And it is important to recognize that the gods do not consist only in an idealization of individual qualities of the human, of force, of moral or immoral character traits, of the tendencies and needs of individuals, but that the inter-individual forms of social life frequently give content to religious conceptions. By taking on their purest and most abstract, but still embodied form, certain sides and certain levels of intensity of social functions shape the objects of religion, so that one can say that religion – aside from everything else that it may be – consists in social forms of relationships, which, detached from their empirical contents, are rendered autonomous and projected onto its own substances.

Indeed, how much the *unity* of the group belongs among the functions to be elaborated religiously can be made clear by the following two considerations. Especially in more primitive epochs, the fact that the group forms a unity is brought about or emphasized by the lack of conflict or competition within it, in contrast to all relationships with those who stand outside it. Now there is perhaps no individual area in which this existential form of non-competing coexistence, the identity of goals and interests, is presented so purely and completely as in the sphere of religion. The peaceful character of internal group life that is emphasized is, after all, only a relative one. There is also an effort, connected with the majority of the strivings even within the group, to exclude fellow competitors from the same goal, to improve the discrepancy between wishes and satisfactions as much as possible, even at the cost of others, or at least to seek the scale of value of one's own deeds and enjoyments in differences with others. It is almost solely within the religious sphere that the energies of individuals can fully realize themselves without coming into conflict with others, because, in the beautiful words of Jesus, there is a place for everyone in God's house.

Although the goal is common to everyone, it provides everyone with the possibility of attainment and does not result in a mutual exclusion, but rather on the contrary a mutual connection. I would mention here the profound way in which the communion gives expression to the fact that religion wishes to achieve the same goals for everyone with the same means for everyone; I would mention above all the feasts which give external visibility to the unity of all who are seized by the same religious fervour – from the crude feasts of primitive religions, where the fusion into a unity ultimately tends to culminate in a sexual orgy, to that purest expression of the *pax hominibus* reaching far beyond the individual group.

The lack of competition which unity prescribes as the life form of the group, but which always only prevails within it relatively and partially, has found the most absolute and intensive realization in the religious sphere. Here, as in the case of faith, one could say that religion represents in substance – in fact, that it virtually consists of – the substantialization of that which regulates group life as form and function. And this once again achieves personal form in the priesthood, which, despite its historical connection with certain social strata, is actually to *all* individuals in its basic conception, constituting by that very fact the intersection and unity of their ideal life contents. Thus, the celibacy of Catholic priests liberates them from any *special* relationship to this or that element or complex of elements, in order thereby to make possible an equal relationship to everyone – just as 'society' or the 'state' stand above all individuals as the abstract unity which has attracted the connections among them to itself. And to mention something quite specific: throughout the Middle Ages, the church offered the great comfort of all philanthropic impulses that it was the reservoir into which every charitable offering was discharged without question. Anyone who would part with property for the benefit of others had no more need to consider what would be the best way for that to happen; instead, there was an all-encompassing central organ between the donors and the needy. Philanthropy, a form of social relation within the group, gained a supra-individual organization and unity within the church.

The other side of this connection, as it were, but pointing to the same issue, is represented by the relationship to 'heretics'. What specifically drives large masses of people to a hatred for, and moral condemnation of, heretics is certainly not the difference in the dogmatic contents of the teaching, which in innumerable cases the masses do not even understand, but rather the fact of the *opposition* of individuals to the totality. The persecution of heretics and dissidents springs from the instinct for the necessary *unity* of the group. Now it is very typical that in many cases of this type the religious deviation could quite well coexist with the unity of the group in all vital matters. But the social impulse for unity has taken on such a pure, abstract and simultaneously substantial form in religion, that it no longer requires any connection with concrete interests; instead, dissidence, as such and by its very idea, seems to threaten unity, that is, the form of life of the group. Just as a palladium or some other symbol of group unity no longer has anything direct to do with the latter, but any attack on it provokes the most violent reactions, so too religion, elevated above all concrete individuality, is the purest form of unity in society – a quality demonstrated by the energy with which even the most irrelevant heresy is combated.

And finally, those inner connections between the individual and his or her group which are called 'moral' offer such deep analogies to the relationship with God, as if the latter were nothing more than a coalescence and modification of the former. The entire mysterious wealth of the former is reflected in the multiplicity of effects in which we feel the divine. The coercive and punishing gods, the loving god, the god of Spinoza, who cannot reciprocate our love, the god who grants or takes away the directives of action and at the same time the strength to follow them – these are indeed the signs under which the moral relationship between the group and its individuals also develops its powers and its antagonisms. For example, let me take as an instance the feeling of dependency, in which people have seen the nature of all religion. The individual feels bound to something general and higher, from which the individual flows and into which they return; but from which the individual also expects uplift and salvation, from which he or she is different, but with which he or she is also identical. All these feelings which meet in the idea of God, as in a focal point, can be traced back to the relationship which individuals have to their species, on the one hand – to the past generations that have transmitted the major forms and contents of their nature to them – and, on the other hand, to the contemporary generation which determines that nature's shape and the degree of its development.

If the theory is correct, according to which all religions originate from ancestor cults, from the reverence for and reconciliation with the soul of our ancestors, particularly those of the hero and the leader, which lives on in the present, then it might confirm this connection; for we are in point of fact dependent on that which existed prior to ourselves and which is concentrated most directly in the authority of the fathers over their descendants. One could say that the idolization of ancestors, and especially of the most active and powerful among them, is the most appropriate expression for the dependency of individuals on the previous past life of the group – no matter what different motifs the consciousness of the people may give to it. Thus, that humility with which the pious man professes to owe everything he has and is to God, to see the source of his being and his strength in Him, can be correctly transferred to the relationship of the individual to the totality. For the human being is not strictly speaking nothing *vis-à-vis* God, but rather a speck of dust, a weak, but still not completely negligible force, a vessel that receptively accommodates every content.

If the nature of a pure love of God lies in the fact that the colourful diversity, all the antagonisms and differences of being and volition and especially of our inner life interests have their origin, and simultaneously their unity, in Him, then we can put the social totality in His place without difficulty. It is, after all, the social totality from which the full wealth of drives springs, which it passes on to us as results of changing adaptations, as the diversity of relationships in which we are involved, as the formation of the organs with which we conceive of the different and often difficult to unite sides of the world – and yet the social group is something sufficiently unified to be viewed as the concrete point of unity of these divergent emanations.

Thus the divine origin of royalty is only the expression for the complete concentration of power in their hands. As soon as social standardization, the objectivization of the totality, has reached a certain level with respect to the individual, it appears to them as a supernatural power; and whether we are still immediately conscious of it as social or it has already shrouded itself in the divine idea, the problem of how much the individual can or must do to fulfil his or her duty, and how much is done by the principle that is transcendent with respect to the individual, occurs in the very same way.

The independence of the individual in relation to the power from which he or she has received the power of *in*dependence, and which indeed determines this objective and the means to it, is the problem in both cases. Thus Augustine places the individual in a historical development with respect to which, in his view, the individual is just as dependent and powerless as with respect to God. The issue of synergism, then, runs through the entire history of the church, just as much as it determines the history of domestic politics. Just as the individual, according to the strict religious interpretation, is only a vessel for the grace or wrath of God, so according to the socialist interpretation, he or she is a vessel for the effects that stem from the general community. Both cases repeat the same basic ethical question as to the essence and rights of the individual, and in both forms the surrender of the latter to the transcendent principle often offers the last satisfaction still possible, if self-reliant individuality possesses no inner viability.[2]

It is very typical of this ranking of religious and ethical – social conceptions that God is conceived of as the personification of those virtues which He demands of people; it is not so much that He *has* the qualities of kindness, justice, forbearance, etc., as that He *is* them. He is perfection presented in substance, as we find it expressed in statements such as, He is 'kindness itself', 'love itself', and so forth. Morality, the set of imperatives concerning the behaviour of human beings with regard to one another, has, as it were, taken permanent shape in Him. Just as practical faith is a relationship between people which forms something absolute over and above this relational form; just as unity is a form of relationship of people living together which can be heightened to that unity of things in personal form as that in which the divine appears – so morality contains those forms of behaviour between one person and another which the interest of the group has sanctioned, so that God, who presents the relative contents in absolute form, represents, on the one hand, the role of the demanding and granting group *vis-à-vis* the individual and, on the other hand, represents in Himself, abstracted from reality and in absolute substantiality, the ethical and social modes of behaviour which the individual must perform.

The relationships of human beings to one another, originating from the most diverse interests, supported by the most contradictory forces, and cast into the widest variety of moulds, are also achieving in their aggregated state, that whose autonomization and relation to an external entity we term religion: in that they become abstract and concrete simultaneously, and in whose dual development precisely that strength resides with which religion acts back upon those relationships. The old conception that God was the absolute, while everything human was relative, here achieves a new meaning:

it is the relations between human beings that find their substantial and ideal expression in the conception of the Godly.

If such investigations, aiming at the foundations of the worldview, are otherwise accompanied by the desire that their scope only be understood in sufficiently comprehensive terms, then on the contrary, the worry here must be that the connections asserted do not seem to be appearing as pretenders to neighbouring areas beyond their self-determined boundaries. They cannot describe the historical genesis of the creation of religion but only display one of its many sources, leaving completely aside the question as to whether the latter, encountering other such sources that also originate from the non-religious area, now produce religion through such a confluence, or whether religion had already found its nature and viability by the time that the sources of religious existence considered here flowed into the stream of religion as tributaries. The efficacy of religion is not bound to any particular historical moment.

Religion as a spiritual reality is also certainly neither a finished thing nor a firm substance, but rather a living process which each soul and each moment must themselves produce, despite all the imperturbability of traditional contents. Precisely in this requirement to draw what has been created by religion continuously into the stream of emotion, whose movements must continually reshape it, just as the continually changing water droplets produce the fixed image of the rainbow – herein is where the power and profundity of religion lie. This is the reason why a genetic explanation of religion must encompass not only the historical origin of its traditions, but also the forces of the present which allow us to acquire the religious treasures we have inherited from our forefathers, so that we can really possess them. Hence, in this sense, there exist real 'origins' of religion, whose emergence and effectiveness live long after the time of the 'origins' of religion.

What is still more important for these investigations, however, than opposing the insinuation here of a historical genetic theory is to exclude any enquiry into the objective truth of religion from that of its circumstances. If one can manage to understand the origination of religion as an event in the life of people from its connections to the inner conditions of that very same life, then the problem has not yet been approached as to whether or not objective reality, lying outside human thought, contains the counterpart and confirmation of that spiritual reality. Thus, the psychology of perception tries to explain how it is possible for our view of the world to be spatially extended in three dimensions, and leaves it to quite different types of investigation to determine whether or not a world of things in themselves in those same forms exists outside of our conceptions. Of course, a point may be reached in which the explanation of inner facticity by means of purely inner conditions is no longer sufficient, but where only an external reality is able to close the causal circle of the inner realities. Yet this possibility or necessity need only affect those who wish to explain the nature and origins of religion completely, but not us, since we were only required to pursue the direction of one of the rays which converge in the focal point of religion.

Finally, we turn to the most important thing: the emotional significance of religion, that is, the effect of the ideas of the divine which reaches into the centre of the mind, is completely independent of all assumptions concerning the manner in which these ideas may have arisen. This is the point of the most serious misunderstandings of all historical and psychological derivations of ideal values. Large circles of people still feel as if the attraction of an ideal deteriorates, as if the dignity of a feeling is degraded, if its origin is no longer an incomprehensible miracle, a creation *ex nihilo* – as if the understanding of evolution could call into question the value of that which has evolved, as if the baseness of the starting point could draw down the attained height of the goal, and as if the unstimulating simplicity of the individual elements could destroy the significance of the product, which consists in the cooperation, formation and interweaving of these elements. This is the foolish and confused attitude which considers human dignity desecrated because human beings descend from a lower animal species, as if this dignity were not based upon what a human being *is*, quite independently of the origins from which they became that which they are. It is this same attitude which will always resist against gaining an understanding of religion from elements that it does not yet consider religion. Precisely that attitude, however, which believes it must uphold the dignity of religion by rejecting its historical and psychological derivation, can be accused of a weakness of religious consciousness. For the inner strength and the emotional depth of the latter must be quite small, if it can consider itself endangered – indeed, even harmed – by the knowledge of its evolution. For just as the genuine and deep love for a person is not nullified by subsequent clarity with regard to the reasons for its emergence and, indeed, shows its triumphant power in the fact that it can survive the loss of its earlier reasons for being – so too all the strength of religious feelings is only demonstrated by the security with which it rests in itself and separates its depth and fervency from all the origins to which knowledge may trace it back.

A FEW WORDS ON SPIRITUALISM

When future times write the history of our century, they might well emphasize two brightly shining points alongside the dark shadows that cover the present times: natural science and social movements. They will depict the first in the security of that which it has achieved and the second in the security of that which it will attain. They will describe the liberation of thought coming from the first and the liberation of the whole of life from the second. They will tell our grandchildren that the conviction of the pervasive conformity to scientific laws penetrated all levels of the people for the first time in our century, and that superstition, the vague fear of supernatural, intangible powers – remnants from youthful periods of the human race – retreated step by step, except among those who had a very evident and very tangible interest in its preservation.

This is how it will perhaps look to a future historian who sees only the great trends of the time, only the major and effective movements. We, who are still in the midst of these things, still notice all sorts of counter-movements and side-currents, emerging and soon disappearing phenomena, which have quite a different character than that main trend of our times, but which are important signs of our times for the contemporary observer and show us that the times are not as uniform as they may later appear to a comprehensive view. Just as reaction, the obstinate clinging to or reversion to past cultural periods, takes its place alongside the great social movement of the times, so also, alongside that progress of natural science and the increased insight into the strict regularity and comprehensibility of all events, we find the belief in the spirits of deceased people who have either returned to earth or have always been with us, and are able to communicate with us as to this and the next world through the mediation of persons with special gifts. This belief and the preoccupation with such matters is called spiritualism, and a person upon whose call the spirits will appear is known as a medium, that is, an intermediary. Before I proceed to depict how the spirits reveal themselves, I wish to mention that thousands of people from all of the civilized countries in Europe and America adhere to spiritualism, that hundreds of books are published on it – in 1870 over one hundred thousand spiritualist books were sold in the United States of America. A great number of periodicals are published solely for the interests of spiritualism, and being a medium is a special 'business', a profession – and sometimes quite a lucrative one. In Germany, Berlin and Munich are the main centres of spiritualism.

The intercourse with spirits takes place in many ways, including in the following manner. The group that wishes to hold a spiritualist séance – three or any other number of people – sits around a table with the medium. If the latter senses the presence of a spirit, then the medium tells it that the alphabet will be recited and that it should knock in response to the letters it wants written down to constitute its statements. Thus, when one reaches a certain letter, starting with A, a knock on the table or the floor is heard. The letter is written down and one starts over again from the beginning and the second letter is obtained, and so on, until a complete sentence is formed which is the answer to the question. Or it is suggested to the spirit that it should respond to yes or no questions with one knock for 'no' and three for 'yes' and two for 'uncertain'.

This is frequently followed by ghostly phenomena: objects fly around the room, often striking the participants painfully, windows are broken, knots are tied or untied in threads – in short, actions follow which appear to come from invisible essences. The communications also often take place with the medium in the condition which was formerly known as 'magnetic sleep', writing sentences dictated by the spirits or written by his hand under their guidance. Additionally, sometimes two blank slate tablets are tied together in the presence of the medium and sealed, and afterwards one finds writing on their inner sides; or objects are removed from sealed boxes with no perceptible damage to the closure, and so forth. Another revelation by the spirits occurs by a person in a deep sleep beginning to speak with his or her own or a different voice – but not for themselves, but rather as a deceased person revealing his or her wishes, prophesies, teachings, and so on through the mouth of the medium. Often the medium names the illnesses of the people present and suggests means for curing them. Finally, the medium may also motivate the spirits to appear in a physical, visible form.

I shall describe a case of the latter type in more detail, since spiritualism takes its most conspicuous form there and also because the person who told it to me is absolutely credible, as are those among whom it happened, so that there is no doubt as to the *facts* reported – only, as we shall see, as to their explanation. The case was related to me several years ago in Frankfurt am Main, and I shall let the narrator speak for himself:

'In a small German regional capital where I lived long ago, I became acquainted with a Mr D., who, as I had previously heard, was involved in spiritualist experiments. This man was absolutely honourable and pure in character and also excused by his position of wealth from any suspicion of wanting to gain advantage of some sort by playing tricks. When we had got to know each other better, I received an invitation from him one day to a spiritualist séance. I found the establishment prepared as follows. One first entered a room furnished in a quite ordinary way where the group gathered together – professors, physicians, members of parliament and so on, in short, people who could not be assumed in advance to be susceptible to some kind of trickery. Adjacent to this room was another, smaller one which had only a single door leading to the room just described. Its windows were closed and it contained only an ordinary table and a few chairs. We investigated this room carefully. It was impossible for anyone to enter this room other than through the first room.

'After we had gone back to the first room and undoubtedly left the second one empty, the door was closed by a curtain. D. sat down in an armchair and fell after a short time into a condition of complete rigidity – his limbs spread out, almost stiff enough to break off, his skin stretched taut, no longer capable of being moved across his bones. At the same time, a knocking was heard in a table. One of those in attendance agreed upon the previously described knocking system with the spirit, and the spirit replied in that way to the question of his identity, "I am Prince H.", the recently deceased provincial ruler. He responded to the request to appear physically: "I would gladly appear, but my enemy B. and others are preventing me". At the same time, one could see the curtain closing off the adjoining room moving considerably, as if someone were pushing against it but could not get through. The movements became more and more violent, and finally an arm and a hand stretched out. I had a personal relationship with the Prince and had sat across from him at table only a short time before, when I had noticed his strangely shaped hand. This was unmistakably the same one, even with the same rings on its fingers. It stretched out of the curtain and tossed a paper into the room. At the same moment, however, a large number of other hands stretched out from behind the curtain and pulled the first one violently back. The paper contained a poem written in the hand of the Prince, with which I was also familiar. Thus the apparation ended. D. slowly came back to his senses, but completely exhausted and worn out. The adjoining room was subsequently inspected and was just as empty as before and the windows were likewise closed. I attended séances at D.'s house quite some time later, but there was never again a visual apparition'.

Thus the testimony of my source, whose personality rules out any doubt as to his credibility. And it must be emphasized particularly that spiritualist phenomena have been noted by the most distinguished and reliable observers, that a number of the greatest scholars, masters of scientific criticism, have attested to the respective facts. Now, of course, a considerable part of them must be dismissed as being based on trickery and conscious fraud. Thus, for instance, corporeal apparitions like the one described above are by no means so frequently attested that one would have to deal with them as a serious matter. In the case related above, the event occurred, as noted, in a first floor flat. The 'spirits', then, can certainly have come in and gone out of the window again, and the fact that the windows were closed before hand and afterward was only sleight of hand. But since Mr D. was certainly not in league with the magicians, but was deceived himself, it can only be assumed that those who really brought about the apparition had some sort of relationship to D. not known to my source and had an interest in his believing in spirits in order to make him a tool of certain, possibly exploitative, purposes.

Aside from such cases, as well as those that can be explained as unconscious self-deception, neurotic processes and the like, there still remain a number that cannot be explained and appear to go beyond the known natural forces. How is one to regard these? I believe first of all that it is justified to leave the entire area unexplored, so long as the phenomena in it are as childish, senseless and indifferent as everything that has been reported so far. All the communications obtained in spiritualist séances from knocking, writing, or in some other way, are silly and meaningless. Whether they stem from spirits or not, no one should bother with such foolishness, no matter where it comes from. If at some time new truths were to be discovered for us in this way, or scientific problems were to be solved or important events were to be predicted, then it will be time to occupy ourselves with it. If one is to throw away an entire, proven, internally consistent worldview such as the scientific one – for that is what spiritualism demands – then it must be worth while. We are entitled, according to the principles of scientific thought, to simply pass by unexplained things, to the extent they are not important and do not promise significant enlightenment. The 'spirits' should first of all prove that they are able to do something besides tell us things we already know, without the roundabout knocking method, or act like children and break window-panes and throw chairs around. Then it will be time to worry about the causes of the apparition and to ask whether it stems from spirits or some other source. In life, after all, we continually set thousands of unexplained events aside if they do not stimulate us by their content or undertake the effort of investigating them. Additionally, it is the case that the spirits only come when they are called. Ordinary everyday life is not interrupted by them and, within it, there are no phenomena that one would have to trace back to the influence of spirits. The spiritualist world is a world unto itself, alongside which the earthly, empirical world continues on its uninterrupted course; and the spiritualist world never intervenes in the latter if it is not specifically called upon to do so. Indeed, we have enough to do with tangible and empirical things, with exploring and shaping them, that we have no need to undertake exploratory travels into a field which, according to experience so far, has produced only superfluous and silly childishness – even though it can still remain an open question as to how much of the spiritualist claims might be true or false.

One thing that is certain, however, is that natural forces which we have not yet recognized are at work in the spiritualist phenomena, but by no means only there. It has only been somewhat over 200 years since we have known about gravity, which brings about the motions of the celestial bodies, and not even 200 years since we have known about electrical force. Who can doubt that there are still innumerable forces in this world which will only become known in the future? Countless numbers of still mysterious things surround us, and the belief that we cannot push forward to yet unknown forces, and that we must rely only on those already known to us, would be just as short-sighted as the view that our social circumstances will always remain the way they are now. But just as we do not progress in the latter realm through the intervention of supernatural powers which are quite outside of our experience, but rather from the development of already planted seedlings or from the more favourable combination of forces which have already been at work, so too the progress of knowledge will not come about by introducing unheard-of creatures that arrange the things in the world arbitrarily and with no connection to prior knowledge, but by proceeding down the already-known paths of knowledge. The history of science shows that research stagnates wherever people attribute events to the effects of spirits and that it progresses only where people look for the causes of material processes only in the material sphere. For long periods it was believed that celestial bodies were held in their orbits by special spirits, and true knowledge of celestial motion began only when, instead of that, the same forces with which we are familiar on earth were recognized as the cause. Just as we look back at the celestial spirits, so some day people will look back in bemusement at the spiritualism of the nineteenth century, which immediately created causative spirits for phenomena that could not yet be explained from known forces.

The really foolish, even incredible aspect of spiritualism is this: it considers its alleged explanation of the knocking, the moving table or telepathy – that spirits are causing them – to be just as certain as the facts themselves, and it would have us believe that if something inexplicable occurs, it could only come from spirits.

Let us now consider the fact that the adherents of spiritualism are by no means to be found in those classes from whom our governmental institutions still withhold so-called higher education, but that it is adhered to by the nobility all the way to the top, by doctors and professors, and by many of the better off middle class. Thus we must ask, how can this be possible? What is the reason why otherwise enlightened people, nourished with all the fruits of science, take childish ghosts seriously and believe in mere suppositions and fantastic images as if they were the most tangible reality?

I must digress a bit in order to explain this peculiarity. Every one of us knows that habituation sets in when one has been occupied with a thing long enough, as well as a desire to extend it further and further. It is difficult to do without that which our mind or heart has consumed for a long time, and, if it is torn away from us, we search for something similar that can fill out the void inside us in the same way. And this occurs just as much in the life of peoples as in that of individuals. If a people were enamoured of certain ideas or feelings for centuries or millennia, the desire for them persists long after the development of knowledge and circumstances have proved the falsity of those ideas.

Many minds cannot free themselves from the past, neither their own nor that of their people, but instead cling to earlier thought and belief, so that if this is made impossible, they reach for something else that is of almost the same type, occupies the same position and stimulates the same feelings. A large part of our population finds itself in this position, now that the advances of knowledge have destroyed the religious and philosophical superstition and the romantic sentiments which inspired past times, or with which the individual was fulfilled during his or her youth. The belief in supernatural entities, in mysterious forces, in spiritual purposes of nature transcending earth life, dominated the human mind for so long that it is unlikely that there would not be relapses into it everywhere. The need for objects that are apparently beyond all tangible and empirical reality is so well rooted as a result of habituation, that, having lost faith in its earlier satisfaction, it now turns to the most peculiar objects.

Thus spiritualism is a remnant of earlier times, that is to say, a consequence of the need for supernatural things to which the mind had adapted, and which now satisfies itself in spiritualism in a new form, after the old ones have become obsolete. There are still all too many people who have not learned to limit themselves to the earth, to seek ideals and the satisfactions of the emotions in it; and they have created spiritualism for themselves like the starving man whose burning desire for food causes him to conjure up sumptuous meals in his feverish fantasies. All science is powerless against this, because the miracle-starved instincts of those who are susceptible to such things are too strong, have been handed down too long and are too deeply rooted to be capable of being dispersed by scientific convictions, which are only of recent vintage, so to speak, and have not yet intervened as deeply and effectively in our worldview as we sometimes believe. It is reserved only for coming ages to have all of their thoughts and feelings penetrated by the results of the sciences. The phenomenon of spiritualism shows that we are still quite far from that point.

One of the highest tasks of humankind is to replace obsolete ideals, hopes and emotional needs with new ones at the right time. Our age has reached such a turning point, where the values of life, the interests of the heart, the intimations and strivings that satisfied earlier times have faded and where it will be seen whether, in an energetic transformation, we will have the strength to transfer our ideals to the social interests that constitute the lodestar of the future – or whether we will stick to the empty husks of the past and attempt to fill them out with absurdities like spiritualism. This spiritualism is itself a ghost of the past, a haunting, returning ghost of childish fairy-tale fantasies and articles of faith long since abandoned. Goethe beautifully expresses this decisive turn:

> The view beyond is barred to mortal ken;
> A fool! who thither turns his blinking eyes
> And dreams he'll find his like above the skies.
> Let him stand fast and look around on earth;
> Not mute is this world to a man of worth.
> Why need he range through all eternity?
> Here he can seize all that he knows to be.
> Thus let him wander down his earthly day;
> When spirits spook, let him pursue his way;
> Let him find fear and bliss as on he stride[s];[3]

But often there is simply no energy left in our bourgeois circles for this decisive turn and that is why countless people flee to spiritualism, the caricature of that beautiful, poetic faith in gods and spirits of earlier days – they must go backward, since they cannot go forward. For the bell has also tolled for the purer and more contemplative forms of faith in the supernatural. Our wishes, our hopes and our satisfactions have returned to earth and find themselves enclosed in the social life that surrounds us and takes up all the forces of its elevation and ennoblement which would otherwise be wasted on the dreams of the supernatural.

Notes to Part IX

1. This functional distinction can, of course, be of very great significance. Socrates had to die for wanting to recreate through the freely enquiring conscience of the individual the same moral life contents which Greek antiquity protected by the strictness of custom and convention.

2. I draw this discussion from my *Einleitung in die Moralwissenschaft* (Introduction to Moral Science), Vol. I.

3. Translator's note: *Faust II*, lines 11, 442–11, 451, translated by George Madison Priest (New York: Knopf. 1940).

BIBLIOGRAPHICAL INFORMATION

'Introduction' to *Philosophical Culture*
'Einleitung' to G. Simmel *Philosophische Kultur, Gesammelte Essais*, Leipzig: W. Klinkhardt 1911, pp. 1–6. A second edition appeared in 1919 published in Leipzig by Alfred Kröner Verlag. To appear shortly in the *Georg Simmel Gesamtausgabe (GSGA)* in volume 10 of the 24 volume critical edition. This English translation by Mark Ritter and David Frisby.

The Concept of Culture
In G. Simmel, *Philosophie des Geldes*, Leipzig: Duncker & Humblot 1907, second enlarged edition, pp. 502–07. See also *Philosophie des Geldes* (*GSGA* vol. 6), Frankfurt: Suhrkamp Verlag, 1989, edited by David P. Frisby and Klaus Christian Köhnke, pp. 617–22. In English in *The Philosophy of Money*, London: Routledge (2nd edn 1990), translated by Tom Bottomore and David Frisby (based on a first draft by Kaethe Mengelberg), pp. 446–50.

On the Essence of Culture
G. Simmel, 'Vom Wesen der Kultur', Österreichische Rundschau, 15, 1908, pp. 36–42 see also G. Simmel, *Aufsätze und Abhandlungen 1901–1908*, vol. 2, Frankfurt: Suhrkamp, 1993, edited by Alessandro Cavalli and Volkhard Krech, pp. 363–73. This English translation original in Peter Lawrence (ed.) *Georg Simmel: Sociologist and European*, Sunbury: Nelson, 1976, pp. 243–49. Translation by D.E. Jenkinson as 'The Meaning of Culture'.

Female Culture
G. Simmel, 'Weibliche Kultur', *Archiv für Sozialwissenschaft und Sozialpolitik*, 33, 1911, pp. 1–36. This translation in 'Female Culture', *Georg Simmel on Women, Sexuality and Love*, New Haven and London: Yale University Press, 1984, pp. 65–101. Translation and introduction by G. Oakes.

The Concept and Tragedy of Culture
G. Simmel, 'Der Begriff und die Tragödie der Kultur', *Logos*, 2, 1911/12, pp. 1–25. Reprinted in G. Simmel, *Philosophische Kultur*, loc.cit., second edn, pp. 223–53. This English translation by Mark Ritter and David Frisby.

The Conflict of Modern Culture
G. Simmel, *Der Konflikt der Modernen Kultur. Ein Vortrag*, Munich & Leipzig: Duncker & Humblot 1918, pp. 48. This translation in P. Lawrence (ed.), *Georg Simmel: Sociologist and European*, Sunbury: Nelson, 1976, pp. 223–42. Translated by D.E. Jenkinson.

The Crisis of Culture

G. Simmel 'Die Krisis der Kultur', *Frankfurter Zeitung*, 13 February 1916. Reprinted in G. Simmel, *Der Krieg und die geistigen Entscheidungen. Reden und Aufsätze*, Munich & Leipzig: Duncker & Humblot, 1917. This translation in P. Lawrence (ed.), *Georg Simmel: Sociologist and European*, Sunbury: Nelson, 1976, pp. 253–66. Translated by D.E. Jenkinson.

The Future of Our Culture

G. Simmel, 'Die Zukunft unserer Kultur', *Frankfurter Zeitung*, 14 April 1909. Translated by Mark Ritter and David Frisby.

The Change in Cultural Forms

G. Simmel, 'Wandel der Kulturformen', *Berliner Tageblatt*, 27 August 1916. English translation by Mark Ritter and David Frisby.

Sociology of the Senses

G. Simmel, 'Soziologie der Sinne', *Die Neue Rundschau*, 18, 1907, vol. 2, pp. 1025–36. See also G. Simmel, *Aufsätze und Abhandlungen 1901– 1908*, vol. 2, Frankfurt: Suhrkamp, 1993, pp. 276–92. English translation by Mark Ritter and David Frisby.

The Sociology of Sociability

G. Simmel, 'Soziologie der Geselligkeit', *Schriften der Deutschen Gesellschaft für Soziologie*, series 1, vol. 1, 1911, pp. 1–16. English translation by Everett C. Hughes reprinted here from 'The Sociology of Sociability', *American Journal of Sociology*, 55, 1949/50, pp. 254–61.

Sociology of the Meal

G. Simmel, 'Soziologie der Mahlzeit', *Berliner Tageblatt*, 10 October 1910, English translation by Mark Ritter and David Frisby.

The Sociology of Space

G. Simmel, 'Soziologie des Raumes', *Jahrbuch für Gesetzgebung, Verwaltung und Volkswirtschaft*, 27, 1903, pp. 27–71. See also G. Simmel, *Aufsätze und Abhandlungen 1901–1908*, vol. 1, edited by L. Rüdiger Kramme, Angela Rammstedt and Otthein Rammstedt, Frankfurt: Suhrkamp, 1995, pp. 132–83. English translation by Mark Ritter and David Frisby.

Bridge and Door

G. Simmel 'Brücke und Tür', *Der Tag*, 15 September 1909. English translation by Mark Ritter as 'Bridge and Door', *Theory, Culture & Society*, 11, 1994, pp. 5–10.

The Metropolis and Mental Life

G. Simmel, 'Die Grossstädte und das Geistesleben', *Jahrbuch der Gehe-Stiftung*, 9, 1903, pp. 185–206. See also G. Simmel, *Aufsätze und*

Abhandlungen 1901–1908, vol. 1, 1995, pp. 116–31. This English translation by Hans Gerth in Kurt H. Wolff (ed.), *The Sociology of Georg Simmel*, Glencoe: Free Press, 1950, pp. 409–24.

The Philosophy of Fashion

G. Simmel, *Philosophie der Mode*, Berlin: Pan Verlag 1905, p. 41. Also in G. Simmel, *Philosophische Kultur*, (second edn) Leipzig: Kröner 1919, pp. 25–57. See also G. Simmel, *Philosophie der Mode. Die Religion. Kant und Goethe, Schopenhauer und Nietzsche*, (*GSGA* vol 10, edited by Michael Behr, Volkhard Krech and Gert Schmidt), Frankfurt: Suhrkamp, 1995, pp. 7–38. This translation by Mark Ritter and David Frisby.

Adornment

See G. Simmel, 'Pychologie des Schmuckes', *Morgen*, 2, 1908, pp. 1685–89. Also G. Simmel, 'Exkurs über den Schmuck' in G. Simmel, *Soziologie*, Leipzig: Duncker & Humblot, 1908, pp. 365–72. See also G. Simmel, *Soziologie*, (*GSGA* vol. 11, edited by Otthein Rammstedt), Frankfurt: Suhrkamp, 1992, pp. 414–21. This English translation by Kurt H. Wolff in Kurt H. Wolff (ed.) *The Sociology of Georg Simmel*, Glencoe: Free Press, 1950, pp. 338–44.

The Problem of Style

G. Simmel, 'Das Problem des Stiles', *Dekorative Kunst*, 16, 1908, pp. 307–16. English translation by Mark Ritter as 'The Problem of Style', *Theory, Culture & Society*, vol. 8, no. 3, 1991, pp. 63–71.

The Alpine Journey

G. Simmel, 'Alpenreisen', *Die Zeit* (Vienna), 4, 13 July 1895. English translation by Sam Whimster as 'The Alpine Journey', *Theory, Culture & Society*, vol. 8, no. 3, 1991, pp. 95–8.

The Adventure

G. Simmel, 'Philosophie des Abenteuers', *Der Tag*, Berlin 7 and 8 June 1910. See also 'Das Abenteuer' in G. Simmel, *Philosophische Kultur* (second edn) Leipzig: Kröner 1919, pp. 7–24. This translation as 'The Adventure' by David Kettler in Kurt H. Wolff (ed.) *Georg Simmel 1858–1918*, Columbus: Ohio State University Press, 1958, pp. 243–58.

On the Psychology of Money

G. Simmel, 'Zur Psychologie des Geldes', *Jahrbuch für Gesetzgebung, Verwaltung und Volkswirtschaft*, 13, 1889, pp. 1251–64. English translation by Mark Ritter and David Frisby.

Money in Modern Culture

G. Simmel, 'Das Geld in der Modernen Kultur', *Zeitschrift des Oberschlesischen Berg und Huttenmännischen Vereins*, 35, 1896, pp. 319–24. See also 'Das Geld in der Modernen Kultur' in G. Simmel, *Aufsätze und Abhandlungen*

1894–1900, (*GSGA* vol. 2, edited by Heinz-J. Dahme and David P. Frisby), Frankfurt: Suhrkamp, 1992, pp. 178–96. This translation by Mark Ritter and Sam Whimster as 'Money in Modern Culture', *Theory, Culture & Society*, vol. 8, no. 3, 1991, pp. 17–31.

The Berlin Trade Exhibition

G. Simmel 'Berliner Gewerbeausstellung', *Die Zeit* (Vienna) 8, 25 July 1896. This translation by Sam Whimster as 'The Berlin Trade Exhibition', *Theory, Culture & Society*, vol. 8, no. 3, 1991, pp. 119–23.

Infelices Possidentes! (Unhappy Dwellers)

P. Liesegang [pseudonym] 'Infelices Possidentes', *Die Zukunft*, 3, 1893, pp. 82–4. This translation by Mark Ritter and David Frisby.

Some Remarks on Prostitution in the Present and in Future

[Anon] 'Einiges über die Prostitution in Gegenwart und Zukunft', *Die Neue Zeit*, 10, 1891/1892, pp. 517–25. Reprinted in H.J. Dahme and K.C. Köhnke (eds), *Schriften zur Philosophie und Soziologie der Geschlechter*, Frankfurt: Suhrkamp, 1985, pp. 60–71. This translation by Mark Ritter and David Frisby.

The Women's Congress and Social Democracy

G. Simmel, 'Der Frauenkongress und die Sozialdemokratie', *Die Zukunft*, 17, 1896, pp. 80–4. Reprinted in H.J. Dahme and K.C. Köhnke (eds) *Schriften zur Philosophie und Soziologie der Geschlechter*, Frankfurt; Suhrkamp, 1985, pp. 133–38. This translation by Mark Ritter and David Frisby.

On the Sociology of Religion

G. Simmel, 'Zur Soziologie der Religion', *Die Neue Deutsche Rundschau* 9, 1898, pp. 111–23. See also 'Zur Soziologie der Religion' in G. Simmel, *Aufsätze und Abhandlungen 1894–1900*, Frankfurt: Suhrkamp, 1992, pp. 266–86. This English translation by Mark Ritter and David Frisby.

A Few Words on Spiritualism

G. Simmel, 'Etwas vom Spiritismus', *Vorwärts*, 12 July 1892. This translation by Mark Ritter and David Frisby.

NAMES INDEX